THE
FORREST J ACKERMAN
OEUVRE

THE
FORREST J ACKERMAN
OEUVRE

*A Comprehensive Catalog of the Fiction, Nonfiction,
Poetry, Screenplays, Film Appearances, Speeches
and Other Works, with a Concise Biography*

CHRISTOPHER M. O'BRIEN

Foreword by Dennis Billows
Essay by Stephen King

McFarland & Company, Inc., Publishers
Jefferson, North Carolina, and London

Frontispiece: Ackerman seated in the Lincoln chair, 1970s (photograph by Walter J. Daugherty, courtesy Mary Ellen Daugherty).

LIBRARY OF CONGRESS CATALOGUING-IN-PUBLICATION DATA

O'Brien, Christopher M., 1980–
The Forrest J Ackerman oeuvre : a comprehensive catalog of the fiction, nonfiction, poetry, screenplays, film appearances, speeches and other works, with a concise biography / Christopher M. O'Brien ; foreword by Dennis Billows ; essay by Stephen King.
p.   cm.
Includes bibliographical references and index.

ISBN 978-0-7864-4984-2

softcover : acid free paper ∞

1. Ackerman, Forrest J — Bibliography.
2. Ackerman, Forrest J.   3. Book collectors — United States — Biography.   4. Collectors and collecting — United States — Biography.   5. Ackerman, Forrest J — Knowledge — Science fiction.   I. Title.
Z8013.35.O27 2012   [Z989.A33]   016.002075 — dc23   2012029676

BRITISH LIBRARY CATALOGUING DATA ARE AVAILABLE

Front cover: facial detail of frontispiece of FJA seated in the Lincoln chair, 1970s (photograph by Walter J. Daugherty, courtesy Mary Ellen Daugherty); robot © 2012 Shutterstock; cover design by David K. Landis (Shake It Loose Graphics)

Manufactured in the United States of America

*McFarland & Company, Inc., Publishers
Box 611, Jefferson, North Carolina 28640
www.mcfarlandpub.com*

In memory of Forry,
and to David A. Kyle and Cuyler W. Brooks, Jr.,
for their untiring assistance.

Table of Contents

Foreword: My Daze
with Forrest J Ackerman

BY DENNIS BILLOWS

When the author of this work told me he was compiling a bibliography of all of Forrest J Ackerman's appearances in print, I shook my head sadly and hoped he wouldn't end up at Arkham Asylum in a cell between the Joker and the Riddler.

Because Forry Ackerman wrote something every day of his life. Every day, first thing in the morning, he took out a piece of paper and wrote "*something*" ten times.

Sorry. I can't help myself. I wrote for *Famous Monsters of Filmland* waaayyy too long.

Forrest J Ackerman wrote his first fan letter in 1929, the same year he was published in a prozine (*SWQ*). His first story, "A Trip to Mars," was published in 1931 when he was only 15 years old and he entered a story-writing contest. His talent would *mushroom* over time, but it was obvious that even at this early age he was a *fun-gi*.

I knew Forrest J Ackerman for 35 years and I saw firsthand how he juggled all the hats he wore (when he wore a hat, which wasn't too often). I worked for him 6 days a week, 9 hours a day, from 1975 to 1978. When I left to pursue my own career plans, I saw him or talked with him on the phone about once a month for all those years after.

I was looking for a career in sci-fi. I asked Forry if he could teach me how to be a punster, editor, and agent, just like him. I said: "Forry, I'm as witty as you are. I can do it. I can be like you." He said: "Den, punning is an art and Art moved to Cleveland last week. Look, I know you have wit, but you're *half* my age ... so ... even if you tried really hard ... you can only be as *half-witted* as I am."

Forry edited *Famous Monsters of Filmland* magazine (the *punniest* magazine ever) and the Ace Books *Perry Rhodan* and *Atlan* science fiction series, and he was a literary agent for science fiction writers like A.E. van Vogt at the time and for writers like Marion Zimmer Bradley in the past.

Of course he would have to squeeze in my lessons when he wasn't being interviewed once a day by reporters (both pro and fan) from all around the world either in person or by phone.

Or when he wasn't giving tours of his awe-inspiring collection of science fiction, fantasy,

1

and horror to someone who just "dropped over" instead of visiting on Open-House Saturdays.

Or when he wasn't writing a contribution to a sci-fi fanzine.

Or when he wasn't attending a movie premiere (he saw every sci-fi, fantasy, and horror movie ever made). Which was probably why Arkham Asylum had a cell with his name waiting for him — they knew it would only take one more Mexican or Philippine horror film...

Or when he wasn't filming a cameo in a new sci-fi film.

Or when he wasn't sharing some of his time with his wife, Wendayne, the translator of the German *Perry Rhodan* books into English.

Or when he wasn't examining a stack of stills or a pile of books or a movie prop brought over by an eager fan to sell or trade.

Or (I came to dread it) ... listen ... there's that sound ... that awful "*ding dong ... ding dong*"... I couldn't help but growl like Karloff in the original *Frankenstein* as a terrible feeling — half-dread, half-excitement, and half gainer — what? Three halfs are more than the sum of the parts? Well, *partsdon* me!—where was I? Oh — it was the postman ringing the front doorbell to deliver the daily bucket of blood ... er ... *mail* (you could always bank on it) — new books to file, new fan mail to answer, new magazines to read, new bills (later in the afternoon "Bill" would swing by to get his misdelivered mail).

Or maybe Forry could teach me between meals at the House of Pies (ironically he never ate the pie, he was only *pie*ous about chocolate shakes and burgers).

Forry had so much energy it's a miracle he wasn't an insomniac. People would ask me if he wandered through his collection in the middle of the night when no one was around, cradling his copy of *The Outsider and Others*, playing with the Martian War Machines from *War of the Worlds*, or running down the aisles of books wearing a Don Post monster mask. Well, I can state right now without any doubt the answer is *No!* If he had, I would have bumped into him, even though it's hard to see out of those tiny holes in the masks ... oops ... *never mind.*

Every day was like Christmas with new items arriving in the mail, new writing or movie projects being offered, new people to meet, new movies to see ... well ... you get the point.

I learned there was only one Forrest J Ackerman and I didn't have his stamina, his generosity, or his enthusiasm.

In the two years that I worked full-time as his archivist, and the remaining years part-time, and after making a daunting attempt to file in a correct and accessible manner all the magazines, clippings, and letters from famous people; and after creating scrapbooks containing film reviews, newspaper articles, promotional material, playbills, and other paper memorabilia (which were auctioned off after his death — the *Karloff, Lugosi, Lon Chaney, Sr., The Invisible Man, Metropolis, Frankenstein, Dracula* scrapbooks and several volumes of Forry's published writings, writings about him, and so much more), this material has vanished as if it was sucked through a wormhole into the Delta Quadrant only to be assimilated by the Borg. But I enjoyed it, so, there you go! I got to read classic movie scripts and was allowed to copy some of them, I filed his movie posters and lobby-cards and I was allowed to photograph whatever I wanted. Forry had a button collection, a stamp collection, a — whew! I'm exhausted just thinking about all that again.

But I miss it.

I left and pursued my own off-the-sci-fi-grid career, but I was hooked. Addicted. I loved sci-fi and Forry needed an archivist. So about twice a month I would drive from Torrance or Orange County, wherever I was living at the time, to Hollyweird, Karloffornia, to the Ackermansion on Glendower Avenue and load up several boxes of papers, take them home with me, and for the next week or two I would file while I watched TV. My wife didn't mind. Well, maybe a little. But she was tolerant.

When a scrapbook or file folder was finished, I would give it to Forry, he would kindly "ooh" and "aah," and I would be rewarded. Oh, the "oohing" and "aahing" was *not* for the amount of work I put into organizing chronologically everything I could find on a subject, or for pasting a clipping into a scrapbook with special art glue that would not bleed through over the years, not even for sliding the clipping and page into a heavyweight sheet protector and alphabetizing it all into a 3-ring loose-leaf binder.

No. Forry "oohed" and "aahed" *because he had so much stuff, that when I presented it to him, in an organized and artistic manner, it was like seeing it for the first time!*

Sometimes I made a collage from duplicate pictures and put it on the front cover of the scrapbook.

I had several collages published in *FM,* and several around the Ackermansion, including a vintage *Buck Rogers* from the 1939 serial with Buster Crabbe made from water-damaged original stills, and I created a huge collage beside Forry's desk of Morris Scott Dollens' original sci-fi art, pictures from George Pal's *War of the Worlds,* space stamps from all over the world, and similar material. Forry labeled it "When Worlds Collage by Dennis Billows" for all the world to see.

Forry trusted me with his collection. I had a key to the Ackermansion all the years he lived there so I could get material whenever my time permitted whether he was there or not. But I usually made the trip when I knew he was there. I wanted to see him.

Forry trusted a lot of people and many betrayed that trust. Many items were stolen from his collection. Most were never recovered. Items like the original sound disks from the 1931 *Frankenstein* and *Murders in the Rue Morgue* were sold to other collectors. I remember we were all mystified how someone, or more likely, several people, were able to steal the front end of the submarine from George Pal's *Atlantis, the Lost Continent.* It was too big and too heavy to put inside the house, so it was outside on the back patio. One morning the front end was gone. It has never turned up.

Most of the stolen items were kept by the thieves, but there was one young boy who stole items only to give them away so he could be popular. His logic was Forry had a lot of stuff, he didn't need it all. He had so much stuff that he wouldn't even know what was missing.

Thieves forgot one important thing.

It didn't belong to them.

I never wanted Forry to wonder if I was the one taking pieces from his collection. So Forry had a standing invitation to visit my home whenever he wanted.

One special Thanksgiving my wife cooked a terrific turkey dinner and I gave Forry a tour of everything in my collection. He knew I had a substantial collection of my own. He saw it not long after we first met when I threw a surprise birthday party at my home for Walt Daugherty, the photographer for *Famous Monsters* and Forry's lifelong friend. Some of the people who attended were A.E. van Vogt and C.L. Moore. I mostly collected comics, and I had 10,000 at the time, but you accumulate things as time goes on. I've added books and magazines and movie posters, things that would turn up at garage sales and swap meets for reasonable prices in very good condition.

I wanted Forry to come over to my house now and then, just to keep our relationship honest. I would ask him to pull any book off the shelf, or look in any box in the garage, or go into any closet just so he could see that his stuff wasn't there.

He liked that. In fact, he found a few things he knew he didn't have and I was happy to give them to him, like a first edition of *Kinsmen of the Dragon* by Stanley Mullen with the incredible Hannes Bok wrap-around dust jacket. I owed him for a lot of joy in my life and it was the least I could do. I was repaid ten times over when he asked me, and a few other personal friends, before an auction, if there was something we personally wanted. I've always been a Clark Ashton Smith and H.P. Lovecraft collector, so I was able to buy a few items like an original Smith statue for a very reasonable price. He could have made twice the money he charged me, but that was Forry — always generous.

One of my great joys was to add to his *Frankenstein* and *Dracula* collections of various book editions and toys. Since I knew what editions he had in his collection (I had filed them, after all), if I ran across a book I suspected he didn't have, I would pick it up. He was always delighted to see something new.

Anyway, the point of this trip down memory lane...

Forry did a lot of things, but the way he made his money was by writing. He was not independently wealthy. He struggled to pay for his science fiction habit; to feed that dinosaur we all called "his collection." And it had a voracious appetite. The way he kept up with the new books and magazines and toys was to write or edit every day. Oh, he traded for items he didn't have from his two-car garage full of duplicates, and he "rented" out stills from his enormous collection when they were needed for a magazine article on science fiction movies in *Playboy*, for example. And he took his 10 percent literary agent's fee for stories he placed for his sci-fi clients. But mostly he earned his money by writing for *Famous Monsters* or *Perry Rhodan* or an article here and there. In fact, there were so many articles, in so many publications, that he had a list of pseudonyms.

Weaver Wright	Clair Helding
Spencer Strong	Katarin Markov Merrit
Jack Erman	Hubert George Wells
Jacques deForest Erman	Nick Beal
Fisher Trentworth	Erdstelulov
Morris & Norris Chapnick	Alden Lorraine
Allis Villette	Claire Voyant
Dr. Acula	Stone T. Farmington
Dr. Ackula	J.C. Lark
The Ackermonster	Fojak
4sJ	Laurajean Ermayne
4e	

And he hinted to me that there were more and listed many of them in his self-published one-shot magazine called *Amazing Forries* in 1976.

There's an interesting story behind the pseudonym Laurajean Ermayne.

In 1946 lesbianism was still "a subject spoken of only in whispers." So Forry deliberately wrote the first lesbian science fiction story. Originally known as "World of Loneliness," it was eventually published as "The Radclyffe Effect." Oddly enough, it was not until 1969 that the Sapphic science fiction story saw print.

In the mid–40s, when he adopted the pen name Laurajean Ermayne, he contributed a large percentage of the stories, articles, poems and reviews to *Vice Versa*, the original underground lesbian journal. Years later, in recognition of his contributions, and at the first public convention of the Daughters of Bilitis in San Francisco (a priest and two members of the vice squad were present, Forry told me), he was accepted as an honorary lesbian.

So much has been written *about* Forrest J Ackerman and his collection, but there's even more out there written **by** *Forrest J Ackerman*.

Some of his writings are gems of wit — and they shouldn't be lost.

Forry's personality shone through his editing on contributions submitted to *Famous Monsters of Filmland*. Before a submitted article was published in *Famous Monsters,* Forry would Ackermanize it. No one who contributed to *FM* was spared because no one could write with that sense of humor, with that sense of wonderment, and no one could generate the excitement for the genre like Forry.

One piece I wrote, and that Forry edited, James Warren rejected. It was titled "Grave of the Vampire," and Warren felt there weren't enough good pictures to accompany a 5,500-word Filmbook. Although 16 photos were sent, only 8 or 9 were exciting enough to use. It was cost prohibitive. And a shame. The movie isn't bad. David Chase's screenplay, upon

Ackerman (left) looks on as Archivist Dennis Billows (right) entertains actress Martine Beswicke, 1970s (photograph by Walter J. Daugherty, courtesy Dennis Billows).

which the Filmbook was based, had a few interesting vampiric twists and although it was made on a low budget, it is still entertaining today.

Forry's editing, how he injected excitement and drama into the sometimes pedestrian writing of others, including my own (later I stopped being a pedestrian, learned to drive a car, and *there you go*), was a wonder to behold, so I kept photocopies of all the articles he changed. It helped me to become a better writer. I contributed more articles to *Famous Monsters of Filmland* and, always keeping in mind Jim Warren's concern for the right mixture of stills to text, I published many articles under my name, under my pseudonym Eric Ashton, and even without any credit. Jim Warren didn't want any name linked with *FM* except Forry's. Again — and rightly so.

I've probably gone on longer than Chris wanted me to. I'm a bit tired. We've meandered down a 35-year road, and it's time to pull over to that motel just ahead. I wish I had Chris's bibliography of Forry to read while I'm trying to sleep tonight, but maybe I can get a newspaper and something to eat before I turn in. Maybe not, it's so deserted around here. I don't see a restaurant. Just the rows of motel cabins. And the ugly old house on the hill silhouetted in the moonlight.

I wonder if this article has captured Forry. I have a few more ideas I want to jot down. I hope the Bates Motel has stationery...

Can anyone capture Forry's enthusiasm, I wonder? That's de*bate*sable.

Dennis Billows *is a writer, an artist, and a fantasy film archivist.* Famous Monsters of Filmland *has published more than 50 of his articles, beginning with issue 115 in 1975. He served as Forrest J Ackerman's personal assistant from 1975 to 1978 and formed a friendship that lasted more than 30 years. He was one of the heirs to the Forrest J Ackerman trust estate.*

Essay: The Importance of Being Forry

BY STEPHEN KING

Let me try to get at the importance of being Forry — to me, at least — by telling you a simplistic little parable. Back there in the European middle age (picture Lon Chaney ringing the bells in *The Hunchback of Notre Dame* to get in the mood, if you want), nobody ate tomatoes. The reason they didn't was because the tomato was thought to be a deadly poisonous fruit — about two bites and you were supposed to drop down with your nostril linings falling out, your hands clutching your swelling neck, your skin turning purple. "*Graaag! Choke!*," as the folks in the old E.C. Comics used to say.

Now suppose you were some more or less typical middle ages dude ... except that *you* had discovered that tomatoes were not only not poisonous, they were *delicious!* No problem with that, you say; that's great, in fact. And so it is ... except that being the only person in the village who knows the truth would have to be both lonely and frustrating. No one is going to come over to *your* hut for spaghetti unless you go back to the traditional butter-and-garlic sauce (which not only wouldn't poison you, it would keep the vampires away). No one is going to join *you* in a bowl of tomato soup, and you would extol the virtues of ketchup in vain.

Now imagine that, after years of putting up with this attitude, a new guy shows up in town ... *and he's selling tomatoes!!!*

If you can imagine your feelings at such a point, you can imagine what I mean by the importance of being Forry, at least as his life has impinged on mine.

As a kid growing up in rural Maine, my interest in horror and the fantastic wasn't looked upon with any approval whatsoever — there went young Steve King, his nose either in a lurid issue of *Tales from the Vault* or an even more lurid paperback of some sort or other — I had gone from Robert Bloch to Frank Belknap Long and from Long to the rest of the so-called Lovecraft Circle. I was, as far as most of my elders were concerned, eating tomatoes ... poison fruit.

And I was pretty much alone in these odd pursuits. I suppose that, if you had discovered monsters and magic and the work of a genius named Ray Harryhausen at the age of nine in New York or Chicago or Cleveland — perhaps even in such smaller cities as Davenport or Tulsa or Melrose — you had a fair chance of finding others who shared the same interests,

7

and that took some of the heat off you. To go back to the original example for a moment, it's harder to come down on one guy for eating the supposedly poisoned fruit when there are six or eight people eating it all at once — the Tomato-Eater's Club, let us say.

Like calls to like, and some of those kids who discovered their mutual liking (but I'm afraid that word is too polite; if you were one of those kids, you know that what I really mean is their mutual *hunger*) for fantasy fans are still getting together, publishing fanzines, sharing rides to conventions ... or organizing their own.

Growing up in a town of nine hundred residents — and fully eight hundred and fifty of them at least seventy, it sometimes seemed — I was pretty much the only tomato-eater around. I was denied the experience of the communal circle, that experience that consists of such wonderful phrases as "Have you read *this?*" and "Yeah, how did you like the part when he —?" and so on.

Imagine, if you will, a whole clique of tomato-eaters getting together once a week or once a month to exchange recipes containing tomatoes ... or inventing new ones. Not bad!

If I had to do it over again, I would change nothing; there are fans who become, in some odd way imprisoned by fandom itself — unlike Forry Ackerman, they are unable to provide the necessary spark which turns fandom into a force with its own identity (an Ackerman competitor, Calvin Beck, possessed the same wonderful spark) — and I wouldn't want that for myself. But I would be lying if I didn't add that it was sometimes lonely, being the only fantasy-horror fan in Durham, Maine, pop. 989. And it sometimes got depressing, listening to adults tell me I was going to "rot my mind" reading that stuff; that it was "nothing but junk"; and, of course, that "you'll never get rich reading stuff like that, Stevie; there's no money in trash like that."

And then, on one wonderful October day in what must have been 1960 or 1961, I discovered that I *wasn't* alone, that there was a whole sub-society of tomatoes-eaters out there ... and that if horror fiction was junk, there were *legions* of people just like me, who thought it was the most fabulous junk ever created.

In those days, as today, twenty years later, the closest moving picture theater to Durham, Maine, is the Ritz, in the smallish city of Lewiston. This place, which I have described elsewhere as "the sleaziest theater in Maine, perhaps in the entire universe," was, nevertheless, the picture-palace of my youth. These days it shows only porno, but when I was a kid it showed what seemed an endless succession of horror pictures — Tom Tryon in *I Married a Monster from Outer Space*, Steve McQueen in *The Blob*, Ray Milland in *X: The Man with the X-Ray Eyes* and *The Last Man on Earth*, Vincent Price in an endless succession of A.I.P. Poe adaptations.

I hitchhiked up to Lewiston to see these films at the Ritz, and then I hitchhiked the seventeen miles back home usually with my mind on fire. And I went alone, because few of my friends had any interest in such weird stuff; certainly not enough interest to hitchhike seventeen miles and maybe not get home until after (*ulp!*) dark. I saw almost all these pictures in the afternoon (remember the good old days when movies played continuously folks?), too, and so the good ol' Ritz was usually almost utterly empty. The natural conclusion was that tomato-stall in the marketplace is never particularly busy when everyone thinks those things are poison.

So, again, imagine my wonder that October day when I found out that there was *someone* — that there were, in fact, *lots* of someones — who not only took books such as Matheson's *The Incredible Shrinking Man* and Bloch's *Yours Truly, Jack the Ripper* seriously, but who took the movies seriously too.

That day was gray and overcast and cold ... but I also remember that, in another way, it was one of the brightest days of my life. I had gone into Freeport with my aunt, who had her weekly shopping to do, and while she did that, I went into the Freeport Variety, which in those days stood hip to hip with L.L. Bean's, to check out the magazines. And there, standing out in a blaze amid such dull companions as *Time, Life, Look, Outdoor Life,* and *The Readers' Digest,* was a magazine with a fiendish rendering of a deliciously horrible creature on its cover. I took it down with a hand that was almost trembling; I really could not *believe* such a thing.

It was, of course, my first issue of Forry Ackerman's *Famous Monsters of Filmland.* The subject of the cover was Claude Rains as the Phantom of the Opera, and it had been executed by the fiendishly talented Basil Gogos. I almost fell over my own feet in my eagerness to get up to the cash register with this wonderful, unbelievable, totally unexpected magazine. The clerk looked at it with a sneer I barely saw and gave me back sixty-five cents from my dollar bill.

Outside, a nasty cold drizzle had begun to fall. I noticed that even less than I had noticed the clerk's sneer. I got into my aunt's car, opened the magazine, feasted my eyes on that utterly *incredible* cover for at least another two minutes ... and at last opened the magazine up. I was *immediately faced with my first outrageous Forrest J Ackerman Pun: the editor's page of that, the November issue, was headed HAPPY THANKSGRAVING!* In the years to follow, I read those puns with a never-ending delight — in one still, Tokyo residents about to be *flambéed* by Godzilla were said by Forry to be "down on their Japan-knees." A still of Joan Crawford from (*Strait-Jacket,* natch) was captioned AX A STUPID QUESTION, GET A BLOODY ANSWER. It was all a part of the inimitable Forry Ackerman style ... and there must have been a lot of us tomato-eaters out there, because *Famous Monsters of Filmland* (or just *FM* to we long-time readers) went from a probable one-shot to a queer sort of American institution ... or what Forry might himself call "a Martian Comical." Ouch!

I didn't just *read* that first issue of *Famous Monsters* (it was actually issue #6 or #7, I believe; the Freeport Variety discovered the magazine late); I *inhaled* it.

Eventually my aunt came back to the car, and I helped her load her stuff into the trunk. She got behind the wheel, saw what I was reading, shook her head severely (as severely as only a second-grade teacher of the *old* school can shake her head), and pronounced it junk.

"Why do you want to fill up your head with such junk, Stevie?" she asked me grimly.

I just shook my head, unable to tell her what my heart knew — that it was *great* junk, *powerful* junk, *liberating* junk. This is an old truth to me now, but in reading the text of the book you now hold, I discovered it in a fresh, exciting way, thanks to Forrest J Ackerman, who writes with the clear and fresh devotion of a real fan ... and that alone is enough to invest his work with a real power, a power so great it would be startling if it were not so clearly benign and loving.

"Just *junk,*" my aunt repeated, more threateningly than before, and I turned the magazine over hoping that with Gogos' gruesomely realistic rendering of Claude Rains out of sight, the whole subject would drift from her mind.

On the back was a large ad extolling the wonders of Venus Flytraps.

CARNIVOROUS PLANTS! The ad screamed.

"Junk," my aunt said more ominously yet, and my mother later concurred. I thought it prudent to slip that copy of *Famous Monsters* behind the loose piece of baseboard behind my bed (the same loose board behind which I would begin to secrete copies of *Cavalier* and *The Adam Bedside Reader* some three years later) so that it would not "disappear" on me. I made that magazine last for at least three weeks. I pored over it; I read and re-read each ad — already The Captain Company was taking on almost mystical overtones in my mind — marveling that one could buy 8-mm horror movies, soundtrack albums, and books such as Charles Beaumont's *The Magic Man* and Sarban's *The Sound of His Horn* that the Freeport Variety had never even *heard* of. I damn near memorized that magazine and it seemed *eons* until the next one was due out. And when I finally saw that next one, I bought it and *ran* back to the car with it, my face one big grin.

Forry was the first, and in the years which followed any number of imitators popped up. Some of them, like *Castle of Frankenstein*, were good ... but not even the best of them had the crazed panache of *Famous Monsters of Filmland* and *Spacemen*, an Ackermagazine which covered the science fiction movies from *Metropolis* to *Forbidden Planet* (and you must remember that in those days films of fantasy, horror and science fiction were very much poor relations; there had been no *Star Wars*, *Alien*, or *The Exorcist* — we had to make due with Marshall Thompson and John Agar instead of Mark Hamill and Harrison Ford).

I finally scraped enough bucks to subscribe to *Spacemen*, and every day I would rush home from school and peer into our RFD box to see if an issue had arrived. And every time I saw the distinctive Warren Publishing Company mailer, it was like someone yelling "Let's have a pizza!" or "You want some ketchup with those fries, kid?" in a land where everyone believed the tomato to be a deadly poison.

And, you know, Forry *was* the best and he *is* the best. Like the magazines he has published, edited, and, in a large part, written, it's possible to say, "Often imitated, but never duplicated." He stood up for a generation of kids who understood that if it was junk, it was *magic* junk. He has always seen the fiction of the fantastic — the stories and the cinema — as a gateway to wonder. His love of the genre is a child's wonder, untouched by the sophistication which eventually corrupts. But this childish love which has been coupled with the enthusiasm of a man who has found the thing which God made him to do and is doing it with a unique style and an energy which never seems to flag.

You'll find all of that in this volume [*Forrest J Ackerman Presents Mr. Monster's Movie Gold*, ed. by Hank Stine], complementing an amazing array of still photographs the way a robust wine complements a good meal. You're going to have a good time, I think.

So grab that ketchup bottle and pour it on!

Stephen King
Halloween 1981

Preface

My lifelong fascination with fantastic genre fiction and cinema led to a general interest in tracing the roots of their expression in twentieth century American culture.

In the late 1990s I conceived the idea for a book of autobiographical essays and memoirs by living authors, editors, and artists who had worked for the science fiction, fantasy, weird fiction, and horror pulp magazines.

The first person I wrote to was Forrest J Ackerman, knowing of his vast collection of pulps, his personal contact with authors of the pulp era and representation of various authors, and inspired by an oft-given quote as in a 1980 interview, "I feel like a sponge that's been around in the science fiction field for fifty-four years now: I should be squeezed while I'm here to get all kinds of information out of me and into print."

Little more than a week later I received a letter in response promising a contribution and suggesting names to contact followed by press clippings, a filmography, and a 23-page single-spaced document listing in no particular order his various accomplishments and an assortment of celebrities and figures he had met. To this day I don't know if he intended this latter item to be the contribution he had promised or not but I wish to emphasize that among this material was not a single flyer, order form or advertisement. He did not look upon me as a potential customer he had hooked.

He offered to forward any correspondence to any of the writers named in his letter as long as I provided self-addressed stamped envelopes. While I appreciated the offer, the thought of buying all that postage to include on two envelopes apiece, which might not even garner a reply, dissuaded me. That he should offer to go to bat for my little project in the midst of all his other activities to me spoke volumes for his character.

I decided to go it alone but in contacting those pulp writers, artists and editors still living at the time, I found that most of the greats had already had their say on the matter, while others begged off due to their health and other factors.

After learning that Ackerman would be attending a not-too-distant convention I made it a point to go and meet him in person. I regret that at the time I still didn't know enough about his background and was not as versed in the history of the field so that I might have asked him better questions.

What I mainly recall is his correcting my pronunciation of authors' names on my list — SEE-OWED-MAHK (Curt Siodmak) and PAY-TAH-YAH (Emil Petaja) to my SY-ODD-MAK and PET-TAHJ-AH—and his taking the time to look over a list of individuals I had hoped to contact, hand-written in my illegible scrawl on lined notebook paper, and his writing in corrections and notations such as "DEAD" next to certain names.

I continued to correspond with him in regard to the project and he even made mention of it in one of his magazine columns of the time.

Choosing to ignore the list of accomplishments he had initially sent, I reminded him of his offer to contribute a memoir and he sent me a more fitting piece for my book, which he titled "My Life in a Time Machine." Ultimately that project never came to fruition but through it I managed to exchange letters with some legendary and now-departed names in science fiction, and I know it might not have gone beyond the status of an idle notion had I not received that early encouragement from Ackerman.

While the publication for which Ackerman is best known, *Famous Monsters of Filmland* (*FM*), was before my time I fully understand its appeal as readers could linger over the copious stills in an age prior to the advent of home video, video sharing and image searches with articles peeling back the layers of mystique surrounding these then little-seen motion pictures.

Though he is remembered for the vast collection he amassed, the influential magazine he edited and his participation in conventions, Ackerman also left a sizeable body of work in print. No one is apt to mistake him for Mark Twain, but Ackerman's small body of fiction displays remarkable compression. As a reportorial presence he was active for eight decades and his journalistic work constitutes some of the earliest reportage on filmmaking in these genres. Anyone who has only encountered his written work in *FM* might be directed to peruse his more serious tributes to fallen figures and an examination of his correspondence reveals a keen mind and a rich cultural awareness.

With regard to this bibliography, I believe that I have given adequate coverage to Ackerman's contributions to fanzines and amateur periodicals, but other areas remain somewhat unclear. Until recently there existed a relative lack of precise information on the contents of *Famous Monsters of Filmland*. The index to the magazine in Dennis Daniel's *Famous Monsters Chronicles* was of great aid in gleaning some idea of issue content but much of the material in the Warren magazines was printed sans credit, or pseudonymously. *The Warren Companion* notes, "Creating any sort of checklist for 'Famous Monsters' is problematic since there's little to distinguish one issue from the other in terms of known contributors." I managed to make contact with a number of surviving contributors to the original magazine and was careful to note the authors of the articles when credited. With respect to the magazine, I am erring on the side of caution and crediting most un-bylined pieces to Ackerman even though some may have been authored by others. Ackerman would regularly rewrite many of the contributions to suit them to the "house" style, and so these are in a sense uncredited collaborations. The timely appearance of David Horne's *Gathering Horror: A Completist Collector's Catalogue and Index for Warren Publishing*, which for the first time fully details the contents of all the various Warren periodicals, proved a godsend in this regard.

The discerning reader will note that two sections of the bibliography—the filmography and discography—do not technically belong, a bibliography being a list of written work. The reasons for including them anyway are two-fold. First, my intention for the book is to be as all-inclusive as possible. Second, considering Ackerman's lifelong interest in and association with the performing arts as well as his expertise on the history of science fiction, fantasy and horror in literature and film, for which expertise he was often sought for comments and interviews, I thought it best to include his appearances in films, various documentaries and talk show programs on these subjects. Ackerman didn't limit himself to the written word, so I thought it fitting I didn't either.

While pains have been taken to make this as complete as possible there yet remain inevitable lacunae particularly in fanzines, foreign publications, reprints, columns, letters, newspaper items, publications on or in Esperanto and items for which copies have not surfaced or information is lacking to determine precisely what Ackerman's contribution was at the time this has gone to press. Any corrections and additions may be addressed to the author care of the publisher. Semicolons within entries have been used to demarcate reprints of items.

Biographically I hope to highlight the remarkable amount of genre figures with whom Ackerman interacted, individuals whose lives spanned three centuries. This portion is necessarily compressed and prevents detailed examination of any one facet but should serve to provide a factually accurate portrait and address certain inaccuracies that have arisen regarding the man.

New material by and about Ackerman continues to be reprinted and released for the first time, which I have sought to reflect in this work.

Ackerman's life story was peopled by a literal "cast of thousands" and my work on this project has accordingly brought me into contact with dozens of individuals. This book could not contain what it does without the generous assistance of the following individuals who have my profound gratitude for fielding inquiries, sharing memories of Ackerman, putting me in contact with others, or providing descriptions or copies of items in their collections: Donn Albright; David Aronovitz; Mike Ashley; George Beahm; Greg Bear; Dennis Billows; Margaret Borst; Ronald V. Borst; Cuyler W. "Ned" Brooks; Bernie Bubnis, Jr.; Judy Cerruti; George "E-gor" Chastain; John L. Coker III; John Robert Colombo; William G. Contento; L. W. Currey; Mary Ellen Daugherty; Paul Davids; Dwight R. Decker; Marsha DeFilippo; Bob Diaz; Vincent Di Fate; Steve Dolnick; Arthur M. Dula; G. John Edwards; Kenneth W. Faig, Jr.; Ernest Farino; Mark Frank; Donald F. Glut; Victoria Hackett; Jonathan Hall; Lee Harris; Ray Harryhausen; David Horne; Dustin Jablonski; Charles Lee Jackson II; Mike Jittlov; Loma Karklins; Earl Kemp; Erle Melvin Korshak; David A. Kyle; the late Verne Langdon; David Langford; Robert Leininger; Robert Lichtman; Brad Linaweaver; Robert A. Madle; Shannon B. Maier; Leonard Maltin; John Mansfield; Linda Ross-Mansfield; Frederick J. Mayer; Michael McCarty; Joe Moe; Timothy C. Moriarty; Lee Neville; Ted Newsom; Charles Nuetzel; Bill Obbagy; Fred Patten; William H. Patterson, Jr.; Dennis Phelps; Wilum H. Pugmire; Juha-Matti Rajala; Kim Reynolds; Gary Don Rhodes; Trina Robbins; Nate Rosenbloom, membership services coordinator of the Cal Alumni Association at UC Berkeley; Dr. Samuel J. Sackett; Andy Sawyer; David Sechrest; Robert Sexton; Richard Sheffield; Perry Shields; M. J. Simpson; John Stanley; Richard Stoner; George Stover; Gary J. Svehla; Greg Theakston; Bill Thomas; James Van Hise; Chuck Verrill; Steve Vertlieb; Carlos Villar; Bill Warren; Stephen C. Wathen; Taral Wayne; Alan White; Douglas M. Whitenack; Tom Whitmore; Isaac Wilcott; Eleanor Wood; Tom Wyrsch; and Raymond F. Young.

I am especially grateful to Stephen King for granting permission to reprint his 1981 essay, which in addition to relating how he discovered Ackerman and *Famous Monsters*, provides an excellent summation of who Ackerman was and what he stood for.

I wish to extend my sincere thanks also to Dennis Billows (who displayed considerable forbearance) for his pun-laden foreword, adding a bit of levity to what might otherwise seem a somewhat stodgy tome.

PART I: BIOGRAPHY

On December 4, 2008, the man Ray Bradbury once pronounced "the most important fan/collector/human being in the history of science-fantasy fiction" quietly passed away.

Forrest James Ackerman was born at 6:22 A.M. on November 24, 1916, in Los Angeles, California.[1] While still in his teens, he dropped the period after his middle initial, leading many to believe it stood for nothing. A 1956 autobiographical piece noted, "The 'J' stands for James. I detest it."[2] An explanation Ackerman offered was that he "was getting interested in numerology, and I tried each of these three names and found that Forrest J was the best numerologically and so dropped the 'ames' in James."[3] One profile stated "he was named after a friend of the family, James Clarke"[4] and indicated he was called Clark as a child.

His father William Schilling Ackerman was born August 27, 1892, in Brooklyn, New York, to Ira Ackerman and the former Rebecca Conkling. As of June 1917 William was employed as clerk at Amalgamated Aluminum and the Ackermans were living at 1115 E. 18th Street. World War I draft registration records indicate William requested to be excused from service because he had to support his family, and later he found employment as a statistician for the Getty Oil Company.

Forrest's mother, Carroll Cridland Ackerman (1883–1977), had been born in Ohio and married William Ackerman on June 16, 1914. Her parents, George Herbert Wyman (1860–1939) and Belle Wyman (1862–1948) — nicknamed "Zululu," a name she made up for herself at the altar on her wedding day — had relocated to California in 1891 where George was employed in the architectural firm of Sumner Hunt. Wyman worked on the design of the Bradbury Building from 1889 to 1893, drawing inspiration from the 1888 Utopian novel *Looking Backward* by Edward Bellamy. The structure, named for millionaire Lewis Bradbury, stands at 304 S. Broadway in Los Angeles, has often been used as a film location and is today on the National Register of Historic Places. Ackerman described the couple as "very much into spiritualism."[5] As an example, George, hesitant to take on the job, relented when he received a message from his long-deceased brother Mark encouraging him to take on the project.

Silent cinema was coming into its own and Forrest Ackerman was privileged to grow up in surroundings that facilitated his natural inclination toward motion pictures. A pivotal early filmgoing experience was *One Glorious Day,* a now-lost film released January 29, 1922, starring Will Rogers, which featured a ghost named "Eck." The next year Ackerman was enthralled by the performance of Lon Chaney, Sr., as Quasimodo in *The Hunchback of Notre Dame.*

A brother Alden Lorraine Ackerman was born February 19, 1924. While the two got on well Ackerman declared his brother "quite the opposite of me."[6]

In the words of H. P. Lovecraft, "horror lifted its grisly visage"[7] in 1925 and Chaney, "The Man of a Thousand Faces," returned as Erik in *The Phantom of the Opera.* The film was a seminal experience not only for Ackerman but for *Psycho* author Robert Bloch and Ray Bradbury as well. Ackerman later met actress Mary Philbin the object of the Phantom's desire, whose career had faded with the coming of the talkies and in 1954[8] Ackerman wrote an oft-anthologized short story "Letter to an Angel" as a tribute to Lon Chaney, Sr. *The Lost World,* which he saw that year, featured pioneering stop-motion effects in a sequence wherein a dinosaur is set loose. This helped further shape his nascent tastes.

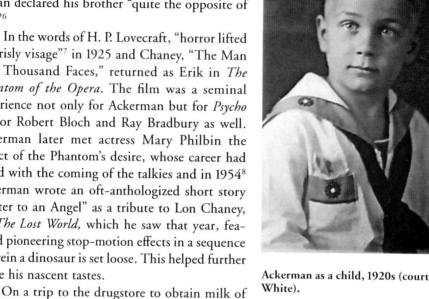

Ackerman as a child, 1920s (courtesy Alan White).

On a trip to the drugstore to obtain milk of magnesia his eye was drawn to the cover of what turned out to be the October 1926 issue of *Amazing Stories.* The magazine, which contained reprints of perennials Jules Verne and H.G. Wells in addition to A. Hyatt Verrill and Garrett P. Serviss, had been in existence a mere six months since its founding by the Luxembourg born Hugo Gernsback. A recent visit to the circus having excited his interest in the varieties of life, nine-year-old Ackerman was intrigued by the strange creature, "a gigantic crustacean ... about three times the size of a human being"[9] by Frank R. Paul illustrating Verrill's "Beyond the Pole." "I think I had so many visions of zebras and various exotic things in my mind, I didn't even know that that was an imaginary creature; I just wanted to read about it."[10] Ackerman recalled he "dutifully bought the medicine"[11] but persuaded his mother to let him return to the store and the soon-to-be ten-year-old made this decisive purchase from a long vanished pharmacy at the corner of Santa Monica and Western.

Being as yet unaware it was a monthly publication Ackerman remembered that he did not purchase another until the August 1927 issue. His having been a reader of *Amazing Stories* since its first year made many consider Ackerman the original American science fiction fan but he was always quick to point to Aubrey MacDermott and others whose interest predated his own.

Ackerman also collected the short-lived *Scientific Detective Monthly,* which attempted to blend two popular genres, and *Ghost Stories* magazine (1926–1932), the product of Gernsback's competitor, pulp magnate Bernarr Macfadden. Grandmother Belle would read these pulp periodicals to Ackerman cover to cover and he was loath to dispose of them. Over eight decades later he remarked, "I was fearful that all of a sudden there wouldn't be any more science fiction, so I figured I better collect as much as I possibly could so I could reread it and remember it."[12]

Ackerman originally housed his burgeoning magazine collection in his grandmother's basement, until his parents forced him to sell them to a neighbor boy.[13] Ackerman so lamented the loss of this "embryonic collection"[14] that his parents were persuaded to let him buy them back. Though he had upgraded from the original, he kept a copy of the October 1926 *Amazing* magazine close at hand all his life and even talked of being buried with it.[15]

Ackerman eventually amassed complete runs of the American science fiction pulps and many international publications containing fantastic fiction from previous eras such as the German-language fantasy magazine *Der Orchideengarten* which ran from 1919 to 1921. This growing hoard was stored in the basement of his 5327 Virginia Avenue residence.

His grandparents also fostered his interest in the cinema and would take him to more than half a dozen films in a single day. Whereas most early science fiction fans focused exclusively on print material, Ackerman's interests were more all-inclusive, and with his proximity to the film industry he began obtaining the autographs of movie stars of the day such as Gary Cooper and his screen crush Marlene Dietrich.

Hollywood-informed sensibilities and its promotional tactics were not lost on him. He absorbed the devices of showmanship in addition to appropriating the hairstyle of Warren William and the handwriting of actress Kay Francis.[16] He was also known to break out into the songs of his musical hero Al Jolson.

One area he showed little enthusiasm for was religion. Ackerman recalled "my well-meaning parents subjected me to 7 different Sunday Schools before I finally rebelled" and ultimately he "became an atheist at 15."[17]

Ackerman attended Sunnyside Elementary School where he received high marks.

William Ackerman's work took the family to San Francisco around 1927 and where they lived at 530 Staples Avenue.

In 1927 Ackerman saw *Metropolis* for the first time, which he cited as his lifelong favorite film. He later described his "all-time pet project" as "the immortalization in print of *Metropolis*"[18] and made it a point to meet its male and female leads Brigitte Helm and Gustav Fröhlich.

He saw *London After Midnight* on its opening day in December 1927. Ackerman would later come into possession of what were believed to be the top hat and teeth worn by Chaney in this lost silent film. Decades later he would participate in an attempt to reconstruct the film from stills in book form.

Ackerman proved adept at sleuthing out pseudonyms, visiting attorney Judson W. Reeves who wrote as "Aladra Septama" and whom he discovered also lived in San Francisco. The preadolescent Ackerman showed up unannounced on Reeves' doorstep but the amused counselor welcomed him, and the author's wife served him with milk and cookies. He also called on author Alfred John Olsen, Jr., of Beverly Hills whose debut in the June 1927 *Amazing Stories* had been "The Four-Dimensional Roller-Press." Writing as Bob Olsen, he had penned a series of entomologically themed works, which Ackerman termed "Antales."[19] Olsen would remark years later, "In all my experiences with science fiction I have never read, seen or known anything that was so amazing as 4e himself. My favorite designation for him was 'God's gift to science fiction writers.'"[20]

At the age of eleven Ackerman in 1928 wrote a 10,000-word story "The Madman of Mars" and serialized it as a fanzine later.

Having followed the *Amazing Stories* letters column "The Reader Speaks," Ackerman wrote in and saw his first published letter of comment appear in the Fall 1929 *Science Wonder*

Quarterly No. 1, the first issue of a companion publication to Gernsback's new science fiction title. The editors tagged this superlative-filled effusion "A New Method of Evaluation." Bursting with praise, the dispatch began, "Although I am only twelve years old, I have taken a delight in reading the magazine you have published for almost the last four years" and assured the staff that the magazine's various features "all meet with my approval."[21]

Coincidentally this was also an offshoot of the publication wherein editor Gernsback, dispensing with the awkward coinage "scientifiction," introduced the term "Science Fiction" from which Ackerman would create his own divisive abbreviation.

Another rare film Ackerman saw was the 1929 "talkie" version of *High Treason* and like many other youths soon to comprise science fiction fandom, in 1929 Ackerman began clipping and collecting Dick Calkins' *Buck Rogers* comic strips from the newspaper, having read the serial by Philip Francis Nowlan in *Amazing* the year before.

Although he felt his grandparents to be more supportive of his interests, he acknowledged that his parents "took pride in seeing their son's name in print."[22] Finding that relatives would purchase the magazines if they contained his letters, he began dashing off a spate of epistles, a feat matched only by Clifford C. Kornoelje who took his nom de plume "Jack Darrow" from a character in the Roy Rockwood books. Historian Sam Moskowitz termed the duo "the most prominent letter-writers of the day," while Jack Speer noted Ackerman and Kornoelje "popularized the letter-every-month habit,"[23] inspiring others to knock them off their pedestals.

In 1929 while lying sick in bed, Ackerman received a letter from Linus Hogenmiller of Farmington, Missouri, who became a steady pen pal and together the two formed the Boys' Scientifiction Club, a lending library for books and magazines. Ackerman made Linus vice president of the club while he himself was its president-librarian. Its secretary-treasurer was Frank Sipos, a Hungarian-American fan who also lived on Ackerman's street. Founded "to promote scientific interest among boys between the ages of 10 and 15, to encourage the reading of Science Fiction and scientific works, and to create a bond of friendship among them,"[24] Ackerman would frequently quip the masculine name was necessary as "female fans were as rare as unicorns' horns."[25]

Ackerman would trade signed cards and copies of author signatures with other fans. Always eager for communication Ackerman confessed, "I once put my name and address in a bottle and threw it in the ocean. Never got an answer."[26]

From 1929 to 1933 Ackerman was on Balboa High School's *Galleon* yearbook staff and contributed vignettes and verse to the school newspaper *The Buccaneer*, sometimes under the pseudonym "Ione Lee Hurd." He was a member of the International Honor Society of High School Journalists[27] and the Quill and Scroll Society. Ackerman graduated from Balboa "8th place in scholastic standing in class of 256."[28]

Ackerman recalled that by this point authors "would write me and tell me what they were working on, where their next story would be published and so on. So I thought, why not disseminate this information to other fans? I didn't have any means other than a typewriter and carbon paper, so I typed up the information, made about six copies, and that's how my first fanzine was born."[29]

Future film producer James H. Nicholson who lived on Lunado Way and attended Balboa High, introduced Ackerman to the process of hectography, and Ackerman published two issues of a hectographed fanzine *The Meteor* in 1930, reproducing the autographs of SF authors including the signatures of Edmond Hamilton and Ray Cummings.[30]

Under Nicholson the club became the Junior Scientific Club, which Ackerman described as "more science-oriented."[31]

Beyond the signatures of science fiction authors, Ackerman obtained manuscripts and magazine cover paintings from the editors and artists. He had issues of the magazines and story clippings specially bound. The first manuscript he received was "The Golden Girl of Munan" from its author Harl Vincent.[32] In many cases Ackerman was the only fan to meet some of these more obscure early science fiction writers (e.g., Austin Hall, the co-author of one of his favorites, *The Blind Spot*). His youthful zeal for hoarding this ephemera would prove a boon though a comprehensive listing was never produced. At this age he also collected stamps and phonograph records.

In August 1930 Ackerman entered into correspondence with Edgar Rice Burroughs, the creator of Tarzan, whose work he first encountered with "The Master Mind of Mars" in the 1927 *Amazing Stories Annual*.

A science fiction musical *Just Imagine* was released November 23, 1930, and Grandmother Belle purchased stills from the production, which he received for his birthday.[33] Recognizing Fritz Lang's name from the credits of *Metropolis* and *Siegfried* he wrote a fan letter to the German film director in 1931 and received a reply and stills.[34] After the filmmaker's passing Ackerman would come to own a monocle, a stuffed toy monkey and other items of Lang's.

In May 1931 Ackerman's contest-winning story "A Trip to Mars" was published on a children's page in the Sunday Supplement section of the *San Francisco Chronicle*. Winning over fifty other entrants, Ackerman was photographed for the paper holding the first issue of *Amazing Stories*.[35]

The first piece of pulp magazine artwork Ackerman obtained was "Midnight Mail Takes off for Mars" from the April–May 1931 issue of the short-lived *Miracle Science and Fantasy Stories* by Elliott Dold, Jr.[36]

On Christmas Day 1931 he saw director James Whale's adaptation of Mary Shelley's *Frankenstein*. Ackerman would recall "a sinister white ambulance" outside the theater and during the screening a woman ran screaming up the aisle when the monster was revealed in green-tinted footage.[37] He stayed on for a second showing and when the same lady repeated her hysterics he realized he had his "first experience of movie hype."[38] Surprisingly Ackerman claimed he was unfamiliar with the novel at the time though he had been informed of its production by Carl Laemmle, Sr. As with *Metropolis*, Ackerman would seek out and make contact with everyone from Jack Pierce, who designed the character's iconic makeup, to Kenneth Strickfaden, who created the electrical equipment for Dr. Frankenstein's laboratory.

By the early 1930s Ackerman had more than 100 correspondents from around the world who received missives from him in his favorite green ink. "Man alive! How do you do it? How do you remember what you've written to each correspondent?" asked his incredulous friend Julius Schwartz in December 1931.[39] This furious epistolary activity would persist in his lifelong efforts to organize and promote communication among aficionados.

Also in the early 1930s Ackerman saw Bela Lugosi performing *Dracula* live at San Francisco's Erlanger Theatre.[40]

Ackerman next held the position of associate editor for *The Time Traveller* in January 1932.[41] Ackerman wrote a list of 32 then-known fantasy films up to that time which appeared on the first page of the first issue, and would continue to cover what he called "imagi-movies." Among the journal's earliest subscribers was Jerome Siegel of Cleveland, Ohio.

Continuing to branch out, in 1932 Ackerman founded a group called Fantasy Fans' Fraternity with Norman Caldwell.[42]

More significantly, in September 1932 Ackerman, in tandem with Julius Schwartz, Mortimer Weisinger, printer Conrad H. Ruppert, and Ruppert's friend Maurice Z. Ingher, incorporated as *Science Fiction Digest* and began publishing a fanzine under that title, the first periodical to carry the titular phrase.[43] Here he functioned as "Scientifilm Editor" carrying on his coverage of "scientifilms" and "imagi-movies," and in this capacity he would report on many then-upcoming films as well as unrealized projects that never appeared and these mentions may be their sole documentation in print. Ackerman credited Weisinger with coining "scientifilms." "Since I didn't think of it first, I promptly came up with 'scientifi-cinema.'"[44]

Schwartz and Weisinger were members of the primigenial metropolitan fan organization "The Scienceers" whose proximity to publishers' offices allowed them to gain firsthand information for their columns "Out of the Ether" and "Weird Whisperings." The canny youths made good use of their surroundings and the duo regularly visited writers and editors, and before long set themselves up as literary agents under the banner of the Solar Sales Service.

In January 1933 Cleveland fan Jerry Siegel's "The Reign of the Superman" appeared in *Science Fiction*, a fanzine he produced on the mimeograph of Glenville High School. Written under the nom de plume Herbert S. Fine, it featured a bindle stiff–turned bald villainous Superman and an intrepid reporter named not Clark Kent but Forrest Ackerman.[45]

Ackerman was made first Honorary Member of the Science Fiction League in 1933. That same year Ackerman saw *Deluge*, directed by Felix E. Feist and starring Sidney Blackmer, an early science fiction disaster film based upon the 1927 novel *Deluge: A Romance* by S. Fowler Wright and believed for years to have been lost. In 1981 Ackerman discovered a print within a cinema archive in Rome.[46]

Also released in 1933 was *King Kong*. Ackerman later owned the pteranodon modeled by Marcel Delgado and would eventually possess the Stegosaurus and the mechanical Brontosaurus models from the film and pass them on to film director Peter Jackson.

From a story called "Adventure in Time" by his future collaborator Henry George Weiss writing as "Francis Flagg" in the April 1930 *Science Wonder Stories*, Ackerman learned of the artificial language Esperanto. Esperanto was created by Polish ophthalmologist Ludwik Lejzer Zamenhof in 1887 and touted as a global language of the future. The notion appealed to Ackerman. In 1933 his grandfather informed him of an Esperanto class being offered at LA City College taught by Arthur Brooks Baker, who had written textbooks on the subject and was the founder of the publication *Amerika Esperantisto*. There Ackerman met Myrtle R. Douglas who went by the nickname "Morojo."[47] Having mastered the tongue Ackerman then set about translating science fiction works into Esperanto.

Early on his predilection for puns and espousal of Esperanto earned him the wrath of Donald A. Wollheim with whom he feuded. The then-disputatious Wollheim was ruthless in his dealings with other fans. Those fans who detested Ackerman's puns were not above childish name-calling themselves. Members of the International Scientific Association fan group called him "Farwest J Sapperman,"[48] while British fan D.R. Smith objected to Ackerman's "portmanteau words"[49] in a piece titled "Hands off English" which ran in the seventh number of fanzine *Novae Terrae* in October 1936, deriding him as "the apostle of a new, simpler language."⁵⁰ Indeed some of Ackerman's fan writings and correspondence are so rife with abbreviations, and other oddities as to be nigh indecipherable.

In 1956 he would reflect, "Years ago I was fanatic about simplifying the English language; now I'm more concerned with a simple tax form."⁵¹

After high school graduation, Ackerman tried to support himself by entering contests.⁵² His parents wished for him to attend college and he applied while operating as a mail-order dealer in books, pulps, tearsheets of stories therefrom, and specialty press items on the side. After experiencing a number of rip-offs, he was hardly any better off so in August 1933⁵³ he entered the University of California, Berkeley, "to study journalism" but, coming to the conclusion he had "nothing further to be learned" he "left after second semester."⁵⁴ Another subject he took was paleontology.

Switching in its second issue to a forum for weird fiction, Charles D. Hornig established *The Fantasy Fan* which ran from September 1933 through February 1935. This printed publication so impressed Hugo Gernsback he hired the seventeen-year-old fan and gave him editorship of *Wonder Stories*.

Ackerman had by now begun appearing as a character in other fan fiction as he had done in "The Reign of the Superman." The first issue of *The Fantasy Fan* contained a short "Earthling Spurns Martian" by Allen Glasser featuring "a young Earthling named Efjay Akkamin." His name appeared in Robert Bloch's "The Ultimate Ultimatum" in the August 1935 *Fantasy Magazine*, and a vignette by Richard G. Kerlin in the letters column of the December 1935 *Wonder Stories*, "The Alien Hah-Rah," told of "the Ackerman-Darrow Scientifictionic Expedition." The thinly disguised duo had previously appeared as "Forrest Jackerman" and "Jack D. Arrow" in "The Return of Tyme," a time travel story by A. Fedor and Henry Hasse in the August 1934 *Wonder Stories*. Still later Arthur C. Clarke penned a serial "A Short History of Fantocracy—1948–1960" featuring "a gigantic, 50,000 horsepower plane, piloted by Clarke and Forrest Ackerman"⁵⁵ in *The Fantast* December 1941.

In the first issue of his journal Hornig initiated "The Boiling Point" with a letter by Ackerman. This immediately landed him in a contretemps with H.P. Lovecraft who would label him "tawdry & press-agent minded"⁵⁶; Clark Ashton Smith; and Lovecraft's young protégé Robert H. Barlow. Ackerman had contended that "Dweller in Martian Depths" in the March 1933 number was ill-suited for an "stf mag" like *Wonder Stories*. Smith, a California poet whose early verse had earned the esteem of George Sterling and Ambrose Bierce had turned to the pulps to put bread on the table for himself and his aging parents. Lovecraft, who had been in correspondence with Smith since 1922 was quick to leap to the defense of his friend and as the debate raged on other readers weighed in and soon called for its surcease. "Either Forrest J Ackerman is daft or an imbecile or a notoriety-seeking clown and knave," wrote Robert Nelson in the November 1933 issue. "I was very grateful that it was a multiple choice; you know, they didn't say it was all four at once,"⁵⁷ Ackerman quipped to an interviewer years after the fact. Bearing no grudges, Ackerman included a story by Barlow in an anthology he edited some six decades later.

Ackerman continued to send a torrent of missives to periodicals under an array of pen names and was not above directing his criticism to the writers themselves. Clark Ashton Smith noted in a letter to August Derleth, "Sometime ago I received a personal letter from him urging me to refrain from contributing this type of material to *W.S.*!"⁵⁸ Later Ackerman befriended Smith and took him on as a client.

Lovecraft remarked to Barlow in private correspondence, "Ackerman represents a millionfold exaggeration of a kind of smart-alec vanity & publicity-seeking which we all have to some extent in youth."[59] The entire "Boiling Point" exchange which ran from September 1933 to February 1934 remained in the memory of the principals and their admirers and was reprinted as a booklet by Necronomicon Press in 1985.

In addition to his verbal jousting Ackerman had a six-part column in *The Fantasy Fan* describing his collection, which by 1933 already included original pieces by Paul ("The Dust of Destruction" cover painting from the February 1931 *Wonder Stories*), Dold, and Leo Morey.[60]

In response to a *Photoplay* magazine ad inviting audience input on their product, Ackerman began corresponding with Carl Laemmle, Sr., the president of Universal Pictures, suggesting science fiction scenarios and stories the studio could adapt.[61] The two exchanged sixty-two letters, and Laemmle wrote a note enabling Ackerman to go to the Universal branch office and "get stills and posters and sound scores."[62] Among the items acquired thus were rare sound discs on which were recorded the soundtracks to *Frankenstein*, *The Mummy*, *Murders in the Rue Morgue*. He later managed to snag the disc for the Paramount film *Dr. Jeckyll and Mr. Hyde*[63] some of which were later purloined from his home during open houses. In time his motion picture related memorabilia came to be augmented by costumes, props, posters, stills, lobby cards, press books, and copies of screenplays.

Ackerman moved back to Los Angeles in 1934[64] living at first with his grandparents, then an apartment at 236½ N. New Hampshire in Hollywood.

As announced in the May 1934 *Wonder Stories* Ackerman was one of two fans to be named among the executive directors of the Science Fiction League listed on the masthead, the others being authors.

The June 1934 issue of *Wonder Stories* contained a letter from David A. Kyle of Monticello, New York, who promised, "Watch for my letter every month, for my middle name — is Ackerman!"[65] The two struck up a correspondence and remained lifelong friends. In emulation of Ackerman's penchant for green ink, Kyle adopted purple ink, signing himself "The Purple Bat."

Nineteen thirty-four saw the release of *Death Takes a Holiday*, another film Ackerman would long remember. He frequently referenced the character of Prince Sirki, portrayed by Fredric March.

Also in 1934 Ackerman's time-travel tale "Dwellers in the Dust" was accepted for *Marvel Tales* by editor William L. Crawford. A Pennsylvania fan who put out a series of semiprofessional publications, Crawford was chronically under-financed and unable to meet deadlines and though he had amassed material from some who were then top names in the field, his printed efforts of the time met with little success. Among the items Crawford did manage to get out were Robert Bloch's first published short story and Lovecraft's first book, an error-riddled edition of *The Shadow Over Innsmouth* through his Visionary Press, a name that was supplied by Ackerman.[66]

In October 1934 Ackerman helped found the Los Angeles chapter of the Science Fiction League, the fourth such chapter to be founded,[67] which became the Los Angeles Science Fantasy Society (LASFS). He would serve as the first director of the organization as well as in a variety of other offices. Ackerman would recall that the initial gathering took place in a fan's garage.[68] Meetings later moved to the Brown Room of Clifton's Cafeteria and still later to the basement of a hotel at 637½ Bixel Street. Ackerman reportedly later "took over the club's leadership in February 1936."[69]

Along with the Philadelphia Science Fiction Society, the organization is one of the longest-running outgrowths of the Gernsback-sponsored Science Fiction League, though its 1940s incarnation was in iconoclastic fan Francis Laney's opinion "one of the twentieth century's great citadels of fuggheadedness."[70] For some years a feature of each meeting was "Forrest Murmurs" wherein Ackerman reported the latest publishing and cinematic scuttle.

Ackerman's persona and level of activity was already becoming a subject for parody. Arthur Wilson "Bob" Tucker wrote a satirical "Report of the 196th Convention" in a letter published in the November 1934 *Wonder Stories*[71] featuring the denizens of "Ackermanville." He placed high, tying with William H. Dellenback and Lewis F. Torrance in the Science Fiction Tests administered in the January 1935 *Wonder Stories*, the results of which were announced later that year. In the 1930s he read the 1928 lesbian-themed novel *The Well of Loneliness* by Radclyffe Hall.

Early in 1935 Ackerman conferred with Universal Studios story editor Dwight Cummins in an attempt to interest him in science fiction properties and adaptations. Cummins advised him such productions would be impractical due to the costs involved. About all that came of the meeting was Cummins' announcement that Universal had acquired the rights to adapt the *Flash Gordon* comic strip as a motion picture serial.[72] In April 1935 Ackerman was invited to the studio premiere of *The Bride of Frankenstein*.

In 1935 Ackerman tried to establish a British chapter of the Science Fiction League in Hayes, Middlesex,[73] while some British fans still bristled at his writing style.

Ackerman crafted a collaboration with C.L. (Catherine Lucille) Moore, whose gender was at first unknown to her colleagues. Centering upon her character Northwest Smith, the story "Nymph of Darkness" appeared in the April 1935 *Fantasy Magazine*. According to Sam Moskowitz, "Ackerman had supplied the idea, of an invisible girl who enlists Smith's aid, and Moore had done the writing."[74]

Ackerman's collaboration with "Francis Flagg" resulted in his first professional sale of fiction with "Earth's Lucky Day." The story appeared in the final issue of *Wonder Stories* March/April 1936 and was built on the pacifist notion of aliens who remove all the world's weaponry. "Time Twister," a further collaborative effort between Ackerman and "Flagg," whose real name was Henry George Weiss, took years to land and did not see print until after Weiss's death.

Trying and failing to secure public relations work for the film studios, Ackerman worked for a time with his father as a statistician for Associated Oil Company. A profile mentions government work as a time-keeper[75] and a stint as a film projectionist as well as his serving as "Civil Service Senior Typist on a Gov't construction project."[76]

In 1937 Ackerman met writer Robert Bloch,[77] already steadily selling to the pulps, who was in the city visiting his correspondent Henry Kuttner and in late June 1937 Ackerman attended the wake of actor Colin Clive at the Edwards Brothers Colonial Mortuary.[78]

Ray Bradbury who had moved to the area from his native Illinois three years before, spotted a notice in a bookstore on Hollywood Boulevard and joined LASFS on September 5, 1937.[79] Ackerman helped to harness his energies and assigned him articles for the club bulletin *Imagination!* "There were so many things he did to change all of our lives," Bradbury remembered at a birthday tribute to Ackerman. Ackerman printed Bradbury's first published short story "Hollerbochen's Dilemma" in the January 1938 *Imagination!* and Bradbury dedicated his short story collection *One More for the Road* to Ackerman. The October 1937

Imagination! was written in "all-out Ackermanese"[80] and the thirteen issues of the bulletin known for its lively letters pages gave free reign to his "Ackernyms."

Stop-motion puppetry enthusiast Ray Harryhausen inquired about some stills displayed at the Hawthorn picture house at which LASFS fan Roy Test, Jr., was employed[81] during a re-release of *King Kong*. He was told they belonged to Ackerman who then lent them to him. Harryhausen drew cover illustrations for *Imagination!* and would soon go to work for George Pal's Puppetoons.

Ackerman gamely tried to keep up with the burgeoning comic book field and "tried to get the first issues of every fantasy comic as it came out but he said the task soon overwhelmed him."[82]

In summer 1939 the first number of Bradbury's *Futuria Fantasia*, bankrolled by Ackerman, appeared. In July Ackerman traveled by train to attend the First World Science Fiction Convention (WorldCon) held in Manhattan concurrently with the World's Fair. He managed on the way to work in some hobnobbing, meeting with J. Harvey Haggard at the first stop in San Bernardino, California.[83]

Met by a group of fans in New York, he was promptly punched in the stomach by the sardonic writer and fan Cyril M. Kornbluth. The rather more welcoming Julius Schwartz arranged for a photo to be snapped by Conrad H. Ruppert of Ackerman shaking hands with his rival from the letters departments "Jack Darrow." Though they had no qualms expressing their opinions in print, both young men feared being asked to give a speech, yet both he and "Darrow" found themselves doing just that when "Darrow" was called to the stands to speak at the convention,[84] Ackerman summoned the courage while still in costume to greet, in Esperanto, the crowd at the World's Fair, saying he was a time traveler from the future.

Another precedent was set when Ackerman donned a "futuristicostume" reminiscent of those worn in the final scenes of the 1936 film *Things to Come*. With its green cape and embroidered "4SJ," he strode the streets looking like a proto-superhero in the company of lady friend and fellow Esperantist Morojo. Bestowing upon the gathering the nickname "NyCon" he there came face to face with the authors and illustrators themselves and put faces to the names of many of his correspondents. Ackerman recalled, "It was a thrill for me to press the flesh of ... the leading SF authors of the day,"[85] and he got to take in another screening of his beloved *Metropolis*.

The convention was not without its downside as six prominent fans were barred from attending but Ackerman commiserated with them at their rumpus in Brooklyn on the 4th[86]

Ackerman made a point to look up the publishing headquarters of the pulps themselves, visiting editor Farnsworth Wright at the offices of *Weird Tales* in company with Ray Bradbury and Erle Melvin Korshak, and calling upon fantasist A. Merritt, then employed with Hearst publications as editor of *The American Weekly*.[87]

Ackerman and Morojo attended a dinner on July 7 for the convention committee and prominent out-of-towners sponsored by Standard Magazines, publishers of *Thrilling Wonder Stories*.[88] Ackerman was among those who produced special fanzines in honor of the convention in exchange for copies of those made by the other participants. "From the NYCon I to the end of World War II Ackerman was #1 fan."[89] For some the convention would mark the crest of their activity but Ackerman would go on to be a record attendee at conventions.

That same month there appeared in *Astounding* "Black Destroyer," marking the debut of Canadian writer A.E. van Vogt who would become Ackerman's star client and whose

The initial meeting of two of the most prolific writers of letters to the science fiction magazines. In the foreground, "Jack Darrow" (Clifford Kornoelje of Chicago, left) shakes hands with "4SJ" Ackerman in his "futuristicostume." First World Science Fiction Convention, New York, July 1939 (photograph by Conrad H. Ruppert, courtesy John L. Coker III).

novel *Slan* was a particular favorite, and in its next issue the magazine carried "Lifeline" by Robert A. Heinlein. Ackerman would be an early champion of Heinlein's work but would come to have an uneasy relationship with him in the ensuing years.

In 1939 Ackerman began issuing *Vom*, or *Voice of the Imagi-Nation*, a "letterzine" continuation of *Imagination!* solely devoted to epistles received. It caused a stir when he featured a nude by Hannes Bok on the cover.[90] In his pioneering work on the history of fandom "Up to Now," Jack Speer recalled *VOM* "was pretty much laid open to any kind of discussions among the readers" and opined that Ackerman "had a disproportionately large part in the work connected with publication" while Francis Laney credited Morojo with "doing most of the drudgery of *VOM* and other Ackerman projects."[91]

In the late 1930s Ackerman heard H.G. Wells give a talk at the Wilshire Ebell club in Los Angeles,[92] while promoting a book on what proved to be one of the final American tours of the British luminary. Wells signed Ackerman's copy of his 1937 novel *Star-Begotten* and Ackerman sought to master a telephonic impression of the author's voice as he knew had been done by a man who had heard Abraham Lincoln speak.

In December 1939 "Nymph of Darkness" was reprinted in *Weird Tales* under editor Farnsworth Wright.

Ackerman secured what must have seemed a dream job at the Academy of Motion Pictures Arts and Sciences, as Superintendent in Charge of Varityping[93] and recalled he "had much to do with the Still & Magazine Dept."[94] but he disliked his superior. One of his other duties was guarding Oscars for *Gone with the Wind*.[95] Ackerman lost the position when he heard of an impending staff walk-out, after which only he and one other employee left.[96] He then worked as a varityper at the Fluor Drafting Company.

Ackerman encountered L. Ron Hubbard in Shep's bookshop on Hollywood Boulevard and upon hearing the various markets Hubbard had already sold to encouraged him to write science fiction.[97] The charismatic Hubbard began spinning an off-the-cuff tale about a future Ice Age and Ackerman was duly impressed.

Ackerman resigned as an executive of the Science Fiction League in January 1940,[98] dissatisfied with the actions of Sam Moskowitz and James V. Taurasi, Sr., who had run the WorldCon. On January 11, 1940, Morojo wrote that Ackerman was "unanimously elected" an "honorary member" of the LASFL. Ackerman was then made a director of the Science Fictioneers, a short-lived organization created by Frederik Pohl through his editorial post at Popular Publications in opposition to the Science Fiction League and inaugurated in the March 1940 issue of *Super Science Stories*.[99] *Novacious*, a fanzine Ackerman began in 1940 (later solely edited by Morojo) ran for seven issues.

Another World Science Fiction Convention was in the works, and the second such event, which Ackerman named the "ChiCon" was held September 1–2, 1940, at the Hotel Chicagoan. Ackerman was among the fans that paraded into the offices of the Chicago *Herald-American* to be photographed in costume,[100] and called on *Weird Tales* cover artist Margaret Brundage, famed for her nudes with Erle Korshak, Walt Liebscher, and Ross Rocklynne.[101]

At the convention Ackerman won a prize as the "Hunchbackerman of Notre Dame," wearing a Quasimodo mask created for him by Ray Harryhausen.[102]

In the 1940s Ackerman had a news column in *Fantasy Fiction Field*, introduced "nonstoparagraphing" into his fan writing, and incorporated red and green ribbon in his typewriter.

At the previous year's World convention, Ackerman nominated Robert A. Heinlein as Guest of Honor for the 3rd World Science Fiction Convention, some seven months before Heinlein would be named most popular SF author in a poll conducted by *Fantasy Fiction Field*.[103] "I was frequently invited to his home and allowed to read his forthcoming masterpieces in manuscript form, and I felt that, given another 12 months, he would be the hottest sf [*sic*] author of the year."[104]

This time the affair was named Denvention I by Wollheim, and held at the Shirley-Savoy Hotel. Future author, critic, and editor Damon Knight, a first-time convention attendee, recalled Ackerman was the only attendee who had then heard of him.[105] At this gathering Ackerman received an early science fiction award in the form of a medal presented by Walter J. Daugherty.

Heinlein gave a rousing speech, which David G. Hartwell described as "legendary"[106] and which was "intended to define the science fiction field for its readers and authors."[107] Heinlein praised science fiction readers for their awareness of cultural change and contended that science fiction held "a distinct therapeutic value" that lay in "its primary postulate that the world does change."[108]

Daugherty recorded Heinlein's "Discovery of the Future" speech and Ackerman transcribed and printed 200 copies as a pamphlet mimeographed in green ink that sold for ten cents. He was amazed to learn the prices a copy commanded years later.[109] Also he 1941 he edited a phonograph fanzine with Walter J. Daugherty.

As wartime conditions worsened, Ackerman shipped paper over to Britain, which was experiencing a shortage of supply, resulting in a "tradition developed in British fandom that Forry Ackerman was to be included in every mailing list and sent a complimentary copy of every British fan publication."[110] He had earlier been made an honorary member of the British Science Fiction Association.[111]

Ackerman stated that he learned of the attack on Pearl Harbor when fan Arthur Louis Joquel II burst into the LASFS clubhouse with the news. He dreaded being drafted for service so he enlisted August 15, 1942.[112]

He drafted a will leaving his collection and $1,000 to launch the Fantasy Foundation, intended as a "Master Library of Imaginative Literature"[113] and asked E. Everett Evans and other fans to tend to his collection during his service.

Cat People was released December 1942 and Ackerman knew and corresponded with French actress Simone Simon (1910–2005).

Ackerman was the first fan to edit a World War II newspaper, the *Ft. McArthur Bulletin Alert* (1942–1945). He later credited his wartime service with forcing him "to juggle half a dozen literary balls in the air at one time"[114] in hectic pace. An army editor reportedly forced Ackerman to fabricate stories, but the paper, which featured work by cartoonists Virgil Partch and Will Gould, won a prize in a national contest. He still sold books by mail to boost his income without much success and, under the pretext of leaving the base to read the proofs, Ackerman surreptitiously attended LASFS meetings, often in uniform.[115]

His brother Alden enlisted January 8, 1943.[116] In March 1943 Ackerman produced *Metalo-Mag*, a fanzine printed on a dog tag. On September 10, 1943, Ackerman met Fritz Lang following a screening held by the American Contemporary Guild.[117]

While still in the service in March 1944 Ackerman began editing *Fantasticonglomeration*, later shortened to *Glom*, for the Fantasy Amateur Press Association and by then had begun composing correspondence on stationery identifying him as a "scientifictionist." Also in 1944 under the imprint of the Fantasy Foundation, he published Jack Speer's *Fancyclopedia*, a detailed lexicography of the jargon that had grown around science fiction fandom.

Nineteen forty-four also marked his first on-screen appearance in a feature film, when he was seen in a cameo in the film *Hey, Rookie*, an adaptation of a Fort MacArthur stage show.

Ackerman served three years, four months, twenty-nine days, and had been promoted to staff sergeant before his discharge. Subsidized by the G. I. Bill, he again attempted and failed to sell his own science fiction stories. Hoping to capitalize on the arrival of the Nuclear Age he wrote a number of short stories with an atomic slant, all of which were slow to sell.[118]

In the 1940s he feuded with Roger Philip Graham, who wrote under pseudonyms such as Rog Phillips and ran "The Club House" column in *Amazing Stories*. Ackerman was particularly opposed to the magazine's continued coverage of the "Shaver Mystery" which posited a hidden subterranean civilization as fact.

On January 1, 1945, Alden Ackerman, a private first class with the 42nd Tank Battalion 11th Armored Division, was killed at the Battle of the Bulge in Belgium. He was awarded the Purple Heart and is interred at Hamm, Luxembourg.

Knowing he was now free of his wartime obligations, fans tried to prod Ackerman to establish the Fantasy Foundation as a working museum in 1946, then bailed out on him one by one.[119] Plans called for storehouses of genre material to be established in various locations.

He continued to bolster his holdings as when editor and collector C.A. Brandt, who had selected material for *Amazing* and *Wonder Stories* and served as literary editor and reviewer, willed his multilingual collection of fantastic literature to Ackerman.[120]

Upon hearing of H.G. Wells's passing in August 1946 Ackerman produced a volume *In Memoriam H. G. Wells 1866–1946* with Arthur Louis Joquel II.

In 1946 Ackerman produced *I Bequeath (to the Fantasy Foundation)* a detailed listing of the first 1,300 items in his collection.

Serving as chairman of PacifiCon I, August 30–September 1, 1946, at the Los Angeles Park View Manor, Ackerman collapsed during the first day of the event and was bedridden for nineteen days from exhaustion,[121] but not before making his presentation for the Fantasy Foundation Thursday, July 4.[122] Though he had proposed an all-female Guest of Honor line-up of C. L. Moore, pulp editor Mary Gnaedinger, and Margaret Brundage[123] this was ignored.

Ackerman included this image of his late brother Alden as the cover to his *Voice of the Imagi-Nation* (VOM), No. 39 (Feb. 1945) (courtesy Robert Lichtman).

In 1946 Ackerman visited Edgar Rice Burroughs in Tarzana in company with E. Everett Evans and "Tigrina." Ackerman asked Tarzan's creator to sign the magazine containing his first published story "Under the Moons of Mars" as "Normal Bean," the pseudonym under which his debut effort had appeared in 1912 but Burroughs instead inscribed it "Norman Ackerman." "Tigrina" was the nickname Ackerman devised for Edythe Eyde an occasional date who also served as minutes taker of the LASFS.

Ackerman is credited with having penned the first lesbian science-fiction story ever published, "World of Loneliness." He also wrote "Kiki" and other lesbian romances in the late 1940s under pseudonym Laurajean Ermayne for the carbon-copied lesbian magazine *Vice Versa*, the first for its audience and published by Eyde using the anagrammatic pseudonym of "Lisa Ben."

Ackerman eventually realized that steady fiction writing was not his forte[124] and that he was more suited to the occasional short-short or vignette. "I feel like nobody took me seriously as a science fiction writer," he lamented.[125]

In 1947 he launched Science Fantasy Agency, filling the vacuum left by his old fanzine associates Mortimer Weisinger and Julius Schwartz who had gone into business as the Solar Sales Service in the 1930s, and who had both moved on to editorial positions in the comic book industry by this time. Like his predecessors, Ackerman exclusively handled science fiction. Operating at a loss for the first year, Ackerman ultimately came to represent a variety of talents as well as the estates of many pulp-era authors, and "was the agent publishers usually approached for the clearance of rights to old-time stories."[126] A number of letters in magazines and articles by Ackerman mention his scrupulous attempts to locate the representatives or heirs of various figures, and author Raymond Z. Gallun recalled that though he didn't really wish to see certain of his pieces reprinted, in each case he received "a copy of the anthology with a check in the leaves" from Ackerman.[127] That same year East Coast writers had founded the Dirk Wylie Literary Agency, which prolific writer Frederik Pohl struggled to keep afloat following the demise of its founder, science fiction fan Joseph Harry Dockweiler.[128]

Though Ackerman was often erroneously cited as being Bradbury's agent, the top-flight authors in the field were already being handled by general agencies (Bradbury was represented by Don Congdon Associates; Arthur C. Clarke by Scott Meredith; while Isaac Asimov represented himself). Bradbury and Asimov did allow him to handle some foreign sales and reprints, though. Faced with these facts, Ackerman took on newer talent and over time he would eventually build up an eclectic clientele of authors, artists and screenwriters. Among the latter was Wyott Ordung, scenarist for the notorious *Robot Monster*.

Utterly disillusioned with his own literary efforts, he contemplated releasing a collection of his unsold short stories as *The Bust of Science Fiction*.[129]

Ackerman drew up contracts, secured illustrative work for clients and arranged story sales and artwork for William L. Crawford's publishing concern Fantasy Publishing Company, Inc.[130] Ackerman was one of several collectors who assisted Dr. J.O. Bailey in compiling information for his pioneering study *Pilgrims Through Space and Time: Trends and Patterns in Scientific and Utopian Fiction* which finally saw print in 1947 after years of gestation, and received similar credit in the likewise trailblazing work, *The Checklist of Fantastic Literature: A Bibliography of Fantasy, Weird and Science Fiction Books Published in the English Language*, the first title issued by the fan-founded Shasta Press.

Another notion Ackerman pushed for was a "Big Pond Fund" to allow foreign fans to attend American conventions, a concept which eventually materialized as the Transatlantic Fan Fund. He raised money for years to get British fan and author Edward John "Ted" Carnell to attend a WorldCon. Ackerman was himself a frequent candidate for the TAFF throughout the 1950s. Ackerman was a guest at the First Annual West Coast Scienti-Fantasy Conference on September 5, 1948, alongside L. Ron Hubbard, mathematician and some-time-science fiction author Dr. Eric Temple Bell, and authoress E. Mayne Hull.

In 1949 he was first called "Mr. Science Fiction" by Willy Ley in an article in the Los Angeles newspaper *The Record*. That same year he met monologist Brother Theodore Gottlieb and through the offices of Tigrina was made an Honorary Lesbian — a "Son of Bilitis" or "SOB" — at a Daughters of Bilitis convention.

Although a 1940 profile characterized him as a "confirmed bachelor,"[131] Ackerman wed Mathilde/Matylde/Matylda "Tilly" Malka Wahrmann Porjes (1912–1990) on June 2, 1950. Born November 4, 1912, in Frankfurt-am-Main, she had served as a nurse in World War II London and had immigrated to the United States in 1947.

Ackerman bestowed upon her a new first and middle name of his coinage: Wendayne Mondelle. Wendayne, who had been a clerk at the book department of the May Company when the two met, taught French and German for two decades at East Los Angeles Junior College and had been a reader of German-language utopian fiction in her youth. Wendayne had previously been married to Fredric Porjes, with whom she had a son, Michael Porjes (1941–2008), while Ackerman had noted that he didn't "care to contribute progeny to posterity."[132] Among other lifestyle changes, Wendayne urged Ackerman to learn to drive.[133]

At the seventh WorldCon in 1949 (the Ohio Cinvention), Ackerman participated in an early TV broadcast on Cincinnati station WLWT emceed by David A. Kyle, featuring

Wendayne and Forrest Ackerman in Germany, 1950s (courtesy Alan White).

famed science fiction author E.E. "Doc" Smith, Jack Williamson, Erle Korshak, Hannes Bok, and Fritz Leiber, Jr., a transcript of which was reproduced in Lloyd Eshbach's book *Over My Shoulder: Reflections on a Science Fiction Era*.[134]

Among the clients Ackerman by now represented was a struggling fan-turned-writer who had recently changed his name from Charles Leroy Nutt to Charles Beaumont. Ackerman could at the onset find no market for his backlog of stories[135] but in the interim supplied him with illustrating work, some of which Beaumont signed as "Chas. McNutt." The two would part ways as Beaumont's fortunes soared when he crashed more lucrative magazine markets and quickly moved on to writing for films and television before a brain disease claimed him at age thirty-eight.

Ackerman visited the set of *Destination Moon* in the company of Heinlein, Henry Kuttner (and his wife C. L. Moore), film director William Cameron Menzies, R.S. Richardson of Wilson Observatory, as well as fans Russ Hodgkins, and Arthur Jean Cox and were shown sets by painter Chesley Bonestell. This ambitious undertaking, based on Heinlein's novel for children *Rocketship Galileo* and on which Heinlein served as science advisor, was helmed by director George Pal, who would christen Ackerman's collection "the Fort Knox of science fiction" and would usher in a decade of science fiction films. Ackerman authored a number of write-ups on the watershed production.

Dr. Samuel J. Sackett recalled upon visiting Ackerman in 1950 that "my wife and I were stunned by the display of nudes in his office."[136]

At the September 1950 Norwescon held in Portland, Ackerman was part of the organizing committee of the Fantasy Writers of America alongside writers Wilson Tucker, Theodore Sturgeon, and anthologist Groff Conklin.[137] *Destination Moon* received a preview there.

In 1951 Forry and Wendayne moved to 915 S. Sherbourne Drive, which Ackerman wasted no time in dubbing "Spacebourne" and "Scarebourne." The move was accomplished with the aid of local fans, Ackerman paying them off in duplicate items from his collection.[138] Ron Haydock reported he then had three garages full, and noted Ackerman's plans to have his home torn down and construct a museum on the site.

In 1951 Ackerman opened his collection to the public and over the years thousands paraded through, often under little to no supervision by its owner. Inevitably items would be stolen from his collection but he never lost the desire to share the material he had accrued.

Ackerman was photographed by Allan Grant for *Life* magazine in April 1951 before his departure for Europe the following month where Ackerman was Guest of Honor at the International Science Fiction Convention in London, also serving in that capacity at the Festival Convention in place of author L. Sprague de Camp.[139] While there he took his first airplane ride, traveling to Belfast to meet leading fan Walt Willis. While in the U.K., Ackerman met S. Fowler Wright whose novel *The World Below* Ackerman had long admired and took him on as a client.[140] Ackerman also visited Agnes Stapledon, the widow of visionary author W. Olaf Stapledon[141] then appeared as Guest of Honor at Germany's BigGerCon 1951.

While overseas on various trips Ackerman made it a point to visit many important sites connected with figures of fantastic literature and film, among them the grave of Jules Verne in Amiens (which had been featured as the masthead of *Amazing Stories*), the urn of Bram Stoker, the grave of Mary Shelley, the home of playwright Karel Čapek who introduced the word "robot" into the language in his *R.U.R.* (Rossum's Universal Robots) and that of *Golem* director Paul Wegener.

Ackerman's father purchased for him the first "Ackermansion" which stood at 915 S. Sherbourne Drive in Los Angeles (courtesy Ronald V. Borst/Hollywood Movie Posters).

Ackerman was on the way to Nolacon I, the Ninth World Science Fiction Convention in September 1951, when he received word that his father William had suffered a fatal stroke.[142] William had attained the rank of vice president of the oil company at which he was employed and Ackerman felt he had passed on "probably feeling that I would never amount to much in life."[143]

On June 28, 1952, Ackerman signed his name to the Preamble to the Science-Fantasy Writers of America, along with a number of authors who met at the U.S. Grant Hotel in San Diego.[144] Ackerman was to serve as secretary but such an organization was not effected until the similarly named Science Fiction Writers of America was formed by Damon Knight in 1965.

TASFiC (the Tenth Annual Science Fiction Convention) was held August 30–September 1, 1952, at Chicago's Hotel Morrison where Hugo Gernsback, who was about to launch what would prove to be his last science fiction magazine, was Guest of Honor. Following the convention Ackerman hosted Walt Willis when he visited California.[145]

Ackerman visited the set of Curt Siodmak's *Donovan's Brain* where he was photographed posing alongside actor Lew Ayres and future first lady Nancy Davis.

In 1953 Ackerman attempted to sell artwork of Mel Hunter (1927–2004) and clients' stories to managing editor Sam Moskowitz at *Science Fiction* + who criticized Ackerman's letter writing style, and sales tactics.[146] Moskowitz had been recruited by Hugo Gernsback to edit what proved to be the final science fiction periodical issued by the pioneering pulp publisher.

Ackerman headed a committee which selected the best science fiction stories of the year for the anthology *Prize Science Fiction*. Anthony Boucher reviewed this title in the August 9, 1953, edition of *New York Herald Tribune*.[147]

Ackerman reported in his Spring 1953 "Scientifilms Preview" column that he had collaborated with Charles Beaumont in adapting the 1926 Henry Gardner Hunting novel *The Vicarion* and that he had written material with *Project Moon Base* writer/producer Jack Seaman for a proposed serial created by E. Mayne Hull and A. E. van Vogt to be titled *Mel Pelton: The Man from the Moon*.

Also in 1953, Ackerman was introduced to Bela Lugosi by Richard Sheffield, Jr., a teenager who had befriended the ailing star. Lugosi visited Ackerman's home where he was played the sound disc from *Murders in the Rue Morgue*. The actor wrote a single word in the guest book, "Amazed."

Ackerman enjoyed the friendship of not only many of these stars themselves but often their families and children as well. Several years later Sheffield sold Ackerman the ring Lugosi wore as Dracula in *Abbott & Costello Meet Frankenstein*, and he would in time come

Ackerman (left) enjoys a visit with Bela Lugosi, 1950s (courtesy Ronald V. Borst/Hollywood Movie Posters).

to acquire an Inverness cape and robe Lugosi wore in films. Amassing hundreds of editions of *Dracula* and *Frankenstein*, he had the signatures of most of the thespians who interpreted the books' monsters for the screen.

In 1953 Ackerman hosted Japanese fan Tetsu Yano, taking him to PhilCon. Yano in turn would donate toward the maintenance of his collection.[148]

At the eleventh World Science Fiction Convention in 1953 Ackerman was the recipient of a newly inaugurated "Annual Science Fiction Achievement Award" (or Hugo Award as they would become better known) for Number One Fan Personality, presented to him by Dr. Isaac Asimov in Philadelphia. Ackerman in turn passed it on to H.J. Campbell for delivery to the British fan Kenneth F. Slater, to whom it had been bequeathed.[149]

The 1950s were boom years for science fiction and Ackerman would fondly recall that in one "magic month"[150] of 1953[151] there were 49 magazines available. Foreign markets for science fiction material continued to open and Ackerman contributed material to a publication called *Häpna!* (Be Astounded!), edited by Swedish fan and writer Sture Lönnerstrand.

Ackerman supplied stories to Chester Whitehorn for a short-lived professional magazine called *Science Fiction Digest*. Among them was S. Fowler Wright's "The Rat," which August Derleth claimed was under contract to Arkham House Publishers, having appeared in the collection *The Throne of Saturn*. After much epistolary wrangling, Ackerman paid to the prizewinning Wisconsin author and founder of the specialty press Arkham House what he termed "blood money."[152] In September 1954 while driving back from Monterrey, Ackerman visited Clark Ashton Smith in the company of David A. Kyle.

In 1954 after hearing "hi-fi" advertised on his car radio, Ackerman coined the term "sci-fi" which would become "anathema to the SF community."[153]

Ackerman introduced "sci-fi" in his column for *Imagination*.[154] A claim has been made that the term was used earlier by Robert A. Heinlein in a letter of October 1, 1949, to his then-agent Lurton Blassingame, which was reproduced with this abbreviation for its printing in the Heinlein collection *Grumbles from the Grave*. The actual text of the letter reveals Heinlein wrote "sci-fic."[155] Ackerman's column on planned and current SF movies "Scientifilm Marquee" continued in *Imaginative Tales* and he would pen similar features in genre publications for the rest of his career.

William Crawford was to edit an aborted magazine *George Pal's Tales of Space Conquest* for which Ackerman planned to supply material[156] and Ackerman negotiated sales of story material to the TV series *Science Fiction Theatre*.

Landing small pieces in a variety of publications, Ackerman employed a host of pseudonyms including Weaver Wright, Hubert George Wells, Dr. Acula, Sylvius Agricola, S. F. Balboa, Jacques DeForest Erman, Stone T. Farmington, Coil Kepac, Alden Lorraine, Forry Rhodan, Spencer Strong, Ray Marlene, Allis Villette, and Astrid Notte for a mass of material in publications from across the globe.

In May 1956 Ackerman received a manuscript and artwork created by Errol Le Cain called "Rapunzel and the Seven Wild Swans," which only surfaced in a 2002 sale.

In 1956 Ackerman had interested publisher George Orick in a publication to be titled *Sci-Fi: Modern Science Fiction*, but *Smart Money*, another publication being underwritten by the same group, failed, and with it Ackerman's project.

Ackerman attended the premiere of *The Black Sleep* with Bela Lugosi and shortly thereafter, on August 18, 1956, attended Lugosi's funeral.[157]

Ackerman introduced special effects technician Paul Blaisdell to his old friend James

Nicholson, who had partnered with Samuel Z. Arkoff in producing films as American International Pictures. Ackerman secured him work illustrating pulp covers and interiors. Blaisdell was the original art director of *Famous Monsters*, but the two had a falling out and Blaisdell went to work for a competing publication, *Fantastic Monsters of the Films*.

In 1956 Ackerman was accused by Robert A. Heinlein of absconding with his Hugo Award for his novel *Double Star*. Ackerman fretted considerably until being assured by convention chairman David Kyle that this could not have happened as the Hugos arrived late that year and photographs showed a dummy model being passed around.[158]

A photograph of Ackerman was featured on the cover of *Other Worlds* March 1957. Ackerman attended the wedding of David A. Kyle at Manhattan's the Church of the Transfiguration in August 1957 and the next month was aboard a fan flight to England for LonCon I, the fifteenth World Science Fiction Convention. A DC-4 Skymaster had been chartered by Kyle in honor of his honeymoon.

In 1957 Ackerman involved himself in a proposed animated film version of J.R.R. Tolkien's *The Lord of the Rings*, written by Morton Grady Zimmerman and Al Brodax. It met with Tolkien's disapproval. Tolkien was awarded the International Fantasy Award at Loncon and together with other fans, Ackerman visited Tolkien on September 4, 1957, presenting him with the award and showing him the treatment, artwork and location photos taken by Ron Cobb. Tolkien was astonished to learn the party had taken a cab all the way from London.

While the film proposal, which predated the trilogy's widespread popularity following its paperback release a decade later, took considerable liberties with the text it did provoke the creator of Middle Earth to put to paper his thoughts on the process of turning his works to film.[159]

A far more fruitful outcome of this trip occurred when Ackerman made a fateful trip to the newsstand while in Paris. Ackerman spotted a magazine, *Cinéma 57* No. 20 dated July/August 1957, which featured a still from *The Werewolf of London* on the cover. Ackerman had been selling reprint rights and contributing articles to a men's magazine called *After Hours* under editor-publisher James Warren and the two met up during a layover in New York. Knowing Warren's appreciation for the Universal horror films, he showed him his French find and Warren suggested a translation be prepared, which he could package as a one-shot.

When Warren learned Ackerman had a treasure trove of memorabilia relating to these films and a personal association with many of their makers, he journeyed to Los Angeles to meet with Ackerman in late November 1957.[160] His claims having been verified, he and Ackerman worked round the clock with Warren grabbing a few hours sleep in a nearby motel. As to the prose style, Ackerman recalled, "I hadn't the slightest intention of being funny about anything. What I had really planned to do ... would be more or less like an encyclopedia."[161]

For his part Warren opined, "Nobody can write fantasy movie features like Forry Ackerman. Nobody."[162]

In January 1958 Wendayne filed for divorce from Ackerman, citing "excessive cruelty," but friction between Ackerman and Wendayne's then-adolescent son was a contributing factor. The couple remained amicable after the divorce and eventually remarried in 1972.

On February 5, 1958,[163] *Famous Monsters of Filmland* hit the newsstands with a cover promising the "most frightening faces" and "the most fearsome monsters ever filmed." Warren had been fearful severe snowstorms would ruin sales of the project[164] but the initial 125,000 copies sold out and an additional 75,000 copies were ultimately printed and sold at a cover price of 35 cents. One contemporary report states 50,000 copies[165] were sold, and the effort was looked upon with disdain by some and termed "Ackerman's folly" by fan and author Richard Lupoff in a letter printed in *Famous Monsters* No. 2.[166] With the success of the first issue, Warren secured backing from Kable News, sales of a *Life* magazine issue[167] with an article covering the popularity of monster fare having convinced the reluctant distributor. Warren had earlier tried to sell them on the idea of a publication to be called *Wonderama* favoring the more encyclopedia-like approach.

Ackerman arranged deals with Nicholson and Arkoff's American International Pictures for writers he represented such as Paul W. Fairman on whose 1955 story "The Cosmic Flame" A.I.P.'s *Invasion of the Saucer Men* was based, and Henry Slesar who authored the 1957 story "Bottle Baby" which provided source material for *Terror from the Year 5000* the following year.

With such fare cleaning up at the drive-in and the old horror films being repackaged into "Shock Theatre" on local TV outlets, a monster zeitgeist was in the air and *Famous Monsters* inspired imitators, among them *Castle of Frankenstein, Monsters of the Movies*, and the German-language magazine *Vampir*. Marvel Comics' Stan Lee got into the act with *Monsters Unlimited, Monsters to Laugh With* and *Monster Madness* and *Monsters of the Movies* a decade later. Charlton Publications had *Horror Monsters, Mad Monsters*, and simply *Monsters* in the U.K. Early on Warren went to court over knock-off *World Famous Creatures*, but the judge dismissed the case.[168] Ackerman was further incensed when former associate Ron Haydock launched an imitator, *Fantastic Monsters of the Films* in 1962.

Scary Monsters publisher Dennis J. Druktenis observed, "*FM* was the premier magazine dedicated to monster movies that spawned many imitators in the early 60's, but was the only one to last 191 issues, 12 yearbooks, 3 paperbacks, 2 convention books and a game book plus other special magazines."[169]

Throughout its run Ackerman injected much of the established terminology and tropes of science fiction fandom into *Famous Monsters of Filmland* as well as information on the making of the films, and gave full rein to his paronomasia. Ackerman claimed he would have preferred a more sophisticated approach but was instructed to write for a younger audience, a method which continued to attract newer generations of readers. In any case its contents included signature features and sayings such as "Fang Mail" and "You Axed for It," "Inside Darkest Acula" and the "Voice of Fiendom." Readers' photographs were run with the caption "Wanted: more readers like..."

A lifelong teetotaler, Ackerman also warned his young readers to avoid substance abuse, agreeing with Sir Arthur C. Clarke, "Science fiction is the only genuine consciousness expanding drug."[170] While it covered the then-current films its focus remained a celebration of the horror films and performers of a generation before and served to instill an appreciation of this body of work with biographical sketches of stars and behind the scenes personnel.

Ackerman would find himself mounting defenses against criticism heaped upon the magazine by parents and educators, figures of authority in the lives of its youthful audience for whom the PTA stood for "Peasants of Transylvania."

Ackerman crafted scenarios for amateur film contests sponsored by the magazine. Paul Davids created a homemade film, *Siegfried Saves Metropolis*, from Ackerman's idea of combining two Fritz Lang titles. Future film critic Leonard Maltin was among the *FM* readers, as were novelist Dean Koontz, film director Frank Darabont, effects technician Dennis Muren, Hollywood make-up artists Joe Blasco and Tom Savini (who would advance the art of prosthetic effects), while still others became film historians or sellers of genre-related collectibles. Readers who displayed special craftsmanship were presented with Master Monster Maker Awards.

Ackerman wrote most of the copy while continuing to produce monthly columns for publications both fan and professional. In author David J. Skal's estimation, "The idiosyncratic and double-jointed diction convinced a large number of aspiring young writers that, hey, language was *fun*—a lesson transmitted all too rarely in the course of a conventional American education."[171]

Mark Evanier opined, "He was to *Famous Monsters* what Hugh Hefner was to *Playboy*—a spokesperson and figurehead, around whose life the entire publication was fashioned."[172]

Despite his newfound editorial duties Ackerman continued to market material for his clients, supplying a copy of the March 1930 issue of *Weird Tales* containing Amelia Reynolds Long's "The Thought Monster" to producer Richard Gordon and arranging the sale of the story for Long[173] which became the motion picture *Fiend Without a Face*. Ackerman represented and handled the film sales of *Curse of the Faceless Man* (1958) and *It! The Terror from Beyond Space* for author Jerome Bixby who wrote short stories and went on to pen episodes of *Star Trek*.

Warren's publishing outfit had expanded with the Captain Company, a sales wing which offered merchandise such as monster masks and model kits to the multitude of loyal fans who had sprung up around the magazine, many of whom would gift Ackerman with and deposit props from their own productions in the ensuing years. "We watched the movies, we bought the magazine, we had to have the models," recalled collector Spencer Brewer.

In the November 1958 installment of "Scientifilm Previews" Ackerman lamented "my very real regret in these crud [sic] new days of earth-in-peril pix is that the authors who pioneered—Hamilton, Cummings, Williamson, Starzl, even John Russell Fearn—are not reaping the yellow harvests of Hollywood gold rather than the Odd-Johnnies Come Lately who do the 'original' stories,'" a sentiment which continued to hold true as concepts were co-opted wholesale for years to come by the film industry from the genre's literature.

In November 1958 Ackerman participated in the 99th birthday of Dr. Adolphe Danziger de Castro who had known Ambrose Bierce and whose stories had been revised by Lovecraft in the 1930s.

In 1959 Ackerman handled the sales of "Time Enough at Last" by Lynn Venable and Paul W. Fairman's "Brothers Beyond the Void" (filmed as "People Are Alike All Over") to *The Twilight Zone*, then in its first season, but despite his best efforts few of the literary properties he represented and wished to see filmed caught the interest of producers, let alone saw production. He long hoped to facilitate big-budget remakes of *Metropolis* and William F. Temple's *The Four-Sided Triangle*, which had been poorly adapted as a film in 1953.

In 1959 Ackerman commissioned Frank R. Paul to have the painting from the October 1926 *Amazing Stories* redone to feature himself greeting the insectoid alien.[174]

In 1959 Ackerman created the E. Everett Evans Memorial Big Heart Award with Walter J. Daugherty. The first was presented to E. E. "Doc" Smith.

On Thanksgiving Day of 1959 Ackerman and Wendayne visited Clark Ashton Smith.[175]

Ackerman attended the eighteenth World Science Fiction Convention, Pittcon, held September 3–5, 1960, at Pittsburgh's Penn-Sheraton Hotel at which there was a display for Warren publications. He presented Sam Moskowitz with the E. E. Evans Big Heart Award, and had the honor of presenting Gernsback himself with a Hugo Award.

In March 1961 Ackerman attended an Annual Open Meeting of ESFA, the Eastern Science Fiction Association where he read his 1929 *Science Wonder Quarterly* letter aloud to Gernsback.

Ackerman leased his file of *Weird Tales* to Douglas Benton, producer of the television series *Boris Karloff's Thriller* which adapted much material from the pulp in its second season.[176]

July 1961 saw the launch of a sister publication to *Famous Monsters* called *Spacemen*, which lasted nine issues until 1964 and covered science fiction films. The first issue sported

Bill Warren (left) and Ackerman stand poolside during their initial meeting at the 19th Worldcon (Seacon) Seattle, September 1961 (courtesy Bill Warren).

a cover by FM's premier artist Basil Gogos and the magazine featured short stories in a section titled "O'Henry's Comet." One submission Ackerman received for this department was a manuscript entitled "The Killer" from a 14-year-old in Maine named Stephen King.[177] Ackerman preserved the tyro effort and duly presented it to be autographed by its bemused author years later.

Ackerman termed the magazine "a miserable financial flop."[178] Timing may have been a factor as *Spacemen* arrived on the scene too late for the science fiction movie boom of the 1950s and a decade and a half too early for *Star Wars*.

Ackerman encouraged future film director Joe Dante, Jr., to expand a letter enumerating what he considered to be the 50 worst horror films into an article which Ackerman titled "Dante's Inferno" and printed in *Famous Monsters of Filmland* No. 18 (July 1962). Reportedly the criticism upset James Nicholson who planned to re-release a number of the films. Thereafter Ackerman was less critical in his remarks on then-current film fare, opting for synopses rather than evaluations.

The 1960s saw the release of *Music for Robots* "An Ack-Coe Chamber Production" which was a spoken word recording featuring 18 minutes of narration by Ackerman on the history of robots in fiction with sound effects and percussion created by Frank Coe on the first side and electronic music and sounds on the reverse. Recorded in Hollywood, this curiosity was carried by the Captain Company and advertised in the magazine.

In August 1963 Ackerman and Wendayne made an 8,700-mile round trip visiting *Famous Monsters* fans across the U.S. on the way to Discon I, the World-Con held in Washington, D.C. This excursion, announced as "Project 6000" in *Famous Monsters* No. 24, invited readers to send invitations to the couple. Around 1,300 responses were received, and Ackerman chose those whose invitations showed the most ingenuity and whose location coincided with his route.

Ackerman at the Seacon art show, September 1961 (courtesy Bill Warren).

Amid other drop-ins, the Ackermans attended a gathering at the Wichita home of Jerry Weist, who was then editing a fanzine called *Movieland Monsters*. Another was with future comic book scribe Doug Murray. The youngsters were thrilled to have the erstwhile editor in their homes viewing their various collections, 8 mm film reels, and homemade horror short films. Several parents thanked him for sparking in their children the desire to read.[179] Also while in route Ackerman visited with his client Amelia Reynolds Long in Pennsylvania.[180]

Another new friend was Dr. Donald A. Reed, the founder of the Count Dracula Society in 1962 and the Academy of Science Fiction, Fantasy and Horror Films, which established the Saturn Awards in 1972. In 1963 Ackerman was the recipient of the Mrs. Anne Radcliffe Award with Boris Karloff from the Count Dracula Society. In the 1960s Ackerman also participated in a literary salon hosted by Terri Pinckard.

Fans gathered in an area restaurant for the Long Beach Science Fiction Convention of 1964 at which Ackerman and Ib J. Melchior were guests. Ackerman was Fan Guest of Honor at the 22nd WorldCon (Pacificon II) held September 1964 in Oakland.

Ackerman subsequently helmed the magazine *Monster World*, which ran for the next

Ackerman (right) poses with actor Vincent Price on the set of *The Raven* (1963). The two hold issues of *Famous Monsters* with both the Price covers (Price holds No. 9. and Ackerman No. 14.).

two years. The initial issue, dated November 1964, contained the first comics to be published by Warren, with an adaptation of "The Mummy" drawn by famed EC Comics artist Wally Wood. Warren's comic magazine line itself would be inaugurated with *Creepy* No. 1 in 1964, which due to its magazine-sized format functioned unhampered by the restrictions of the Comics Code Authority self-imposed by the industry in 1954. The periodical was not much of a success and Ackerman conceded, "*Monster World* might as well have said *Famous Monsters* on the cover, though, as it was virtually the same articles."[181] Folding in 1966, its ten-issue run was incorporated into the numbering of the parent magazine *Famous Monsters*.

Ackerman (left) visits with actor Edward van Sloan (1882–1964) in November 1963 (courtesy Ronald V. Borst/Hollywood Movie Posters).

Left to right: G. John Edwards, actor Edward van Sloan and Ackerman, November 1963 (courtesy G. John Edwards).

Ackerman appeared as a technician in an android factory in the feature film *The Time Travelers* directed by his friend Ib J. Melchior. He is heard throwing in a reference to "keeping our *Spacemen* happy." Ackerman would continue to have walk-on bits in dozens of productions in the decades to come, many of them helmed by former readers of the magazine. No matter the paucity of production values or conception Ackerman was game and he hoped to be listed by Guinness World Records as cameo king though he admitted, "I don't always know when somebody's going to ask me to do a little cameo for them whether it'll be a film that I would take any pride in appearing in."[182]

Ackerman's loose association with the film industry continued, and he wrote dialogue for actor John Carradine to speak in *The Wizard of Mars* helmed by David L. Hewitt.

Further travels took Ackerman to Loncon II held in late August 1965 at the London Mount Royal Hotel. Following the Loncon he visited the Netherlands at the invitation of P. Hans Frankfurther[183] and in September the New England Science Fiction Association (NESFA) held a convention in Boston named "Boskone" after alien pirate antagonists in the "Lensman" saga of E. E. Smith, where he lunched with Isaac Asimov.[184] With each flight he took during this Ackerman had himself insured to the maximum amount available for air travel passengers with fans and longtime friends named as beneficiaries.

Ackerman on the set of the 1964 film *The Time Travelers* in his role as an android technician (courtesy Ronald V. Borst/Hollywood Movie Posters).

September 18, 1965, marked the New York Monstercon at the Loew's Midtown Motor Inn. The following month Don Post, Sr., and Verne Langdon presented Ackerman with duplicate life-masks of the classic horror stars, which he had mounted by Walt Daugherty. Eventually Ackerman acquired life masks of many other Hollywood film performers not excluding one of himself "when I was alive."

In March 1966 Ackerman attended a ceremony of the Praed Street Irregulars, a society formed of admirers of the "Solar Pons" series of Sherlock Holmes pastiches, honoring their author August Derleth. Fritz Leiber, Jr., Bradbury, Bloch and Ackerman were inducted into the Irregulars by Sir Alvin Germeshausen.

Also in March 1966 the Count Dracula Society again honored Ackerman along with Lon Chaney, Jr., Robert Bloch, and Magic Castle founder Milt Larsen. Later that year the Los Angeles Science Fantasy Society began presenting the "Forry Award" for Lifetime Achievement in the field of Science Fiction.

In 1966 Ackerman approached Greenleaf Classics, whose operators William Hamling and Earl Kemp had arisen out of fandom, with the idea for novelizations of more titillating genre film fare heavily laden with stills and marketed as a series of erotic paperbacks. Only two titles saw print, one of which was written by Edward D. Wood, Jr., and based upon his script for the film *Orgy of the Dead* for which Ackerman provided a "Special Introduction." In subsequent years a cult arose around the fabled filmmaker inadvertently creating a collectible out of the Wood volume.

Ackerman often quipped that he functioned as the "illiterary agent" of Edward D. Wood, Jr., and would find himself on the receiving end of late night phone calls from the often inebriated writer-producer-director.[185]

Greg Bear, for whom Ackerman would devise the pen name "G. Reginald Urso,"[186]

met Ackerman at the Westercon that year and would write tributes to Karloff for *Famous Monsters* before embarking on a career as a professional science fiction writer which would garner him several awards.

Bill Warren, who had discovered Ackerman's "Scientifilm Marquee" column in *Imaginative Tales* and soon became an avid reader of *Famous Monsters*, was by then living in the city and wrote for the magazine and functioned as Ackerman's assistant for a time.[187] Another visitor to the Sherbourne house from whom Ackerman commissioned works was a talented amateur named Phil Tippet who would go on to realize creatures

Ackerman (left) and Boris Karloff regard one another, late 1960s (photograph by Walter J. Daugherty, courtesy Mary Ellen Daugherty).

such as the Rancor in *Return of the Jedi* among hundreds of effects for special effects house Industrial Light & Magic.[188]

In the fall of 1966[189] Ackerman scripted "An Evening with Boris Karloff and his Friends" for Decca Records. The idea had been that of Verne Langdon, but Karloff was displeased with his version and the project was almost scrapped until Langdon prevailed upon Ackerman to salvage the effort. The actor was satisfied with Ackerman's version written overnight and Ackerman was forever tickled that "for one magic hour of my life every word that came out of the mouth of Boris Karloff, I put into it."[190]

It would not be the last time this occurred, as Ackerman made uncredited contributions to a script written in part by *Mad* magazine creator Harvey Kurtzman for the 1967 feature *Mad Monster Party?* directed by Jules Bass and for which Boris Karloff voiced "Baron Boris von Frankenstein." Ackerman had long admired the hardworking performer whom he first met backstage at a Hollywood performance of the play *On Borrowed Time*.[191]

Forry! A Special Publication Presented to Forrest J. Ackerman, on the Occasion of the 50th Anniversary of His Birthday prepared by Fred Patten for the Los Angeles Science Fiction Society was a special 82-page fanzine which included tributes by Bradbury, van Vogt, Asimov, Harl Vincent, August Derleth, and more. Editor Patten would recall, "It was printed on the LASFS Rex Rotary mimeograph, and it was so thick we had trouble stapling it."[192]

In the autumn of 1966 Ackerman suffered a "series of heart attacks he had on his way to a 50th birthday" party.[193] Ackerman had thrown a series of birthday parties, one of which, attended by 200 persons was a Testimonial Banquet held in the Hollywood Room of the Hollywood Knickerbocker Hotel on December 2, 1966.

He spoke at the 5th annual Count Dracula Society dinner February 18, 1967, and later in 1967 he edited the collection *Monsters* by A. E. van Vogt, the first book to feature his byline, albeit a paperback. Ackerman was to have appeared opposite Karloff as Laing, the character portrayed by Ernest Thesiger in the 1933 original in an Alex Gordon-produced remake of *The Ghoul*.[194] Likewise Ackerman missed out on having a role in the 1967 Lon Chaney, Jr./John Carradine anthology vehicle *Dr. Terror's Gallery of Horrors* when funding ran out before the segment could be shot.[195]

Ackerman visited the set of *The Incredible Invasion* where photos were taken by Daugherty, but found himself dismayed by the filming conditions of the micro-budgeted motion picture. Even to the end, Karloff's acting was so convincing as he feigned a cardiac episode that Ackerman and others observing the scene almost ran to his aid.[196]

Ackerman appeared as a character that year in Philip José Farmer's explicit Essex House novel *The Image of the Beast*.

In the late 1960s Ackerman was involved in a Dracula Society banquet honoring Lon Chaney, Jr., and Ackerman was the First Guest of Honor at the Golden State Comic-Minicon held in March 1970 at the U.S. Grant Hotel and the Golden State Comic-Con in August, forerunners of the massive San Diego Comic-Con International. At the 26th World-Con in 1968 he was inducted into the order of the Knights of St. Fantony.

Boris Karloff passed away February 2, 1969. "By that night I was deluged with requests for Karloff material,"[197] and in short order Ackerman prepared a paperback tribute called *The Frankenscience Monster*. It appeared later that year from Ace Books and contained appreciations from Bradbury, Robert Bloch, Fritz Lang, actors Vincent Price, Christopher Lee, and Lon Chaney, Jr., and reprinted material from *Famous Monsters*. He later lamented, however, that "the heart of my *Frankenscience Monster* book was cut out before it ever reached print."[198]

Later in the year he released a collection of his short stories and collaborations *Science Fiction Worlds of Forrest J Ackerman and Friends* through Powell Publications under editor Charles Nuetzel as part of a short-lived line, which included editions of classic science fiction texts with introductions by Ackerman.

In 1969 Ackerman began editing the Perry Rhodan series for Ace Books, which his wife translated[199] from German, assisted at times by her brother Siegmund "Sig" Wahrman, Dwight R. Decker, and others. Inaugurated in 1961 by Walter Ernsting and K-H Scheer writing as "Clark Darlton," the long-running episodic adventures proved internationally popular.

In the paperback series, which ran from April 1969 to January 1978, Ackerman reintroduced his "Scientifilm World" column and made them more into the style of magazines tagging them "maga-books," reprinting Golden Age era science fiction stories and material from the fanzines including the all-star round-robin "Cosmos" as back-up material. As the years wore on the relationship became strained when the German publisher began to demand higher licensing fees.[200] Eighteen additional volumes (numbers 119 through 137) were released and sold to subscribers under the imprint of Master Publications, which had been established by the Ackermans.

In March 1969 Ackerman attended the Second International Film Festival of Rio de Janeiro as part of a concurrent science fiction program. The affair had authors such as Arthur C. Clarke, Bloch, Harlan Ellison, Heinlein, Frederik Pohl, Harry Harrison, Roger Zelazny, and British writer J. G. Ballard as honored guests as well as film directors Fritz Lang, George Pal, Roger Corman and Roman Polanski. After a screening of *Metropolis*, Fritz Lang instructed the audience to direct all their questions to Ackerman.

Ackerman found himself thinking about a request from James Warren on the flight to Rio. Warren's comic magazine line had grown considerably and Warren proposed Ackerman devise a "mod witch," rejecting Ackerman's suggestion "Miss Terry." Recalling the suggestion on the flight and never having a strong affinity for comics, Ackerman nonetheless created Vampirella of planet Drakulon. A female alien born a vampire, she wore a costume designed by underground comix artist Trina Robbins. The premiere issue was dated September 1969 and was bolstered by a distinctive Frank Frazetta cover painting.

Ackerman scripted the first two stories, with Archie Goodwin and others eventually assuming the writing duties. The character proved popular and an Aurora model kit was produced and a film version announced by Britain's Hammer Films to star Barbara Leigh, who posed as the character for several covers.

Ackerman enjoyed getting together with Ray Harryhausen again during the promotion of *The Valley of Gwangi*.[201] By the decade's end, the Sherbourne house had become so filled (including the kitchen) that Ackerman had moved into a nearby apartment with Wendayne.[202]

Ackerman was conferred with an Honorary Doctor of Literature from Scotland's St. Andrews University at the Eighth Annual Mrs. Anne Radcliffe Awards Dinner on April 25, 1970.

Ackerman attended the 28th WorldCon, Heicon '70, held that August in Heidelberg, Germany. In 1971 he made an appearance on *The Merv Griffin Show* alongside Vincent Price, John Carradine, Don Post, Glenn Strange, and Frank Gorshin.[203]

Ackerman performed in *Dracula vs. Frankenstein* for director Al Adamson as "Dr. Beaumont" and gave the name "Zandor Vorkov" to the stockbroker-turned-actor Roger Engel, who portrayed the immortal Count in the muddled production.

The Ackermans introduced the German science fiction series *Perry Rhodan* to American audiences in the 1970s (courtesy George Chastain).

Of more lasting consequence he cameoed in *Schlock*, where he was shown seated munching popcorn in a movie theater before being joined by the film's gorilla-suited director John Landis. Landis would similarly feature Ackerman in cameos in many of his later productions, beginning with *The Kentucky Fried Movie* in 1977. "Forry's extraordinary generosity is what I remember best about him," Landis recalled.[204] Richard A. "Rick" Baker, to whose surname Ackerman would append "monster maker," designed the costume Landis wore. Baker, who had begun reading *Famous Monsters* with the third issue, would receive the first Academy Award for Best Makeup and go on to win the award in that category multiple times.

Ackerman assisted Walt Lee in the compilation of his three-volume 1972 *Reference Guide to Fantastic Films*. Ackerman remarried Wendayne in 1972.[205]

Ackerman kept up his long-enduring convention-going. His and Wendayne's travels took them to the third Speculation Conference held in June 1972 at the University of Birmingham and they also attended EuroCon 1 in Trieste, Italy that July. Ackerman acknowledged, "I frequently say, nowadays, that I am a quart bottle into which the world is daily trying to pour a gallon, and I go to bed each night dissatisfied because of the three-fourths that has spilled over, usually into limbo."[206]

In 1972 he won the Evans-Freehafer Award for his years of service to the LASFS and on November 24, 1972, a 100-film retrospective was organized to celebrate Ackerman's 56th birthday by the husband-and-wife fans the Trimbles and held at Cocoanut Grove and at which were presented the Georges Méliès Awards.

Ackerman edited an anthology of what he felt to be the *Best Science Fiction for 1973*. The title was poorly received and Ackerman claimed the publishers chopped 25 percent out of the collection. Reviewer Richard Delap, writing in *The Journal of the Washington S.F. Association* found Ackerman's "juvenile, perilously inane and vulgar attempts at humor" to be "offensive."

That year Ackerman penned what he felt to be the briefest ever science fiction story "Cosmic Report Card: Earth" appearing in *Vertex: The Magazine of Science Fiction*, June 1973. The one-letter vignette sold to *Vertex* editor Donald J. Pfeil for $100, and Ackerman managed to sell it several additional times.

When Ackerman suggested Pfeil reprint Robert A. Heinlein's "Discovery of the Future" speech in *Vertex*, which he felt then most likely to be in the public domain, it appeared in the April 1973 issue. Heinlein wrote a November 17, 1973, letter to Ackerman, closing with the underlined passage, "Keep your hands off my property."[207]

In August 1973[208] the Ackermans purchased a Spanish villa in Los Feliz Hills near Griffith Park at 2495 Glendower Avenue, the former home of actor Jon Hall, who had portrayed the Invisible Man and Tarzan knock-off "Ramar of the Jungle." Its new owner hailed it as "Son of Ackermansion"[209] and Ackerman lost no time filling the "seventeen room, four story home with three garages"[210] nicknaming its basement "Grislyland." His Cadillac, bearing the license plate "Sci Fi," had to be parked outside the collectible-filled "GarageMahal."

Opposite, top: **Ackerman always stood ready to offer a tour of his treasures (courtesy Ernest Farino/Archive Editions).** *Opposite, bottom:* **Ackerman, as "bad Dr. Beaumont," stands between actors John Bloom (left, as Frankenstein's monster holding *Famous Monsters* No. 56) and Roger Engel (acting under the name "Zander Vorkov," holding the 1970 *Famous Monsters Fearbook*, and dressed as Dracula) during the making of the 1971 schlockfest *Dracula vs. Frankenstein* (courtesy Douglas M. Whitenack).**

Ackerman (right) with collector and historian Sam Moskowitz, perhaps the only man whose collection of literary material rivaled his own (courtesy John L. Coker III).

When second-generation fan Heidi Saha began appearing at conventions dressed as Vampirella, Warren issued a special pictorial publication *An Illustrated History of Heidi Saha: Fantasy Fandom's Famous Femme*. Ackerman had served as "creative consultant and script polisher" for *Horror Hall of Fame: A Monster Salute*, a television special hosted by Vincent Price which aired in February 1974.

In 1973 Ackerman moved into the "Son of Ackermansion" (courtesy Perry Shields).

Warren and his publishing operation were profiled in an April 25, 1974, article for *Rolling Stone* called "Citizen Pain."

Ackerman was designated Guest of Honor at the first exclusive Famous Monsters Convention held November 1974 at the Hotel Commodore. The convention was mounted with the assistance of Phil Seuling, a schoolteacher with experience staging comic book conventions in the area. A poster and program book for the event were produced, reproducing Ken Kelly's cover artwork for *Famous Monsters* No. 119.

Ackerman continued to be lauded, receiving the Inkpot Award from the San Diego ComiCon 1974, obliging as Guest of Honor of Lunacon 1974, and journeying to the 32nd World Science Fiction Convention, Discon II at the Sheraton Park Hotel in Washington, D.C., where he was co-recipient of the First Fandom Hall of Fame Award with Sam Moskowitz.

In October 1975 he appeared on *The Mike Douglas Show* and attended the first World Fantasy Convention in Providence, Rhode Island, honoring H. P. Lovecraft. In November of that year he attended another Famous Monsters Convention. Also in 1975 Ackerman appeared on Tom Snyder's *Tomorrow* show with actor Peter Cushing.

On December 29, 1975, Ackerman delivered a eulogy for pulp publisher Leo Margulies, and as the pulp writers and early fans of his generation began to die off he saw to it that notices appeared in the fan press even if the personalities were by then largely forgotten.

Ackerman (left) clowns around with actor Vincent Price on the set of *The Horror Hall of Fame* television special, 1974 (courtesy Alan White).

Publisher James Warren (left) and Ackerman (right) recoil from fan Patrick Butkas, costumed as Thomas Edison's 1910 *Frankenstein* at the 1974 Famous Monsters Convention (courtesy Douglas M. Whitenack).

Ackerman was to have edited *The Bicentennial Man*, an anthology that was going to contain works by big-name science fiction authors, including a play by Bradbury and a story by Philip José Farmer. Isaac Asimov's titular contribution won the Hugo and Nebula awards and was later expanded to a novel and filmed. The project, originated by his friend Naomi Gordon-Magaziner, floundered when backing fell through after the well-to-do couple bankrolling the endeavor divorced.[211]

In 1976 Ackerman had a replica of the "robotrix" from *Metropolis* built by special effects artist Robert Short and Bill Malone, who was a former mask maker for Don Post and who later directed films.[212] Ackerman nicknamed "her" *Ultima Futura Automaton* after the initials of the studio that had produced the film, UFA.

Shelves designed by Walt Daugherty housed many film props in the Glendower Ackermansion (courtesy Perry Shields).

In August 1976 *Starlog*, a slickpaper successor to *Spacemen*, appeared on the crest of another boom in science fiction moviemaking and science fiction film and media-oriented publications proliferated.

Ackerman attended the first World Science Fiction Writers Conference held September 24–26, 1976, at Dublin's Burlington Hotel and together with David A. Kyle and fan John Flory, Ackerman created the Science Fiction and Fantasy Film Society which sought to present Star Fire Awards to Fritz Lang and George Pal.

Ray Bradbury (left) and Ackerman lean against Ackerman's Cadillac bearing the license plate "Sci Fi" (courtesy Ronald V. Borst/Hollywood Movie Posters).

He received the Science Fiction Hall of Fame Award that year and in November 1976 celebrated his 60th birthday at the Century Plaza Hotel. That same year he issued *Amazing Forries*, a special Warren publication under the banner of Metropolis Press in honor of his birthday. The publication featured Frank R. Paul's October 1926 *Amazing Stories* cover swipe, and on the back a mock *TIME* magazine "Man of the Year" cover painting of Ackerman that he asked artist Josh Kirby to produce gave a tongue-in-cheek touch to what might otherwise have been seen as unbridled egotism.

Ackerman received the Academy of Science Fiction Films Award in January 1977, and he attended Lunacon in April.[213]

On September 7, 1977, Ackerman took part in a 25th anniversary celebration held at the Holly Theater in Hollywood for *The War of the Worlds* with George Pal, Anne Robinson, and stunt performer Mushy Callihan.[214]

In the 1970s 250 items from Ackerman's collection were displayed in Tokyo in nine different department stores for three months, a promotion from which a souvenir book was produced.

In September 1978 he appeared at the Fantasy Film Celebration in Pittsburgh and in the fall of 1978 traveled to Spain and Portugal[215] to judge at a film festival in Sitges, Spain.

Ackerman scripted segments of a comic strip "Jeanie of Questar" that Ackerman created for the eponymous publication *Questar*.

In 1980 then-Mayor Tom Bradley visited the Ackermansion and tentatively accepted Ackerman's offer to donate the collection to the city of Los Angeles. The mayor dispatched four librarians to catalogue the collection but soon abandoned efforts. Ackerman received a commendation from Bradley and other offers came from the city of Monterey. Meanwhile Ackerman obtained some impressive names for the board of directors while Bradbury tried to persuade Rocketdyne to take Ackerman's collection, to no avail.

In May 1980 Ackerman delivered a eulogy for George Pal at Holy Cross Mausoleum. In his last years, the special-effects pioneer had been stymied in launching projects and had died suddenly. Ackerman additionally had a star named after Pal.

Later in May Ackerman received the Frank R. Paul Award from Kubla Khanate. Michael Alan "Mick" Garris, then a publicist, arranged for a press conference on John Carpenter's 1980 release *The Fog* to be held at the Ackermansion.[216]

In May 1982 Ackerman journeyed to Russia with a group of science fiction fans,[217] including author Joe Haldeman and his wife, longtime fans Clifton Amsbury and Art Widner, as well as *Locus* publisher Charles N. Brown.

In 1982 Ackerman appeared with some items from his collection on the nationally syndicated Merv Griffin talk show.

No. 190 marked the last issue of *Famous Monsters of Filmland* to appear under Ackerman's editorship as Ackerman had resigned the post in August 1982.[218] Chief among the reasons given for his disenfranchisement were his complaints concerning his salary, which he claimed had failed to rise in proportion with the escalating cost of living.[219] By now distributed by Independent News, the periodical faced competition from full-color publications such as *Fangoria*, a sister magazine to *Starlog* which reveled in the visceral fare which Ackerman himself deplored, though he would be a sporadic contributor to both. A sole issue co-edited by Timothy Moriarty and Randy Palmer followed before the publication expired. Warren Publishing Co. itself ceased operations in early 1983.

By this time other projects closer to his childhood interest occupied his working time

Top: Ackerman displays the head and shoulders of "The Creature from the Black Lagoon" used in *Revenge of the Creature* (courtesy Kim Reynolds). *Bottom:* Ray Harryhausen (left) and Ackerman admire a casting of the Ymir, Harryhausen's creation for the film *20 Million Miles from Earth* (courtesy Ernest Farino/Archive Editions).

and in 1982 Ackerman conceived of presenting retroactive honors to overlooked genre stories from the pulp era. He had First Fandom members vote on works from *Amazing Stories* to determine the recipients of the Gernsback Awards and edited what he hoped to be the first of a multi-volume anthology series devoted to getting them back into print. In the first volume he included "Beyond the Pole," the first science fiction story he ever read.

In May 1983 he attended a 50th Anniversary screening of *King Kong* at Grauman's Chinese Theater which displayed props and items relating to the feature from his collection.

In 1983 he was briefly involved in a short-lived revival of *Weird Tales* but more significantly was able to realize a long-standing wish[220] to produce a book showcasing each of Lon Chaney Sr.'s "thousand faces."

At the behest of its director John Landis, in October 1983 Ackerman appeared in the landmark music video for Michael Jackson's "Thriller." What is arguably his most widely seen cameo proved to be a holdover of his role in *Schlock* and Ackerman can be seen munching popcorn in the same seat of the Palace Theater behind the late King of Pop before Jackson and his date exit the theater.

Even if he himself was not seen on camera, items from Ackerman's collection would later appear as set dressing in films such as *Fright Night*, *The Bodyguard* (the robotrix), and *House of 1000 Corpses*. In the 1980s he served as a contributing editor on *Fantasy Book*, a fiction magazine unrelated to William Crawford's earlier publication of the same title.

In 1984 the Ackermans planned to visit French SF author Claude Avice, who wrote under the pseudonym Pierre Barbet[221] and whom he represented. Wendayne had translated his *Games Psyborgs Play* for DAW books in 1973. Ackerman was present at the 42nd World-Con, L.A.con II, in Anaheim and was Fan Guest of Honor at LosCon Eleven held that November at the Pasadena Hilton.

December 1984 inaugurated Forrest J Ackerman's *Monster Land*, a successor to *Famous Monsters* under publisher Hal Schuster who was known for a series of unauthorized television episode guides and publications relating to *Star Trek* and other series. Aimed at the fan market, it was one of several attempts to revive the format. It failed not only because audiences had grown more sophisticated in their knowledge of special effects techniques but also because the market was saturated; by this point, many books had been written on the classic American horror films and their stars, and these books were filled with the stills and information that had been the mainstay of Ackerman's magazine. Although not enamored of the level of gore and violence of the 1980s horror films, Ackerman correctly predicted nostalgia would arise for Freddy and Jason, the boogeymen of the nascent slasher genre.

Weary of the lack of acceptance for his coinage in 1985 he offered $100 to anyone to come up with a word "to describe sleazy, exploitative pseudo-SF" in place of "sci-fi."[222]

A 70th birthday party was held November 21, 1986, at the Biltmore Hotel and in 1987 Ackerman attended the centennial of Esperanto in Poland.

The New York auction house Guernsey's approached Ackerman about selling his collection. Believing his collection was at one point to go to Disney, Ackerman thinned out much of the more erotic artwork of Frank Frazetta, and Boris Vallejo,[223] supplementing this with film props, posters, and many first edition volumes in addition to L. Ron Hubbard items and Bradbury manuscripts.

Ackerman put a total of 2,000 items in 105 boxes up for bidding. Held December 12–13, 1987, at the Puck Building, the Guernsey's auction grossed a touted figure of over $550,000[224] but many individual items such as the first printed appearances of the Superman and Tarzan characters failed to realize a fraction of their worth. Selling this material off at a considerable loss must have been heartbreaking and he termed it "a complete financial catastrophe and a personal tragedy." The item that wound up realizing the highest price proved to be a hand-written screenplay for *The Wizard of Oz*, which fetched $40,000. However, a handsome catalog was produced that featured photographs and descriptions of the items and included tributes from Stephen King, Ray Bradbury and Steven Spielberg.

Ackerman continued to entertain notions that the remainder of his collection would be preserved in toto. German investors purchased portions of his collection. Other abortive plans included "a joint Superman/science fiction museum"[225] in Cleveland and a home for the collection at the site of the present Museum of the Moving Image.

In late 1987 the Ackermans were victims of a "mugging in Naples, Italy" in which Wendayne was injured. Days later she suffered a stroke, resulting in partial paralysis.

In January 1990 Ackerman underwent prostate and gallstone operations.[226] Wendayne Mondelle Ackerman passed away at home March 5, 1990. She had refused to continue undergoing dialysis for kidney ailments and succumbed to renal failure. Joe Moe, a fan and friend of Ackerman's, moved in as a paying tenant at the Glendower house following Wendayne's passing. He accompanied Ackerman to conventions and assisted in the upkeep of the home and collection.

In 1990 Ackerman began working with Ray Ferry, who had produced a documentary on Ackerman and *Famous Monsters of Filmland*, in marketing a line of products including videos, trading cards, and a calendar.

Ackerman seen in his role as "Judge Rhinehole" playfully raises his gavel above the head of *Nudist Colony of the Dead* director Mark Pirro (courtesy Pirromount Pictures).

In September 1990 he was presented with an award, which Ackerman named the "Grimmy," on another "Horror Hall of Fame" show televised from Universal Studios and hosted by Freddy Krueger actor Robert Englund who called Ackerman "the Hugh Hefner of Horror."

While in Wellington, New Zealand, for the "Forrycon," film director Peter Jackson managed to snag Ackerman for a cameo in his zombie epic *Braindead* (released in America as *Dead Alive*). In the early 1990s Philip J. Riley edited a number of volumes in the MagicImage Filmbooks series, which printed the original screenplays for the Universal horror films coupled with stills.

In 1992 Ackerman served on the Editorial Advisory Committee of *Futures Past: A Visual Guidebook to Science Fiction History* edited by Jim Emerson and dedicated to the pulp era, and as a contributing editor to *Expanse*, a Baltimore semiprozine.

As of 1992 Ackerman's collection was to go to Berlin and be housed at the Hotel Esplanade, but the investors backed out. Later he also talked of a floating museum to be placed next to the RMS *Queen Mary*[227] and efforts by the University of California, Riverside, to acquire his book collection came to naught. The vicissitudes over the ultimate fate of his collection caused him much grief.

A 35th Anniversary Famous Monsters of Filmland Convention was held in Arlington, Virginia, in May 1993. Ray Bradbury, Harryhausen, writer Curt Siodmak, and many remaining actors from classic horror and science fiction productions were in attendance. A poster advertising the event was designed by Frank Kelly Freas and a special 200th issue of *Famous Monsters of Filmland* was produced as a tie-in giveaway to attendees, which proved well received, and a revival began to be considered.

In the years since his passing a cult had swelled around Edward D. Wood, Jr., and his films, and in 1994 a biopic was released on the cross-dressing would-be-auteur. Ackerman took issue with the film's portrayal of a foul-mouthed Lugosi (insisting the Hungarian performer never swore in his presence) and in its depiction of Lugosi harboring animosity toward Karloff.

In May 1995 Ray Ferry sponsored a monster convention in Hollywood at the Universal Sheraton Hotel. Ackerman thereafter broke ties with Ferry in No-

Forrest J Ackerman (left) and David Ackerman Kyle, friends for more than seven decades, at the 50th World Science Fiction Convention in Orlando, 1992 (photograph by John L. Coker III).

Left to right: Walt Daugherty, Ray Ferry, and Ackerman at the unveiling of the 200th issue of *Famous Monsters* during the 35th Anniversary Famous Monsters convention, May 1993 (courtesy Douglas M. Whitenack).

vember 1995[228] amidst disagreements over Ackerman's compensation and credit in the magazine.

Ackerman received the Service Award of the Academy of Science Fiction, Fantasy & Horror Films in 1995 and in early 1996 he delivered the eulogy at early science fiction fan Aubrey MacDermott's funeral.

He was Guest of Honor at the April 1996 Chiller Theatre convention and received the magazine's Living Legend Award and was also Guest of Honor at PulpCon 25. In the 1990s *Spacemen* was revived as a companion to *Cult Movies* magazine along with a new title, *Spacewomen.*

On September 12, 1996, he participated in a tribute to Academy Award-winning makeup effects technician Dick Smith who had authored a guide to special effects make-up for Warren years before.

Harris Comics revived *Vampirella* in the 1990s introducing the character to a new generation, and Roger Corman's Concorde-New Horizons finally adapted *Vampirella* as a telefilm airing on Showtime Networks in September 1996. Directed by Jim Wynorski, it showcased Talisa Soto as the titular vampiress and featured a character called "Forry Ackerman."

Offering a simulated tour of his collection and featuring video commentary by Ackerman, the CD-ROM *Forrest J Ackerman's Museum of Science Fiction, Horror and Fantasy* released by Marlin Entertainment/Hobby Software in 1997 was intended to suffice for those who couldn't make a visit in person.

In 1997 Haunted Hollywood held a "Monster Bash" convention to celebrate Ackerman's 80th birthday attended by the descendents of the Universal horror stars: Sara Karloff, Bela Lugosi, Jr., and Ron Chaney, on July 18–20 in Ligonier, Pennsylvania. Ackerman was honored by the Horror Writers of America with the Bram Stoker Lifetime Achievement Award in 1997.

Also in 1997 he established a website called "Forrest J Ackerman's Wide Webbed World" which featured contests, games, a maze, and scans of signatures from famed genre figures.

At the August 1999 Monster Rally sponsored by Gary Svelha, Ackerman received the Carl Laemmle Monster Rally Award. He attended the 5th Fantastisk Film Festival that September heading the festival's jury[229] and also attended the Perry Rhodan Millennial Worldcon.

Ackerman had brought suit against Ray Ferry in January 1997[230] and in the spring of 2000 the case went to trial at the Superior Court of the State of California. At issue were charges of "breach of contract, libel, trademark infringement"[231] and the rights to the pseudonym "Dr. Acula." The trial brought several noted figures with Ray Bradbury testifying for Ackerman, and author Harlan Ellison against. A verdict was reached May 10, 2000, and though the jury ruled in Ackerman's favor, Ferry declared bankruptcy and Ackerman subsequently failed to recover the awarded amount.

Ackerman rang in 2001 at the Playboy Mansion, and under Sense of Wonder Press a series of reprints and anthologies appeared that year. Ackerman read the eulogy at the funeral of Dr. Donald Reed who passed away in March.

Still more honors came to him in the first decade of the century; in 2001 Ackerman won a Moxie! Tribute Award at the Santa Monica Film Festival in June; was Guest of Honor at the "Halfway to Hollywood" film festival in Kansas City, Missouri; was one of the guests of honor at Fanex 15 held July 2001 in the Baltimore Hunt Valley Inn; and was Guest of Honor at the August 2001 Festival of Fantastic Films #12 in Manchester.

Ackerman celebrated his 85th birthday with a party at The Friar's Club in Beverly Hills for which a special commemorative publication was produced, "*It's Alive @ 85.*"

Ackerman's health took a sudden turn for the worse early in 2002. One report stated "Forry's medical crisis began in April when the chair he was sitting in collapsed and he struck his head."[232] Shortly thereafter Ackerman began experiencing ischemic episodes which proved to be the first sign of a cerebral clot and that led him to be hospitalized where he underwent brain surgery to remove the clot. He was treated at Kaiser Permanente Hospital, Hollywood, and transferred to Amberwood Convalescent Hospital in May. While recovering in a rehab facility Ackerman developed renal septicemia.

The World Fantasy Convention presented Ackerman its 2002 Life Achievement Award. In September 2002 Ackerman sold off most of the collection from the Glendower home, with many of his items appearing on the auction website eBay. "Their loss was like losing the library at Alexandria,"[233] lamented his artist friend Anton Brzezinski.

Some took exception to Ackerman's unwillingness to restore the props in his collection and the authenticity and provenance of some of the items have been called into question[234] but the sheer comprehensiveness and scope of his lifetime accumulation is undeniable.

In 2002 Ackerman received the Rondo Hatton Classic Horror Award and in November celebrated his 86th birthday at the China Inn in Glendale, California.

Ackerman moved to a bungalow he called the mini–Ackermansion or the Acker Mini-Mansion in Los Feliz, retaining a limited selection of favorite showpieces. Having sold off many of his originals, Ackerman still displayed a number of re-creations of Frank R. Paul artwork by Anton Brzezinski from whom he had commissioned over 200 such works. "What he had left were the most sentimental, intimate things that he treasured," recalled collectibles dealer Joe Maddalena.[235]

His health having somewhat improved, Ackerman was Special Guest of Honor at the 13th World Horror Convention at Kansas City, Missouri, in April 2003. With Brad Linaweaver, Ackerman put together a book of science fiction cover artwork *Worlds of Tomorrow: The Amazing Universe of Science Fiction Art* for Collectors Press and he co-edited *Womanthology* with Pam Keesey for Sense of Wonder Press in 2003.

A good deal of Ackerman's film-related material went under the hammer via Julien's Auctions November 15, 2003.

A tribute to Ackerman was held at the American Cinematheque on February 11, 2004. Ackerman had plaques installed on 153 seats at Grauman's Egyptian Theatre honoring his friends and favorites in the film industry.

Ackerman served on the Advisory Board of Directors of the Science Fiction Museum and Hall of Fame which opened in 2004, a partial realization of his lifelong dream underwritten by Microsoft co-founder Paul G. Allen. Also in 2004 he was awarded a place in the Monster Hall of Fame at the Rondo Hatton Classic Horror Awards.

Some of the *King Kong* models Ackerman owned went to Peter Jackson whose remake of the film was released that year and Ackerman put in an appearance at the 2005 Monster Bash. Facing declining health and hearing loss, Ackerman continued to make personal appearances, to attend screenings and to appear on-camera in interviews for documentaries and DVD extras.

In August 2005 Ackerman scalded himself while bathing at the 63rd WorldCon-Interaction in Glasgow and was treated at the Glasgow Royal Infirmary. The following year he was able to attend the much closer 64th World Science Fiction Convention held August 26, 2006, in Anaheim where he was presented with the newly renamed Forrest Ackerman Big Heart Award. Health problems continued to plague him and he was hospitalized in September 2006 with a kidney stone. In February 2007 Ackerman broke his hip. Later that year Monster Bash began presenting their Forry Award and he was the subject of a documentary *Famous Monster: Forrest J Ackerman*. Earl Roesel of Kentucky struck up a friendship with Joe Moe on the Internet message board for *Scarlet Street* magazine and became another caretaker for Ackerman.[236]

Ackerman continued to attend Comic-Con and was at the San Diego Convention Center's yearly gathering in July 2008 where actor Benicio Del Toro requested a meeting with Ackerman in preparation for his turn as *The Wolf Man*. A 50th Anniversary *Famous Monsters* panel with James Warren and Verne Langdon was held July 26 and a tribute to Ackerman appeared in the October 2008 issue of *Rue Morgue* magazine.

In 2008 Ackerman had been diagnosed with congestive heart failure, and continued to be cared for by Joe Moe and visiting nurses. A major setback occurred when Ackerman could no longer taste his food, which dampened his spirits, and he eventually elected to forego measures to treat his condition.

In late October he asked to see James Warren and Verne Langdon and as word of his condition spread, fans were encouraged to write. Ackerman recorded a "Final Video Farewell" for his fans and was mistakenly reported as having passed away in November by the website of the British Fantasy Society.

Ackerman succumbed to heart failure at 11:58 P.M. on December 4, 2008. He had long before stated he wished to die an "actifan"[237] and was interred at Forest Lawn Memorial Park in Glendale with a marker reading "Sci-Fi Was My High."

Ray Harryhausen lamented, "When I moved to Europe I hardly ever saw him except at various conventions."[238] Prometheus Entertainment head Kevin J. Burns was named a trustee of Ackerman's estate. There were "17 beneficiaries" of Ackerman's will, including a waitress from his favorite restaurant, the House of Pies.

Genre magazines dedicated entire issues to his memory and the news garnered space in major newspapers while the Internet saw a tremendous outpouring of sympathy. Conventions held testimonials and panel discussions on his life and influence. James Warren wrote a tribute in verse.

Ackerman (left) and Richard Sheffield, display the Bela Lugosi opera cape and silk and velvet house robe Sheffield had sold him years before (circa 2005) (courtesy Richard Sheffield).

On January 24, 2009, the LASFS had a memorial to him and the American Cinematheque's Aero theater held a Forrest J Ackerman Memorial Double Feature of *Frankenstein* and *The Mummy* on February 5. On March 8, 2009, the Cinematheque held a memorial tribute for Ackerman in the Egyptian Theatre emceed by filmmaker Tim Sullivan, which was attended by Ray Bradbury, John Landis, Brad Linaweaver, Joe Moe, Bill Warren, director Guillermo del Toro, David J. Skal, Carla Laemmle, author and former client George Clayton Johnson, and Ron Chaney.

Los Angeles auction house Profiles in History handled the Forry Ackerman Estate Auction, held April 30 and May 1, 2009. Among the items offered were his treasured *War of the Worlds* ship and the Lugosi ring and garments.

Joe Moe was honored

for his service in care of Ackerman at the Seventh Annual Rondo Hatton Classic Horror Awards. A new version of *Famous Monsters of Filmland* launched in 2010 dedicated its initial issue to Ackerman and highlighted his film roles.

NOTES TO BIOGRAPHY

1. I am indebted to Paul Davids for supplying information from Ackerman's birth certificate.
2. Ackerman, "Introducing the Author," p. 131.
3. Michael Copner and Coco Kiyonaga, "Nights of Futures Past," *Cult Movies* No. 37, p. 60.
4. *Imagination!* July 1938.
5. <http://replay.web.archive.org/20061012152434/http://4forry.best.vwh.net/ouija.htm>.
6. Ackerman, "My Brother," *Voice of the Imagi-Nation* (*VOM*) No. 39, February 1945.
7. Joshi, *I Am Providence*, p. 588.
8. Ackerman, *Science Fiction Worlds* (1969), p. 195.
9. Ross, *Contemporary Authors*, p. 13.
10. Ibid.
11. Elliot, "Take me home, little boy...," *Questar*, p. 46.
12. Corupe, *Rue Morgue*, p. 18.
13. Sackett, "The Ackerman Story," *Fantastic Worlds,* Fall-Winter 1952, pp. 5–6.
14. "Meet the Fan," pp. 25–26.
15. Blass, *Chiller*, p. 35.
16. Ross, p. 12.
17. Ackerman (as Paul Linden), "Ackermonster Strikes Again ... 13 Years Later," p. 5.
18. Druktenis, "The Ackermonster, Forrest J Ackerman," *Scary Monsters* No. 3, p. 14.
19. Ackerman, "Notes on Bob Olsen."
20. Olsen, *Fantastic Worlds*, Spring 1953, p. 28.
21. Ackerman, "A New Method of Evaluation," *Science Wonder Quarterly*, Fall 1929, p. 136.
22. Ross, p. 13.
23. Speer, *Up to Now.*
24. Linus Hogenmiller, Letter, *Astounding Stories of Super-Science*, January 1931.
25. Ackerman, "Through Time and Space with Forry Ackerman (Part 1)," *Mimosa* No. 16, December 1994.
26. Ackerman, "Lon Chaney Shall Not Die," "*It's Alive!@85*," p. 6.
27. "Meet the Fan."
28. Ackerman, Filler, *Amazing Forries*, p. 29.
29. Corupe, *Rue Morgue*, p. 18.
30. Ackerman, Letter, *Amphipoxi* No. 8.
31. Druktenis, p. 15.
32. Ackerman (as Linden), "Ackermonster Strikes Again ... 13 Years Later," p. 10.
33. Ackerman, *Movie Gold*, p. 87.
34. Ackerman, "Through Time and Space with Forry Ackerman (Part 6)," p. 29.
35. Ross, p. 13.
36. Ackerman, "My Science Fiction Collection Part Two."
37. Ackerman, "Monster Mosaic," p. 6.
38. Ibid.
39. Quoted in Robert L. Beerbohm, "The Big Bang Theory of Comic Book History," *Comic Book Marketplace*, Vol. 2, No. 50 (August 1997) p. 52.
40. Ackerman often recalled this as occurring in 1932. According to Lugosi scholar Gary Don Rhodes, "I think Forry was off on the date. Bela didn't play SF that year, or in 1930 or 1931, for that matter. He did play Oakland in 1930. But his two main appearances in SF as Drac came in 1928 and 1929." E-mail to author, 31 October 2010.
41. Often erroneously cited as the first science fiction fan magazine, the designation goes to Jerome Siegel's *Cosmic Stories*.
42. Moskowitz, *The Immortal Storm*, p. 15; Siclari, *Science Fiction Reference Book*, p. 89.
43. Moskowitz, *Explorers of the Infinite*, p. 329.
44. Ackerman, "An Imagi-Movie Odyssey," *Worlds of Horror*, p. 2.
45. Siegel as Herbert S. Fine, "The Reign of the Superman," *Science Fiction* Vol. 1, No. 3 (January 1933), pp. 13–14.
46. John T. Soister, *Up from the Vault: Rare Thrillers of the 1920s and 1930s*, p. 150.
47. Ackerman, "Esperanto, the Universalanguage."

48. Madle, *David A. Kyle*, p. 192.

49. D. R. Smith, "Hands Off English," p. 4.

50. Ibid.

51. Ackerman, "Introducing the Author," *Imaginative Tales*, May 1956, p. 131.

52. Sackett, "The Ackerman Story," pp. 7–8.

53. Nate Rosenbloom, "Mr. Ackerman enrolled at UC Berkeley 8/1/1933 and was undeclared," e-mail to author 14 September 2010. Most sources have previously dated Ackerman's enrollment to 1934–35.

54. Ackerman, "Filler," p. 29.

55. Moskowitz, "The Immortal Storm II," *Fantasy Commentator* 47+48, p. 282.

56. Lovecraft to Barlow, 16 March 1935, *O Fortunate Floridian*, p. 218.

57. Grayson, "At the Castle of the Effjay of Akkamin," p. 16.

58. Smith to August Derleth 4 August 1933, *Selected Letters of Clark Ashton Smith*, Ed. David E. Schultz and Scott Connors (Sauk City WI: Arkham House, 2003), p. 214.

59. Lovecraft to R. H. Barlow, 29 November 1933, *Floridian*, p. 89.

60. "My Science Fiction Collection."

61. Correspondence Ackerman received from Laemmle can be seen on the Special Features of the DVD *The Sci Fi Boys* and a January 13, 1933, letter from Laemmle to Ackerman is reproduced in *Famous Monster of Filmland* Vol. 2 (Hollywood Publishing Company, 1991), p. 133.

62. Ross, p. 14.

63. Ackerman, "My Science Fiction Collection Part Six — Conclusion," *The Fantasy Fan* Vol. 1, No. 6 (February 1934), p. 94.

64. Ackerman, "Through Time and Space with Forry Ackerman (Part 8)," *Mimosa* No. 23, January 1999.

65. Kyle, From a Young Fan, *Wonder Stories*, June 1934, p. 117.

66. Ackerman (as Linden), "Ft, Knox," p. 20.

67. Ross, p. 15.

68. Ackerman, "Through Time Part 1."

69. "Proofreading The Philadelphia Story," *File 770* No. 133, Ed. Mike Glyer (Monrovia, CA: December 1999), p. 8.

70. Laney, *Fan-Dango* No. 21.

71. Bleiler, *Science-fiction: The Gernsback Years*, p. 188.

72. Ackerman, *Gosh! Wow!*, pp. 447–450.

73. Hansen, *THEN*.

74. Moskowitz, *Seekers of Tomorrow*, p. 312.

75. "Meet the Fan."

76. Ackerman, "War of the Words," *Amazing Forries*, p. 13.

77. Bloch, *Once Around the Bloch*, p. 98.

78. Gregory William Mank, *Hollywood Cauldron*, p. 150.

79. Moskowitz, *Seekers*, p. 355.

80. Warner, "All Our Yesterdays 13," *Opus* No. 6 (July 1952).

81. Ackerman, "Potpourri by 4e," *Futurian War Digest* Vol. 1, No. 9 (June 1941).

82. Charles Lieurance, "Night of the Ackermonster," *Amazing Heroes* No. 153 (November 15, 1988), p. 47.

83. Ackerman, "My Life in a Time Machine."

84. Gorecki, "An Afternoon with Jack Darrow," p. 37.

85. Ackerman, "1939 — Nycon I, New York City," *Noreascon Three Souvenir Book*, p. 58.

86. Moskowitz, *Storm*, p. 244.

87. Ackerman, "Through Time, Part 1."

88. Moskowitz, *Storm*, pp. 222, 225–226.

89. Eney, TOP FAN, *Fancyclopedia II*.

90. Ackerman, *Amazing Forries*, p. 31.

91. Laney, *Ah!, Sweet Idiocy!*, p. 36.

92. Ackerman, *Movie Gold*, p. 185. There has been considerable confusion as to the exact date this event occurred. Ackerman stated he heard Wells in 1938 at the Wilshire Ebell club in Los Angeles (*Mr. Monster's Movie Gold*, p. 185). In the seventh installment of his autobiographical column "Through Time and Space with Forry Ackerman" (*Mimosa* No. 22, June 1998) Ackerman gave the date as 1939, while stationery Ackerman employed in the mid-1960s which listed his accomplishments in a sidebar gave the date as 1940 (see the 1974 LunaCon program book and *Amazing Forries*, p. 14). In an interview Ackerman recalled Robert A. Heinlein also attended the Wells talk and the author did mention this in an 8 November 1940 letter to brother J. Clare Heinlein (ms, The Robert A. and Virginia Heinlein Archives, UC Santa Cruz [misdated 1941 in files]). My thanks to William H. Patterson, Jr., for this information.

93. "Meet the Fan."

94. Ackerman, *Forrest J Ackerman, Famous Monster of Filmland* (1986), p. 113.
95. Ackerman, "The Ackermonster Chronicles," *Cult Movies* No. 34 (2001), p. 66.
96. Sackett, "The Ackerman Story," p. 8.
97. Gary Fisher, "An Interview with Forrest J Ackerman," 1997, <http://www.armchair.com/warp/ackerman.html>.
98. Ackerman, Letter, *Le Zombie* No. 24 (February 24, 1940), p. 3.
99. Moskowitz, "Inside Madle: A Fan for All Seasons," p. 57.
100. These photos never ran in the paper.
101. Ackerman, "A Visit with Margaret Brundage."
102. Ackerman, "Through Time," Part 2.
103. Moskowitz, *Seekers*, p. 203.
104. Ackerman, 1940—Chicon I, *Noreascon Three*, pp. 68–69.
105. Knight, Knight Piece, *Hell's Cartographers*, p. 107.
106. David G. Hartwell, *Age of Wonders*.
107. Ibid.
108. Ibid.
109. Ackerman, "Through Time," Part 2.
110. Willis, "The Harp that Once or Twice."
111. Hansen, "Chapter 1 The 1930s: GENESIS," *THEN*.
112. U.S. World War II Army Enlistment Records, 1938–1946.
113. Eney, *Fancyclopedia II*.
114. Ross, p. 13.
115. Cox, "A Few Words About an Old Friend," pp. 5, 59.
116. U.S. World War II Army Enlistment Records, 1938–1946.
117. Ackerman, "At Long Last," *Venus* Vol. 1, No. 1, Ed. Lora Crozetti, June 1944, p. 14.
118. Sackett, "Ackerman Story," p. 9.
119. Sackett, "Ackerman Story," p. 11.
120. Warner, *All Our Yesterdays* (1969), p. 72
121. Ackerman, "Through Time, part 3," *Mimosa* 18, pp. 22–24.
122. Laney, "Pacificon Diary."
123. Ackerman, "Through Time, part 3."
124. Sackett, "Ackerman Story," p. 6.
125. Corupe, *Rue Morgue*, p. 28.
126. Eshbach, *Over My Shoulder*, p. 55.
127. Davin, "Pioneer in the Age of Wonder," p. 87.
128. Pohl, *The Way The Future Was*, p. 177.
129. Introduction, *Science Fiction Worlds of Forrest J Ackerman and Friends*, p. 10.
130. Eshbach, p. 252.
131. Meet the Fan, p. [2?].
132. Ackerman, "Introducing the Author," p. 131.
133. Ackerman, "Things That Have Warmed...," *Amazing Forries*, p. 24
134. Eshbach, pp. 86–98.
135. Zicree, *The Twilight Zone Companion*, p. 77.
136. Sackett, "Confessions of an American Science Fiction Fan," unpublished article.
137. Siclari, "Science Fiction Fandom," p. 111.
138. Haydock, "From Fandom to Infinity," *Escape*, p. 16.
139. Hansen, "Volume 2, Chapter 1," *THEN*.
140. Ackerman, "The Aug and I," p. 61.
141. Ackerman, "The Far-Out Philosopher of Science Fiction," *Science Fiction Worlds of Forrest J. Ackerman and Friends*, p. 127. Ackerman misremembered her name as "Zelda."
142. Linden, "Ackermonster Strikes Again," *Amazing Forries*, p. 5.
143. Elliot, "Take Me Home...," p. 46.
144. *Science-Fiction Fantasy Horror: The World of Forrest J Ackerman at Auction*, p. 49.
145. Walt Willis, "My Life in Fandom."
146. Moskowitz, "The Return of Hugo Gernsback Part IV," *Fantasy Commentator* Nos. 55–56, Spring 2003, pp. 208–210.
147. Moskowitz, "The Return of Hugo Gernsback Part IV," *FC* 55–56, Spring 2003, p. 233.
148. Ackerman, *Amazing Forries*, p. 20.
149. Decades later Ackerman recalled, "I really don't know who took possession of the trophy.... The most obvious individual would have been H.J. Campbell, who was going back home to England after the convention, and would have been in a position to deliver it to Ken Slater" ("Through Time and Space with Forry Ackerman (Part 3)," *Mimosa* No. 18, May 1996).

150. Ackerman, "From Ghetto to Glory The Science Fiction Story," *Science-Fiction Fantasy Horror: The World of Forrest J Ackerman at Auction*, p. 18.

151. I am indebted to Mike Ashley for pinpointing this year.

152. Ackerman, "The Aug and I," p. 62.

153. Hansen, "Chapter 10 The Mid 1970s: THE BASTARD OFFSPRING OF SCIENCE FICTION MONTHLY," *THEN*.

154. "*Target Earth!* will be the screen title of 'Deadly City,' the sci-fi story authored by Paul W. Fairman under his penname Ivar Jorgenson" (Ackerman, "Fantasy Film Flashes," *Imagination* Vol. 5, No. 12, December 1954, p. 109).

155. Christopher Kovacs, "This Week In Words: Coining 'Sci-Fi.'"

156. Ashley, *Transformations*, p. 68.

157. Ackerman, "Through Time, Part 6," *Mimosa* No. 21, December 1997.

158. Coker, *David A. Kyle: A Life*, p. 15.

159. The treatment and other materials are now housed at Marquette University.

160. Ackerman, "Introduction By FJA — The Man Who Collected Himself," *Fantasy Magazine Index*, p. 6.

161. Ackerman, "Through Time, Part 5," *Mimosa* No. 20, May 1997.

162. Cooke, "The Making of a Monster Mogul," *Comic Book Artist* Vol. 1, No. 4 (Spring 1999), p. 21.

163. *Science-Fiction Fantasy Horror: The World of Forrest J Ackerman at Auction*, p. 116.

164. "WORST COLD WAVE OF YEAR GRIPS CITY; Blizzard Sweeps Upstate — Mercury to Stay Low" read a front page headline of *The New York Times* for 10 February 1958. "HALF OF U.S. SWEPT BY SNOW AND COLD; 42-Inch Fall and Minus-33 Temperature Recorded Snow and Cold Hit Half of U.S." reads another a week later.

165. Robert A. Madle, "Bob Madle's American Letter," *Nebula Science Fiction,* No. 40, May 1959.

166. Lupoff, Letter, *Famous Monsters* No. 2, p. 6.

167. "Ghastly Look of a Film Fad," *LIFE* 11 November 1957, pp. 16–17.

168. Ackerman, *Forrest J Ackerman, Famous Monster of Filmland* (1986), p. 27.

169. Dennis J. Druktenis, Editorial, *Scary Monsters* No. 3, p. 3.

170. Arthur C. Clarke, "Of Sand and Stars."

171. Skal, *The Monster Show*, p. 274.

172. Evanier, "Forrest J Ackerman, R.I.P."

173. Ackerman, *Gosh! Wow!*, p. 531.

174. Elsewhere Ackerman wrote that this work was commissioned from Paul "during the last year of his life" (*Science Fiction Worlds*. p. 190).

175. Ackerman to August Derleth, 13 December 1959.

176. Alan Warren, *This Is a Thriller*, p. 14.

177. King, *On Writing*, p. 35.

178. Ackerman, *Famous Monster*, p. 131.

179. Monster Mosaic, *Essential Monster Movie Guide*, p. 18.

180. Ackerman, *Gosh!*, p. 531.

181. Corupe, *Rue Morgue*, p. 24.

182. Grayson, p. 17.

183. Jaap Boekestein, "Dutch and Flemish Fandom, Fifties and Sixties."

184. Asimov, *In Joy Still Felt*, p. 376.

185. Grey, *Nightmare of Ecstasy*, p. 121.

186. Greg Bear, "Forrest J Ackerman," *Locus* Vol. 62, No. 1, Whole No. 576, p. 59.

187. Warren, "Famous Monsters, Forry Ackerman, and Other Stuff," *Famous Monster Chronicles*, p. 165.

188. Tippet, <http://www.aintitcool.com/node/39346>.

189. Scott A. Nollen, *Boris Karloff: A Gentleman's Life*, p. 242.

190. Ackerman, Monster Mosaic, p. 10.

191. Blass, "One Famous Monster of an Interview," p. 35. For the play see Buehrer, pp. 15, 24; Nollen, pp. 237–238.

192. Patten, E-mail to author.

193. Ackerman, "The Ackermonster Strikes Again," *Amazing Forries*, p. 9.

194. Ackerman, *Movie Gold*, p. 143.

195. Weaver, *Eye on Science Fiction: 20 Interviews with Classic SF and Horror Filmmakers*, p. 188.

196. Ed Grant, "Forry's a Jolly Good Fellow," *VideoScope*, p. 41.

197. Introduction, *Science Fiction Worlds of Forrest J Ackerman and Friends*, p. 9.

198. Ackerman, "Hello," *Amazing Forries*, p. 1.

199. During the 1970s Wendayne had also translated American editions of *Solaris* author Stanislaw Lem's novel *The Invincible* and *Hard to Be a God* by Boris and Arkady Strugatsky.

200. Elton T. Elliott, "The Ackerman Interview," *Science Fiction Review* No. 27, p. 46.

201. Bill Warren, online posting, 19 February 2009, Classic Horror Film Board, <http://monsterkid classichorrorforum.yuku.com/sreply/387801/Forrest-J-Ackerman>.

202. Theakston, *Famous Monsters Chronicles*, p. 16.

203. Ackerman, *Movie Gold*, p. 198.

204. Landis, "Forry Ackerman Estate Auction." Profiles in History Hollywood Auction, p. 172.

205. "Wendayne Ackerman," *Science Fiction Chronicle: The Monthly SF and Fantasy Newsmagazine* Vol. 11, No. 8, Ed. Andrew I. Porter (May 1990), pp. 10, 12.

206. Ackerman, "The Aug and I," *IS*, p. 61.

207. Heinlein to Ackerman, 17 November 1973, ms, The Robert A. and Virginia Heinlein Archives, UC Santa Cruz.

208. Lee Harris, "Fun Forry Facts to Know and Tell," *Scary Monsters,* No. 70, p. 71.

209. Austin, *Thrust*, p. 19.

210. Ross, p. 13.

211. "Forrest J Ackerman's Crimson Chronicles," *Scarlet Street* No. 33, 1999.

212. Bembaron, "A Visit with the King of Eerie," *Synn Watch*, p. 18.

213. Asimov, *In Joy Still Felt*, p. 768.

214. Weaver, *Double Creature Feature Attack*, pp. 304–305.

215. Elliott, p. 46.

216. Garris, <http://www.aintitcool.com/node/39346>.

217. Ackerman, "Through Time, Part 9," *Mimosa* No. 24, August 1999.

218. Ackerman (as Linden), "Ackerman Quits Famous Monsters!" *Fangoria* 24 (December 1982), p. 26.

219. Ackerman, "Through Time, Part 5."

220. Ross, p. 16.

221. *Cloud Chamber,* 29 July 1984.

222. David Langford, "INFINITELY IMPROBABLE," *Ansible* 42, March 1985.

223. Alan White, p. 14.

224. Edwards and Clute, p. 4.

225. Austin, *Thrust*, p. 19.

226. Fan Newsnotes, *Science Fiction Chronicle*, Vol. 11, No. 6, March 1990.

227. Bembaron, p. 17.

228. David Langford, "The Cottage of Eternity," *Ansible* No. 104, March 1996.

229. "Through Time, Part 10."

230. Ferry, *Life Is But a Scream!*, p. 299.

231. Stephen Jones, "Introduction," *The Mammoth Book of Best New Horror 13*, pp. 39–40.

232. "Forry Has Left the Building — Not the Planet," *File 770* No. 142, Ed. Mike Glyer (Monrovia, CA: June 2003), p. 6.

233. Mallarm, *False Memories: Adventures of the Living Dali*, p. 47.

234. Ferry, *Life Is But a Scream!*, pp. 127–128, 340.

235. Alicia Lozano, "Forrest J. Ackerman's scary treasures part of Hollywood auction."

236. Joe Moe, "Horrorwood Babbles On: The Ackermansion, Gone?..."

237. "Meet the Fan."

238. Steve Vertlieb, "Ray Harryhausen on Forry Ackerman's Passing," online posting.

SOURCES

Ackerman, Forrest J. "The Ackermonster Chronicles." *Cult Movies*. No. 34. 2001.

_____. "The Aug and I." *IS* No. 4. Ed. Tom Collins. Meriden, CT: October 1971.

_____. "Esperanto, the Universalanguage." <http://classic-web.archive.org/web/20051210041403/4forry.best.vwh.net/>.

_____. "The Far-Out Philosopher of Science Fiction." *Science Fiction Worlds of Forrest J Ackerman and Friends*. Reseda, CA: Powell Publications, 1969.

_____. "Filler You Can Skip." *Amazing Forries: This Is Your Life, Forrest J Ackerman*. Hollywood, CA: Metropolis Publications/Warren, 1976. p. 29.

_____. *Forrest J Ackerman, Famous Monster of Filmland*. Pittsburgh, PA: Imagine, 1986.

_____. *Forrest J Ackerman Presents Mr. Monster's Movie Gold: A Treasure Trove of Imagi-Movies*. Ed. Hank Stine. Virginia Beach, VA: Donning, 1981.

_____. "Forrest J Ackerman's Crimson Chronicles." *Scarlet Street*. No. 33. Ed. Richard Valley. Glen Rock, NJ: R.H. Enterprises, 1999.

_____. "From Ghetto to Glory The Science Fiction Story." *Science-Fiction Fantasy Horror: The World of Forrest J Ackerman at Auction*. pp. 18–19.

_____. "An Imagi-Movie Odyssey." *Worlds of Horror*. No. 2. Ed. Darren Gross. Electric Publishing, August 1989. pp. 2–3.

_____. "In Contemplation Of My Inevitable Demise." <http://www.aintitcool.com/node/39346>.

_____. "Introducing the Author." *Imaginative Tales*. Vol. 3, No. 3. Ed. William L. Hamling. Evanston, IL: Greenleaf, May 1956.

_____. "Introduction By FJA — The Man Who Collected Himself." *Fantasy Magazine Index*. Delbert W. Winans. Baltimore, MD: Delbert W. Winans, March 1977. pp. 4–6.

_____. Letter. *Amphipoxi*. No. 8. Ed. Billy H. Pettit. The Hague, Netherlands: 1968.

_____. Letter to August Derleth. 13 December 1959. August W. Derleth Papers. Madison, WI: State Historical Society of Wisconsin.

_____. "Lon Chaney Shall Not Die." *"It's Alive!@85."* Ed. Jeffrey Roberts & George Chastain. A MonsterBoom Special Publication, November 2001. p. 6.

_____. "Monster Mosaic." *The Essential Monster Movie Guide: A Century of Creature Features on Film, TV, and Video*. Stephen Jones. London: Titan Books, 1999; Billboard Books, 2000.

_____. "My Life in a Time Machine." Unpublished article.

_____. "My Science Fiction Collection Part Two." *The Fantasy Fan*. Vol. 1, No. 2. Ed. Charles D. Hornig. Elizabeth, NJ: Charles D. Hornig, October 1933. p. 29.

_____. "My Science Fiction Collection Part Six — Conclusion." *The Fantasy Fan*. Vol. 1, No. 6. Ed. Charles D. Hornig. Elizabeth, NJ: Charles D. Hornig, February 1934. p. 94.

_____. "A New Method of Evaluation." *Science Wonder Quarterly*. Vol. 1, No. 1. Ed. Hugo Gernsback. Mt. Morris, IL: Stellar Publishing, Fall 1929. p. 136.

_____. "Notes on Bob Olsen." *The Fantasy Fan*. Vol. 2, No. 1. Whole No. 13. Ed. Charles D. Hornig. Elizabeth, NJ: Charles D. Hornig, September 1934. pp. 11, 15.

_____. "Potpourri by 4e." *Futurian War Digest*. Vol. 1, No. 9. Ed. J. Michael Rosenblum. Leeds, UK: June 1941.

_____. "Through Time and Space with Forry Ackerman (Part 8)." *Mimosa* No. 23. Gaithersburg, MD: January 1999.

_____. "A Visit with Margaret Brundage." *The Weird Tales Collector*. No. 3. Ed. Robert Weinberg. Chicago, IL: 1978. p. 17.

Ackerman, Forrest J (as Paul Linden). "Ackerman Quits Famous Monsters! 'Acksclusive' to FANGORIA The Most Incredible Article We — Or Any Other Filmonster Magazine — Has Ever Published!" *Fangoria*. No. 24. December 1982.

_____. "Forrest J Ackerman #1 Everything." Unpublished.

Adams, Ron. "Give This Kid Anything He Wants!" *MonsterMad*. No. 1. Ed. George Chastain. Morgantown, WV: July 1997. pp. 8–11.

Ashley, Mike. *Transformations: The Story of the Science Fiction Magazines from 1950 to 1970*. Liverpool: Liverpool University Press, 2005.

Asimov, Isaac. *In Joy Still Felt: The Autobiography of Isaac Asimov, 1954–1978*. Garden City, NY: Doubleday, 1980.

Bear, Greg. "Forrest J Ackerman." *Locus*. Vol. 62, No. 1. Whole No. 576. p. 59.

Beerbohm, Robert L. "The Big Bang Theory of Comic Book History." *Comic Book Marketplace*. Vol. 2, No. 50. Coronado, CA: Gemstone Publishing, August 1997. pp. 48–60.

Bembaron, Jeffrey Mark. "Interview. A Visit with the King of Eerie." *Synn Watch: The Magazine of Esoteric Entertainment*. Longwood, FL: Paragon, 1999. pp. 17–20.

Blass, Terry. "One Famous Monster of an Interview." *Chiller Theatre*. Vol. 1, No. 5. Ed. Kevin Clement. Rutherford, NJ: Chiller Theatre, 1996.

Bleiler, Everett F., and Richard Bleiler. *Science-fiction: The Gernsback Years: A Complete Coverage of the Genre Magazines Amazing, Astounding, Wonder, and Others from 1926 Through 1936*. Kent, OH: Kent State University Press, 1998.

Bloch, Robert. *Once Around the Bloch: An Unauthorized Autobiography*. New York: Tor, 1993.

Boekestein, Jaap. "Dutch and Flemish fandom, fifties and sixties." <http://www.fanac.org/Fan_Histories/Netherlands/>.

Buard, Jean-Luc. "Georges Gallet: An Obituary." *Fantasy Commentator*. Vol. IX, No. 1. Whole No. 49. Ed. A. Langley Searles. Bronxville, NY: A. Langley Searles, Fall 1996. pp. 45–48.

Carpenter, Humphrey. *Tolkien: A Biography*. Boston: Houghton Mifflin, 1977.

Clarke, Arthur C. "Of Sand and Stars." *The Sentinel*. New York: Berkley, 1983.

Coker, John L., ed. *David A. Kyle: A Life of Science Fiction Ideas and Dreams*. Orlando, FL: Days of Wonder Publishers, 2006.

_____. *A Gathering to Honor Forrest J Ackerman Presented by David A. Kyle and Friends*. Orlando, FL: Days of Wonder Publishers, 2006.

Cooke, Jon B. "The Making of a Monster Mogul 'Someone Has to Make it Happen,' The James Warren Interview: The Emperor of Horror Speaks!" *Comic Book Artist*. Vol. 1, No. 4. Raleigh, NC: TwoMorrows, Spring 1999. pp. 13–43.

Copner, Michael, and Coco Kiyonaga. "Nights of Futures Past: An Intimate Interview: Forrest J Ackerman." *Cult Movies*. No. 37. January 2001. pp. 58–61.

Davin, Eric Leif. "Pioneer in the Age of Wonder: An Interview with Raymond Z. Gallun." *Fantasy Commentator*. Vol. 6, No. 2. Whole No. 38. Ed. A. Langley Searles. Bronxville, NY: A. Langley Searles, Fall 1988. pp. 78–97.

Delap, Richard. "The 'Best' Anthologies: 1973." *The WSFA Journal (The Journal of the Washington S.F. Association)* No. 84. December 1974.

Druktenis, Dennis J. "The Ackermonster, Forrest J Ackerman." *Scary Monsters*. No. 3. Highwood, IL: Dennis Druktenis Publishing & Mail Order, June 1992.

_____. Editorial. *Scary Monsters*. No. 3. Highwood, IL: Dennis Druktenis Publishing & Mail Order, June 1992.

Edwards, Malcolm J., and John Clute. "Ackerman, Forrest J(ames)." *The Encyclopedia of Science Fiction*. Ed. John Clute and Peter Nicholls. New York: St. Martin's, 1993. pp. 3–4.

Eney, Richard H. *Fancyclopedia II*. Alexandria, VA: Operation Crifanac, 1959.

Eshbach, Lloyd A. *Over My Shoulder: Reflections on a Science Fiction Era*. Philadelphia: Oswald Train Publisher, 1983.

Evanier, Mark. "Forrest J Ackerman, R.I.P." <http://www.newsfromme.com/archives/2008_12_05.html#016 305>.

Evans, E. Everett. "Denvention Dope." *Le Zombie*. No. 41. August 1941.

Ferry, Ray. *Life Is But a Scream! The True Story of the Rebirth of Famous Monsters of Filmland*. North Hills, CA: Karmanirhara Publications, 2000.

Fisher, Gary. "An Interview with Forrest J Ackerman." 1997. <http://www.armchair.com/warp/ackerman.html>.

"Focus on Warren Comics Magazines." *Hero Illustrated*. No. 5. Lombard, IL: Warrior Publications, November 1993.

"Forry Has Left the Building — Not the Planet." *File 770*. No. 142. Ed. Mike Glyer. Monrovia, CA: June 2003. p. 6.

Garris, Mick. Untitled post. <http://www.aintitcool.com/node/39346>.

"Ghastly Look of a Film Fad." *LIFE*. 11 November 1957. pp. 16–17.

Glasser, Allen. "Earthling Spurns Martian! Inhabitant of Neighboring Planet Doubts Visitor's Origin." *The Fantasy Fan*. Vol. 1, No. 1. Elizabeth, NJ: September 1933.

Gorecki, Dave. "An Afternoon with Jack Darrow." *The 14th Alternative*. Spring 1990. pp. 36–37.

Grey, Rudolph. *Nightmare of Ecstasy: The Art and Life of Edward D. Wood, Jr.* Los Angeles: Feral House, 1994.

Hall, Halbert W. *Science Fiction Book Review Index 1929–1973*. Detroit: Gale Research, 1975.

Hansen, Rob. "Chapter 1 The 1930s: Genesis." *THEN*. <http://www.ansible.co.uk/Then/then_1-1.html>.

_____. "Chapter 10 The Mid 1970s: The Bastard Offspring of Science Fiction Monthly." *THEN*. <http://www.ansible.co.uk/Then/then_4-2.html>.

Harryhausen, Ray, and Tony Dalton. *Ray Harryhausen: An Animated Life*. New York: Billboard Books, 2004.

Hartwell, David G. *Age of Wonders: Exploring the World of Science Fiction*. New York: Walker and Company, 1984.

Haydock, Ron. "From Fandom to Infinity." *Escape! (Into The Whirls of Fandom)*. Vol. 1, No. 1. Ed. Ron Haydock and Larry Byrd. Santa Ana, CA: West Coast Zines, January 1961. pp. 13–18.

Heinlein, Robert A. Letter to Forrest J Ackerman. 17 November 1973. Manuscript, The Robert A. and Virginia Heinlein Archives, UC Santa Cruz.

Hogenmiller, Linus. Letter. *Astounding Stories of Super-Science*. Vol. V, No. 1. Ed. Harry Bates. Readers' Guild, January 1931.

Holmberg, John-Henri. "Sture Lönnerstrand." *Science Fiction Chronicle*. Vol. 21, No. 3. June/July 2000. p. 62.

Horne, David. *Gathering Horror: A Completist Collector's Catalogue and Index for Warren Publishing*. Concord, CA: Phrona Press, 2010.

Jackson, Peter. "Peter Jackson Eulogizes Uncle Forry..." <http://www.aintitcool.com/node/39356>.

Jones, Stephen. "Introduction: Horror in 2001." *The Mammoth Book of Best New Horror 13*. New York: Carroll & Graf, 2002. pp. 39–40.

Joshi, S. T. *I Am Providence: The Life and Times of H. P. Lovecraft*. 2 Volumes. New York: Hippocampus Press, 2010.

King, Stephen. *On Writing: A Memoir of the Craft*. New York: Scribner, 2000.

Knight, Damon. "Knight Piece." *Hell's Cartographers: Some Personal Histories of Science Fiction Writers*. Ed. Brian W. Aldiss and Harry Harrison. New York: Harper & Row, 1975.

Kovacs, Christopher. "This Week in Words: Coining 'Sci-Fi.'" December 9, 2008. <http://file770.com/?p=710>.

Kyle, David A. "From a Young Fan." *Wonder Stories*. Vol. 6, No. 1. Springfield, MA: Continental, June 1934. p. 117.

Landis, John. "Forry Ackerman Estate Auction." *Profiles in History Hollywood Auction 36*. p. 172.

Laney, Francis T. *Ah!, Sweet Idiocy!* F. T. Laney and C. Burbee for FAPA, 1948.

_____. "I'm Terrified of Fans." *Fan-Dango.* No. 21. Spring 1949.

_____. "Pacificon Diary." *Fan-Dango.* No. 13. (FAPA) Fall 1946.

Langford, David. "Infinitely Improbable." *Ansible.* No. 42. Reading, Berkshire, UK: March 1985.

_____. "The Cottage of Eternity." *Ansible.* No. 104. Reading, Berkshire, UK: March 1996.

Lovecraft, H. P. *O Fortunate Floridian: H. P. Lovecraft's Letters to R. H. Barlow.* Ed. S. T. Joshi and David E. Schultz. Tampa: University of Tampa Press, 2007.

Lozano, Alicia. "Forrest J. Ackerman's Scary Treasures Part of Hollywood Auction." Hero Complex — Los Angeles Times. 29 April 2009. <http://herocomplex.latimes.com/2009/04/29/forrest-j-ackermans-scary-treasures-go-to-the-auction-block/>.

Lupoff, Richard. Letter. *Famous Monsters of Filmland.* Vol. 1, No. 2. Philadelphia: Central Publications, September 1958. p. 6.

Madle, Robert A. "Bob Madle's American Letter." *Nebula Science Fiction.* No. 40. Ed. Peter Hamilton. Glasgow: May 1959.

_____. "David A. Kyle: The Man Who Evolved — From The Purple Bat to The Grey Lensman." *David A. Kyle: A Life of Science Fiction Ideas and Dreams.* Ed. John L. Coker III. Orlando, FL: Days of Wonder Publishers, 2006.

Mallarm, Gabrielle. *False Memories: Adventures of the Living Dali: The Surreal Biography of Anton Brzezinski.* iUniverse, 2005. pp. 44–47.

Maltin, Leonard. "Getting Movie Crazy: Talking with Leonard Maltin." <http://scoop.diamondgalleries.com/public/default.asp?t=1&m=1&c=34&s=265&ai=67610&arch=y&ssd=3/8/2008%2012:01:00%20PM>.

Mank, Gregory William. *Hollywood Cauldron: 13 Horror Films from the Genres's Golden Ag*e. Jefferson, NC: McFarland, 1994.

Miller, Stephen T., and William G. Contento. *Science Fiction, Fantasy, & Weird Fiction Magazine Index (1890– 2007).* CD-Rom. Oakland, CA: Locus Press, 2008.

Moe, Joe. "Horrorwood Babbles On: The Ackermansion, Gone? Puns Fail Me..." <http://www.dreadcentral.com/news/31540/horrorwood-babbles-on-the-ackermansion-gone-puns-fail-me>.

Moskowitz, Sam. *Explorers of the Infinite.* Westport, CT: Hyperion, 1974.

_____. *The Immortal Storm: A History of Science Fiction Fandom.* Westport, CT: Hyperion, 1974.

_____. "The Immortal Storm II (Part II)." *Fantasy Commentator.* 47 & 48. Vol. VIII, Nos. 3 & 4. Ed. A. Langley Searles. Bronxville, NY: Fall 1995.

_____. "Inside Madle — A Fan for All Seasons." *SunCon: The Thirty-Fifth World Science Fiction Convention Program Book.* Miami Beach, FL: Worldcon 35, 1977. p. 52–57.

_____. "The Return of Hugo Gernsback Part IV." *Fantasy Commentator.* 55–56. Bronxville, NY: Spring 2003.

_____. *Seekers of Tomorrow.* Westport, CT: Hyperion, 1974.

Nollen, Scott A. *Boris Karloff: A Gentleman's Life.* Baltimore, MD: Midnight Marquee, 1999.

Olsen, Bob. "Did You Say Reminisce?" *Fantastic Worlds.* Vol. 1, No. 3. Ed. Sam Sackett. Spring 1953. p. 28.

Palmer, Randy. *Paul Blaisdell, Monster Maker: A Biography of the B Movie Makeup and Special Effects Artist.* Jefferson, NC: McFarland, 1997.

Patten, Fred. E-mail to author. 19 November 2008.

"Proofreading The Philadelphia Story." *File 770.* No. 133. Ed. Mike Glyer. Monrovia, CA: December 1999. p. 8.

Rhodes, Gary Don. E-mail to author. 31 October 2010.

Rosenbloom, Nate. E-mail to author. 14 September 2010.

Ross, Jean W. "Interview with Forrest J Ackerman." *Contemporary Authors.* Volume 102. Detroit: Gale Research, 1980. pp. 13–16.

Sackett, Sam. "The Ackerman Story." *Fantastic Worlds.* Vol. 1, No. 2. Fall-Winter 1952. pp. 5–13.

_____. "Confessions of an American Science Fiction Fan." Unpublished Article.

Shuster, Fred. "Addams Family, Move Over — Forrest J Ackerman's House Is Really a Museum." *Daily News of Los Angeles.* Wednesday 31 May 1989.

Siclari, Joe. "Science Fiction Fandom." In Tymn, Marshall B. *The Science Fiction Reference Book.* Mercer Island, WA: Starmont House, 1981.

Skal, David J. *The Monster Show: A Cultural History of Horror.* New York: Norton, 1993.

Smith, Clark Ashton. *Selected Letters of Clark Ashton Smith.* Ed. David E. Schultz and Scott Connors. Sauk City WI: Arkham House, 2003.

Smith, D. R. "Hands Off English." *Novae Terrae.* Vol. 1, No. 7. Ed. Maurice K. Hanson. pp. 4–5.

Smith, Don G. *Lon Chaney, Jr.: Horror Film Star, 1906–1973.* Jefferson, NC: McFarland, 1996.

Soister, John T. *Up from the Vault: Rare Thrillers of the 1920s and 1930s.* Jefferson, NC: McFarland, 2004.

Speer, Jack. *Up to Now.* 1938. (fanzine)

Tippet, Phil. Untitled post. <http://www.aintitcool.com/node/39346>.

Tolkien, J. R. R. *The Letters of J. R. R. Tolkien.* Ed. Humphrey Carpenter and Christopher Tolkien. Boston: Houghton Mifflin, 1981.

Vertlieb, Steve. "Ray Harryhausen on Forry Ackerman's Passing." Online posting. 18 February 2009. Horror Headlines: Forrest J Ackerman Final Farewells Classic Horror Film Board. <http://monsterkidclassichor rorforum.yuku.com/topic/20552/t/Forrest-J-Ackerman.html?page=23>.

Waite, Ronald N. "Enchanted Forrest." *Polaris One.* Vol. 2, No. 1. Spring 1980. pp. 2–15.

Warner, Harry, Jr. *All Our Yesterdays: An Informal History of Science Fiction Fandom in the Forties.* Chicago: Advent Publishers, 1969.

_____. "All Our Yesterdays 13." *Opus.* No. 6. July 1952.

Warren, Alan. *This Is a Thriller: An Episode Guide, History and Analysis of the Classic 1960s Television Series.* Jefferson, NC: McFarland, 1996.

Warren, Bill. "Famous Monsters, Forry Ackerman, and Other Stuff." *Famous Monster Chronicles.* Ed. Dennis Daniel with Jim Knusch. Albany, NY: FantaCo Enterprises, 1991. p. 165.

_____. Online posting. 19 February 2009. Classic Horror Film Board. <http://monsterkidclassichorrorfor um.yuku.com/sreply/387801/Forrest-J-Ackerman>.

Weaver, Tom. *Double Creature Feature Attack: A Monster Merger of Two More Volumes of Classic Interviews.* Jefferson, NC: McFarland, 2003.

_____. *Eye on Science Fiction: 20 Interviews with Classic SF and Horror Filmmakers.* Jefferson, NC: McFarland, 2003.

Weller, Sam. *The Bradbury Chronicles: The Life of Ray Bradbury.* New York: William Morrow, 2005.

"Wendayne Ackerman." *Science Fiction Chronicle: The Monthly SF and Fantasy Newsmagazine.* Vol. 11, No. 8. Ed. Andrew I. Porter. May 1990. pp. 10, 12.

White, Alan, ed. *Mr. Monster: A Tribute to Forrest J Ackerman.* Las Vegas: Alan White, 2009.

Willis, Walt. "The Harp that Once or Twice." *Science-Fiction Five-Yearly.* No. 8. Ed. Lee Hoffman, Patrick Hayden and Teresa Nielsen Hayden. November 1986.

_____. "My Life In Fandom." <www.smithway.org/fstuff/walt.html>.

Zicree, Marc Scott. *The Twilight Zone Companion.* Los Angeles: Silman-James Press, 1992.

PART II : BIBLIOGRAPHY

BOOKS

1 *Ackermanthology! 65 Astonishing, Rediscovered Sci-Fi Shorts.* Los Angeles, CA: General Publishing Group, 1997; *Ackermanthology: Millennium Edition.*

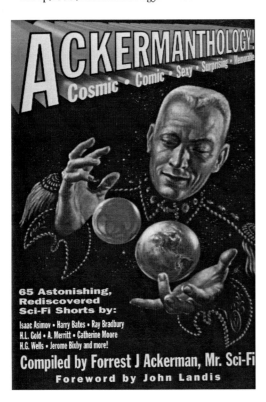

The cover of *Ackermanthology! 65 Astonishing, Rediscovered Sci-Fi Shorts* (1997) [1], a collection of short stories and vignettes culled from over 60 years of periodical selections.

Rockville, MD: Sense of Wonder Press, 2000. (*365 Science Fiction Short Short Stories.* [Editor with Jean Stine] Stamford, CT: Longmeadow Press, 1995. Announced, evidently not published and became *Ackermanthology!*)

2 *Amazing Forries: This Is Your Life, Forrest J Ackerman.* Hollywood, CA: Metropolis Publications, 1976. 36 pp. (autobiographical booklet in honor of

Back cover of *Amazing Forries* [2], portrait by Josh Kirby.

Cover of *Amazing Forries: This Is Your Life, Forrest J Ackerman* (Metropolis Publications, 1976) [2], an autobiographical volume celebrating Ackerman's 60th birthday).

60th birthday, contains reprints of stories, articles and many stills)

3 *Best Science Fiction for 1973*. (Editor) New York: Ace, 1973.

4 *The Boiling Point*. West Warwick, RI: Necronomicon Press, April 1985. 9 pp. (reprints Ackerman's letters and readers' letters in response to Ackerman's criticism of Clark Ashton Smith from the "Boiling Point" column in 1930's fanzine *The Fantasy Fan*)

5 *Book of Weird Tales*. Ed. [With Cliff Lawton.] Burnley, Lancashire, England: Veevers and Hensman Ltd., n.d. Autumn 1960.

6 *Dr. Acula's Thrilling Tales of the Uncanny*. [As Dr. Acula.] Rockville, MD: Sense of Wonder Press, 2004.

7 *Famous Forry Fotos: Over 70 Years of Acker-Memories*. Rockville, MD: Sense of Wonder Press, 2001. (captions throughout by Ackerman)

8 *Film Future: Twenty Classic Science Fiction Stories Which Morphed into Movies*. London: Orion Media, 1998; *Science-Fiction Classics: The Stories That Morphed into Movies*. New York: TV Books Inc., 1999. [446 pp.]

9 *Forrest J Ackerman, Famous Monster of Filmland*. Introduction by Vincent Price. Pittsburgh, PA: Imagine, Inc. 1986. [152 pp.] (covering the first fifty issues of *Famous Monsters*, contains tributes, excerpts and reprints from editorials and readers' letters)

10 *Forrest J Ackerman, Famous Monster of Filmland #2*. Volume II (Issues #51–100) Universal City, CA: Hollywood Publishing Company, 1991. 162 pp. (continuation of earlier Imagine volume covering *Famous Monsters* 51–100, reprints of material) [Foreword by Bill Warren; "Otherwords" by Steven Spielberg and Stephen King, Afterword by Philip J. Riley]

11 *Forrest J Ackerman Presents Donovan's Brain*. Curt Siodmak. Mill Valley, CA: Pulpless.com, 1999.

12 *Forrest J Ackerman Presents Hauser's Memory*. Curt Siodmak. Mill Valley, CA: Pulpless.com, 1999.

13 *Forrest J Ackerman Presents This Island Earth*. Raymond F. Jones. Mill Valley, CA: Pulpless.com, 1999.

14 *Forrest J Ackerman's Fantastic Movie Memories: Forrest Ackerman's Treasure Trove of Imagi-Movies*. Canoga Park, CA: New Media Books, 1985. (booklet) 100 pp. (similarly titled but separate item from above)

15 *Forrest J Ackerman's World of Science Fiction*. Los Angeles, CA: General Pub. Group., 1997. [Introduction by John Landis]; London: Aurum Press, 1998; as *Science-Fiction*. Köln: Taschen, 1998. (German); *Science-Fiction*. Köln: Evergreen Benedikt Taschen Verlag, 1998 (French).

16 *The Frankenscience Monster: Everything You Could Possibly Wish to Know About the Late, Great Boris Karloff*. New York: Ace Publishing Corporation, 1969. [Illustrations by Verne Tossey]

17 *The Gernsback Awards 1926*. Vol. 1. Los Angeles, CA: Triton Books, 1982; *The Gernsback Awards 1926*. Vol. 1. Wildside Press, 2003.

18 *Gosh! Wow! (Sense of Wonder) Science Fiction*. New York: Bantam, 1982. [introductions to each story, material about the authors reprinted from letters pages and fanzines]

19 *I, Vampire: Interviews with the Undead*. (Editor, with Jean Stine) Stamford, CT: Longmeadow Press. 1995. [235 pp.]; Clemmons, NC: Renaissance E Books, 2001.

20 *James Warren Presents Famous Monsters of Filmland Strike Back!* New York: Paperback Library, 1965. (uncredited)

21 *James Warren Presents Son of Famous Monsters of Filmland*. New York: Paperback Library, 1965. (uncredited)

Top: Cover of *The Gernsback Awards* [17], the first volume of what was to have been a series retroactively honoring early pulp science fiction and its creators. *Bottom:* Cover of *I, Vampire: Interviews with the Undead* [19] a theme anthology Ackerman co-edited with Jean Stine.

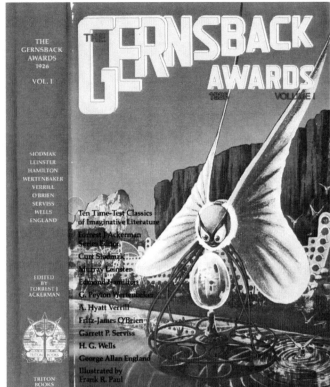

22 *James Warren Presents the Best from Famous Monsters of Filmland.* New York: Paperback Library, 1964. (uncredited)

23 *Lon of 1000 Faces.* Beverly Hills, CA and Pangbourne, Bershire, England: Morrison, Raven-Hill Co., 1983. 286 pp; Rockville, MD: Sense of Wonder Press, 2003. [a dream project for Ackerman]

24 *Martianthology: An Ackermanthology of Sense of Wonder Stories.* Sense of Wonder: 2003. [complied by Ackerman, Edited by Anne Hardin]

25 *Las Mejores Historias de Horror.* Barcelona: Editorial Bruguera, 1969; 1971; 1972; 1973; 1974; 1975.

26 *Metropolis Souvenir Book: A Fascinating Look at Life, Strife & Super Science in the year 2026.* Tokyo: Tsurumoto Room Co., 1978.

27 *Monsters.* A. E. van Vogt. (Editor) New York: Paperback Library, 1965; 1967; 1970; London: Transworld Pub. / Corgi Books, 1970; Corgi Books, 1977; *Les Monstres.* [translated by Denis Verguin] Paris: Belfond, 1974; Paris: Ed. J'ai lu, 1990.

28 *New Eves: Science Fiction about the Extraordinary Women of Today and Tomorrow.* (Editor, with Janrae Frank and Jean Stine) Stamford, CT: Longmeadow Press, 1994. [427 pp.]

29 *The Pirate and Other Poems: By a Valedictorian.* Rochester, MI: The Pretentious Press, 1990. (verse and graduation speech, 16 pp., 126 copies printed)

30 *Rainbow Fantasia: 35 Spectrumatic Tales of Wonder.* Rockville, MD: Sense of Wonder Press, 2001.

31 *Reel Future: The Stories that Inspired 16 Classic Science Fiction Movies.* Ed. with Jean Marie Stine. New York: Barnes & Noble Books, 1994; Science Fiction Book Club, 1994. [538 pp.]; *Die Vergangenheit der Zukunft: Die Originalstories hinter den*

grossen Science-fiction-Filmen. Nürnberg: Burgschmiet Verlag, 1998.

32 *A Reference Guide to American Science Fiction Films.* Volume 1. [With A. W. Strickland.] Bloomington, IN: T.I.S. Publications Division, 1981. [397 pp.] (covers silent films produced between 1897–1929, profusely illustrated with stills; series never continued)

33 *Science Fiction Worlds of Forrest J Ackerman and Friends.* Reseda, CA: Powell Publications, 1969; *Expanded Science Fiction Worlds of Forrest J Ackerman & Friends PLUS.* Rockville, MD: Sense of Wonder Press. 2002. (contains seven additional stories)

34 *Sense of Wonder Science Fiction.* Illustrated by E. J. Gold. Sirius Science Fiction, 1993. (revision of earlier "Gosh! Wow! volume) [423 pp.]

35 *Souvenir Book of Mr. Science Fiction's Fantasy Museum.* New York: Kodansha, 1978.

36 *Worlds of Tomorrow: The Amazing Universe of Science Fiction Art.* [With Brad Linaweaver.] Portland, OR: Collectors Press, 2004.

Cover of *New Eves: Science Fiction about the Extraordinary Women of Today and Tomorrow* (1994) [28].

CONTRIBUTIONS TO PERIODICALS

Short Stories/Fiction

37 "All Cremated Equal." *Fantastic Worlds.* Vol. 1. No. 1. Stockton, CA: Fantastic Worlds / S. J. Sackett, Summer 1952.

38 "And Then the Cover Was Bare." *Science Fiction Worlds of Forrest J Ackerman and Friends.* Reseda, CA: Powell Publications, 1969; *Expanded Science Fiction Worlds of Forrest J Ackerman & Friends PLUS.* Rockville, MD: Sense of Wonder Press, 2002.

39 "Atomic Error." *Shangri-La; Slant.* No. 3. Spring 1950. Ed. Walter A. Willis. Belfast, N. Ireland: Oblique, 1950. p. 4; *Other Worlds Science Stories.* Ed. Raymond A. Palmer. Clark Publishing Company, July 1950; as "Atom-irrtum." *Utopia Sonderband I.* Rastatt, Baden, Germany: Erich Pabel Verlag, 1956.

40 "Atomigeddon 2419 A.D." *Vertex.* Vol. 1. No. 2. Ed. Donald J. Pfeil. Los Angeles: Mankind Publishing Company, June 1973. (contained within the editor's Introduction to "The Shortest Science Fiction Story Ever Told"); *Worlds in Small.* Ed. John Robert Colombo. Vancouver, B. C., Canada: Cacanadadada Press, 1992; *Miniatures: An Anthology of Miniature Literary Compositions.* Ed. John Robert Colombo. Shelburne, Ontario: Battered Silicon Dispatch Box, 2006. (play on the first Buck Rogers story, "Armageddon 2419 A.D." by Philip Francis Nowlan)

41 "La Atomomonumento." (revision of Theodore Sturgeon's "Memorial" from April 1946 *Astounding Science Fiction*) *Fantasticonglomeration; Glom.* No. 4. April 1946; as "El Monumento Atómico." *Los Cuentos Fantasticos.* Vol. 3. No. 33. Agosto 1951; *Las Mejores Historias de Horror.* Barcelona: Editorial Bruguera, 1969, 1971, 1972, 1973, 1974, 1975; as "The Atomic Monument" *Science Fiction Worlds of Forrest J. Ackerman and Friends.* Reseda, CA: Powell Publications, 1969; *Expanded Science Fiction Worlds of Forrest J Ackerman & Friends PLUS.* Rockville, MD: Sense of Wonder Press, 2002.

42 "Atoms and Stars." *Nebula Science Fiction.* Vol. 1. No. 2. Ed. Peter Hamilton. Glasgow: Crownpoint Publications. Spring 1953.

43 "Behind the Ate Ball: A Martian Oddity." [As by Anon.] *Marvel Science Stories.* Vol. 2. No. 4. Whole No. 8. November 1950; as "A Martian Oddity." *Science Fiction Worlds of Forrest J Ackerman and Friends.* Reseda, CA: Powell Publications, 1969; *Adam.* Knight Publishing Corporation, August 1973; *Ackermanthology! 65 Astonishing, Rediscovered Sci-Fi Shorts.* Los Angeles, CA: General Publishing Group. 1997; *Ackermanthology: Millennium Edition 65 Astonishing, Rediscovered Sci-Fi Shorts.* Rockville, MD: Sense of Wonder Press, 2000; *Expanded Science Fiction Worlds of Forrest J Ackerman & Friends PLUS.* Rockville, MD: Sense of Wonder Press. 2002; *Martianthology: An Ackermanthology of Sense of Wonder Stories.* Rockville, MD: Sense of Wonder Press, 2003.

44 "Being of Blasphemy." [As Laurajean Ermayne.] [original publication unknown]; as "Entity of blasphemy" translated by José María Claramunda Bes. *Las Mejores Historias de Horror.* Barcelona: Editorial Bruguera, 1969; 1971; 1972; 1973; 1974; 1975.

45 "The Big Sleep." Other Worlds Science Stories. Ed. Raymond A. Palmer. Clark Publishing Company, May 1950; *Science Fiction Worlds of Forrest J Ackerman and Friends.* Reseda, CA: Powell Publications, 1969; *Expanded Science Fiction Worlds of Forrest J Ackerman & Friends PLUS.* Rockville, MD: Sense of Wonder Press. 2002.

46 "Chaney Speaks Again." *Scarlet Street.* No. 7. Summer 1992. p. 18. (on a dream Ackerman had)

47 "Changed Choice." *The Buccaneer.* San Francisco, CA: Balboa High School, 16 March 1933. (vignette about character Weaver Right in the Year 2000; This is the *The Buccaneer* item Ackerman recalled as "Suicide in the Year 2000" [see: *Gosh! Wow!,* p. 436.])

48 "The Cosmic Kidnappers." [As S. F. Balboa with Christian Vallini.] *Evolutionary Rag.* Vol. 1. No. 2. Nevada City, CA: IDHHB, Inc., 1993; *Ackermanthology! 65 Astonishing, Rediscovered Sci-Fi Shorts.* Los Angeles, CA: General Publishing Group. 1997; *Expanded Science Fiction Worlds of Forrest J Ackerman & Friends PLUS.* Rockville, MD: Sense of Wonder Press, 2002.

49 "Cosmic Report Card: Earth." as "El Cuento de Cinca Ficcion mas Corto Que se ha Escrito Nunca." ("The World's Shortest Science Fiction Story") *Labirintos do Amanhã–Coleção Infinitos.* Brazil: Myths, 1964; [As Monitor 4SJ AKA MAN.] *Vertex: The Magazine of Science Fiction.* Vol. 1. No. 2. Ed. Donald J. Pfeil. Los Angeles: Mankind Publishing Company, June 1973; (As "The Shortest Science Fiction Story Ever Told.") *Tomorrow, and Tomorrow, and Tomorrow...* Ed. Bonnie L. Heintz, Frank Herbert, Donald A. Joos, Jane Agorn McGee. Holt, Rinehart and Winston, 1974; (As "The Shortest SF Story Ever Told") *Perry Rhodan No. 29.*

A World Gone Mad. Clark Darlton. New York: Ace Books, September 1973; London: Futura, 1977; as "Résultat de l'Exame, d'Entrée dans la Fédération Galactique: Planète Terre..." *Univers 02 — ANTHOLOGIE.* No. 614. September 1975; *Worlds in Small.* Ed. John Robert Colombo. Vancouver, B. C., Canada: Cacanadadada Press, [Ronsdale Press] 1992; *Ackermanthology! 65 Astonishing, Rediscovered Sci-Fi Shorts.* Los Angeles, CA: General Publishing Group, 1997; *Ackermanthology: Millennium Edition 65 Astonishing, Rediscovered Sci-Fi Shorts.* Rockville, MD: Sense of Wonder Press, 2000; *Miniatures: An Anthology of Miniature Literary Compositions.* Ed. John Robert Colombo. Shelburne, Ontario: Battered Silicon Dispatch Box, 2006.

50 "Death Rides the Spaceways." *Authentic Book of Space.* Ed. H. J. Campbell. London: Hamilton & Co., 1954. (review of *Riders to the Stars*???)

51 "Dhactwhu!— Remember?" [With Robert A. W. Lowndes as by Jacques DeForest Erman and Wilfred Owen Morley.] *Super Science Stories.* Ed. Ejler Jakobsson. Niagra Falls, NY: Fictioneers, Inc. April 1949; UK: 1949; *Science Fiction Worlds of Forrest J Ackerman and Friends.* Reseda, CA: Powell Publications, 1969; *Perry Rhodan. No. 44. The Pseudo One.* Clark Darlton. New York: Ace, April 1974; *Expanded Science Fiction Worlds of Forrest J Ackerman & Friends PLUS.* Sense of Wonder Press, 2002.

52 "Don of Flame." *Slant.* No. 6. Walter A. Willis. Winter 1952. p. 55.

53 "Donovan's Idee." (Donovan's Brainstorm) *Utopia Sonderband I.* Rastatt, Baden, Germany: Erich Pabel Verlag, 1956; "Donovan's Brainstorm." *Authentic Science Fiction.* (1950s); *The New York Post.* 3 April 1955.

54 "Dracula 2000." [As by Sathanas Rehan (G. John Edwards) and Viktor Vesperto.] *Famous Monsters of Filmland.* No. 55. Warren, May 1969; *Las Mejores Historias de Horror.* Barcelona: Editorial Bruguera, 1969; 1971; 1972; 1973; 1974; 1975; *Famous Monsters of Filmland.* No. 101. Warren, September 1973.

55 "Dwellers in the Dust." *Fantasy Book.* Vol. 1 No. 4. Ed. Garret Ford. Los Angeles: Fantasy Publishing Co., Inc., November 1948; [As "Los Moradores del Polvo."] *Los Cuentos Fantasticos.* Vol. 2. No. 11. January 1949; *Science Fiction Digest.* Vol. 1. No. 1. Ed. Chester Whitehorn. Specific Fiction, Corp. 1954. (revised version); "Die Zeltreise." *Utopia Science Fiction Magazine.* No. 5; *Science Fiction Worlds of Forrest J Ackerman and Friends.* Reseda, CA: Powell Publications, 1969; *Perry Rhodan. No. 48,* New York: Ace, June 1974; *Expanded Science Fiction Worlds of Forrest J Ackerman & Friends PLUS.* Rockville, MD: Sense of Wonder Press. 2002.

56 "Earth Can Be Fair." (Concluding Installment) [as Hubert George Wells] *Other Worlds Science Stories.* Raymond A. Palmer, Ed. Clark Publishing Company, October 1950.

57 "Earth's Lucky Day." [With Francis Flagg.] *Wonder Stories.* March/April 1936; as "El Día más Afortunado de la Tierra." *Los Cuentos Fantasticos.* Vol. 2. No. 11. January 1949; *Fantastic Story Magazine.* Vol. 2. No. 2. Springfield, MA: Best Books/A Thrilling Publication. Spring 1951; *Spaceway Science Fiction.* May/June 1969. (revised version); *Perry Rhodan. No. 46. Again Atlan!* New York; Ace, 1974; *Expanded Science Fiction Worlds of Forrest J Ackerman & Friends PLUS.* Ed. Forrest J Ackerman. Sense of Wonder Press, 2002.

58 "An Experiment with Time." [With Francis Flagg.] *Fantasy Magazine.* Vol. 2. No. 5. Whole No. 17. January 1934.

59 "The Flight of the Good Ship Clarissa." [As "One Who Should Know Better."] *Futuria Fantasia.* No. 3. Ed. Ray Bradbury. Los Angeles, CA: Winter 1940. p. 7; *Futuria Fantasia.* Ray Bradbury. Los Angeles: Graham, 2007.

60 "The Girl Who Wasn't There." [With Tigrina (Edythe Eyde) and William F. Nolan and Charles E. Fritch.] *Gamma.* Vol. 1. No. 1. Ed. Charles E. Fritch. North Hollywood, CA: Star Press, Inc. 1963. [as by Forrest J. Ackerman]. *Science Fiction Worlds of Forrest J Ackerman and Friends.* Reseda, CA: Powell Publications, 1969. pp. 129–134; "La Ragazza non C'Era." ("The Little Girl Who Wasn't There") *Il Meglio della Fantascienza.* Italy: 1971; *Expanded Science Fiction Worlds of Forrest J Ackerman & Friends PLUS.* Rockville, MD: Sense of Wonder Press. 2002. [further re-written version for *Gamma* by editor William F. Nolan and Charles E. Fritch involving removal of lesbian element)]

61 "The Great Goddess LN–OR." *Outworlds.* Vol. 5. No. 1. Whole No. 19. Wadsworth, OH: Bill Bowers, January 1974. p. 727.

62 "Great Gog's Grave." [With Donald A. Wollheim.] *Fantasy Book.* Vol. 1 No. 2. Ed. Dennis Mallonee & Nick Smith. Long Beach/Pasadena, CA: Fantasy Book Enterprises, December 1981; *Expanded Science Fiction Worlds of Forrest J Ackerman & Friends PLUS.* Rockville, MD: Sense of Wonder Press, 2002.

63 "The Hazy Hord[e]." [As Weaver Wright with Francis Flagg.] *Imagination!* No. 2. Los Angeles: Los Angeles Science Fiction League, November 1937.

64 *"The Hazy Hord."* [As Weaver Wright with Francis Flagg.] Imagination! Vol. 1. No. 3. December 1937. p. 9.

65 "The Incredible Olympian." [As S. F. Balboa.] *Scienti-Snaps.* Vol. 2. No. 3. Ed. Walter E. Marconette. Dayton, OH: April 1939.

66 "Kiki." *Vice Versa.* Ed. Edythe Eyde [as "Lisa Ben"]. CA: December 1947.

67 "The Lady Takes a Powder." [As Weaver Wright with Edythe Eyde.] *Inside.* No. 3. Ed. Ronald L. Smith. September 1953; as by "Karlon Torogsi as told to Tigrina" *Science Fiction Worlds of Forrest J Ackerman and Friends.* Reseda, CA: Powell Publications, 1969. pp. 135–142; *Expanded Science Fiction Worlds of Forrest J Ackerman & Friends PLUS.* Rockville, MD: Sense of Wonder Press. 2002.

68 "The Last Dangerous Game." *The Buccaneer.* San Francisco, CA: Balboa High School, Thursday 2 March 1933. (an absurdist vignette; the title is a play on *The Most Dangerous Game*)

69 "The Last Man on Earth: Variation, No. 97." *Miniatures: An Anthology of Miniature Literary Compositions.* Ed. John Robert Colombo. Shelburne, Ontario: Battered Silicon Dispatch Box, 2006.

70 "Laugh, Clone, Laugh." [With A. E. van Vogt.] *Science Fiction Worlds of Forrest J Ackerman & Friends.* Reseda, CA: Powell Publications, 1969; *More Than Superhuman.* Dell, 1971; NEL, 1975; *Expanded Science Fiction Worlds of Forrest J Ackerman & Friends PLUS.* Sense of Wonder Press, 2002.

71 "Letter to an Angel." *Science Fiction Worlds of Forrest J Ackerman and Friends.* Reseda, CA: Powell Publications, 1969; (translated by Miguel Giménez Sales) *Las Mejores Historias de Horror.* Barcelona: Editorial Bruguera, 1969; 1971; 1972; 1973; 1974; 1975; *Famous Monsters of Filmland.* No. 96. March 1973; *Amazing Forries: this is your life, Forrest J. Ackerman.* (London, England) Hollywood, CA: Metropolis Publications, 1976. pp. 33–35; "It's Alive!@85." Ed. Jeffrey Roberts & George Chastain. A MonsterBoom Special Publication, November 2001. pp. 7–10; *Expanded Science Fiction Worlds of Forrest J Ackerman & Friends PLUS.* Rockville, MD: Sense of Wonder Press, 2002.

72 "The Man Who Was Thirsty." *Science Fiction Worlds of Forrest J Ackerman and Friends.* Reseda, CA: Powell Publications, 1969; *Adam.* Vol. 17. No. 6. Ed. Don Pfeil. July 1973; as "The Shaggy Werewolf" [As Sylvius Agricola.] *Perry Rhodan. No. 41. The Earth Dies.* Clark Darlton. New York: Ace, March 1974.; *Expanded Science Fiction Worlds of Forrest J Ackerman & Friends PLUS.* Rockville, MD: Sense of Wonder Press, 2002.

73 ["Me and the Mite." (As Carl F. Burk.)] *Specula.* Ed. Arthur Louis Joquel, II. 1941; "Me and the Mite." [As Alden Lorraine.] *New Worlds.* Vol. 1. No. 2. Ed. John Carnell. London: Pendulum Publications, Ltd. October 1946; as "Micro-Man." [As Weaver Wright.] *Fantasy Book.* Vol. 1. No. 1. Ed. Garret Ford. Los Angeles: Fantasy Publishing Company, Inc. July 1947; as "Micro-Hombre" *Los Cuentos*

Fantasticos. Vol. 2. No. 11. January 1949; as "Micro Man." *The New York Post.* 24 April 1955; *Science Fiction Worlds of Forrest J Ackerman and Friends.* Reseda, CA: Powell Publications, 1969; *Expanded Science Fiction Worlds of Forrest J Ackerman & Friends PLUS.* Rockville, MD: Sense of Wonder Press. 2002.

74 "Una mujer nerviosa de 1970." [A Nervous Girl of 1970] [As Weaver Wright.] *Los Cuentos Fantasticos.* No. 38. Mexico: 1 Abril 1952; *The Great Male Robbery.* [As Weaver Wright.] *After Hours.* Vol. 1 No. 4. Ed. James Warren. Philadelphia: Jay Publishing Co., Inc. 1957; "Ora di Schiacciamento." ("The Crush Hour.") Italy; "You Can't Be Too Carful." (unknown).

75 "The Mute Question." *Other Worlds Science Stories.* Ed. Raymond A. Palmer. Clark Publishing Company, September 1950; *Adventures in Tomorrow.* Ed. Kendell Foster Crossen. New York: Greenberg: Publisher, 1951; Belmont, 1968; as "La Pregunta Silente." [as Níck Beal] *Los Cuentos Fantasticos.* Vol. 2. No. 22. 15 Noviembre 1949; *Authentic Science Fiction Monthly.* Vol. 1. No. 53. London, England: Hamilton & Co. (Stafford) Ltd. January 1955; as "Die Frage de Mutanten." *Utopia Sonderband.* No. 1. Rastatt, Baden, Germany: Erich Pabel Verlag, 1956; as "Pergunta sem Cabeça." *Labirintos do Amanhã-Coleção Infinitos.* Brazil: Myths, 1964; *If This Goes On.* Ed. Charles Nuetzel. Beverly Hills: CA: Book Co. of America, 1965; *Après ... La Guerre Atomique.* Verviers: Gérard, 1970; *Adam.* Vol. 17. No. 5. Ed. Donald J. Pfeil. Los Angeles: Knight Publishing Corp., June 1973; *Mutants.* Ed. Robert Silverberg. Nashville, TN: Thomas Nelson & Sons, 1974; Tompkins, Robert. *Futurescapes: Explorations in Fact and Science Fiction.* Toronto: Methuen, 1977. pp. 95–; as "Bij Gebrek Aan ... Antwoord" (Dutch) *Sprong Naar Omega: 20 verhalen van SF-grootmeesters.* Ed. Albert van Hageland. Zele: D.A.P. Reinaert, 1978; (revised) *Evolutionary Rag.* Vol. 1. No. 2. Nevada City, CA: IDHHB, Inc., 1993.

76 "My Friend, the Night." [As Laurajean Ermayne.] *Vice Versa.* Ed. Edythe Eyde [as "Lisa Ben"]. CA: October 1947. pp. ii-12.

77 "The Mystery of the Boardwalk Asylum." [As "Jack Erman."] *Outré.* Vol. 1. No. 2. Ed. Francis J. Litz. August 1939.

78 "Nada nuevo bajo el Sol." ["Nothing new under the sun."] *Los Cuentos Fantasticos.* No. 25. Mayo 1950.

79 "The Naughty Venusienne." [As Spencer Strong] with "Morgan Ives" (Marion Zimmer Bradley). *Caper.* Vol. 1. No. 3. December 1956. pp. 16–17, 21; [As by "Otis Kaye" and "Morgan Ives"], as "Stygg Flicka fran Venus." *Raff.* Sweden: February 1958; *Expanded Science Fiction Worlds of Forrest J Ack-*

erman & Friends PLUS. Rockville, MD: Sense of Wonder Press. 2002.

80 "The Night You Were Wed." [As Laurajean Ermayne.] *Vice Versa.* Ed. Edythe Eyde [as "Lisa Ben"]. CA: November 1947.

81 "No Time Like the Future." *Shangri L'Affaires.* No. 37. Ed. Charles Burbee. August 1947; *Marvel Science.* Vol. 3. No. 1. New York: Stadium Publishing Corp., November 1950. [As Spencer Strong???]; *Los Cuentos Fantasticos.* Vol. 3. No. 6; *Las Mejores Historias de Horror.* Barcelona: Editorial Bruguera, 1969; 1971; 1972; 1973; 1974; 1975; *Perry Rhodan No. 34. SOS: Spaceship Titan!* Kurt Brand. New York: Ace, November 1973; London: Orbit, 1978.

82 "Nymph of Darkness." [With C. L. Moore.] *Fantasy Magazine.* Vol. 4. No. 5. No. 29. April 1935; *Weird Tales.* Vol. 34. No. 6. Ed. Farnsworth Wright. Popular Fiction Publishing Co., Inc. December 1939; *La Nymphe des Ténèbres. Les Meilleurs Recits de Weird Tales Periode 1938/42.* Ed. Jacques Sadoul. Paris: J'ai Lu, 1975. Nº 923 — Février 1979; as "La Ninfa del Tenebre." *Nova SF Anthology.* [Italy]: 1980; *Denvention Two Program Book [The 39th World Science Fiction Convention].* Ed. Phil Normand. Denver, CO: Denvention Two, 1981. pp. 28–33; *Gosh! Wow (Boy-oh-Boy)! Science Fiction.* New York: Bantam, 1982. pp. 489–503; *Fantasy Book.* Vol. 3. No. 1, No. 11, Ed. Dennis Mallonee & Nick Smith. Pasadena, CA: Fantasy Book Enterprises, March 1984; *Echoes of Valor II.* Ed. Karl Edward Wagner. New York: Tor, 1989; 1993; *Womanthology.* Ed. Forrest J Ackerman & Pam Keesey. Rockville, MD: Sense of Wonder Press, 2003; *Northwest of Earth: The Complete Northwest Smith.* Seattle: Planet Stories, 2008; SFBC, 2009.

83 "Pre-Hysteric." *Utopian.* Vol. 1. No. 6. Ed. R. J. Banks, Jr. June 1952.

84 "The Record." [With Ray Bradbury.] *Futuria Fantasia.* Vol. 1 No. 1. Summer 1939. Ed. Ray Bradbury. Los Angeles, CA: Summer 1939. *Science Fiction Worlds of Forrest J Ackerman and Friends.* Reseda, CA: Powell Publications, 1969. pp. 170–177; *Expanded Science Fiction Worlds of Forrest J Ackerman & Friends PLUS.* Ed. Forrest J Ackerman. Sense of Wonder Press, 2002; *Futuria Fantasia.* Ray Bradbury. Los Angeles: Graham, 2007.

85 "The Red Button." [With Arthur L. Widner, Jr.] *Fanfare.* No. 10. Ed. Arthur L. Widner, Jr. December 1943.

86 "Sabina." *Nebula Science Fiction.* Vol. 2. No. 1. Whole No. 5. Ed. Peter Hamilton. Glasgow: Crownpoint Publications, September 1953. [pp. 38-?]

87 "A Sad Story of the Future." *The Fantasy Fan.* Vol. 1. No. 7. Ed. by Charles D. Hornig. Elizabeth,

NJ: Charles D. Hornig, March 1934; *Yawning Vortex: The Tsathoggua Press Journal of Weird Fiction.* Ed. Perry M. Grayson. Vol. 1. No. 3. West Hills, CA: Tsathoggua Press, February 1995; *The Fantasy Fan — The Fans' Own Magazine (September, 1933–February, 1935; Vol. 1, Nos. 1–12; vol. 2, Nos. 13–18.* n.p., n.d. Tacoma, WA[?]: Lance Thingmaker, 2010.

88 "Skyball." *The Buccaneer.* San Francisco, CA: Balboa High School, Thursday 26 January 1933. (projects a future Balboa High class playing a new type of sport; This is *The Buccaneer* item Ackerman recalled as "Wing Ball" [Gosh! Wow!, p. 436.])

89 "The Skyscraper Kidnappers." [As S. F. Balboa.] *Perry Rhodan. No. 20. The Thrall of Hypno.* Clark Darlton. New York: Ace, December 1972. (written in Ackerman's youth for a cover contest from the November 1929 *Science Wonder Stories*)

90 "Social Séance." *Polaris.* Vol. 2. No. 1. Ed. Paul Freehafer. December 1940.

91 "Stars and Atoms." *Canadian Fandom.* No. 29. Ed. Beak Taylor.[?] June 1956.

92 "A Stitch in Time." *Women of Intrigue.* No. 3. Los Angeles: Art Enterprises, Inc., 196–.

93 "The Survivor." [As Spencer Strong.] *Perry Rhodan. No. 18. Menace of the Mutant Master.* Kurt Mahr. New York: Ace Books, 1972.

94 "Synopsis." *Vortex.* No. 2. Ed. Gordon M. Kull and George R. Cowie. San Francisco, CA: Fansci Pubafi, 1947. p. 82.

95 "Technocrazy." *The Buccaneer.* San Francisco, CA: Balboa High School, Thursday 16 February 1933. (vignette on the foibles of a future world run by Technocracy)

96 "These Were Their Lives: Count Down to Doom." [as Viktor Vesperto] [With Charles Nuetzel.] *Famous Monsters of Filmland.* 1962. Vol. 3. No. 6. Whole No. 15. Philadelphia: Central Publications, Inc., January 1962. [p. 45]; *Monster World.* No. 8. Warren, May 1966; *Science Fiction Worlds of Forrest J Ackerman and Friends.* Reseda, CA: Powell Publications, 1969; *Expanded Science Fiction Worlds of Forrest J Ackerman & Friends PLUS.* Rockville, MD: Sense of Wonder Press. 2002.

97 "These Were Their Lives: Curiosity Killed the Bat." [As Weaver Wright with Ronald Budovec.] *Famous Monsters of Filmland.* No. 19. September 1962; *Famous Monsters of Filmland.* No. 49. May 1968. (about Dracula)

98 "These Were Their Lives: Litter to a Werewolf." [As K. Vazau Virlup.] *Famous Monsters of Filmland.* Vol. 5. No. 4. Whole No. 25. Warren Publishing, October 1963. p. 29; *Famous Monsters of Filmland.* No. 110. Warren, September 1974; *Famous*

Monsters of Filmland. No. 158. Warren, October 1979.

99 "These Were Their Lives: Silver Threats Among the Gold." [As by Peter Wang and "Spencer Strong."] *Famous Monsters of Filmland.* Vol. 5. No. 2. Whole No. No. 23. June 1963. p. 21; *Famous Monsters of Filmland.* No. 93. October 1972. p. 69. [Wolf Man short story, revision of "Wolfbane and Sagebrush" submitted by Ronald Matthies]

100 "Time of the Medusa." [With Norbert Novotny.] *Adam.* Knight Publishing Corporation, February 1974.

101 "Time to Change." [With Marcial Souto; originally "Mirror Image"] 1968. *Science Fiction Worlds of Forrest J Ackerman and Friends.* Reseda, CA: Powell Publications, 1969; *Expanded Science Fiction Worlds of Forrest J Ackerman & Friends PLUS.* Rockville, MD: Sense of Wonder Press, 2002.

102 "The Time Twister." [As Weaver Wright] with Francis Flagg. *Thrilling Wonder Stories.* Ed. Sam Merwin, Jr. New York: Standard Magazines Inc./ A Thrilling Publication, October 1947; as "Y El Tiempo Marcha Adalente." *Los Cuentos Fantasticos.* No. 12. 1949; *The New York Post.* 29 January 1956; (revised as) "Strangers in a Strange Time" in: *Perry Rhodan. No. 23. Peril on Ice Planet.* Kurt Mahr. New York: Ace, April 1973; *Expanded Science Fiction Worlds of Forrest J Ackerman & Friends PLUS.* Sense of Wonder Press, 2002.

103 "To Serf MAN." [As Coil Kepac.] *Perry Rhodan. No. 50: Attack from the Unseen.* New York: Ace Books, July 1974; *Ackermanthology! 65 Astonishing, Rediscovered Sci-Fi Shorts.* Los Angeles, CA: General Publishing Group. 1997; *Ackermanthology: Millennium Edition 65 Astonishing, Rediscovered Sci-Fi Shorts.* Rockville, MD: Sense of Wonder Press, 2000.

104 "A Trip to Mars." *San Francisco Chronicle.* 24 May 1931.

105 "Twin of Frankenstein." [With "Mary W. Shelley."] *Famous Monsters of Filmland.* No. 35. Warren, October 1965. pp. 17–19. (prose version of monster movie maker contest script included within article "Amateur Monster Movie Makers." See entry 157.)

106 "A Typical Terran's Thought When Spoken to by an Alien from the Planet Quarn in Its Native Language." [With Daryl F. Mallett.] *The ISFA Newsletter.* Nov. 1990; *Worlds in Small.* Ed. John Robert Colombo. Cacanadadada Press, 1992; *Miniatures: An Anthology of Miniature Literary Compositions.* Ed. John Robert Colombo. Shelburne, Ontario: Battered Silicon Dispatch Box, 2006.

107 "What an Idea!" *Authentic Science Fiction Monthly.* Vol. 1. No. 30. Ed. Herbert J. Campbell.

London: Hamilton & Co. (Stafford) Ltd., February 1953.

108 "Winner Take All." [With Jill Taggart.] *Miniatures: An Anthology of Miniature Literary Compositions.* Ed. John Robert Colombo. Shelburne, Ontario: Battered Silicon Dispatch Box, 2006.

109 "World of Loneliness." [Laurajean Ermayne] (as "Mundo de Soledad.") Mexico: Los Cuentos Fantasticos. July 8 1948. (revised as "The Radclyffe Effect") *Science Fiction Worlds of Forrest J Ackerman and Friends.* Reseda, CA: Powell Publications, 1969; *Expanded Science Fiction Worlds of Forrest J Ackerman & Friends PLUS.* Rockville, MD: Sense of Wonder Press, 2002.

110 ["Yvala." (with C. L. Moore as Amaryllis Ackerman) *Weird Tales.* Ed. Farnsworth Wright. Popular Fiction Publishing Co., Inc. February 1936; *Womanthology.* Ed. Forrest J Ackerman & Pam Keesey. Rockville, MD: Sense of Wonder Press, 2003.]

Nonfiction

111 "A. E. van Vogt." *The Universe Maker.* A. E. van Vogt. New York: Ace, 1967; 1974; 1976.

112 "Abbott & Costello Meet Frankenstein." *Famous Monsters of Filmland.* No. 105. Warren, March 1974.

113 "About Amelia Reynolds Long." *Science Fiction—The Advance Guard of Future Civilization.* Vol. 1. No. 3. Ed. Jerome Siegel. Cleveland, OH: January 1933. p. 14. (female pulp writer, notes the appearance of her story "Omega" in *Amazing Stories* July 1932)

114 "About the Next Issue." *Shangri-La.* No. 12. CA: July 1949.

115 "The Ace of Space." *Spacemen.* Vol. 1. No. 4. Philadelphia: Spacemen, Inc., July 1962; *Spacemen 1965 Yearbook.* Warren Publishing Co., 1964. (Flash Gordon)

116 "Ack Is Back." *Monster Bash.* No. 7. 2007. p. 2.

117 "The Ackerman Chronicles." *Cult Movies.* No. 33. Ed. Buddy Barnett. Hollywood, CA: Cult Movies, 2000. p. 66.

118 "The Ackerman Chronicles." *Science Fiction Chronicle: The Monthly SF and Fantasy Newsmagazine.* Vol. 3. No. 6. Ed. Andrew Porter. March 1982. p. 5.

119 "The Ackerman Chronicles." *Science Fiction Chronicle: The Monthly SF and Fantasy Newsmagazine.* Vol. 3. No. 9. Ed. Andrew Porter. New York: June 1982. 6–7.

120 "The Ackerman Chronicles." *Science Fiction Chronicle: The Monthly Science Fiction and Fantasy Newsmagazine.* Vol. 3. No. 10. Ed. Andrew Porter. New York: July 1982. pp. 4–5.

121 "The Ackerman Chronicles." *Science Fiction Chronicle: The Monthly SF and Fantasy Newsmagazine.* Vol. 4. No. 2. Ed. Andrew Porter. November 1982. p. 5. (reports on his visit to Dracula's castle in Romania)

122 "The Ackerman Chronicles." *Science Fiction Chronicle: The Monthly Science Fiction and Fantasy Newsmagazine.* Vol. 4. No. 3. Ed. Andrew Porter. December 1982. p. 5.

123 "Ackerman on Harryhausen." *FXRH: Special Visual Effects Created by Ray Harryhausen.* No. 3. Ed. Ernest D. Farino and Sam Calvin. Irving, TX: Talos Publications, June 1972. pp. 4–5; *The FXRH Collection.* Los Angeles: Archive Editions, 2012. (transcript of remarks by Ackerman and Robert Bloch from a panel held at the July 1971 D'Con)

124 "Ackerman Quits Famous Monsters! 'Acksclusive' to FANGORIA The Most Incredible Article We — Or Any Other Filmonster Magazine — as Ever Published!" [As Paul Linden.] (in a self-interview "The Ackermonster Talks" on why he left *Famous Monsters*)

125 "The Ackerman Report. [As "Mr. Science Fiction."] *Fantasy Times.* No. 177. Ed. James V. Taurasi, et al. May 1, 1953. p. 7.

126 "The Ackerman Report." [As Mr. Science Fiction.] *Fantasy Times.* No. 186. (2nd September 1953 issue) pp. 2, 8.

127 "The Ackerman Report." [As Mr. Science Fiction.] *Fantasy Times.* No. 192. (2nd December 1953 issue)

128 "The Ackerman Report." [As Mr. Science Fiction.] *Fantasy Times.* No. 193. (1st January 1954 issue)

129 "The Ackerman Report." *Fantasy Times.* Vol. 8. No. 15. [Whole] No. 183. Ed. James V. Taurasi. Fandom House Publication. First August 1953 Issue. pp. 2–4. (The All-Ackerman Issue)

130 "The Ackerman Report: It Was Champagne for Chad Oliver on 1 Nov. 52." [As "Mr. Science Fiction."] *Fantasy Times.* Vol. 7 No. 21. No. 165. November 1952. p. 6. (on the wedding of author Oliver)

131 "The Ackerman Report." *Science Fiction Chronicle.* Vol. 2. No. 9. Ed. Andrew Porter. June 1981. pp. 6–7. (on recent sales for Ackerman and clients, general SF news)

132 "Ackermanese." *Amazing Forries: this is your life, Forrest J Ackerman.* Hollywood, CA: Metropolis Publications/Warren, 1976. p. 26.

133 "Ackermonster, Alien Astronaut in Starstruck." *Famous Monsters of Filmland*. No. 157. Warren, September 1979. pp. 36–40. (on a science fiction TV pilot in which Ackerman had a cameo)

134 "The Ackermonster Chronicles." *Cult Movies*. No. 29. 1999. p. 65.

135 "The Ackermonster Chronicles." *Cult Movies*. No. 34. 2001. p. 66.

136 "The Ackermonster in Frankenstein's Domain." *Famous Monsters of Filmland*. No. 111. Warren, October 1974.

137 "The Ackermonster Strikes!" *Famous Monsters of Filmland*. Vol. 5. No. 2. Whole No. No. 23. June 1963 p. 2. (photos of Ackerman with Boris Karloff, Peter Lorre and Vincent Price)

138 "The Ackermonster Strikes Again ... 11 Years Later." [As Paul Linden.] *Famous Monsters of Filmland Convention Book*. Warren/Phil Seuling, November 1974.

139 "The Ackermonster Strikes Again ... 13 Years Later." [As Paul Linden.] *Amazing Forries: this is your life, Forrest J Ackerman*. Hollywood, CA: Metropolis Publications/Warren, 1976. pp. 3–10; as "The Amazing Ackermonster." [As Paul Linden.] *Famous Monsters of Filmland*. No. 200. Orange, NJ: Dynacomm, May 1993. pp. 58–65. (updated/expanded version)

140 "The Ackermonster's Die-ry." *Cult Movies*. No. 39. 2003. p. 65.

141 "Acknowledgements." *Forrest J Ackerman Presents Mr. Monster's Movie Gold: A Treasure Trove of Imagi-Movies*. Ed. Hank Stine. Virginia Beach, VA: Donning Co. 1981. pp. 202–203.

142 "Adlib from Ackerman." *Fantasy Advertiser*. Vol. 2. No. 1. Ed. Gus Wilmorth & Roy A. Squires. June 1947.

143 "Advance Vision." *Stardust*. Ed. W. Lawrence Hamling. Vol. 1. No. 2. May 1940. p. 15. (profile of Robert A. Heinlein)

144 "After Shocks? We Got 3500 of 'Em." *Famous Monsters of Filmland*. No. 202. No. Hollywood, CA: Dynacomm, Spring 1994.

145 "Afterword." [As F. J. Ackerman.] *Gosh! Wow (Boy-oh-Boy)! Science Fiction*. pp. 163–164. (to H. L. Gold's "Inflexure")

146 "Afterword." *Best Science Fiction for 1973*. New York, New York: Ace, 1973. p. 268.

147 "Afterword." *Souvenir Book of Mr. Science Fiction's Fantasy Museum*. New York: Kodansha, 1978. p. 78.

148 "Alice in Monster Land." *Famous Monsters of Filmland*. Vol. 1. No. 1. Philadelphia: Central Publications, Inc., 1958. pp. 10–23; *Famous Monsters Yearbook*. No. 1. Summer-Fall 1962; *James Warren Presents The Best from Famous Monsters of Filmland*. New York: Paperback Library, 1964; *Famous Monsters 1968 Yearbook*. Warren, 1967; *Famous Monsters of Filmland*. No. 100. New York: Warren Publishing Co. August 1973; *Famous Monsters of Filmland Convention Book*. Warren, November 1974; *Forrest J Ackerman's Monsterama*. No. 1. Seattle, WA: Fantagraphics Books, May 1991. pp. 9–21; *Famous Monsters of Filmland*. Vol. 1. No. 1. Filmland Classics, January 2008. pp. 10–23. (replica edition)

149 "Alien." *Famous Monsters of Filmland*. No. 155. Warren, July 1979; *Warren Presents Alien Invasions Comix*. No. 3. Warren, August 1979. p. 8. [issue numbered 3 on the cover but considered seventh issue in the series]

150 "Alien." *Famous Monsters of Filmland*. No. 156. Warren, August 1979; *Warren Presents Movie Aliens Illustrated*. (*Warren Presents*. No. 4.) Warren, September 1979. *Warren Presents The Official Exclusive Horror Movie Yearbook 1981 Collector's Edition*. Warren, February 1981.

151 "The Alien Strikes Again." *Famous Monsters of Filmland*. No. 158. Warren, October 1979.

152 "Alien Will Get You If You Don't Watch Out!" *Famous Monsters of Filmland*. No. 157. Warren, September 1979.

153 "The Aliens Are Coming!" *Famous Monsters of Filmland*. No. 142. Warren, April 1978.

154 "All Shock Up." *Famous Monsters of Filmland*. Vol. 1. No. 4. August 1959. pp. 40–45. (TV horror film host Zacherley); *Famous Monsters of Filmland*. Vol. 1. No. 4. Filmland Classics, May 2008. pp. 40–45. (replica edition)

155 "All Star Cast Editorial from the Spaceship A2Z." *Perry Rhodan*. 43. *Life Hunt*. Kurt Brand. New York: Ace, April 1974.

156 "The Alligator People." *Famous Monsters of Filmland*. Vol. 1. No. 5. Philadelphia: Central Publications, Inc., November 1959. [pp. 44–47]; *James Warren Presents Son of Famous Monsters of Filmland*. New York: Paperback Library, 1965. (uncredited); *Famous Monsters of Filmland*. No. 36. Warren, December 1965. pp. 10–13.

157 "Amateur Monster Movie Makers." *Famous Monsters of Filmland*. No. 35. Warren, October 1965. pp. 14–19. (includes "Twin of Frankenstein" prose story. See entry 105.)

158 "The Amazing Ackermonster." [As Paul Linden.] *Famous Monsters of Filmland*. Vol. 5. No. 3. Whole No. 24. Warren Publishing, Inc., August 1963. [pp. 24–32.] (sub-titled "You Asked for It: FM's Editor Viewed & Interviewed in the 'Ackermansion of Horrorwood'")

159 "The Amazing Ackermonster." [As Paul Linden.] *Famous Monsters of Filmland.* Vol. 5. No. 4. Whole No. 25. Warren Publishing, Inc., October 1963. pp. 58–66. (part 2)

160 "The Amazing Ackermonster." [As Paul Linden.] *Famous Monsters of Filmland.* No. 26. Warren Publishing, Inc., January 1964. pp. 28–33. (self-written profile by Ackerman)

161 "Amazing Science Adventures." [By P. E. Jones and F. J. Ackerman.] *Marvel Science.* Vol. 3. No. 1. Ed. R. O. Erisman. New York: Stadium Publishing Corp., November 1950.

162 "The Amazing Star Wars Robots." *Famous Monsters of Filmland Star Wars Spectacular.* Warren Publishing Co., October 1977.

163 "'The American Olaf Stapledon': Forrest J Ackerman's Tribute to Robert A. Heinlein." *File 770.* No. 79. Ed. Mike Glyer. Van Nuys, CA: April 1989. p. 21.

164 [American SF and lexicon.] *Authentic Science Fiction.* No. 28. December 1952.

165 "An American Werewolf in London." *Famous Monsters of Filmland.* No. 177. Warren, September 1981; *Film Fantasy Yearbook 1982 Collector's Edition.* Warren, March 1982. (preview)

166 "An American Werewolf in London." *Famous Monsters of Filmland.* No. 178. Warren, October 1981.

167 "An American Werewolf in London." *Famous Monsters of Filmland.* No. 180. Warren, January 1982. (interviews)

168 "The Amityville Horror." *Famous Monsters of Filmland.* No. 157. Warren, September 1979. (preview)

169 "Among the Magazines: The Palmer Hoax." [As Geoffrey Giles with Walter Gillings.] *Science-Fantasy Review.* Vol. 4. No. 17. Winter 1949–1950. pp. 10–14. (on the "Shaver Mystery")

170 "And Now the Noose." *Famous Monsters of Filmland.* No. 99. Warren, July 1973.

171 "...And Prejudices." *Amazing Forries: this is your life, Forrest J Ackerman.* Hollywood, CA: Metropolis Publications/Warren, 1976. p. 32.

172 "And So We End an Age." *Photon.* No. 24. Ed. Mark Frank. Atomic Enterprises, 1974. (on Lon Chaney, Jr.)

173 "And So We End an Age." [With Wendayne Ackerman.] *Perry Rhodan: In the Center of the Galaxy.* New York: Ace Books, January 1978.

174 "Andy Warhol's Frankenstein." *Famous Monsters of Filmland.* No. 112. Warren, December 1974. (negative film review)

175 "An Anecdote." *The Fantasy Fan.* Volume 2. No. 5. Whole No. 17. Ed. Charles D. Hornig. Elizabeth, NJ: January 1935. p. 79; *The Fantasy Fan—The Fans' Own Magazine (September, 1933—February, 1935; Vol. 1, Nos. 1–12; vol. 2, Nos. 13–18.* n.p., Tacoma, WA[?]: Lance Thingmaker, 2010. (concerns Bob Olsen)

176 "Animals, Creatures, & Things." *Famous Monsters of Filmland.* No. 55. Warren, May 1969; *Famous Monsters of Filmland.* No. 141. Warren, March 1978; *Famous Monsters of Filmland.* No. 158. Warren, October 1979.

177 "Announcement from Ackerman Dept." *Le Zombie.* No. 20. 30 December 1939. p. 4. ("Public Headache Dept." criticizing the reportage of Sam Mokowitz in *Fantasy News*)

178 "The Ape and the Ape Girl." *Famous Monsters of Filmland.* No. 33. Warren, May 1965. pp. 13–15.

179 "Ark Vader meets Darth Raider." *Famous Monsters of Filmland.* No. 177. Warren, September 1981; *Film Fantasy Yearbook 1982 Collector's Edition.* Warren, March 1982. (*Raiders of the Lost Ark*)

180 "Arthur C. Clarke's Tour of Heidiville." *An Illustrated History of Heidi Saha: Fantasy Fandom's Famous Femme.* New York: Warren Publishing Co., 1973.

181 "Arthur Louis Joquel." *Luna Monthly.* No. 52. Ed. Franklin M. Dietz, Jr. Oradell, NJ: Frank Dietz & Ann Dietz, May 1974. p. 8. (obituary)

182 "Ask Uncle Forry." *Stoner's Monster Mayhem.* No. 2. Ed. Richard Stoner. Spring 1996. p. 7. (Q&A column)

183 "Ask Uncle Forry." *Stoner's Monster Mayhem.* No. 3. Ed. Richard Stoner. Summer 1996. p. 6.

184 "Ask Uncle Forry." *Stoner's Monster Mayhem.* No. 5. Ed. Richard Stoner. Winter 1997. p. 5.

185 "Ask Uncle Forry." *Stoner's Monster Mayhem.* No. 6. Ed. Richard Stoner. Spring 1997. p. 5.

186 "Ask Uncle Forry." *Stoner's Monster Mayhem.* No. 7. Ed. Richard Stoner. October 1997. p. 6.

187 "Astronautics in England." *The Fantasite.* Vol. 2. No. 5. Ed. Phil Bronson. May-June 1943. (on the British Interplanetary Society)

188 "Asylum." *Famous Monsters of Filmland.* No. 97. Warren, April 1973. (preview)

189 "At Long Last." *Venus.* Vol. 1. No. 1. Ed. Lora Crozetti. June 1944. pp. 11–14. (on meeting Fritz Lang)

190 "At the Earth's Core." *Famous Monsters of Filmland.* No. 129. Warren, October 1976. (preview)

191 "Atomicon Report." *Shangri L'Affaires*. No. 28. Ed. Arthur Louis Joquel II. February 1946. pp. 2–3.

192 "The Attack of 'Mr. Black.'" *Famous Monsters of Filmland*. No. 44. May 1967; *Famous Monsters of Filmland*. No. 101. Warren, September 1973. (*The Creature Walks Among Us*)

193 "Attack of the Giant Tarantula." *Famous Monsters of Filmland*. No. 44. Warren, May 1967; *Famous Monsters of Filmland*. No. 90. Warren, May 1972.

194 "Au Revoir, Capt. Nemo." *Famous Monsters of Filmland*. No. 103. Warren, December 1973. (obituary of actor Robert Ryan)

195 "The Aug and I." *Is*. No. 4. Ed. Tom Collins. Meriden, CT: October 1971. pp. 61–61. (memoir of August Derleth)

196 "Author's Note." *Forrest J Ackerman Presents Mr. Monster's Movie Gold: A Treasure Trove of Imagi-Movies*. Ed. Hank Stine. Virginia Beach, VA: Donning Co. 1981. p. 13.

197 "Authors' Note." *New Eves: Science Fiction about the Extraordinary Women of Today and Tomorrow*. Stamford, CT: Longmeadow Press, 1994.

198 "The Awakening It'll Open Your Eyes!" *Famous Monsters of Filmland*. No. 170. New York: Warren Publishing Co., January 1981. pp. 39–41. (on film adaptation of Bram Stoker's novel *The Jewel of Seven Stars* which is heavily quoted throughout)

199 "Aye, Rocket." *Space Magazine*. Ed. Clyde T. Hanback. Vol. 1. No. 2. Washington D.C.: Clyde T. Hanback in affiliation with the American Rocketry Association, Spring 1950. pp. 6–7, 23–24. (*Destination Moon*)

200 "Baby Frankenstein." *Famous Monsters of Filmland*. No. 127. Warren, August 1976.

201 "Badder Late Than Never from the Weirdprocessor of Dr. Akula." *Fangoria*. No. 26. March 1983. pp. 34–35. (on the centennial of Bela Lugosi's birth accompanied by stills)

202 "Baron Blood." *Famous Monsters of Filmland*. No. 97. Warren, April 1973. (preview)

203 "Barrack Bunk." *The Fort MacArthur Bulletin*. Friday 5 February 1943. p. 3-A.

204 "A Basic Science Fiction Library, a Symposium." (contributor) *The Arkham Sampler*. Vol. 2. No. 1. Ed. August Derleth. Sauk City, WI: Arkham House, Winter 1949; *Arkham House Sampler (2010)*. Sauk City, WI: Arkham House/The August Derleth Society, 201. (responses to questionnaire)

205 "Batman and the Super Hero Stars." *Monster World*. No. 10. Warren, September 1966.

206 "Battle Beyond the Stars." *Famous Monsters of Filmland*. No. 170. Warren, January 1981. pp. 20–25. (preview)

207 "Battle for the Planet of the Apes." *Famous Monsters of Filmland*. No. 108. Warren, July 1974.

208 "Battle of the Frankensteins." *Monster World*. Vol. 1. No. 1. Warren, November 1964; *Famous Monsters of Filmland 1971 Fearbook*. Warren, 1970.

209 "Battle of the Giant Beetle." *Monster World*. No. 3. Warren, April 1965.

210 "Battlestar Galactica." *Famous Monsters of Filmland*. No. 150. Warren, January 1979.

211 "Battlestar Galactica Revisited." *Famous Monsters of Filmland*. No. 157. Warren, September 1979.

212 "B.C. = Before Conan." *Famous Monsters of Filmland*. No. 184. Warren, June 1982.

213 "The Beastmaster." *Famous Monsters of Filmland*. No. 186. Warren, August 1982; *Film Fantasy Yearbook 1983 Collector's Edition*. Warren, March 1983. (preview)

214 "Beasts, Creatures & Things." *Famous Monsters of Filmland*. No. 65. Warren, May 1970.

215 "The Beasts of Tarzan." *Famous Monsters of Filmland*. Vol. 3. No. 4. Whole No. 13. Philadelphia: Central Publications, Inc., August 1961. pp. 54–59; *James Warren Presents Son of Famous Monsters of Filmland*. New York: Paperback Library, 1965; *Famous Monsters of Filmland*. No. 93. Warren, October 1972.

216 "Beauties and Beasts." *Showcase*. Vol. 1. No. 4. Alta-Glamour Inc. North Hollywood, CA: American Art Agency [Parliament], 1961.

217 "Beauty Escapes the Beast." *Famous Monsters of Filmland*. No. 113. Warren, January 1975. (obituary of Ilona Massey)

218 "The Beginning of Famous Monsters." *Fantasy Journal*. No. 4. Ed. Jim Hollander, Bob Greenberg. February 1963; *Forrest J Ackerman, Famous Monster of Filmland*. Pittsburgh, PA: Imagine, Inc. 1986. p. 11.

219 "Behind the Ape Ball." *Monster World*. No. 8. Warren, May 1966; *Famous Monsters of Filmland*. No. 54. Warren, March 1969.

220 "Behold: Margaret Brundage." *The Alchemist*. No. 5. Ed. Lew Martin, Roy Hunt and Charles Ford Hansen. February 1941. pp. 13–15; as "A Visit with Margaret Brundage." *The Weird Tales Collector*. No. 3. Ed. Robert Weinberg. Chicago, IL: 1978. p. 17. (*Weird Tales* cover artist)

221 "Bela Lugosi." *Famous Monsters of Filmland*. No. 92. Warren, September 1972.

222 "Beneath the Planet of the Apes." *Famous Monsters of Filmland*. No. 80. Warren, October 1970;

Famous Monsters of Filmland. No. 149. Warren, November 1978.

223 "Berlin's Army Show Scores Smash at RC." *The Fort MacArthur Bulletin.* Friday 5 February 1943. pp. 1-A–2-A.

224 "The Best Science Fiction Film Ever Made!" *Famous Monsters of Filmland Star Wars Spectacular.* Warren Publishing Co., October 1977.

225 "Better Late Than Never." *Wonderama Annual 1993 — First Issue, Forgotten Futures.* New York: Pure Imagination, 1993. (Editorial)

226 "Beware the Eyes." *Famous Monsters of Filmland.* No. 28. May 1964. Warren Publishing, Inc., pp. 62–64. (*Children of the Damned* preview)

227 "Beware the Frogs." *Famous Monsters of Filmland.* No. 91. Warren, July 1972. (1972 film *Frogs*)

228 "Beyond the Planet of the Apes." *Famous Monsters of Filmland.* No. 103. Warren, December 1973. (obituary of producer Arthur P. Jacobs)

229 "The Big One." *Fantasy Times.* No. 161. September 1952. p. 4. (report on 10th WorldCon)

230 "Big Pond Fund." *Philcon News.* No. 2. Ed. Robert A. Madle & Jack Agnew. Philadelphia: May 1947. p. 4.

231 "The Birth of a Notion." *Forrest J Ackerman, Famous Monster of Filmland.* Pittsburgh, PA: Imagine, 1986. pp. 9–23. (outlines the creation of *Famous Monsters of Filmland* with reprints and photographs); *Famous Monsters 1992 Coverart Calendar.* Raygen Entertainment, 1991. (text excerpt); *Famous Monsters of Filmland: The Annotated No. 1.* Movieland Classics, LLC, 2011. pp. 7–11.

232 "The Birthday Boys." *Famous Monsters of Filmland.* No. 154. Warren, June 1979.

233 "Birthday Greetings from 3700 BC to 2001 AD." *Famous Monsters of Filmland.* No. 156. Warren, August 1979.

234 "Birthday Witches." *Famous Monsters of Filmland.* No. 157. Warren, September 1979.

235 "Birthday Witches." *Famous Monsters of Filmland.* No. 164. Warren, June 1980.

236 "Birthday Witches." *Famous Monsters of Filmland.* No. 166. Warren, August 1980.

237 "Birthday Witches." *Famous Monsters of Filmland.* No. 167. Warren, September 1980.

238 "Birthday Witches." *Famous Monsters of Filmland.* No. 169. Warren, November 1980.

239 "Birthday Witches." *Famous Monsters of Filmland.* No. 170. Warren, January 1981. p. 15.

240 "Birthday Witches." *Famous Monsters of Filmland.* No. 172. Warren, April 1981.

241 "Birthday Witches." *Famous Monsters of Filmland.* No. 173. Warren, May 1981.

242 "Birthday Witches." *Famous Monsters of Filmland.* No. 174. Warren, June 1981.

243 "Birthday Witches." *Famous Monsters of Filmland.* No. 175. Warren, July 1981.

244 "Birthday Witches." *Famous Monsters of Filmland.* No. 176. Warren, August 1981.

245 "Birthday Witches." *Famous Monsters of Filmland.* No. 177. Warren, September 1981.

246 "Birthday Witches." *Famous Monsters of Filmland.* No. 180. Warren, January 1982.

247 "Birthday Witches." *Famous Monsters of Filmland.* No. 182. Warren, April 1982.

248 "Birthday Witches." *Famous Monsters of Filmland.* No. 183. Warren, May 1982.

249 "Birthday Witches." *Famous Monsters of Filmland.* No. 184. Warren, June 1982.

250 "Birthday Witches." *Famous Monsters of Filmland.* No. 185. Warren, July 1982.

251 "Birthday Witches." *Famous Monsters of Filmland.* No. 186. Warren, August 1982.

252 "Birthday Witches." *Famous Monsters of Filmland.* No. 187. Warren, September 1982.

253 "Birthday Witches." *Famous Monsters of Filmland.* No. 187. Warren, September 1982.

254 "Birthday Witches." *Famous Monsters of Filmland.* No. 190. Warren, January 1983. p. 11.

255 "BK Reviews." *Imagination!* Vol. 1. No. 1. October 1937. p. 11.

256 "The Black Cat." *Famous Monsters of Filmland.* No. 67. Warren, July 1970; (part 1) *Famous Monsters of Filmland.* No. 134. Warren, May 1977; (part 2) *Famous Monsters of Filmland.* No. 135. Warren, July 1977. (filmbook)

257 "The Black Heart of Dorian Gray." *Famous Monsters of Filmland.* No. 37. Warren, February 1966; *Famous Monsters of Filmland.* No. 51. Warren, August 1968; *Famous Monsters of Filmland.* No. 89. Warren March 1972; *Famous Monsters of Filmland.* No. 137. Warren, September 1977. pp. 40–41. [51, 89]

258 "The Black Hole." *Famous Monsters of Filmland.* No. 154. Warren, June 1979.

259 "The Black Sleep Takes Tamiroff!" *Famous Monsters of Filmland.* No. 98. Warren, May 1973. (Akim Tamiroff)

260 "The Black Sleep Takes Tor Johnson." *Famous Monsters of Filmland.* No. 90. Warren, May 1972. (obituary)

261 "Black Zoo." *Famous Monsters of Filmland.* Vol. 5. No. 2. Whole No. No. 23. June 1963. pp. 18–20; *Famous Monsters of Filmland.* No. 41. Warren, November 1966. pp. 26–28; *Famous Monsters of Filmland.* No. 89. Warren March 1972. (preview of 1963 film)

262 "Blacula." *Famous Monsters of Filmland.* No. 95. Warren, January 1973; *Dracula '79.* (*Warren Presents.* No. 5.) Warren, September 1979. (preview)

263 "Blade Runner." *Famous Monsters of Filmland.* No. 185. Warren, July 1982. (preview)

264 "The Bloch Sleep." *Famous Monsters of Filmland.* No. 205. N. Hollywood, CA: Dynacomm, December 1994. p. 3.

265 "Blood Banquet." *Famous Monsters of Filmland.* No. 145. Warren, July 1978. (Count Dracula Society function)

266 "Blood Creature!" *Famous Monsters of Filmland.* No. 37. Warren, February 1966; *Famous Monsters of Filmland 1971 Fearbook.* Warren, 1970.

267 "Blood Feast in Draculand: Elvira Day." *Forrest J Ackerman's Monster Land.* No. 2. [Canoga Park, CA: New Media Pub. Co.] April 1985. pp. 19–21. (23rd Annual Count Dracula Society Banquet)

268 "Blood from the Mummy's Tomb." *Famous Monsters of Filmland.* No. 98. Warren, May 1973.

269 "Blood of Frankenstein/Horror of the Blood Monsters." *Famous Monsters of Filmland.* No. 80. Warren, October 1970.

270 "Bob Olsen Dead at 71." *Fantasy Times.* No. 248. Ed. James V. Taurasi. June 1, 1956. p. 6.

271 "The Bogie Man Will Get You!" *Famous Monsters of Filmland.* No. 116. Warren, May 1975.

272 "Bones from the Hood." *Famous Monsters of Filmland.* No. 209. N. Hollywood, CA: Dynacomm, August/September 1995. p. 3.

273 "The Boogey Man." *Famous Monsters of Filmland.* No. 172. Warren, April 1981. (preview)

274 "Boris Karloff, Gentle Monster 1887–1969." *Photon.* No. 17. Ed. Mark Frank. New York: Atomic Enterprises, 1968 [sic]; "The King Has Answered Prince Sirki's Call." *The Frankenscience Monster.* New York: Ace Publishing Corporation, 1969. pp. 56–59.

275 "Boris Karloff: Out of This World." *Spacemen.* Vol. 2. No. 3. Whole No. 7. Warren Publishing, Inc., September 1963.

276 "Borrowed Time Ends." *Famous Monsters of Filmland.* No. 173. Warren, May 1981. (obituary of actress Beulah Bondi)

277 "The Bounty Hunter ... Wants You!" *Famous Monsters of Filmland.* No. 177. Warren, September 1981. (actor Jeremy Bulloch)

278 "The Boy Who Became a Monster." *Famous Monsters of Filmland.* Vol. 1. No. 3. Philadelphia: Central Publications, Inc., April 1959; *Famous Monsters of Filmland 1965 Yearbook.* No. 3. Warren, 1965.

279 "Boys Will Be Beasts." *James Warren Presents Famous Monsters of Filmland Strike Back!* New York: Paperback Library, 1965

280 "Bradbury's Best." *Starlog.* No. 84. O'Quinn Studios, July 1984. pp. 65, 96. (Saul Bass short film adaptation of Ray Bradbury's "Frost and Fire")

281 "The Brain That Would Not Die." *Famous Monsters of Filmland.* Vol. 4. No. 19. Philadelphia: Central Publications, Inc., September 1962; *Famous Monsters of Filmland.* No. 49. Warren, May 1968.

282 "Brave Nude World." *American Sunbather.* Mays Landing, NJ: American Sunbathing Association, 1961. pp. 16–19; *Fantastic.* Ed. Harry Harrison. Flushing, NY: Ultimate Publishing Co., Inc., May 1968.

283 "The Bride of Dr. Frankenstein." *Famous Monsters of Filmland.* No. 100. Warren, August 1973. p. 64. (Ackerman's interview of Mae Clarke)

284 "The Bride of Frankenstein." *Famous Monsters of Filmland.* Vol. 4. No. 6. Whole No. 21. February 1963; *Famous Monsters of Filmland 1967 Yearbook.* Warren, 1966.

285 "Bride of the Monster." *Monster World.* No. 5. Warren, October 1965; *Famous Monsters of Filmland.* No. 131. Warren, January 1977. (filmbook)

286 "Brontosaurus Battle!" *Monster World.* No. 9. New York: Warren, July 1966; *Famous Monsters of Filmland.* No. 137. Warren, September 1977. (*One Million Years B.C.*)

287 "A Brush with Genius." *Omni.* Vol. 13. No. 9. Ed. Keith Ferrell. June 1991. pp. 65–69, 84. (Frank R. Paul)

288 "Buck Rogers." *Famous Monsters of Filmland.* No. 155. Warren, July 1979.

289 "Buck Speaks!" *Famous Monsters of Filmland.* No. 160. Warren, January 1980. (interview of actor Gil Gerard)

290 "Burlesque Escapade." [As Weaver Wright.] *Sex & Censorship Magazine.* Vol. 1. No. 2. San Francisco, CA: Mid-Tower Publishing. Corp. 1958.

291 "Burn, Witch Burn!" *Sex & Censorship Magazine.* Volume 1. No. 2. San Francisco, CA: Mid-Tower Publishing. Corp. 1958; *Science Fiction Worlds of Forrest J Ackerman and Friends.* Reseda, CA: Powell Publications, 1969; *Expanded Science Fiction Worlds of Forrest J Ackerman & Friends PLUS.* Ed. Forrest J Ackerman. Sense of Wonder Press, 2002. [on the artwork of Rosaleen Norton (1917–1979)]

292 "By Jupiter, It's Outland." *Famous Monsters of Filmland.* No. 177. Warren, September 1981; *Film Fantasy Yearbook 1982 Collector's Edition.* Warren, March 1982.

293 "The Cabinet of Dr. Caligory." *Famous Monsters of Filmland.* No. 104. January 1974. (about Robert Bloch)

294 "The California Scene." [As Morris Chapnick.] *Science Fiction Times.* No. 465. April 1969. p. 5.

295 "Calling All Ache Heads." [As Forrest J. Eggerman with James Warren.] *Famous Monsters of Filmland.* Vol. 2. No. 7. Philadelphia: Central Publications, Inc., June 1960.

296 "Calling All Boy Spooks." *Famous Monsters of Filmland.* No. 36. Warren, December 1965. (Editorial)

297 "Calling Dr. Death." *Famous Monsters of Filmland.* No. 99. Warren, July 1973. (J. Carroll Naish)

298 "Can You Scare Up an Answer to This?" *Monster World.* Vol. 1. No. 2. New York: Warren, January 1965. (Editorial)

299 "Captain Sterner St. Paul Meek." *Gosh! Wow (Boy-oh-Boy)! Science Fiction.* p. 165. (introduction to Meek's "Futility")

300 "Captive Wild Women." *Famous Monsters of Filmland.* No. 81. Warren, December 1970.

301 "Capturing the Catman." *Famous Monsters of Filmland.* No. 33. Warren, May 1965. pp. 38–39.

302 "Carry On, Monsters." *Famous Monsters of Filmland.* No. 33. Warren, May 1965. pp. 44–51.

303 "The Case of the Baroque Baby Killer — A Teenage Chum Rattles Some Skeletons in the Closet of Ray Bradbury." *Shangri-La.* No. 14. CA: October 1949. [also Self-Published, 1949.?]

304 "The Case of the Lonely Grave Robber." *Famous Monsters of Filmland.* No. 6. Philadelphia: Central Publications, Inc., February 1960. pp. 34–37; (on Miami horror host M. T. Graves); *Famous Monsters of Filmland.* Vol. 1. No. 4. Filmland Classics, May 2008. pp. 34–37. (replica edition)

305 "Cast of Characters." *Famous Monsters of Filmland Star Wars Spectacular.* Warren Publishing Co., October 1977.

306 "Cast of Characters and Creators." *Close Encounters of the Third Kind.* Warren Publishing Co., January 1978.

307 "Castle of Terror." *Famous Monsters of Filmland.* No. 33. Warren, May 1965. pp. 63–71; *Famous Monsters of Filmland.* No. 66. Warren, June 1970; *Famous Monsters of Filmland.* No. 138. Warren, October 1977. (on William Castle.)

308 "Castle of Terrors." *Famous Monsters of Filmland.* No. 44. Warren, May 1967.

309 "Casually Speaking." *The Fort MacArthur Bulletin.* Friday 5 February 1943. p. 2-A.

310 "The Cat and the Canary." *Famous Monsters of Filmland.* No. 167. Warren, September 1980.

311 "The Cat Creeps ... Again!" *Famous Monsters of Filmland.* No. 155. Warren, July 1979.

312 "Cat People." *Famous Monsters of Filmland.* No. 184. Warren, June 1982.

313 "The Cat ... The Canary ... & The Comedian." *Famous Monsters of Filmland.* No. 145. Warren, July 1978. (obituary of actress Getrude Astor)

314 "Catherine L. Moore." [As Jack Erman.] *Imagination!* No. 2. November 1937. [interview]

315 "Catherine Moore Remains Hospitalized." *Science Fiction Chronicle: The Monthly Science Fiction and Fantasy Newsmagazine.* Vol. 7. No. 1. Ed. Andrew I. Porter. October 1985. p. 25. (reports on the condition of Moore)

316 "Caveman." *Famous Monsters of Filmland.* No. 175. Warren, July 1981. (preview)

317 "Centenarian Passes." *Science Fiction Times.* No. 313. (Second April 1959 issue) (obituary of author Gustaf Adolf de Castro Danziger)

318 "Chad Oliver Has Had a Daughter, Kimberly." *National Fantasy Fan.* 15. February 1956.

319 "Chamber of Horrors." *Famous Monsters of Filmland.* No. 44. Warren, May 1967.

320 "Chandu the Magician." *Famous Monsters of Filmland.* No. 80. Warren, October 1970; *Famous Monsters of Filmland.* No. 138. Warren, October 1977.

321 "Chaney Happy Returns." *Famous Monsters of Filmland.* No. 163. Warren, May 1980. (birthdays)

322 "The Change of the Leech Woman." *Famous Monsters of Filmland.* No. 34. Warren, August 1965. pp. 68–69; *Famous Monsters of Filmland.* No. 66. Warren, June 1970.

323 "The Changeling: A Haunting Saga of the Spirit World." [As Eddie Tauris Laite.] *Famous Monsters of Filmland.* No. 165. Warren, July 1980. pp. 28–35.

324 "Charles D. Hornig Speaks in L. A." *Science Fiction Chronicle.* Vol. 2. No. 2. Ed. Andrew Porter. November 1980. p. 3. (reports on speech given by early science fiction fan)

325 "Charles Laughton: 1899–1962." *Famous Monsters of Filmland.* Vol. 5. No. 1. Whole No. 22. April 1963. p. 11.

326 "Cheer for Chaney!" *Famous Monsters of Filmland.* No. 98. Warren, May 1973. (inviting readers to write the then-ailing Lon Chaney, Jr.)

327 "Cheesecake 'N Ice Scream." *Candid*. No. 7. Hollywood, CA: Sari Publishing Co. 1960. (monster movie actresses)

328 "Chevy Chases Modern Problems." *Famous Monsters of Filmland*. No. 183. Warren, May 1982.

329 "Chris Lee, Danforth's Pal & Supermen." [As Paul Linden.] *Famous Monsters of Filmland*. No. 135. Warren, July 1977. (inductees into the Science Fiction, Horror and Fantasy Hall of Fame)

330 "Clash of the Titans." *Famous Monsters of Filmland*. No. 175. Warren, July 1981; *Film Fantasy Yearbook 1982 Collector's Edition*. Warren, March 1982.

331 "Close Encounters of the Third Kind." *Famous Monsters of Filmland*. No. 136. Warren, August 1977. (preview)

332 "Close Encounters of the Third Kind." *Famous Monsters of Filmland*. No. 141. Warren, March 1978.

333 "Close Encounters of the Weird Kind." *Famous Monsters of Filmland*. No. 147. Warren, September 1978. pp. 30–34.

334 "Close Encounters of the Weird Kind." *Famous Monsters of Filmland*. No. 169. Warren, November 1980.

335 "Close Encounters Special Effects." *Close Encounters of the Third Kind*. Warren Publishing Co., January 1978; *House of Horror*. No. 1. Warren, April 1978; *Famous Monsters of Filmland*. No. 144. Warren, June 1978.

336 "The Clown at Midnite." (by "the staff of Famous Monsters") *Famous Monsters of Filmland*. Vol. 3. No. 3. Whole No. 12. Philadelphia: Central Publications, Inc., June 1961. p. 3.

337 "Cold Water and No Soap." [As Jack Erman.] *Science-Fiction Collector*. Vol. 5. No. 4. Whole No. 28. Ed. John V. Baltadonis. Philadelphia: November-December 1939.

338 "Colin Clive Reveals ... I Hate Horror Films!" *Famous Monsters of Filmland*. No. 208. No. Hollywood, CA: Dynacomm, May 1995. pp. 18, 21. (Ackerman's prefatory remarks to vintage Clive interview)

339 "Collector's Corner: Stop Me Before I Collect More!" *Futures Past*. No. 1. Ed. Jim Emerson. Convoy, OH: The Write Answer, 1992. p. 39.

340 "College of Scientifictional Knowledge." *Fantasy Stories*. Ed. Curtis Mitchell. New York: Magabook, Inc., November 1950. [p. 80.]

341 "Collision Course." *Spacemen*. Vol. 1. No. 1. Philadelphia, PA: Spacemen, Inc. July 1961; *Spacemen 1965 Yearbook*. Warren Publishing Co., 1964;

Famous Monsters of Filmland. No. 140. Warren, January 1978. (1951 film *When Worlds Collide*)

342 "Coming Soon!" *Imagination!* Vol. 1. No. 1. October 1937. p. 14.

343 "Commander Hanson Dead at 72." *Luna Monthly*. No. 14. Ed. Ann F. Dietz. Oradell, NJ: July 1970. p. 9. (author Sewell Peaslee Wright)

344 "Comrade Connie." *Days of Wonder: Remembering Sam Moskowitz and Conrad H. Ruppert*. John L. Coker III. Orlando, FL: Days of Wonder Press, 1998. p. 16; *Tales of the Time Travelers: Adventures of Forrest J Ackerman and Julius Schwartz*. Ed. John L. Coker, III. Orlando, FL: Days of Wonder Publishers, 2009. (reminiscence of Conrad H. Ruppert, printer of early fan publications)

345 "Conan Is Coming!" *Famous Monsters of Filmland*. No. 179. Warren, November 1981. (preview)

346 "Conan the Barbarian." *Famous Monsters of Filmland*. No. 185. Warren, July 1982; *Film Fantasy Yearbook 1983 Collector's Edition*. Warren, March 1983.

347 "Confessions of a Science Fiction Addict." *After Hours*. Vol. 1. No. 4. 1957. Ed. James Warren. Jay Publishing Co., Inc; *Science Fiction Worlds of Forrest J Ackerman and Friends*. Reseda, CA: Powell Publications, 1969; *Expanded Science Fiction Worlds of Forrest J Ackerman & Friends PLUS*. Rockville, MD: Sense of Wonder Press. 2002.

348 "Congrats." *Imagination!* Vol. 1. No. 1. October 1937. p. 3.

349 "[Contest!] Fantascience Filmaze." *Fantasy Magazine*. Vol. 6. No. 4. No. 38. Jamaica, NY: September 1936. (contest matching stars with film titles, with/as(?) D. H. Green)

350 "Contest!" *Perry Rhodan*. No. 9. *Quest Through Space and Time*. Clark Darlton. New York: Ace, November 1971, 1974; London: Futura Publications, 1975.

351 [contribution] *Ad Astra*. No. 3. September 1939.

352 [contribution, as Carroll Wymack] *Voice of Imagi-Nation*. (VOM) Vol. 1. No. 2. Los Angeles, CA: Los Angeles Science Fantasy Society (L.A.S.F.S.), April 1939.

353 [contribution] *Black Market Magazine*. No. 8. San Diego, CA: Black Market Productions, 1987.

354 [contribution] *The Comet*. Ed. Tom Wright. Vol. 1. No. 1. January 1940.

355 [contribution] *Comics Buyers Guide*. No. 887. 16 November 1990. (on Wendayne Ackerman)

356 [contribution] *Etherline*. No. 57. Ed. Ian J. Crozier. AFPA for Melbourne Science Fiction Group, Australia: 1955.

357 [contribution] *Fandom Speaks*. Vol. 1. No. 1. Ed. Rex Ward & Jack Clements. October 1947.

358 [contribution] *Fantasy Digest*. Vol. 1. No. 6. [Ed. T. E. Dikty? Fred Shroyer?] August-September 1939.

359 [contribution] *Fantasy Fictioneer*. No. 2. Ed. Sully Roberds. January 1940. ("Official Organ of the Illini Fantasy Fictioneers")

360 [contribution] *Future: The Magazine of Science Adventure*. Vol. 1. No. 3. Ed. Harold Zimmerman. July 1978.

361 [contribution] *Gaylaxicon V Program Book*. Rockville, MD: 1994.

362 [contribution] *Guilty Pleasures: The Magazine of Forbidden Films and Erotic Horror*. No. 2. Ed. Todd Tjersland. Threat Theatre International, Summer 1997. (Forrest J Ackerman writes about 80 years of erotic horror)

363 [contribution] *IF!* Vol. 1. No. 4. Ed. Conrad A. Pederson. October 1948.

364 [contribution] *Noreascon Two, The 38th World Science Fiction Convention*. Cambridge, MA: Noreascon Two, 1980.

365 [contribution] *Nuz from Home*. Vol. 1. No. 13. Ed. Walter Dunkelberger. Fargo, ND: 1943.

366 [contribution] *Paradox*. Ed. Frank Wilimczyk. No. 2. Fall 1942.

367 [contribution] *Sci Fi News and Reviews*. No. 2. Feb.-Mar. 1980.

368 [contribution] *Science-Fiction Monthly*. No. 15. Melbourne, Australia: Atlas Publications Pty. Ltd., November 1956.

369 [contribution] *Spacewarp*. Ed. Arthur H. Rapp. 1947.

370 [contribution] *Star Rover*. Ed. Van H. Splawn. No. 5. Summer 1946.

371 [contribution] *Stellar Tales*. Vol. 1. No. 1. Ed. Len Moffatt. Winter 1941.

372 [contribution] *Tesseract*. Vol. 2. No. 2. Ed. C. Hamilton Bloomer, Jr. San Francisco: Science Fiction Advancement Association, February 1937.

373 [contribution] *Ultra*. Ed. Eric F. Russell. Australia, 1940.

374 [contribution] *Vampire*. No. 9. Ed. Joseph Kennedy. June 1947.

375 [contribution] *The Variant*. Ed. Allison Williams. February 1947.

376 [contribution on Boris Karloff] *Visions: The Magazine of the Atlanta Fantasy Faire*. No. 5. 1984.

377 [contribution on Dr. Frankenstein actor Colin Clive by Ackerman] *Novacious*. No. 1. December 1938. Ed. Forrest J Ackerman & Morojo [Myrtle R. Douglas].

378 [contribution on his leaving the Science Fiction League] *Science Fiction Weekly*. Ed. Robert W. Lowndes. Vol. 1. No. 1. 18 February 1940.

379 [contribution on the fantasy market] *Fantasy Advertiser*. Vol. 2. No. 2. Ed. Gus Wilmorth & Roy A. Squires. August 1947.

380 [contribution on the surprise success of *Famous Monsters*] *Mimsy*. No. 1. Ed. Steve Tolliver. 1958.

381 "Cosmic Editorial by Guest Captain of the KLR." *Perry Rhodan No. 34. SOS: Spaceship Titan!* Kurt Brand. New York: Ace, November 1973; London: Orbit, 1978.

382 "Cosmiclubs." *Perry Rhodan. No. 46. Again Atlan!* K. H. Scheer. New York: Ace, May 1974.

383 "Cosmiclubs." *Perry Rhodan. No. 62. The Last Days of Atlantis*. K. H. Scheer. New York: Ace, January 1975.

384 "Cosmiclubs." *Perry Rhodan. No. 67. Crimson Universe*. K. H. Scheer. New York: Ace, April 1975.

385 "Cosmiclubs for Rhofans." *Perry Rhodan. No. 57. A Touch of Eternity*. Clark Darlton. New York: Ace, November 1974.

386 "Co-Star Reunited with Chaney in Death." *Famous Monsters of Filmland*. No. 138. Warren, October 1977. (actress Joan Crawford)

387 "The Costumes." *The Stunning Scientifan*. Vol. 1 No. 1. Ed. J. J. Fortier. Fall 1939.

388 "Count Dracula Society Awards." [As "Vespertina Torgosi."] *Luna Monthly*. No. 31. Ed. Ann F. Dietz. Oradell, NJ: December 1971. p. 12.

389 "Count Dracula's Vampire Ring." *Famous Monsters of Filmland*. No. 30. Warren Publishing Co., September 1964. p. 70; *Famous Monsters of Filmland*. No. 92. Warren, September 1972; *Dracula '79. (Warren Presents. No. 5.)* Warren, September 1979.

390 "Count Yorga, Vampire." *Famous Monsters of Filmland*. No. 91. Warren, July 1972.

391 "Creeping Ahead." *Famous Monsters of Filmland*. No. 98. Warren, May 1973.

392 "The Creeping Flesh." *Famous Monsters of Filmland*. No. 31. Warren Publishing Co., December 1964. pp. 30–37.

393 "Creepy's Loathsome Lore: Boris Karloff." *Creepy*. No. 27. Warren, June 1969; *Creepy Archives*. Volume 6. Dark Horse, 2010. pp. 36–37.

394 "Crimson Chronicles." *Scarlet—The Film Magazine*. Vol. 1. No. 1. Cleona, PA: 2008. (on Richard Valley)

395 "Crimson Chronicles." *Scarlet—The Film Magazine.* No. 2. Cleona, PA: February 2009.

396 "Crimson Chronicles." *Scarlet Street.* No. 22. Ed. Richard Valley. 1996. pp. 42–43. (column)

397 "Crimson Chronicles." *Scarlet Street.* No. 23. Ed. Richard Valley. 1996. pp. 53–54. (on Simone Simon)

398 "Crimson Chronicles." *Scarlet Street.* No. 24. Ed. Richard Valley. 1997. pp. 23–24.

399 "Crimson Chronicles." *Scarlet Street.* No. 25. Ed. Richard Valley. 1997. p. 41.

400 "Crimson Chronicles." *Scarlet Street.* No. 26. Ed. Richard Valley. 1997. pp. 15, 79.

401 "Crimson Chronicles." *Scarlet Street.* No. 27. Ed. Richard Valley. 1998. (on a Dutch film festival screening of *The Phantom of the Opera*)

402 "Crimson Chronicles." *Scarlet Street.* No. 28. 1998. p. 18. (on actress Gloria Stuart, etc.)

403 "Crimson Chronicles." *Scarlet Street.* No. 29. Ed. Richard Valley. 1998. p. 20. (on a 65th anniversary screening of *King Kong*)

404 "Crimson Chronicles." *Scarlet Street.* No. 30. Ed. Richard Valley. 1998. p. 19. (on Maureen O'Sullivan)

405 "Crimson Chronicles." *Scarlet Street.* No. 31. Ed. Richard Valley. 1998. p. 17. (on his travels)

406 "Crimson Chronicles." *Scarlet Street.* No. 33. Ed. Richard Valley. Glen Rock, NJ: R.H. Enterprises, 1999. pp. 44–47.

407 "Crimson Chronicles." *Scarlet Street.* No. 34. Ed. Richard Valley. Glen Rock, NJ: R.H. Enterprises, 1999. p. 17.

408 "Crimson Chronicles." *Scarlet Street.* No. 35. Ed. Richard Valley. 1999. p. 33.

409 "Crimson Chronicles." *Scarlet Street.* No. 36. Ed. Richard Valley. Glen Rock, NJ: R.H. Enterprises, 2000. p. 38. (on Vincent Price)

410 "Crimson Chronicles." *Scarlet Street.* No. 39. 2000. pp. 32, 77. (Ackerman Remembers Curt Siodmak, screenwriter of *The Wolf Man*)

411 "Crimson Chronicles." *Scarlet Street.* No. 51. 2004. p. 39.

412 "Crimson Chronicles." *Scarlet Street.* No. 52. 2005. p. 51.

413 "Crimson Chronicles." *Scarlet Street.* No. 53. 2005. p. 16.

414 "Crimson Chronicles." *Scarlet Street.* No. 54. 2005. pp. 13, 17. (on *King Kong*, Ackerman's hospitalization in Glasgow)

415 "Crimson Chronicles." *Scarlet Street.* No. 55. 2006.

416 "The Critic's Crypt." *Famous Monsters of Filmland.* No. 96. Warren, March 1973.

417 "The Critic's Crypt." *Famous Monsters of Filmland.* No. 98. Warren, May 1973.

418 "The Critic's Crypt." *Famous Monsters of Filmland.* No. 100. Warren, August 1973.

419 "The Critic's Crypt." *Famous Monsters of Filmland.* No. 103. Warren, December 1973.

420 "The Critic's Crypt." *Famous Monsters of Filmland.* No. 108. Warren, July 1974.

421 "The Critic's Crypt." *Famous Monsters of Filmland.* No. 113. Warren, January 1975.

422 "The Critic's Crypt." *Famous Monsters of Filmland.* No. 120. Warren, October 1975.

423 "Cry of the Banshee." *Famous Monsters of Filmland.* No. 90. Warren, May 1972.

424 "The Crystal Ball Sees All for Early '63." *Famous Monsters of Filmland.* Vol. 4. No. 6. Whole No. 21. February 1963.

425 "The Crystal Cherry Tree." [As Gorgo "whoosh" N. Tomb.] *Famous Monsters of Filmland.* Vol. 3. No. 2. Whole No. 11. Philadelphia: Central Publications, Inc., April 1961. pp. 7–14. (this piece may have been authored by Giovanni Scognamillo)

426 "Curse of the Demon." *Famous Monsters of Filmland.* No. 38. Warren, April 1966. pp. 24–27; *Famous Monsters of Filmland.* No. 145. Warren, July 1978.

427 "The Curse of the Katzman People." *Famous Monsters of Filmland.* No. 106. Warren, April 1974. (Sam Katzman)

428 "The Curse of the Mummy's Tomb." *Famous Monsters of Filmland.* No. 41. Warren, November 1966. pp. 12–15.

429 "Curse of the Werewolf." *Famous Monsters of Filmland.* Vol. 3. No. 3. Whole No. 12. Philadelphia: Central Publications, Inc., June 1961. [pp. 34–39]; *James Warren Presents Son of Famous Monsters of Filmland.* New York: Paperback Library, 1965; *Famous Monsters of Filmland 1965 Yearbook.* No. 3. Warren, 1965.

430 "Cyclops and Lollipops." *Famous Monsters of Filmland.* Vol. 2. No. 7. Philadelphia: Central Publications, Inc., June 1960. [pp. 24–32]; as "The Incredible Shrinker of Men." *Famous Monsters of Filmland: Yearbook No. 2.* [1964] Warren Publishing Co., December 1963; *James Warren Presents Famous Monsters of Filmland Strike Back!* New York: Paperback Library, 1965 (*Dr. Cyclops*)

431 "The Daleks Are Coming!" *Famous Monsters of Filmland.* No. 44. Warren, May 1967; *Famous Monsters of Filmland.* No. 124. Warren, April 1976.

432 "The Daleks Invade England." *Famous Monsters of Filmland.* No. 38. Warren, April 1966. pp. 52–58; *Famous Monsters of Filmland.* No. 129. Warren, October 1976.

433 "Dark House Takes Douglas." *Famous Monsters of Filmland.* No. 180. Warren, January 1982. (obituary of actor Melvyn Douglas)

434 "Dark Intruder." *Famous Monsters of Filmland.* No. 39. Warren, June 1966. pp. 29–31.

435 "Dark Shadows." *Famous Monsters of Filmland.* No. 52. Warren, October 1968; *Famous Monsters of Filmland.* No. 125. Warren, May 1976.

436 "Dark Shadows: It Haunts Again!" *Famous Monsters of Filmland.* No. 187. Warren, September 1982.

437 "Daughter of Exorcist." *Famous Monsters of Filmland.* No. 122. Warren, January 1976. (*Beyond the Door*)

438 "Dave Prowse." *Famous Monsters of Filmland.* No. 153. Warren, May 1979.

439 "David H. Elder." *Science Fiction Chronicle: The Monthly SF and Fantasy Newsmagazine.* Vol. 9. No. 2. Ed. Andrew I. Porter. November 1987. p. 16. (obituary of Pittsburgh area fan)

440 "David L. Fox." *Science Fiction Chronicle: The Monthly Science Fiction and Fantasy Newsmagazine.* Vol. 7. No. 11. Ed. Andrew I. Porter. August 1986. p. 18. (California fan)

441 "Davis Is a Devil!" *Famous Monsters of Filmland.* No. 171. Warren, March 1981. (Sammy Davis, Jr.)

442 "The Day the 'Post' Master of Maskville Trapped the Acker-Monster." *Famous Monsters of Filmland.* No. 45. Warren, July 1967.

443 "Day the World Ended." *Monster World.* No. 8. Warren, May 1966.

444 "Dead Eyes of London." *Monster World.* No. 10. New York: Warren, September 1966.

445 "Deadlines from Karloffornia; A Column by Forrest J Ackerman." *Cult Movies.* No. 17. 1996. p. 66.

446 "Deadlines from Whollyweird." *Cult Movies.* No. 19. / *Spacemen.* No. 1. Cult Movies Publishing, 1997. pp. 5–6.

447 "Dean of the Horror Directors Tod Browning: 1882–1962." *Famous Monsters of Filmland.* Vol. 5. No. 1. Whole No. 22. April 1963. pp. 38–43, 46–47. (obituary for Browning, actually born 1880)

448 "Dear Lydia van Vogt." *Cult Movies.* No. 31. 2000. pp. 62–63. (memoriam of A. E. Van Vogt)

449 "Death of a Phantom." *Famous Monsters of Filmland.* No. 134. Warren, May 1977. (obituary of Jack Cassidy)

450 "Death of a Vampire." *Famous Monsters of Filmland.* No. 147. Warren, September 1978. pp. 36–37. (obituary of actor Barry Atwater)

451 "Death of a Witch." *Famous Monsters of Filmland.* No. 103. Warren, December 1973. (obituary of Veronica Lake)

452 "Death Takes David Bruce." *Famous Monsters of Filmland.* No. 132. Warren, March 1977.

453 "Death Takes George Zucco." *Famous Monsters of Filmland.* Vol. 3. No. 4. whole No. 13. Philadelphia: Central Publications, Inc., August 1961. [pp. 52–53.]

454 "Death Takes Horror Director!" *Famous Monsters of Filmland.* No. 102. Warren, October 1973. (Edgar G. Ulmer)

455 "Death's Duo." *Famous Monsters of Filmland.* No. 155. Warren, July 1979. (obituaries of Hungarian director Steve Sekely and effects artist Adam Beckett)

456 "Deep Inside *The Black Hole.*" *Famous Monsters of Filmland.* No. 162. Warren, April 1980.

457 "Delgado Dies." *Famous Monsters of Filmland.* No. 133. Warren, April 1977. (obituary of *King Kong* sculptor Marcel Delgado)

458 "Dens of Demons." *Monster World.* No. 6. Warren, January 1966; *Famous Monsters of Filmland.* No. 50. July 1968. New York: Warren Publishing Co., 1968; *Famous Monsters of Filmland.* No. 67. Warren, July 1970.

459 "Destination Moon." *Other Worlds Science Stories.* Ed. Raymond A. Palmer. Clark Publishing Company, May 1950. p. 147. (essay on the film)

460 "Destroy All Monsters." *Famous Monsters of Filmland.* No. 64. Warren, April 1970; *Famous Monsters of Filmland.* No. 114. Warren, March 1975.

461 "The Detroit Convention." *Fantastic Universe.* Vol. 12. No 3. Ed. Hans Stefan Santesson. Great American Publications, Inc., January 1960.

462 "The Devil and Max Devlin." *Famous Monsters of Filmland.* No. 173. Warren, May 1981. (preview)

463 "Devil Bat." *Famous Monsters of Filmland.* No. 50. July 1968. New York: Warren Publishing Co., 1968; *Famous Monsters of Filmland.* No. 86. Warren, September 1971; *Famous Monsters of Filmland.* No. 137. Warren, September 1977. pp. 52–54.

464 "The Devil Commands." *Famous Monsters of Filmland.* No. 46. Warren, September 1967; *Famous Monsters of Filmland.* No. 84. Warren, June 1971.

465 "Devils of Darkness." *Famous Monsters of Filmland*. No. 111. Warren, October 1974.

466 "The Devil's Rain." *Famous Monsters of Filmland*. No. 120. Warren, October 1975. (filmbook)

467 "Diary of a Monster." *Famous Monsters of Filmland*. No. 64. Warren, April 1970. pp. 42–47.

468 "Did You Know?" *Fantasy Book*. Vol. 1 No. 1. Ed. Garret Ford. (William L. Crawford) Fantasy Publishing Company, Inc. July 1947.

469 "The Die-ry of a She-Fiend." *Famous Monsters of Filmland*. No. 174. Warren, June 1981.

470 "Dinosaurus!" *Famous Monsters of Filmland*. No. 40. Warren, August 1966. pp. 8–14; *Famous Monsters of Filmland 1970 Year Book/Fearbook*. Warren, 1969; *Famous Monsters of Filmland*. No. 119. Warren, September 1975.

471 "Disneyland's House of Horrors." *Famous Monsters of Filmland*. No. 82. Warren, February 1971.

472 "Dizzy Dean." [As "Mr. Science Fiction."] *Fantastic Worlds*. Vol. 2. No. 1. No. 5. Ed. Sam J. Sackett & Stewart Kemble. Los Angeles, CA: Fall 1953. pp. 9, 11.

473 "DL 4833." *The Frankenscience Monster*. New York: Ace Publishing Corporation, 1969. pp. 171–174. (title refers to the album code number for *An Evening with Boris Karloff and His Friends*)

474 "Do You Believe This Story?" *Famous Monsters of Filmland*. No. 37. Warren, February 1966; *Famous Monsters of Filmland*. No. 59. Warren, November 1969. (Bela Lugosi's haunted house)

475 "Do You Know Ed Earl Repp?" *The Time Traveller*. Vol. 1. No. 5. June 1932.

476 "Dr. Acula Rides (Writes) Again." *Cult Movies*. No. 32. 2000. pp. 82–83.

477 "Dr. Acula's Diary." *Cult Movies*. No. 35. 2001. p. 65.

478 "Dr. Acula's Diary." *Cult Movies*. No. 36. 2001. p. 66.

479 "Dr. Acula's Diary." *MonsterZine.com The Horror Movie Magazine You Can Really Sink Your Teeth Into*. Issue No. 1. October-December 2000. <http://www.monsterzine.com/200010/dr_acula.html>(column)

480 "Dr. Ackula's Diary." *MonsterZine.com The Horror Movie Magazine You Can Really Sink Your Teeth Into*. Issue No. 6. <http://www.monsterzine.com/200201/ackula.php>

481 "Dr. Acula's House of Horrors!" *James Warren Presents Son of Famous Monsters of Filmland*. New York: Paperback Library, 1965.

482 "Dr. Blood's Coffin." *Famous Monsters of Filmland*. No. 45. Warren, July 1967.

483 "Doctor Cyclops Is Dead." *Famous Monsters of Filmland*. No. 52. Warren, October 1968. (obituary of actor Albert Dekker)

484 "Dr. Frankenstein, The Ackermonster, and the Wolf Man." *Famous Monsters of Filmland*. No. 133. Warren, April 1977. (transcript of Ackerman's appearance on *The Tomorrow Show* with actor Peter Cushing and Leonard Wolf. See entry 2878.)

485 "Dr. Jekyll & Mr. Hyde." *Famous Monsters of Filmland*. Vol. 3. No. 2. Whole No. 11. Philadelphia: Central Publications, Inc., April 1961.

486 "Dr. Jekyll & Mr. Hyde." *Famous Monsters of Filmland*. No. 34. Warren, August 1965. pp. 42–55; *Famous Monsters of Filmland*. No. 54. Warren, March 1969; *Famous Monsters of Filmland*. No. 188. New York: Warren Publishing Co., October 1982. pp. 36– (history of adaptations)

487 "Dr. Jekyll and Mr. Hyde." *Famous Monsters of Filmland*. No. 62. Warren, February 1970. (filmbook of 1932 version)

488 "Dr. Jekyll and Sister Hyde." *Famous Monsters of Filmland*. No. 94. Warren, November 1972.

489 "Dr. Jekyll Hydes Again." *Famous Monsters of Filmland*. No. 167. Warren, September 1980. (*Dr. Heckyl and Mr. Hype*)

490 "Dr. Paul Bearer." *Famous Monsters of Filmland*. No. 144. Warren, June 1978. (TV horror host)

491 "Dr. Terror's House of Horrors." *Monster World*. No. 6. Warren, January 1966. (preview)

492 "Doctor X." *Monster World*. No. 8. Warren, May 1966.

493 "Donovan's Brain." *Perry Rhodan. No. 22. The Fleet of the Springers*. Kurt Mahr. New York: Ace Books, March 1973; London: Futura, 1977.

494 "Don't Be a Droop-Out." *Famous Monsters of Filmland*. No. 34. Warren, August 1965. p. 3.

495 "Don't Look Now But a Monster Is Reading This Magazine!" [As "The Monster's Keeper."] *Famous Monsters of Filmland*. No. 2. Philadelphia: Central Publications, Inc., September 1958. p. 3.

496 "Don't Read This on Friday the 13th." *Famous Monsters of Filmland*. No. 163. Warren, May 1980; *Warren Presents The Official Exclusive Horror Movie Yearbook 1981 Collector's Edition*. Warren, February 1981. (preview of original 1980 film)

497 "Dorian Gray Strikes Again." *Famous Monsters of Filmland*. No. 94. Warren, November 1972.

498 "Double the Pleasure, Double the Fun." *Perry Rhodan. No. 109. The Stolen Spacefleet*. Clark Darlton. / *Perry Rhodan. No. 110. Sgt. Robot*. Kurt Mahr. New York: Ace Books, March 1977.

499 "Dracula." *Famous Monsters of Filmland.* Vol. 5. No. 1. Whole No. 22. April 1963. pp. 52–61; Famous Monsters of Filmland. No. 49. Warren, May 1968; *Famous Monsters of Filmland.* No. 92. Warren, September 1972; Dracula '79. (*Warren Presents. No. 5.*) Warren, September 1979; *Famous Monsters of Filmland.* No. 178. Warren, October 1981. (part 1)

500 "Dracula." *Famous Monsters of Filmland.* Vol. 5. No. 2. Whole No. No. 23. June 1963. pp. 28–43; as "Trail of Dracula." *Famous Monsters of Filmland.* No. 110. Warren, September 1974. (part 2)

501 "Dracula After Death!" *Famous Monsters of Filmland.* No. 97. Warren, April 1973.

502 "Dracula at Home." [As Tip Tracton.] *Famous Monsters of Filmland.* No. 173. Warren, May 1981.

503 "Dracula Award." *Famous Monsters of Filmland.* Vol. 5. No. 2. Whole No. No. 23. June 1963. p. 9.

504 "Dracula Dead at 73." *Fantasy Times.* No. 254. Ed. James V. Taurasi, Sr. [& Ray Van Houten]. Paterson, NJ: Fandom House: September 1956. pp. 3, 10; *The Road to Veletrium.* No. 47. Yucca Valley, CA: James van Hise, October 2002. (Bela Lugosi obituary)

505 "Dracula Flies Again." [As Paul Linden.] *Famous Monsters of Filmland.* No. 43. Warren, March 1967; *Famous Monsters of Filmland.* No. 119. Warren, September 1975.

506 "Dracula Has Risen from the Grave." *Famous Monsters of Filmland.* No. 59. Warren, November 1969; *Dracula '79.* (*Warren Presents. No. 5.*) Warren, September 1979.

507 "Dracula 1979." *Famous Monsters of Filmland.* No. 157. Warren, September 1979; *Dracula '79.* (*Warren Presents. No. 5.*) Warren, September 1979.

508 "Dracula Plays Frankenstein." *Monster World.* No. 3. Warren, April 1965.

509 "Dracula — Prince of Darkness." *Monster World.* No. 10. New York: Warren, September 1966.

510 "Dracula Returns!" *Famous Monsters of Filmland.* No. 37. Warren, February 1966; *Famous Monsters of Filmland 1970 Year Book/Fearbook.* Warren, 1969. (The Curse of Dracula)

511 "Dracula Strikes Again!" *Famous Monsters of Filmland.* No. 107. Warren, May 1974.

512 "Dracula, TV." *Famous Monsters of Filmland.* No. 106. Warren, April 1974; *Dracula '79.* (*Warren Presents. No. 5.*) Warren, September 1979. (Dan Curtis TV film *Bram Stoker's Dracula*)

513 "Dracula II: Prince of Darkness." *Monster World.* No. 6. Warren, January 1966. (preview)

514 "Dracula vs. Frankenstein." *Famous Monsters of Filmland.* No. 89. Warren March 1972.

515 "Dracula's Guests." *Scarlet Street.* No. 38. Ed. Richard Valley. Glen Rock, NJ: 2000. pp. 34–35. (Ackerman's memories of Bela Lugosi)

516 "Dracula's Victim Dies." *Monster World.* No. 5. Warren, October 1965. p. 32. (actress Helen Chandler)

517 "Dragonslayer." *Famous Monsters of Filmland.* No. 176. Warren, August 1981; "Spotlight on 'Dragonslayer.'" *Sword & Sorcery Comix.* (*Warren Presents. No. 13.*) Warren, October 1981; *Film Fantasy Yearbook 1982 Collector's Edition.* Warren, March 1982. (preview)

518 "Drip Drip Drip: Bloody Terrors." *Famous Monsters of Filmland.* No. 99. Warren, July 1973.

519 "DYKTAWO!— Remember?" [As Weaver Wright.] *Glom.* No. 13. May 1949. (on the genesis of Ackerman's short story collaboration with Robert A. W. Lowndes)

520 ["The Earl of Hell"]??? *Shangri-La.* Vol. 1. No. 1. March-April 1940.

521 "EARTHQUAKE! Ackermansion Style a Day After Report by Forry Ackerman." *Luna Monthly.* No. 22. Ed. Ann F. Dietz. Oradell, NJ: March 1971. p. 4. (on the damage sustained to his Sherbourne residence)

522 "EBC." *Shangri L'Affaires.* No. 29. Ed. Charles Burbee. April 1946.

523 "EBC." *Shangri L'Affaires.* No. 30. Ed. Charles Burbee. May 1946.

524 "Ed Says." *Imagination!* Vol. 1. No. 1. October 1937. p. 4.

525 "Edgar Rice Burroughs: How the Famous Martian Series Began." *Fantasy Review.* Vol. 2. No. 12. December 1948/January 1949. pp. 16–19.

526 "Editorial." *Forrest J Ackerman's Monster Land.* No. 6. [Canoga Park, CA:] New Media Publishing, Inc., December 1985. pp. 2, 25.

527 "Editorial." *Forrest J Ackerman's Monsterland.* No. 7. [Canoga Park, CA:] New Media Publishing, Inc., February 1986. pp. 2, 41.

528 "Editorial." *Glom.* No. 3. February 1946. p. 1. (FAPA fanzine)

529 [Editorial] *Voice of the Imagi-Nation* (*VOM*). No. 19. November 1941; *DNQ.* No. 21. Ed. Taral and Victoria Wayne. Ontario: August 1979.

530 "The Editorial." [With Raymond A. Palmer.] *Imagination.* Ed. Raymond A. Palmer. Evanston, IL: Clark Publishing Company, October 1950.

531 "Editorial: The Ackermonster in Edgar Allan Poland." *Forrest J Ackerman's Monster Land.* No. 5. [Canoga Park, CA:] New Media Publishing, Inc., October 1985. p. 4.

532 "Editorial: Ackolades & Ackrimony." *Forrest J Ackerman's Monster Land.* No. 3. Studio City, CA: New Media Pub. Co., June 1985. p. 3.

533 "Editorial: Fear Warning." *Forrest J Ackerman's Monster Land.* No. 2. [Canoga Park, CA: New Media Pub. Co.], April 1985. p. 3.

534 "Editorial: Filmonster Fanomenon." *Forrest J Ackerman's Monsterama.* No. 2. Seattle, WA: Fantagraphics Books, Spring 1992. p. 3.

535 "Editorial: Forry's Foreign Fantasy Film Feast: Madrid's Imagfic 85: Flick or Treat? No, Flicks and Treats! Forry Reports from Spain." *Forrest J Ackerman's Monster Land.* Vol. 1. No. 4. Canoga Park, CA: New Media Publishing, Inc., August 1985. pp. 4–5. (on Madrid International Film Festival)

536 "Editor's Note." *Famous Monsters of Filmland.* No. 35. Warren, October 1965. p. 22. (precedes Terri Pinckard's article "Monsters Are Good For My Children — Yours Too!")

537 "Editor's Note." *Famous Monsters of Filmland.* No. 200. Orange, NJ: Dynacomm, May 1993. p. 90. (on Ronald V. Borst)

538 "The Editors Space." *Spacemen.* Vol. 1. No. 2. Philadelphia: Spacemen, Inc., September 1961.

539 "The Editors Space." *Spacemen.* Vol. 1. No. 3. Philadelphia: Spacemen, Inc., April 1962.

540 "The Editors Space." *Spacemen.* Vol. 1. No. 4. Philadelphia: Spacemen, Inc., July 1962.

541 "The Editors Space." *Spacemen.* Vol. 2. No. 1. Whole No. 6. Philadelphia: Spacemen, Inc., January 1963.

542 "The Editors Space." *Spacemen.* Vol. 2. No. 3. Whole No. 7. Warren Publishing, Inc., September 1963.

543 "Edmond Hamilton." *Gosh! Wow (Boy-oh-Boy)! Science Fiction.* New York: Bantam, 1982. pp. 65–66. (remarks precede Hamilton's "The Eternal Cycle")

544 "Edmond Hamilton." *Xenophile.* No. 30. Ed. Nils Hardin. St. Louis, MO. March 1977; *A Guide to the Fanzines Pulp, Xenophile, Nemesis, Inc. and Golden Perils.* James Van Hise. Yucca Valley, CA: 1997. p. 11. (obituary)

545 "Edwin Baker." *Locus.* No. 84. Ed. Charles and Dena Brown. Bronx, NY: 25 May 1971. p. 1. (obituary)

546 "EEE: Great Fan Dies." *Science Fiction Times.* No. 305. (December 1958 issue)

547 "The Eggs and I." *Two Dozen Dragon Eggs.* Donald A. Wollheim. Powell, September 1969; *Two Dozen Dragon Eggs.* Donald A. Wollheim. Dennis Dobson, July 1977.

548 "Eight for Eternity." *Famous Monsters of Filmland.* No. 47. Warren, November 1967. (obituaries)

549 "Eight Great B'day Boys." *Famous Monsters of Filmland.* No. 153. Warren, May 1979.

550 "Elena Vasquez." *Science Fiction Chronicle: The Monthly SF and Fantasy Newsmagazine.* Vol. 9. No. 2. Ed. Andrew I. Porter. November 1987. p. 16. (obituary)

551 "Ellison Roasted, Toasted." *Science Fiction Chronicle: The Monthly Science Fiction and Fantasy Newsmagazine.* Vol. 7. No. 12. Ed. Andrew I. Porter. September 1986. pp. 30, 32.

552 "Elma Wentz." *Luna Monthly.* No. 31. Ed. Ann F. Dietz. Oradell, NJ: December 1971. p. 11.

553 "The Empire Strikes Back." *Famous Monsters of Filmland.* No. 156. Warren, August 1979. (preview)

554 "The Empire Strikes Back: An Inner View of Outer Space." *Famous Monsters of Filmland.* No. 165. Warren, July 1980; *Famous Monsters of Filmland.* No. 177. Warren, September 1981. (interview with Donald F. Glut who wrote the film's novelization)

555 "The Empire Strikes Gold (Now It Can Be Told)." *Famous Monsters of Filmland.* No. 166. Warren, August 1980; *Warren Presents: Empire Encounters Comix.* Ed. Chris Adames. Warren Publishing Co., Inc. November 1980. pp. 14–21. (includes comments from George Lucas and cast)

556 "The End of Endora." *Famous Monsters of Filmland.* No. 112. Warren, December 1974. (obituary of Agnes Moorehead)

557 "An End to Banality: It's Curtains for Space Opera." *Fantasy Review.* Vol. 1. No. 4. Ed. Walter Gillings. Aug-Sep 1947.

558 "Epilog: Coming Attractions." *Science Fiction Worlds of Forrest J Ackerman and Friends.* Reseda, CA: Powell Publications, 1969; *Expanded Science Fiction Worlds of Forrest J Ackerman & Friends PLUS.* Rockville, MD: Sense of Wonder Press. 2002.

559 "Epizodoj Esperantaj." *The Planeteer.* Vol. 2. No. 1. Ed. James Blish. East Orange, NJ: September 1936. (in English and Esperanto)

560 "Die Ersten Opfer." *Utopia Sonderband.* No. 1. Rastatt, Baden, Germany: Erich Pabel Verlag, 1956. (The First Leap: "Riders to the Stars")

561 "Escape from the Planet of the Apes." *Famous Monsters of Filmland.* No. 85. Warren, July 1971.

562 "Esperanto: Its Relation to Scientifiction." *Novae Terrae.* Vol. 1. No. 6. Ed. Maurice K. Hanson and Dennis A. Jacques. Nuneaton, UK: Nuneaton Science Fiction League, August 1936.

563 "E.T.—The Extra-Terrestrial." *Famous Monsters of Filmland.* No. 185. Warren, July 1982. (preview)

564 "Ether Eeries." [As Dr. Acula.] *Imagination!* Vol. 1. No. 9. June 1938. p. 11.

565 "Ether Eeries." [As Dr. Acula.] *Imagination!* Vol. 1. No. 10. July 1938.

566 "Ether Eeries." [As Dr. Acula.] *Imagination!* Vol. 1. No. 11. August 1938. p. 10.

567 "Ether Eeries." [As Dr. Acula.] *Imagination! The Fanmag of the Future with a Future!* Vol. 1. No. 12. Los Angeles: Los Angeles Chapter — Science-Fiction Association, September 1938. p. 11.

568 "Even Dr. Jekyll Hydes from—Altered States—" *Famous Monsters of Filmland.* No. 170. Warren, January 1981.pp. 16–18. (illustrated with stills from 1974 film *The Mutations*)

569 "Excalibur." *Famous Monsters of Filmland.* No. 176. Warren, August 1981.

570 "Exclusion Act—#2!!" *The Fantasite.* Vol. 2. No. 2. Ed. Phil Bronson. MN: May-June 1942.

571 "Exclusive Famous Monsters Movie Preview: 13 Ghosts." *Famous Monsters of Filmland.* No. 8. September 1960. [pp. 34–40]; *James Warren Presents Son of Famous Monsters of Filmland.* New York: Paperback Library, 1965.

572 "Exorcist Actor Dies." *Famous Monsters of Filmland.* No. 127. Warren, August 1976. (obituary of actor Lee J. Cobb)

573 "Eye Popping News." *Famous Monsters of Filmland.* Vol. 5. No. 1. Whole No. 22. April 1963. pp. 8–10, 13.

574 "Eye to the Future." *Famous Monsters of Filmland.* No. 28. Warren Publishing, Inc., May 1964. (previews)

575 "The Eyes of March." *Famous Monsters of Filmland.* No. 207. N. Hollywood, CA: Dynacomm, March 1995. p. 3.

576 "Fabulous Ackermemories of Filmland." *The Scream Factory.* No. 18. The Deadline Publications, Autumn 1996. (on *Famous Monsters of Filmland* No. 101)

577 "Face of Fire from the House of Wax." *Famous Monsters of Filmland.* No. 36. Warren, December 1965. pp. 54–55; *Famous Monsters of Filmland.* No. 59. Warren, November 1969.

578 "Face That Launched a 1000 Shrieks." *Lon of 1000 Faces.* Beverly Hills, CA and Pangbourne,

Bershire, England: Morrison, Raven-Hill Co., 1983. pp. 44–46; Rockville, MD: Sense of Wonder Press, 2003.

579 "Face to Face with the Forgotten Frankenstein." *Monster World.* No. 5. Warren, October 1965.

580 "Faces." *Forrest J Ackerman's Fantastic Movie Memories: Forrest Ackerman's Treasure Trove of Imagi-Movies.* Canoga Park, CA: New Media Books, 1985.

581 "Faces That Launched 1,000 Shrieks." *Monster World.* No. 4. Warren, June 1965.

582 "Facing 1946." *The Fort MacArthur Bulletin; Glom.* No. 3. February 1946. p. 3.

583 "Facing the Music." *Amazing Forries: this is your life, Forrest J Ackerman.* Hollywood, CA: Metropolis Publications/Warren, 1976. p. 19.

584 "Fade to Black." *Famous Monsters of Filmland.* No. 171. Warren, March 1981; *Warren Presents The Official Exclusive Horror Movie Yearbook 1981 Collector's Edition.* Warren, February 1981. (preview)

585 "Faint Brays from a Tied Jackass (!?)." *Venus.* Vol. 1. No. 1. Ed. Lora Crozetti. June 1944.

586 "Famous Fantasy Fans." *Marvel Tales.* Vol. 1. No. 5. Ed. William L. Crawford. Everett, PA: Fantasy Publications, Summer 1935.

587 "Famous Monsters #70 to 79." *Scary Monsters.* No. 21. Highwood, IL: Dennis Druktenis Publishing & Mail Order, Inc., 1996. pp. 121–124. (piece on *Monster World*)

588 "Famous Monsters Wants You!" *Famous Monsters of Filmland.* No. 98. Warren, May 1973.

589 "Famous Morsels of Fantaland." [As J. Forester Eckman.] *Science Fiction Times.* No. 365. (First July 1961 issue). p. 4.

590 "Famous Morsels of Fantaland." [As J. Forester Eckman.] *Science Fiction Times.* No. 374. (Second November 1961 issue).

591 "Famous Munsters of Tickle-vision." *Monster World.* Vol. 1. No. 2. New York: Warren, January 1965; *Famous Monsters of Filmland.* No. 88. Warren, January 1972. (TV's *The Munsters*)

592 "The Fan-Mirror." *Le Zombie.* Ed. Bob Tucker. Vol. 2. No. 9. Whole No. 21. January 13, 1940. (news items as "FJA")

593 "Fantascience Filmart." [As "Claire Voyant."] *Imagination!* Vol. 1. No. 11. August 1938. p. 7.

594 "Fantascience Filmart." *Imagination!* Vol. 1. No. 1. October 1937. p. 10.

595 "Fantascience Filmart." *Imagination!* Vol. 1. No. 2. November 1937.

596 "Fantascience Filmart." *Imagination!* Vol. 1. No. 3. December 1937. p. 15.

597 "Fantascience Filmart." *Imagination!* Vol. 1. No. 4. January 1938.

598 "Fantascience Filmart." *Imagination!* Vol. 1. No. 5. February 1938.

599 "Fantascience Filmart." *Imagination!* Vol. 1. No. 6. March 1938. p. 5.

600 "Fantascience Filmart." *Imagination!* No. 7. April 1938. p. 5.

601 "Fantascience Filmart." *Imagination!* Vol. 1. No. 8. May 1938.

602 "Fantascience Filmart." *Imagination!* Vol. 1. No. 9. June 1938. p. 5.

603 "Fantascience Filmart." *Imagination!* Vol. 1. No. 10. July 1938.

604 "Fantascience Filmart." *Imagination! The Fanmag of the Future with a Future!* Vol. 1. No. 12. Los Angeles: Los Angeles Chapter — Science-Fiction Association, September 1938. p. 7. (cover by Ray Harryhausen)

605 "Fantascience Filmsnaps." *Fantasy Magazine.* Vol. 6. No. 4. No. 38. Jamaica, NY: September 1936.

606 "Fantascience Flashes." [As "Claire Voyant."] *Imagination!* No. 8. May 1938. p. 5.

607 "Fantascience Flashes." [As "Claire Voyant."] *Imagination!* Vol. 1. No. 10. July 1938.

608 "Fantascience Flashes." [As "Ev. Reware."] *Imagination!* Vol. 1. No. 2. November 1937.

609 "Fantascience Flashes." *Imagination!* Vol. 1. No. 3. December 1937. p. 3.

610 "Fantascience Flashes." *Imagination!* Vol. 1. No. 11. August 1938. p. 3.

611 "Fantastic Frankensteins from France." *Famous Monsters of Filmland.* No. 35. Warren, October 1965. pp. 38–44; *Famous Monsters of Filmland.* No. 54. Warren, March 1969.

612 "Fantastic Futurama." *Famous Monsters of Filmland.* No. 91. Warren, July 1972.

613 "Fantastic Planet." *Famous Monsters of Filmland.* No. 112. Warren, December 1974.

614 "Fantastic Voyage." *Famous Monsters of Filmland.* No. 43. Warren, March 1967; *Famous Monsters of Filmland 1969 Year Book/Fearbook.* New York: Warren Publishing Co., 1968; *Famous Monsters of Filmland.* No. 138. Warren, October 1977.

615 "Fantasy Books." [With Charles R. Tanner.] *Fantastic.* Ed. Harry Harrison. Flushing, NY: Ultimate Publishing Co. Inc., August 1968.

616 "Fantasy Circle." (anonymous, with Barbara Bovard) *Astonishing Stories.* Vol. 4. No. 2. Ed. Alden H. Norton. Chicago, IL: Fictioneers, Inc., February 1943.

617 "Fantasy Film Awards." *Famous Monsters of Filmland.* No. 153. Warren, May 1979.

618 "Fantasy Film Festival." *Famous Monsters of Filmland.* No. 151. Warren, March 1979. (event held in Spain)

619 "Fantasy Film Flashes." *Famous Monsters of Filmland.* No. 148. Warren, October 1978.

620 "Fantasy Film Flashes." *Imagination: Stories of Science Fiction and Fantasy.* Vol. 3. No. 2. Ed. William L. Hamling. Evanston, IL: Greenleaf Publishing Company, September 1951.

621 "Fantasy Film Flashes." *Imagination: Stories of Science Fiction and Fantasy.* Vol. 3. No. 2. Ed. William L. Hamling. Evanston, IL: Greenleaf Publishing Company, March 1952.

622 "Fantasy Film Flashes." *Imagination-Stories of Science Fiction and Fantasy.* Vol. 4. No. 3. Ed. William L. Hamling. Evanston, IL: Clark Publishing Co., Greenleaf Publishing Company, April 1953.

623 "Fantasy Film Flashes." *Imagination-Stories of Science Fiction and Fantasy.* Vol. 4. No. 7. Whole No. 21. Ed. William L. Hamling. Evanston, IL: Greenleaf Publishing Company, August 1953. pp. 140–143.

624 "Fantasy Film Flashes." *Imagination.* Vol. 5. No. 12. Ed. William L. Hamling. Greenleaf Publishing Company, December 1954. pp. 107–110.

625 "Fantasy Film Flood." *Famous Monsters of Filmland.* No. 159. Warren, November 1979.

626 "Fantasy Film Forecasts." *Fantasy Magazine.* Vol. 4. No. 5. No. 29. Ed. Julius Schwartz. Jamaica, NY: April 1935.

627 "Fantasy Filmarquee." *Forrest J Ackerman's Monster Land.* No. 2. [Canoga Park, CA: New Media Pub. Co.], April 1985. pp. 5–6.

628 "Fantasy Filmarquee." *Forrest J Ackerman's Monster Land.* No. 3. Studio City, CA: New Media Pub. Co., June 1985. pp. 5–6.

629 "Fantasy Filmarquee: The Shapes of Things to Come." *Forrest J Ackerman's Monster Land.* No. 1. Canoga Park, CA: New Media Publishing, Inc., December 1984. pp. 9–10.

630 "Fantasy Filmcon 1975." [As Paul Linden.] *Famous Monsters of Filmland.* No. 120. Warren, October 1975.

631 "Fantasy Flanguage." *What is Science Fiction Fandom?* Ed. Al Ashley. National Fantasy Fan Federation, 1944. pp. 26–35.

632 "The Fantasy Foundation: Forrest J Ackerman's Archive of the Fantastic." *Special Collections.*

2(1/2): 111–118. Fall/Winter 1982; *Science/Fiction Collections: Fantasy, Supernatural & Weird Tales.* Ed. Hal W. Hall. New York: The Haworth Press, 1983. pp. 111–118; *Historical Journal of Film, Radio, and Television.* 16, No. 1. (1996) Dorchester-on-Thames, Oxford, UK: Carfax Pub. Co. in association with the International Association for Audio-Visual Media in Historical Research and Education. p. 27

633 "Fantasy Marquee." *The Acolyte.* No. 14. Spring 1946. pp. 20–22.

634 "Fantasy Marquee." *The Acolyte.* No. 13. Winter 1946. pp. 18–21; *After Midnight.* No. 19. Ed. Reg Smith. Santa Ana, CA: May 1981. p. 6. [*Zombies on Broadway, Jungle Captive*]

635 "Fantasy's Prodigy." [as Geoffrey Giles (with Walter Gillings).] *Fantasy Review.* Vol. 3. No. 15. Ed. Walter Gillings. Ilford, Essex, UK: Summer 1949. (profile of Ray Bradbury)

636 "The Far-Out Philosopher of Science Fiction." [dust-jacket commentary for Olaf Stapledon's *Worlds of Wonder, three tales of fantasy.* Los Angeles, CA: Fantasy Publishing Co., 1949]; *Science Fiction Worlds of Forrest J Ackerman and Friends.* Reseda, CA: Powell Publications, 1969; *Expanded Science Fiction Worlds of Forrest J Ackerman & Friends PLUS.* Rockville, MD: Sense of Wonder Press. 2002.

637 "Farewell, Dear Frieda." *Famous Monsters of Filmland.* No. 128. Warren, September 1976. (obituary of actress Frieda Inescort)

638 "Farewell, Jack." *Famous Monsters of Filmland.* No. 103. Warren, December 1973. (Jack Hawkins)

639 "Farewell, Michael Dunn." *Famous Monsters of Filmland.* No. 105. Warren, March 1974.

640 "Farewell, Rod Serling." *Famous Monsters of Filmland.* No. 121. Warren, December 1975. (obituary)

641 "Farewell to a Super Fan, James Nicholson." (part 1) *Famous Monsters of Filmland.* No. 97. Warren, April 1973. (obituary of A. I. P. producer James H. Nicholson)

642 "Farewell to a Super Fan, James Nicholson." (part 2) *Famous Monsters of Filmland.* No. 98. Warren, May 1973.

643 "Farewell to Edward G. Robinson." *Famous Monsters of Filmland.* No. 100. Warren, August 1973.

644 "Farewell to Ford." *Famous Monsters of Filmland.* No. 41. Warren, November 1966. pp. 10–11. (Wallace Ford)

645 "Farewell to the Master." *Famous Monsters of Filmland.* No. 88. Warren, January 1972. (Michael Rennie obituary)

646 "Farewell to the Master." *The Frankenscience Monster.* New York: Ace Publishing Corporation, 1969. pp. 8–11. (on Boris Karloff)

647 "Farewell to the Master." *In Memoriam H. G. Wells.* Ed. Ackerman and Arthur Louis Joquel II. Los Angeles, CA: 1946.

648 "Farflite of the Future." *Spaceways.* Vol. 1. No. 1. Ed. Harry Warner, Jr. November 1938. (on Esperanto translation of pamphlet on space travel by Ernest G. Dodge)

649 "Fat Fare for Film Fiends." *Famous Monsters of Filmland.* No. 154. Warren, June 1979.

650 "Father of Kong, Farewell Willis O'Brien in Memoriam, 2 March 1886–8 November 1962." *Famous Monsters of Filmland.* Vol. 5. No. 1. Whole No. 22. April 1963. pp. 27–29; "Willis O'Brien: Father of Kong Farewell." *Famous Monsters of Filmland.* No. 110. Warren, September 1974; *King Kong Cometh!* Paul A. Woods. London: Plexus Publishing Limited, 2005. pp. 102–106.

651 "Father of Modern SF Films." *Famous Monsters of Filmland.* No. 167. Warren, September 1980. (obituary of George Pal)

652 "The Fear of the Year Is Here!" *Famous Monsters of Filmland Year Book/Fearbook.* Warren, 1969.

653 "The Fear of the Year Is Here! Famous Monsters 1970 Fearbook Can You Take It?" *Famous Monsters of Filmland 1970 Year Book/Fearbook.* Warren, 1969.

654 "Fear Today and Gaunt Tomorrow." *Famous Monsters of Filmland.* No. 174. Warren, June 1981. (previews)

655 "The Fear-Jerkers Are Coming." *Famous Monsters of Filmland.* No. 86. Warren, September 1971.

656 "Fiend." *Famous Monsters of Filmland.* No. 172. Warren, April 1981. (preview)

657 "Fifty-Foot Woman Dies." *Famous Monsters of Filmland.* No. 139. Warren, December 1977. (actress Allison Hayes)

658 "Filler You Can Skip." *Amazing Forries: this is your life, Forrest J Ackerman.* Hollywood, CA: Metropolis Publications/Warren, 1976. p. 29.

659 "Film News." [With Leon Stone.] *Etherline.* No. 69. Ed. Ian J. Crozier. Australia: 195-

660 "Film Tricks." *Utopia-Science-Fiction-Magazine.* No. 3. Rastatt, Baden, Germany: Erich Pabel Verlag, 1956.

661 "Filmfax Hall of Fame: The Most Memorable Hollywood Personalities Last Stop for Mrs. Forrest J Ackerman: Rocket to the Rue Morgue:

Cinemastronaut Wendayne Departs for Another World." *Filmfax: The Magazine of Unusual Film & Television.* No. 21. July 1990. pp. 84–87. (reprints Wendayne Ackerman's article "Rocket to the Rue Morgue" with additional material by Forrest Ackerman)

662 "Filmfax Uncovers: Lost Rarities of Film and Television from Decades Past: Forrest J Ackerman Remembers: The Thief of Bagdad." *Filmfax: The Magazine of Unusual Film & Television.* No. 19. March 1990. pp. 42–49.

663 "Filmfax Uncovers: Lost Rarities of Film and Television from Decades Past: Up from the Depths of Time: Helivision." *Filmfax: The Magazine of Unusual Film & Television.* No. 23. November 1990. pp. 40–41. [Ackerman uncovers *Helivision*]

664 "Filmonster Forecast." *Famous Monsters of Filmland.* No. 136. Warren, August 1977.

665 "Filmonster News." *Famous Monsters of Filmland.* No. 54. Warren, March 1969.

666 "Filmonsters of Tomorrow." *Famous Monsters of Filmland.* No. 61. Warren, January 1970.

667 "Filmrecension." *Häpna!* Sweden: May 1954. (*Project Moonbase*)

668 "Filmrecension." *Häpna!* Sweden: March 1955. (*Gog*)

669 "Filmrecension." *Häpna!* Sweden: July-August 1955. (*This Island Earth*)

670 "Films in the Future." *Inside.* No. 5. Ed. Ron Smith. January 1954.

671 "Filmuseum #1." *Famous Monsters of Filmland.* No. 111. Warren, October 1974. (Paris Cinematheque museum)

672 "The Final Conflict." *Famous Monsters of Filmland.* No. 172. Warren, April 1981. (*Omen III: The Final Conflict* preview)

673 "Fires of Death." *Famous Monsters of Filmland.* No. 81. Warren, December 1970.

674 "First Famous Monsters Convention." [As Paul Linden.] *Famous Monsters of Filmland.* No. 116. Warren, May 1975.

675 "The First Fan Magazine." *The Fanscient.* Vol. 1. No. 2. Ed. Donald B. Day. Portland, OR: Portland Science-Fantasy Society, Winter 1948.

676 "The First Men on the Moon." *The Fanscient.* Vol. 4. No. 12. Ed. Donald B. Day. Portland, OR: Summer 1950. (*Destination Moon*)

677 "First of the Swordcery Sagas Hawk the Slayer." *Famous Monsters of Filmland.* No. 170. New York: Warren Publishing Co., January 1981. p. 43.

678 "The First to Receive a 'Grimmy'!: An Accolade for the Ackermonster." [As "Paul Linden" with Pittman Matthis.] *Forrest J Ackerman Famous Monster of Filmland #2.* Volume II (Issues #51–100) Universal City, CA: Hollywood Publishing Company, 1991. pp. 149–154.

679 "The First World Science Fiction Convention and 1939 World's Fair." *David A. Kyle: A Life of Science Fiction Ideas and Dreams.* Ed. John L. Coker, III. Orlando, FL: Days of Wonder Publishers, 2006. pp. 154–155.

680 "FJA's Top 20." *Famous Monsters of Filmland.* No. 142. Warren, April 1978. (Ackerman's favorite genre films from 1958–1977)

681 "Flash Gordon." *Famous Monsters of Filmland.* No. 171. Warren, March 1981.

682 "Flashes from Forrie." *The Time Traveller.* Vol. 1. No. 5. June 1932.

683 "Flashy Gordon Attracts the World." [As Weaver Wright with Ron Haydock.] *Famous Monsters of Filmland.* No. 14. October 1961. [pp. 17–24]; *Famous Monsters of Filmland.* No. 101. Warren, September 1973. (Bert I. Gordon)

684 "Flavia Paulon." *Science Fiction Chronicle: The Monthly SF and Fantasy Newsmagazine.* Vol. 8. No. 11. Ed. Andrew I. Porter. August 1987. p. 10. (obituary of Italian film festival promoter)

685 "Fleischer Dies." *Famous Monsters of Filmland.* No. 159. Warren, November 1979. (animator Max Fleischer)

686 "The Flesh Eaters." *Famous Monsters of Filmland.* No. 29. July 1964. Warren Publishing, Inc., pp. 20–25.

687 "Florence Marly Dead." *Famous Monsters of Filmland.* No. 152. Warren, April 1979. p. 57.

688 "Flying Disc Man from Mars." *Spacemen.* Vol. 2. No. 1. Whole No. 5. Philadelphia: Spacemen, Inc., October 1962. pp. 48–51; *Spacemen 1965 Yearbook.* Warren Publishing Co., 1964.

689 "Flying Disc Man from Mars." *Spacemen.* Vol. 2. No. 1. Whole No. 6. Philadelphia: Spacemen, Inc., January 1963. (Part 2); *Spacemen 1965 Yearbook.* Warren Publishing Co., 1964.

690 "Foolosophy." *Imagination!* Vol. 1. No. 3. December 1937. p. 8.

691 "Foolosophy — Scientifriction." *Imagination!* Vol. 1. No. 1. October 1937. p. 6.

692 "For Your Eyes Only!" *Famous Monsters of Filmland.* No. 177. Warren, September 1981.

693 "The Forbidden World of the Mutant." *Famous Monsters of Filmland.* No. 185. Warren, July 1982. (preview)

694 "Forecast." *Imagination!* Vol. 1. No. 3. December 1937. p. 14.

695 "Forecast." *Imagination!* Vol. 1. No. 9. June 1938. p. 18.

696 "Foreign Fanzines." *Fantasy Annual.* Los Angeles: 1948. pp. 112–113.

697 "Foreword." *Horror Biz.* No. 7. 2001. p. 5. (precedes article "London After Midnight: 75 Years of Silence" by Michael T. Koneful)

698 "Forgotten Frankensteins." *Forrest J Ackerman Presents Mr. Monster's Movie Gold: A Treasure Trove of Imagi-Movies.* Ed. Hank Stine. Virginia Beach, VA: Donning Co. 1981. pp. 104–113.

699 "Forrest J. Ackerman Presents Science Fiction on the Air!" *The Time Traveller.* Vol. 1. No. 5. June 1932.

700 "Forrest J Ackerman Remembers: The 1939 World Science Fiction Convention and 1939 World's Fair." *Days of Wonder: Remembering Sam Moskowitz and Conrad H. Ruppert.* John L. Coker III. Orlando, FL: Days of Wonder Press, 1998.

701 "Forrest J. Ackerman reports on Destination Moon." *Science-Fantasy Review.* Vol. 4. No. 18. Ed. Walter Gillings. Ilford, Essex, UK: Spring 1950.

702 "Forrest J Ackerman Selects..." *Expanse.* No. 3. Ed. Steven E. Fick. Baltimore, MD: Summer 1994.

703 "Forrest J. Ackerman Visits Edgar Rice Burroughs." *Fantasy Review.* Vol. 2. No. 12. Ed. Walter Gillings. Ilford, Essex, UK: Dec. 1948-January 1949. pp. 16–19; as "A visit with Edgar Rice Burroughs." *Edgar Rice Burroughs' Fantastic Worlds.* Ed. James van Hise. Yucca Valley, CA: James Van Hise, 1996; 2005.

704 "Forrest J. Ackerman Writes from America." *Authentic Science Fiction.* No. 23. Ed. L. G. Holmes. London: Hamilton & Co. (Stafford) Ltd., July 1952.

705 "Forrest J Ackerman Writes from Hollywood." *Science Fiction News.* No. 5. Ed. Graham Stone. Sydney: May 1953. p. 3. (concerns SF radio broadcast)

706 "Forrest J Ackerman's List of the 11 Kings of Horror Films." *The Book of Movie Lists.* Gabe Essoe. Westport, CT: Arlington House, 1981; New York: Crown Publications, Inc. 1981. p. 153.

707 "Forrest J Ackerman's Nine Favorite Science Fiction Movie Nude Scenes." *The SF Book of Lists.* Ed. Malcolm Edwards & Maxim Jakubowski. New York: Berkeley, 1982. p. 258.

708 "Forrest J Ackerman's Sci-Fi Monsters." *Cult Movies.* No. 19. Cult Movies Publishing, 1997.

709 "Forrest Murmurings." *To the Stars.* No. 0. Ed. John & Bjo Trimble. Los Angeles, CA: Methuselah Press, August 1983.

710 "The Forrest Prime Evil." *Famous Monsters of Filmland.* No. 104. Warren, January 1974; as "Afterword: The Forrest Prime Evil." *Forrest J Ackerman Presents Mr. Monster's Movie Gold: A Treasure Trove of Imagi-Movies.* Ed. Hank Stine. Virginia Beach, VA: Donning Co. 1981. pp. 184–198. (horror film stars)

711 "Forry Ackerman Remembers the Miracle Man." *House of Hammer.* No. 26. Ed. Dez Skinn. London: Top Sellers, Ltd./Quality Communication, 1983. pp. 11–12. (article on Lon Chaney, Sr.)

712 "Forry Ackerman's Crimson Chronicles." *Scarlet Street.* No. 41. 2001. pp. 35, 78.

713 "Forry Ackerman's Crimson Chronicles." *Scarlet Street.* No. 47. 2002. p. 49. (on Peter Lorre)

714 "Forry Ackerman's Crimson Chronicles." *Scarlet Street.* No. 48. 2003. p. 63. (on *The Fly* and its author George Langelaan)

715 "Forry Dies!" *Famous Monsters of Filmland.* No. 173. Warren, May 1981. (on a misreport of Ackerman's death)

716 "Forry Faces." *Forrest J Ackerman's Monster Land.* No. 1. Canoga Park, CA: New Media Publishing, Inc., December 1984. p. 50. (contest entrants' photographs)

717 "Forry Story." *Philcon Memory Book.* 1947. (*Tympani*)

718 "Forry Tales." *The Tana Leaflet: Unofficial Publication of The Count Dracula Society.* No. 1. Ed. Kristian W. Vosburgh. Los Angeles: October 1973. p. 12. (notes on Ackerman's recent publications and doings)

719 "Forry's Folly." *Famous Monsters of Filmland.* No. 100. Warren, August 1973.

720 "Forry's Stories." [With Dennis Billows.] *Famous Monsters of Filmland: The Annotated No. 1.* Movieland Classics, LLC, 2011. pp. 16–23.

721 "Forry's World." *Science Fiction Horror & Fantasy Sci Fi News & Reviews.* Vol. 1. No. 1. Nov/Dec 1979. p. 11. (news column)

722 "Forry-warned Is Forry-armed." *Glom.* No. 12. November 1948. (Editorial)

723 "Forryword." *First Karloffornia Monster Convention.* Ed. Harry Douthwaite. 1961.

724 "Forryword." *Forrest J Ackerman Famous Monster of Filmland #2.* Volume II (Issues #51–100). Universal City, CA: Hollywood Publishing Company, 1991. (entirely different from that of *Directed by Jack Arnold* and *Famous Monsters Chronicles*)

725 "The Fort Knox of Science Fiction." [As Paul Linden.] *Science-Fiction Fantasy Horror: The World of Forrest J Ackerman at Auction.* New York: Guernsey's, 1987.

726 "Forthcoming Fantasy Films." [As Forrest de Hollywood.] *New Concept.* Ed. Harry Loren Sinn. December 1944.

727 "Forthcoming Fantasy Films." *Fan Slants.* Vol. 1. No. 1. Ed. Mel Brown. September 1943.

728 "4E's Fave Films, 1978–96." *Screem.* No. 8. Ed. Darryl Mayeski. 1996. pp. 14–17. (Ackerman's Top 20 Favorite Films from 1978–1996)

729 "The Four Faces of Dr. Who." *Famous Monsters of Filmland.* No. 155. Warren, July 1979.

730 "400 Fete Bradbury at Banquet." *Science Fiction Chronicle.* Vol. 2. No. 11. Ed. Andrew Porter. August 1981. p. 14. (brief piece on May 1981 banquet honoring the author)

731 "Four New Fright Films." *Famous Monsters of Filmland.* No. 163. Warren, May 1980; as "Three New Fright Films." *Warren Presents The Official Exclusive Horror Movie Yearbook 1981 Collector's Edition.* Warren, February 1981. (previews of *The Orphan, Silent Scream, The Coming, Dominique*)

732 "The 4SJ Chronicles." *Bjo Trimble's Sci-Fi Spotlite. (formerly Space Time Continuum)* No. 1. March 1996.

733 "The 4SJ Chronicles." *Bjo Trimble's Sci-Fi Spotlite.* No. 2. April 1996.

734 "The 4SJ Chronicles." *Bjo Trimble's Sci-Fi Spotlite.* No. 3. June 1996.

735 "Frankenstein." [With G. John Edwards.] *Famous Monsters of Filmland.* No. 56. Warren, July 1969; *Famous Monsters of Filmland.* No. 178. Warren, October 1981.

736 "Frankenstein and the Monster from Hell." *Famous Monsters of Filmland.* No. 113. Warren, January 1975. (preview)

737 "Frankenstein and the Vampires!" *Famous Monsters of Filmland.* No. 96. Warren, March 1973. (*The Horror of Frankenstein*)

738 "Frankenstein Conquers the World!" *Famous Monsters of Filmland.* No. 39. Warren, June 1966. pp. 9–24; *Famous Monsters of Filmland.* No. 114. Warren, March 1975.

739 "Frankenstein Filmbook." [As Weaver Wright with Tom Mula.] *The Frankenscience Monster.* New York: Ace Publishing Corporation, 1969. pp. 129–148.

740 "Frankenstein Flashbacks: Castle of Frankenstein Meets Famous Monsters!" *Castle of Frankenstein.* No. 26. Highwood, IL: Dennis Druktenis Publishing & Mail Order, Inc., Summer 1999. (two photos of Ackerman with *Castle of Frankenstein* founder Calvin Thomas Beck and a letter of explanation from Ackerman to Dennis Druktenis)

741 "Frankenstein Meets the Space Monster." *Famous Monsters of Filmland.* No. 39. Warren, June 1966. pp. 34–37.

742 "Frankenstein Meets the Wolfman." *Famous Monsters of Filmland.* No. 42. Warren, January 1967; *Famous Monsters of Filmland.* No. 96. Warren, March 1973.

743 "Frankenstein —1910." *Famous Monsters of Filmland.* Vol. 5. No. 2. Whole No. No. 23. June 1963. pp. 44–45.

744 "Frankenstein ... 1970." *Monster World.* No. 4. Warren, June 1965.

745 "Frankenstein, 1973." *Famous Monsters of Filmland.* No. 104. January 1974.

746 "Frankenstein, part 2." [With G. John Edwards.] *Famous Monsters of Filmland.* No. 57. Warren, September 1969; *Famous Monsters of Filmland.* No. 178. Warren, October 1981.

747 "Frankenstein, part 3." [With G. John Edwards.] *Famous Monsters of Filmland.* No. 60. Warren, December 1969; *Famous Monsters of Filmland.* No. 178. Warren, October 1981.

748 "The Frankenstein Story." *Famous Monsters of Filmland.* Vol. 1. No. 1. Philadelphia: Central Publications, Inc., 1958. pp. 24–35; *Famous Monsters Yearbook.* No. 1. Summer-Fall 1962; *James Warren Presents The Best from Famous Monsters of Filmland.* New York: Paperback Library, 1964; *Famous Monsters 1968 Yearbook.* Warren, 1967; as The Frankenscience Monster" *Forrest J Ackerman's Monsterama.* No. 1. Seattle, WA: Fantagraphics Books, May 1991. pp. 23–32; *Famous Monsters of Filmland.* Vol. 1. No. 1. Filmland Classics, January 2008. pp. 24–35. (replica edition)

749 "Frankenstein's Bebe or Brigitte and the Beast." *Hi-Life.* May 1959. (piece about Brigitte Bardot)

750 "Friday the 13th, Part II." *Famous Monsters of Filmland.* No. 174. Warren, June 1981; *Film Fantasy Yearbook 1982 Collector's Edition.* Warren, March 1982. (preview)

751 "Fright Films to Come." *Famous Monsters of Filmland.* No. 30. Warren Publishing Co., September 1964. pp. 7–12.

752 "Fritz Lang." *Famous Monsters of Filmland.* No. 121. Warren, December 1975. (invites readers to send birthday greetings)

753 "The Fritz LANGlanguage, Or on the Set with the Man Who Made 'The Girl in the Moon.'" *Shangri L'Affaires.* No. 15. Ed. Charles Burbee. June 1944. (on a visit by Ackerman and Morojo to the set of Lang's *The Woman in the Window*)

754 "From Beyond the Grave John Andrews Strikes Again! A Tale of Woe (by FJA)." *Cult Movies.* No. 6. 1992. pp. 36–37.

755 "From Ghetto to Glory the Science Fiction Story." *Science-Fiction Fantasy Horror: The World of Forrest J Ackerman at Auction.* New York: Guernsey's, 1987. pp. 18–19.

756 "From the Captain of the Cellship Attica." *Perry Rhodan. No. 32. Challenge of the Unknown.* Clark Darlton. New York: Ace. October 1973.

757 "From the Captain of the Markron R4B." *Perry Rhodan. No. 18. Menace of the Mutant Master.* Kurt Mahr. New York: Ace Books, 1972.

758 "From the Captain of the Spaceship 4SJ." *Perry Rhodan. No. 27. Planet of the Gods.* Kurt Mahr. New York: Ace, August 1973; London: Futura Publications, 1977.

759 "From the Captain of the Spaceship Vern 2E." *Perry Rhodan. No. 31. Realm of the Tri-Planets.* K. H. Scheer. New York: Ace, October 1973; London: Futura Publications, 1973.

760 "From the Captain of the Stardust 4E." [As Forry Rhodan.] *Perry Rhodan. No. 14. Venus in Danger.* Kurt Mahr. New York: Ace, June 1972. 1974.

761 "From the Captain of the Stardust 4E." [As Forry Rhodan.] *Perry Rhodan. No. 19. Mutants vs. Mutants.* Clark Darlton. New York: Ace, November 1972; London: Futura, 1976.

762 "From the Captain of the Stardust 4E." [As Forry Rhodan.] *Perry Rhodan. No. 20. The Thrall of Hypno.* Clark Darlton. New York: Ace, December 1972; London: Futura, 1976.

763 "From the Captain of the Stardust 4E." [As Forry Rhodan.] *Perry Rhodan. No. 21. The Cosmic Decoy.* K. H. Scheer. New York: Ace, January 1973.

764 "From the Captain of the Stardust 4SJ." *Perry Rhodan. No. 26. Cosmic Traitor.* Kurt Brand. New York: Ace, July 1973.

765 "From the Captain of the Stardust 4SJ." *Perry Rhodan. No. 33. The Giant's Partner.* Clark Darlton. New York: Ace, November 1973.

766 "From the Captain of the Stardust 4SJ." *Perry Rhodan. No. 35. Beware the Microbots.* Kurt Mahr. New York: Ace, December 1973.

767 "From the Crypt of Forrest J Ackerman." *Graveyard Examiner: The Official Newsletter of the FJA/Famous Monsters Club.* Vol. 1. No. 2. Dynacomm, 1994.

768 "From the Heart of Darkest Ackula: A Personal Message From the Dreaded Ackermonster Himself." *Famous Monsters of Filmland.* No. 100. Warren, August 1973. p. 50; *Forrest J Ackerman Famous Monster of Filmland #2.* Volume II (Issues #51–

100) Universal City, CA: Hollywood Publishing Company, 1991. p. 97.

769 "From There to Eternity." *Gosh! Wow (Boy-oh-Boy)! Science Fiction.* New York: Bantam, 1982. pp. 435–437.

770 "Fueling the Future." *Worlds of Tomorrow: The Amazing Universe of Science Fiction Art.* [With Brad Linaweaver.] Portland, OR: Collectors Press, 2004. pp. 55–56.

771 "The Funhouse." *Famous Monsters of Filmland.* No. 173. Warren, May 1981. (preview)

772 "Future Fantasia Film Forecast." *Famous Monsters of Filmland.* No. 164. Warren, June 1980.

773 "Future Fantastic Filmarvels." *Famous Monsters of Filmland.* No. 80. Warren, October 1970.

774 "Future Fiction O.K. Now Heinlein No Model — Critic." *Fantasy Review.* Vol. 2. No. 8. Ed. Walter Gillings. Ilford, Essex, UK: April-May 1948. p. 1.

775 "Future Film Fear." *Famous Monsters of Filmland.* No. 100. Warren, August 1973.

776 "Future Fright Films." *Famous Monsters of Filmland.* No. 34. Warren, August 1965. pp. 7–14.

777 "Future Fright Flicks." *Famous Monsters of Filmland.* No. 185. Warren, July 1982.

778 "Future Tense." *Famous Monsters of Filmland.* Vol. 5. No. 4. Whole No. 25. Warren Publishing, Inc., October 1963. pp. 8–13.

779 "'Future World' Convention." [As Weaver Wright.] *Glom.* No. 6. January 1947. pp. 1–3. (rejected article Ackerman sent to mainstream outlets promoting and explaining the World Science Fiction Convention)

780 "The Futurescope." *Famous Monsters of Filmland.* No. 183. Warren, May 1982.

781 "Futureworld." *Famous Monsters of Filmland.* No. 129. Warren, October 1976.

782 "Futuria Fantasia." *Famous Monsters of Filmland.* No. 170. Warren, January 1981. pp. 12–14.

783 "Futuria Fantasia Film Flashes." *Famous Monsters of Filmland.* No. 157. Warren, September 1979.

784 "Galactica or Star Wars, Which Is Best?" *Famous Monsters of Filmland.* No. 150. Warren, January 1979.

785 "A Galaxy in Flames." *Famous Monsters of Filmland Star Wars Spectacular.* Warren Publishing Co., October 1977.

786 "Garage Mahal." *Forrest J Ackerman's Monsters & Imagi-Movies.* Ed. Robert V. Michelucci. Canoga Park, CA: New Media Pub. Co., 1985. p.

55?. (advertisement for items then available from Ackerman)

787 "Geoffrey Giles Writes About Books." [As Geoffrey Giles with Walter Gillings.] *Fantasy Review.* Ed. Walter Gillings. Volume 1. No. 4. August-September 1947. pp. 17–18.

788 "Geoffrey Giles Writes About Books." [As Geoffrey Giles with Walter Gillings.] *Fantasy Review.* Vol. 1. No. 5. (Incorporating *Scientifiction* and *To-Morrow Magazine of the Future*). Ilford, Essex, UK: Oct.-Nov. 1947.

789 "Geoffrey Giles Writes About Books." [As Geoffrey Giles with Walter Gillings.] *Fantasy Review.* Vol. 2. No. 7. (Incorporating *Scientifiction* and *To-Morrow Magazine of the Future*). Ilford, Essex, UK: Feb.-March. 1948. pp. 17–19.

790 "Geoffrey Giles Writes About Books." [As Geoffrey Giles with Walter Gillings.] *Fantasy Review.* Vol. 2. No. 7. Ed. Walter Gillings. Ilford, Essex, UK: April-May 1948. pp. 17–18.

791 "Geoffrey Giles Writes About Books." [As Geoffrey Giles with Walter Gillings.] *Fantasy Review.* Vol. 2. No. 9. Ed. Walter Gillings. Ilford, Essex, UK: Jun.-Jul. 1948. pp. 17–18.

792 "Geoffrey Giles Writes About Books: Fantasy Publishers Join Forces in Drive for Bigger Sales." [As Geoffrey Giles with Walter Gillings.] *Fantasy Review.* Vol. 3. No. 14. Ed. Walter Gillings. Ilford, Essex, UK: Apr.-May 1949. (Associated Fantasy Publishers)

793 "George Lucas: Our Hero." *Famous Monsters of Filmland Star Wars Spectacular.* Warren Publishing Co., October 1977.

794 "The Ghastrological Horrorscope." [As "Ghostradamus."] *Famous Monsters of Filmland.* Vol. 2. No. 8. Philadelphia: Central Publications, Inc., September 1960. [pp. 9–20]; *Famous Monsters of Filmland 1965 Yearbook.* No. 3. Warren, 1965; *Famous Monsters of Filmland 1972 Fearbook.* Warren, 1971.

795 "Ghidrah!" *Monster World.* No. 7. March 1966; *Famous Monsters of Filmland.* No. 137. Warren, September 1977. pp. 6–10.

796 "Ghost in the Invisible Bikini." *Monster World.* No. 10. New York: Warren, September 1966.

797 "The Ghost of Frankenstein." *Famous Monsters of Filmland.* No. 48. Warren, February 1968.

798 "The Ghost of Post." *1975 Famous Monsters of Filmland Convention Book*; *Famous Monsters of Filmland.* No. 123. Warren, March 1976. (mask maker Don Post, Sr.)

799 "The Ghost, Son of Frankenstein." *Forrest J Ackerman's Fantastic Movie Memories: Forrest Ackerman's Treasure Trove of Imagi-Movies.* Canoga Park, CA: New Media Books, 1985.

800 "Ghost Story." *Famous Monsters of Filmland.* No. 181. Warren, March 1982. (preview)

801 "Giants from Japan." *Famous Monsters of Filmland.* No. 30. Warren Publishing Co., September 1964. pp. 42–48; *Famous Monsters of Filmland.* No. 110. Warren, September 1974.

802 "Giger the Great." *Famous Monsters of Filmland.* No. 158. Warren, October 1979. (artist H. R. Giger)

803 "The Girl in the Moon Part 1." *Spacemen.* Vol. 1. No. 3. Philadelphia: Spacemen, Inc., April 1962. (Fritz Lang's *Frau im Mond* a.k.a. *By Rocket to the Moon*)

804 "The Girl in the Moon Part 2." *Spacemen.* Vol. 1. No. 4. Philadelphia: Spacemen, Inc., July 1962.

805 "Girls Will Be Ghouls." *Famous Monsters of Filmland.* Vol. 1. No. 2. Philadelphia: Central Publications, Inc., September 1958. [pp. 38–43]; *Famous Monsters of Filmland: Yearbook.* No. 2. [1964] [Warren Publishing Co.], December 1963; *James Warren Presents The Best from Famous Monsters of Filmland.* New York: Paperback Library, 1964.

806 "Glad They Were Born." *Famous Monsters of Filmland.* No. 150. Warren, January 1979.

807 "Glenn Strange Dies." *Famous Monsters of Filmland.* No. 104. Warren, January 1974.

808 "The Glowing Goal." [With Donald A. Wollheim as Forry Rhodan.] *Perry Rhodan. No. 10. The Ghosts of Gol.* Kurt Mahr. New York: Ace, December 1971, 1972, 1974.

809 "Go Jira, Go!" *Famous Monsters of Filmland.* No. 206. N. Hollywood, CA: Dynacomm, Jan./Feb. 1995. pp. 30–38. [pp. 37–38 comprise Mark Patrick Carducci's interview of Tony Randel, uncredited co-writer of *Godzilla 1985: The Legend Is Reborn*]

810 "God Busters." [As Erick Freyor.] *Futuria Fantasia.* No. 2. Ed. Ray Bradbury. Los Angeles, CA: Fall 1939. p. 11; *Futuria Fantasia.* Ray Bradbury. Los Angeles: Graham, 2007.

811 "Godzilla! King of the Creatures!" *Famous Monsters of Filmland.* No. 35. Warren, October 1965. pp. 46–56; *Famous Monsters of Filmland.* No. 114. Warren, March 1975.

812 "Godzilla vs. Bionic Monster." *Famous Monsters of Filmland.* No. 135. Warren, July 1977.

813 "Godzilla vs. the Smog Monster." *Famous Monsters of Filmland.* No. 91. Warren, July 1972; *Famous Monsters of Filmland.* No. 158. Warren, October 1979.

814 "Godzilla vs. The Thing." *Monster World.* Vol. 1. No. 2. New York: Warren, January 1965. (*Mothra vs. Godzilla* preview)

815 "Golden Age Classics: Rarities from the Early Years of Hollywood: One Glorious Day: Forry Recalls an 'Ek'toplasmic Fantasy from The Silent Era, Featuring some Spirited Effects." *Filmfax: The Magazine of Unusual Film & Television.* No. 9. 1987. pp. 23–26. (on the 1922 film *One Glorious Day*)

816 "Golden Age Classics: Rarities from the Early Years of Hollywood Horror: Seven Footprints to Satan: FJA Resurrects a Lost Monsterpiece of the Cinemacabré." *Filmfax: The Magazine of Unusual Film & Television.* No. 7. June/July 1987. pp. 28–31, 59. (on film adaptation of A. Merritt novel *7 Footprints to Satan*)

817 "Golden Age Classics: Rarities from the Early Years of Hollywood: The Bat Whispers." [With Additional Information by Michael Stein.] *Filmfax: The Magazine of Unusual Film & Television.* Vol. 1. No. 12. October 1988. pp. 18–21, 56. (on *The Bat Whispers* & *The Bat*)

818 "The Golden Voyage of Sinbad." *Famous Monsters of Filmland.* No. 106. Warren, April 1974.

819 "The Golem." *Monster World.* No. 8. Warren, May 1966; *Famous Monsters of Filmland.* No. 89. Warren March 1972; *Famous Monsters of Filmland.* No. 127. Warren, August 1976; *Famous Monsters of Filmland.* No. 158. Warren, October 1979.

820 "Gone but Not Forgotten." *Famous Monsters of Filmland.* No. 163. Warren, May 1980.

821 "The Gordons Will Get You!" *Famous Monsters of Filmland.* No. 35. Warren, October 1965. (Alex, Richard & Ruth Alexander Gordon)

822 "Gorgo the Gargantuan." *Famous Monsters of Filmland.* Vol. 3. No. 2. Whole No. 11. Philadelphia: Central Publications, Inc., April 1961. [pp. 25–30]; *Famous Monsters of Filmland 1965 Yearbook.* No. 3. Warren, 1965; *Famous Monsters of Filmland.* No. 50. July 1968. New York: Warren Publishing Co., 1968; *Famous Monsters of Filmland.* No. 168. Warren, October 1980.

823 "Grafologyarns." [As Zhan Dark.] *Imagination! The Fanmag of the Future with a Future!* Vol. 1. No. 12. Los Angeles: Los Angeles Chapter — Science-Fiction Association, September 1938. p. 11.

824 "Gray Mauser [*sic*] Award to Marion Z. Bradley." *Science Fiction Chronicle: The Monthly Science Fiction and Fantasy Newsmagazine.* Vol. 3. No. 2. Ed. Andrew Porter. November 1981. p. 19. (award named for Fritz Leiber's character the Gray Mauser)

825 "Great Horror Figure Dies." *Famous Monsters of Filmland.* No. 31. Warren Publishing Co., December 1964. pp. 40–51. (Edward Van Sloan)

826 "Great Lugosi Mystery." *Famous Monsters of Filmland.* No. 40. Warren, August 1966. pp. 28–30; *Famous Monsters of Filmland.* No. 92. Warren, September 1972.

827 "The Great Man Is Gone." *Famous Monsters of Filmland.* No. 132. Warren, March 1977. (obituary for Fritz Lang)

828 "Greetings to the (Extended) Bat Pack from Forry Ackerman." *Midnight Marquee.* No. 37. Ed. Gary J. Svehla. Albany, NY: Fantaco Enterprises, Inc., 1988.

829 "Gremlin Grumblin's." *The Fort MacArthur Bulletin.* Friday 5 February 1943. p. 2-A.

830 "The Grim Reaper." *Famous Monsters of Filmland.* No. 180. Warren, January 1982. (*Antropophagus* preview)

831 "Grue's News." *Famous Monsters of Filmland.* No. 57. Warren, September 1969.

832 "Guess Again." *Forrest J Ackerman's Monster Land.* No. 1. Canoga Park, CA: New Media Publishing, Inc., December 1984. pp. 49. (photo contest)

833 "Guess What Happened to Count Dracula." *Famous Monsters of Filmland.* No. 95. Warren, January 1973.

834 "Guest Riders in the Sky." *Spacemen.* Vol. 1. No. 1. Philadelphia, PA: Spacemen, Inc. July 1961; *Spacemen 1965 Yearbook.* Warren Publishing Co., 1964. (*Riders to the Stars*)

835 "Guide to Monsterland." *Famous Monsters of Filmland.* No. 142. Warren, April 1978.

836 "Gustav Fröhlich." *Science Fiction Chronicle: The Monthly SF and Fantasy Newsmagazine.* Vol. 9. No. 6. Ed. Andrew I. Porter. March 1988. pp. 12, 14. (obituary of *Metropolis* star)

837 "Guy Endore, Theodore Pratt, Arthur K. Barnes." *Luna Monthly.* No. 12. Ed. Ann F. Dietz. Oradell, NJ: May 1970. pp. 5–6. (obituaries)

838 "Half a Life." *Famous Monsters of Filmland.* No. 172. Warren, April 1981. (obituary of actor Steve McQueen)

839 "'Half-Boy' Eck Robbed." *Science Fiction Chronicle: The Monthly SF and Fantasy Newsmagazine.* Vol. 9. No. 10. Ed. Andrew I. Porter. July 1988. p. 8. (*Freaks* star Johnny Eckhardt)

840 "The Hallmark Hall of Hammer." *Famous Monsters of Filmland.* No. 208. No. Hollywood, CA: Dynacomm, May 1995. pp. 60–63. (on Hammer Films)

841 "Halloween Happenings." *Famous Monsters of Filmland.* No. 179. Warren, November 1981.

842 "Halloween Planet." *Famous Monsters of Filmland.* No. 179. Warren, November 1981.

843 "The Halloween Screen." *Famous Monsters of Filmland*. Vol. 1. No. 5. Philadelphia: Central Publications, Inc., November 1959. [pp. 9–19]; *Famous Monsters of Filmland 1967 Yearbook*. Warren, 1966.

844 "Halloween III: Season of the Witch." *Famous Monsters of Filmland*. No. 189. November 1982; *Film Fantasy Yearbook 1983 Collector's Edition*. Warren, March 1983.

845 "The Hammer of Horror." *Monster World*. No. 5. Warren, October 1965; *Famous Monsters of Filmland*. No. 53. Warren, January 1969.

846 "Happy Birthday, Dear Alonzo! Chaney Is 100!" *Fangoria*. No. 27. O'Quinn Studios, May 1983. pp. 38–41. (on Lon Chaney, Sr., whose first name Ackerman mistakenly believed to have been Alonzo)

847 "Happy Birthday Dear Phantom!" *Famous Monsters of Filmland*. No. 98. Warren, May 1973. (in recognition of what would have been Lon Chaney Sr.'s 90th birthday)

848 "Happy Birthday to —." *The Fort Mac-Arthur Bulletin*. Friday 5 February 1943. p. 3-A.

849 "Happy Birthdays." *Famous Monsters of Filmland*. No. 159. Warren, November 1979.

850 "Happy Birthdays." *Famous Monsters of Filmland*. No. 160. Warren, January 1980.

851 "Happy Fourth of Ghoul Eye." [With James Warren.] *Famous Monsters of Filmland*. Vol. 2. No. 8. Philadelphia: Central Publications, Inc., September 1960. [p. 3.]

852 "Happy Thanksgraving!" *Famous Monsters of Filmland*. Vol. 3. No. 1. No. 10. Philadelphia: Central Publications, Inc., January 1961. (Editorial)

853 "Harlequin." *Famous Monsters of Filmland*. No. 175. Warren, July 1981.

854 "Harpy Birthdays." *Famous Monsters of Filmland*. No. 162. Warren, April 1980.

855 "Harpy Days Are Here Again." *Famous Monsters of Filmland*. No. 50. July 1968. New York: Warren Publishing Co., 1968.

856 "Harpy New Fear." *Famous Monsters of Filmland*. No. 206. N. Hollywood, CA: Dynacomm, Jan./Feb. 1995. p. 3.

857 "Harpy New Year." [As "Dr. Acula and His Assistant 'Furry' Ackerman."] *Famous Monsters of Filmland*. Vol. 2. No. 1. Whole No. 6. Philadelphia: Central Publications, Inc., February 1960; *Famous Monsters of Filmland*. Vol. 2. No. 1. Whole No. 6. Filmland Classics, May 2008. pp. 46–49. (replica edition)

858 "Harryhausen's Titans." *Famous Monsters of Filmland*. No. 169. Warren, November 1980.

859 "Have a Lark with Quark." *Famous Monsters of Filmland*. No. 144. Warren, June 1978. (TV sci-fi comedy series *Quark*)

860 "Have You a Skeleton in Your Closet?" [As Dr. Acula.] *Famous Monsters of Filmland*. No. 29. Warren Publishing, Inc., July 1964.

861 "He Died on Halloween." *Famous Monsters of Filmland*. No. 27. Warren Publishing, March 1964. p. 47. (actor Henry Daniell)

862 "He Fought Donovan's Brain & Dr. Moreau's Manimals: Dead at 75." *Famous Monsters of Filmland*. No. 130. Warren, December 1976. (obituary of actor Richard Arlen)

863 "He Took Them to Kong's Island." *Famous Monsters of Filmland*. No. 37. Warren, February 1966; *Famous Monsters of Filmland 1971 Fearbook*. Warren, 1970. (actor Frank Reicher)

864 "He Unmasked for It!" *Monster World*. No. 7. Warren, March 1966.

865 "He Walked with Death." *Famous Monsters of Filmland*. No. 139. Warren, December 1977. (obituary of actor Ricardo Cortez)

866 "He Wrote 'Souls Aspace.'" *Science Fiction Digest*. Vol. 2. No. 4. Ed. Julius Schwartz. Jamaica, NY: Conrad H. Ruppert, December 1933. (about Joseph William Skidmore)

867 "Head of Horror." *Famous Monsters of Filmland*. No. 27. Warren Publishing, March 1964. pp. 44–46. (*The Madmen of Mandoras*)

868 "Headlines from Horrorsville." *Famous Monsters of Filmland*. No. 201. No. Hollywood, CA: Dynacomm, Fall 1993.

869 "Headlines from Horrorsville." *Famous Monsters of Filmland*. No. 202. No. Hollywood, CA: Dynacomm, Spring 1994.

870 "Headlines from Horrorsville." *Famous Monsters of Filmland*. No. 203. No. Hollywood, CA: Dynacomm, August/September 1994. pp. 50–51.

871 "Headlines from Horrorsville." *Famous Monsters of Filmland*. No. 204. No. Hollywood, CA: Dynacomm, November 1994. pp. 58–59.

872 "Headlines from Horrorsville." *Famous Monsters of Filmland*. No. 205. N. Hollywood, CA: Dynacomm, December 1994. pp. 60–61.

873 "Headlines from Horrorsville." *Famous Monsters of Filmland*. No. 206. N. Hollywood, CA: Dynacomm, Jan./Feb. 1995. pp. 60–61.

874 "Headlines from Horrorsville." *Famous Monsters of Filmland*. No. 207. N. Hollywood, CA: Dynacomm, March 1995. pp. 60–61.

875 "Headlines from Horrorsville." *Famous Monsters of Filmland*. No. 208. No. Hollywood, CA: Dynacomm, May 1995. pp. 68–69.

876 "Headlines from Horrorsville." *Famous Monsters of Filmland*. No. 209. N. Hollywood, CA: Dynacomm, August/September 1995. p. 64.

877 "Headlines from Horrorsville." *Famous Monsters of Filmland*. No. 210. No. Hills, CA: Dynacomm, Nov./Dec. 1995. p. 66.

878 "Headlines from Whollyweird." *Cult Movies*. No. 21. Summer 1997. p. 4.

879 "Headlines from Whollyweird." *Cult Movies*. No. 19. / *Spacemen*. No. 1. p. 4. (on Ackerman's 80th birthday party)

880 "Headlines from Whollyweird." *Cult Movies*. No. 22. 1997. pp. 74–75.

881 "Headlines from Whollyweird." *Cult Movies*. No. 23. 1997. p. 28.

882 "The Hearse." *Famous Monsters of Filmland*. No. 169. Warren, November 1980; *Warren Presents the Official Exclusive Horror Movie Yearbook 1981 Collector's Edition*. Warren, February 1981.

883 "Heartbeeps." *Famous Monsters of Filmland*. No. 179. Warren, November 1981. (preview)

884 "Heartbeeps Heartbeeps." *Famous Monsters of Filmland*. No. 181. Warren, March 1982.

885 "Heeeere's New Years! Full of Sci-Fi & Fears!" *Famous Monsters of Filmland*. No. 182. Warren, April 1982.

886 "'Heid' & Go Chic." *An Illustrated History of Heidi Saha: Fantasy Fandom's Famous Femme*. New York: Warren Publishing Co., 1973.

887 "Heidi, Ho!" *An Illustrated History of Heidi Saha: Fantasy Fandom's Famous Femme*. New York: Warren Publishing Co., 1973.

888 "Helen Beaumont." *Locus*. No. 84. Charles and Dena Brown. Bronx, NY: 25 May 1971. p. 1. (obituary)

889 "Hell in the Heavens." *Famous Monsters of Filmland*. No. 124. Warren, April 1976. (1975 film *The Hindenburg*)

890 "Hell Night." *Famous Monsters of Filmland*. No. 180. Warren, January 1982. (preview)

891 "Hello!" *Amazing Forries: this is your life, Forrest J Ackerman*. Hollywood, CA: Metropolis Publications, 1976. p. 1. (in honor of 60th birthday)

892 "Help Stamp out Monsters." *Famous Monsters of Filmland*. Vol. 1. No. 3. Philadelphia: Central Publications, Inc., April 1959. (Editorial)

893 "Henry M. Eichner." *Luna Monthly*. No. 31. Ed. Ann F. Dietz. Oradell, NJ: December 1971. p. 11. (obituary of Atlantis scholar)

894 "Her Famous Friends." *An Illustrated History of Heidi Saha: Fantasy Fandom's Famous Femme*. New York: Warren Publishing Co., 1973.

895 "Here 'It' Is: The Winner of FM's 1973 Monster Make-Up Contest. *Famous Monsters of Filmland*. No. 100. Warren, August 1973.

896 "Here's Heidi!" *An Illustrated History of Heidi Saha: Fantasy Fandom's Famous Femme*. New York: Warren Publishing Co., 1973.

897 "Here's Looking at You Kid." *Famous Monsters of Filmland*. No. 203. No. Hollywood, CA: Dynacomm, August/September 1994. p. 3.

898 "He's Gone to Other Space." *Famous Monsters of Filmland*. No. 142. Warren, April 1978. (Richard Carlson)

899 "Hey Young Monster Lovers!" *Monster World*. No. 5. Warren, October 1965.

900 "Hidden Horrors." *Famous Monsters of Filmland*. Vol. 3. No. 4. Whole No. 13. Philadelphia: Central Publications, Inc., August 1961. [pp. 38–39]; *Famous Monsters of Filmland 1965 Yearbook*. No. 3. Warren, 1965. (photo of Claude Rains as the unmasked *Phantom of the Opera*)

901 "Hidden Horrors." *Famous Monsters of Filmland*. Vol. 3. No. 5. Whole No. 14. Philadelphia: Central Publications, Inc., October 1961. [p. 26.] (*Forbidden Planet* "monster from the Id")

902 "Hidden Horrors." *Famous Monsters of Filmland*. No. 35. Warren, October 1965. p. 45. (Mrs. Bates from *Psycho*)

903 "The Hidden Horrors of Mr. Sardonicus." [As "James Ackerman and Forrest J. Warren."] Inside Ackerman. *Famous Monsters of Filmland*. Vol. 4. No. 2. Whole No. 17. Philadelphia: Central Publications, Inc., May 1962. [p. 2.]

904 "Hi-Fi Sci-Fi on TV of Wars and Awards." *Famous Monsters of Filmland*. No. 143. Warren, May 1978. pp. 46–49. (Science Fiction, Fantasy & Horror Award Program)

905 "Highlights in Terra's Future History." *Perry Rhodan*. No. 40. *Red Eye of Betelgeuse*. Clark Darlton. New York: Ace, February 1974.

906 "Hi-Lites of Local Leag Life." *Imagination!* Vol. 1. No. 1. October 1937. p. 9.

907 "Hip! Hip! Forre'..." [As Paul Linden.] *Filmfax: The Magazine of Unusual Film & Television*. Vol. 1. No. 6. March/April 1987. pp. 6–8, 24. (on Ackerman's 70th birthday)

908 "His Last Voyage." *Famous Monsters of Filmland*. No. 138. Warren, October 1977. (obituary of actor Stephen Boyd)

909 "History of Famous Monsters From the Mouth of Forrest J Ackerman." *GUTS The Magazine with Intestinal Fortitude*. No. 4. Ed. Rob & Jeff Gluckson. September 1968. pp. 14–15.

910 "The History of Robots." *Interface Age.* Cerritos, CA: McPheters, Wolfe & Jones, April 1978.

911 "Hitchcock Is Gone!" *Famous Monsters of Filmland.* No. 167. Warren, September 1980. (Sir Alfred Hitchcock obituary)

912 "Hollycon 1." *Locus.* Ed. Dena and Charlie Brown. 11 May 1973.

913 "Holly-weird or Bust." [With Ray Ferry.] *Famous Monsters of Filmland.* No. 202. No. Hollywood, CA: Dynacomm, Spring 1994. pp. 18–21. (interview with Elvira)

914 "Hollywood Film Museum to Capture Kong, Feature Frankenstein." *Famous Monsters of Filmland.* Vol. 5. No. 4. Whole No. 25. Warren Publishing, Inc., October 1963. pp. 22–23.

915 "Hollywood on the Moon." *Amazing Stories.* Ed. Howard Browne. Ziff-Davis Publishing Company, June 1950; *Amazing Stories Quarterly.* Ziff-Davis Publishing Company, Winter 1950.

916 "Hoot 'n' Holler Department." *The Fort MacArthur Bulletin.* Friday 5 February 1943. p. 2-A.

917 "Horrib-Lee Yours." *Famous Monsters of Filmland.* Vol. 1. No. 4. August 1959. pp. 46–49; *Famous Monsters of Filmland: Yearbook No. 2.* [1964] [Warren Publishing Co.], December 1963; *James Warren Presents the Best from Famous Monsters of Filmland.* New York: Paperback Library, 1964; *Famous Monsters of Filmland.* Vol. 1. No. 4. Filmland Classics, May 2008. pp. 46–49. (replica edition)

918 "Horror Castle." *Famous Monsters of Filmland.* No. 44. Warren, May 1967; *Famous Monsters of Filmland 1970 Year Book/Fearbook.* Warren, 1969; *Famous Monsters of Filmland.* No. 90. Warren, May 1972.

919 "Horror Classics Veteran Hollywood Personalities from Decades Past — Elsa Lanchester Remembered: Forrest J Ackerman Recalls His Favorite Femonster." *Filmfax: The Magazine of Unusual Film & Television.* Vol. 1. No. 6. March/April 1987. pp. 25–27.

920 "Horror Express." *Famous Monsters of Filmland.* No. 112. Warren, December 1974. (preview)

921 "The Horror Express." *Famous Monsters of Filmland.* No. 173. Warren, May 1981. (previews)

922 "Horror Hall of Fame." *Famous Monsters of Filmland.* No. 109. Warren, August 1974. (1974 TV special)

923 "Horror Hall of Fame." *Famous Monsters of Filmland.* No. 142. Warren, April 1978. (James Warren's receipt of the Science Fiction, Horror & Fantasy Hall of Fame award)

924 "The Horror Horizon." *Famous Monsters of Filmland.* No. 190. Warren, January 1983. pp. 6–10.

925 "Horror Hotel." *Famous Monsters of Filmland.* No. 40. Warren, August 1966. pp. 16–19; *Famous Monsters of Filmland.* No. 63. Warren, March 1970; *Famous Monsters of Filmland.* No. 119. Warren, September 1975.

926 "Horror of Dracula, Jr." *Famous Monsters of Filmland.* No. 47. Warren, November 1967.

927 "The Horror Show." *Famous Monsters of Filmland.* No. 154. Warren, June 1979.

928 "Horrors Ahead!" *Famous Monsters of Filmland.* No. 112. Warren, December 1974.

929 "Horror's Hottest Newcomer." *Famous Monsters of Filmland.* Vol. 3. No. 4. Whole No. 13. Philadelphia: Central Publications, Inc., August 1961. [pp. 46–51.] (Bob Burns)

930 "Horror's New Hotshot." *Famous Monsters of Filmland.* No. 179. Warren, November 1981. (director David Cronenberg)

931 "Horrors of Spider Island." *Famous Monsters of Filmland.* No. 34. Warren, August 1965. pp. 23–29. (German film)

932 "Horrorwood Screamiere." *Famous Monsters of Filmland.* No. 33. Warren, May 1965. pp. 40–42. (coverage of *The Tomb of Ligeia* premiere)

933 "House at the End of the World." *Famous Monsters of Filmland.* No. 32. Warren, March 1965. (1965 film released as *Die, Monster, Die!*)

934 "The House in the Twilight Zone." *Famous Monsters of Filmland.* No. 81. Warren, December 1970.

935 "The House in the Twilight Zone." (part 1) [As Paul Linden.] *Famous Monsters of Filmland.* No. 142. Warren, April 1978. (on the "Son of Ackermansion")

936 "The House in the Twilight Zone." (part 2) [As Paul Linden.] *Famous Monsters of Filmland.* No. 143. Warren, May 1978. pp. 50–57.

937 "The House in the Twilight Zone." *Science Fiction Worlds of Forrest J Ackerman and Friends.* Reseda, CA: Powell Publications, 1969; *Expanded Science Fiction Worlds of Forrest J Ackerman & Friends PLUS.* Rockville, MD: Sense of Wonder Press. 2002.

938 "House of Dark Shadows." *Famous Monsters of Filmland.* No. 82. Warren, February 1971. (preview)

939 "House of Dracula." *Famous Monsters of Filmland.* No. 43. Warren, March 1967; *Famous Monsters of Filmland.* No. 84. Warren, June 1971. (filmbook)

940 "House of Wax." *Famous Monsters of Filmland.* No. 45. Warren, July 1967; *Famous Monsters of Filmland.* No. 149. Warren, November 1978.

941 "The House that Dripped Blood." *Famous Monsters of Filmland.* No. 86. Warren, September 1971; *Famous Monsters of Filmland.* No. 137. Warren, September 1977. pp. 20–25; *Famous Monsters of Filmland.* No. 158. Warren, October 1979.

942 "How Hollywood Creates a Monster." *Famous Monsters of Filmland.* Vol. 1. No. 1. Philadelphia: Central Publications, Inc., 1958. pp. 44–51. (on Paul Blaisdell); *Famous Monsters of Filmland.* Vol. 1. No. 1. Filmland Classics, January 2008. pp. 44–51. (replica edition)

943 "How to Go to the Devil." *Famous Monsters of Filmland.* No. 123. Warren, March 1976. (the North American Science Fiction Convention)

944 "How to Hurt a Guy." *Monster World.* No. 9. New York: Warren, July 1966. p. 47.

945 "How to Make a Monster." *Famous Monsters of Filmland.* No. 163. Warren, May 1980. (filmbook)

946 "How to Make a Mummy Chaney Takes the Wrap." *Famous Monsters of Filmland.* No. 94. Warren, November 1972.

947 "The Human Monster." *Famous Monsters of Filmland.* No. 45. Warren, July 1967; *Famous Monsters of Filmland.* No. 119. Warren, September 1975.

948 "Humanoids from the Deep." *Famous Monsters of Filmland.* No. 165. Warren, July 1980. (preview)

949 "Hunch-Facts of Notre Dame." *Famous Monsters of Filmland.* No. 37. Warren, February 1966; *Famous Monsters of Filmland 1969 Year Book/Fearbook.* New York: Warren Publishing Co., 1968.

950 "The Hunchback of Notre Dame." [With Janet Reid and G. John Edwards-uncredited.] *Famous Monsters of Filmland.* No. 33. Warren, May 1965. pp. 20–37; *Famous Monsters of Filmland.* No. 55. Warren, May 1969; *Famous Monsters of Filmland.* No. 119. Warren, September 1975. (Ackerman acknowledged the assistance of Reid and Edwards with this filmbook in the "Monster Mail Call" of *Famous Monsters* No. 34, p. 6.)

951 "The Hunchback of Yokohama?" *Famous Monsters of Filmland.* No. 26. Warren Publishing, Inc., January 1964. p. 2.

952 "The Hunchbacks of Notre Dame, part 1." *Famous Monsters of Filmland.* No. 83. Warren, April 1971.

953 "The Hunchbacks of Notre Dame, part 2." *Famous Monsters of Filmland.* No. 84. Warren, June 1971.

954 "Hyde from the Sun." *Famous Monsters of Filmland.* No. 32. Warren, March 1965. (*The Hideous Sun Demon*)

955 "I Bid You Welcome!— Dr. Ackula." *Forrest J Ackerman's Monsterama.* No. 1. Seattle, WA: Fantagraphics Books, May 1991. p. 1. (Editorial)

956 "I Remember Morojo." *Myrtle Rebecca Douglas: An Appreciation.* (February 1965 FAPA mailing)

957 "I Was a Tin Age Robot." [As "McKanical Mann."] *Famous Monsters of Filmland.* Vol. 3. No. 6. Whole No. 15. Philadelphia: Central Publications, Inc., January 1962. pp. 16–22; *James Warren Presents Famous Monsters of Filmland Strike Back!* New York: Paperback Library, 1965; *Famous Monsters of Filmland.* No. 93. Warren, October 1972; *Famous Monsters of Filmland.* No. 168. Warren, October 1980.

958 "Ideas, Etc." *The Buccaneer.* San Francisco, CA: Balboa High School, Thursday 16 February 1933. (humorous riffs on the names of some of Ackerman's high school classmates)

959 "If We Don't End War, War Will End Us." *Worlds of Tomorrow: The Amazing Universe of Science Fiction Art.* Portland, OR: Collectors Press, 2004. pp. 135–136.

960 "If You Knew Julie." Theakston, Greg & Evanier, Mark. *Julius Schwartz Non-Surprise Party Program Book August 4, 1989.* (song tribute to editor Julius "Julie" Schwartz sung to the tune of "If You Knew Susie")

961 "I'm Through." [As Foo E. Onya.] *Futuria Fantasia.* No. 2. Ed. Ray Bradbury. Los Angeles, CA: Fall 1939; *Futuria Fantasia.* Ray Bradbury. Los Angeles: Graham, 2007.

962 "Imagi-Movie Marvels." *Famous Monsters of Filmland.* No. 187. Warren, September 1982.

963 "An Imagi-Movie odyssey." *Worlds of Horror.* No. 2. Ed. Darren Gross. Electric Publishing, August 1989. pp. 2–3. (installment of what was to have been a column)

964 "Imagi-Movies." *Fan Slants.* Vol. 1. No. 2. Ed. Mel Brown. February 1944.

965 "Imagi-Movies." *Polaris.* No. 1. Ed. Paul Freehafer. December 1939.

966 "Imagi-Movies." *Polaris.* Vol. 1. No. 3. Ed. Paul Freehafer. June 1940.

967 "Imagi-nik-nax." *Imagination!* Vol. 1. No. 3. December 1937. p. 3.

968 "Imagi-nik-nax." [As Weaver Wright.] *Imagination!* Vol. 1. No. 10. July 1938.

969 "In Memoriam: Dorothy B. Stratten." *Famous Monsters of Filmland.* No. 172. Warren, April 1981.

970 "In Memoriam — Harl Vincent." *Nebula Award Stories 4*. Ed. Poul Anderson. New York: Doubleday 1969; *Nebula Award Stories 4*. Ed. Poul Anderson. UK: Panther, 1971; *Nebula Award Stories Four*. Ed. Poul Anderson. New York: Pocket, 1971.

971 "In Memoriam: J W S." [With Bob Olsen.] *Imagination!* Vol. 1. No. 5. February 1938. p. 3. [writer Joseph William Skidmore (1890–1938)]

972 "In Memoriam: William L. Crawford (1911–1984)." *Fantasy Book*. Ed. Dennis Mallonee & Nick Smith. Pasadena, CA: Fantasy Book Enterprises, June 1984. (longtime fan, editor, and founder of Visionary Press, FPCI., etc)

973 "In the Beginning (The First Decade)." *Gosh! Wow (Boy-oh-Boy)! Science Fiction*. New York: Bantam, 1982.

974 "In the Days of the Dinosaurs." *Famous Monsters of Filmland*. No. 43. Warren, March 1967; *Famous Monsters of Filmland*. No. 88. Warren, January 1972; *Famous Monsters of Filmland*. No. 94. Warren, November 1972.

975 "The Incredible Shrinking Woman." *Famous Monsters of Filmland*. No. 172. Warren, April 1981. (preview)

976 "Infirmary Blues." *The Fort MacArthur Bulletin*. Friday 5 February 1943. p. 3-A.

977 "Ingrid Pitt." *Famous Monsters of Filmland*. No. 122. Warren, January 1976.

978 "Innside Darkst Ackernam [*sic*]: Etaoin Shrdlu Qwertyuiop?" *Famous Monsters of Filmland*. Vol. 5. No. 3. Whole No. 24. Warren Publishing, Inc., August 1963. p. 3; *Forrest J Ackerman, Famous Monster of Filmland*. Pittsburgh, PA: Imagine, 1986. pp. 104–105.

979 "Inside Ackerman." *Famous Monsters of Filmland*. Vol. 3. No. 5. Whole No. 14. Philadelphia: Central Publications, Inc., October 1961. [p. 3.]

980 "Inside Ackerman." *Famous Monsters of Filmland*. Vol. 4. No. 1. Whole No. 16. Philadelphia: Central Publications, Inc., March 1962. [p. 3.] (on the return of Warren's briefcase)

981 "Inside Ackerman." *Famous Monsters of Filmland*. Vol. 4. No. 2. Whole No. 17. Philadelphia: Central Publications, Inc., May 1962. [p. 4.]

982 "Inside Ackerman." [as Forrest K Akermann] [*sic*] *Famous Monsters of Filmland*. No. 18. Philadelphia: Central Publications, Inc., July 1962. [p. 3]; *Forrest J Ackerman, Famous Monster of Filmland*. Pittsburgh, PA: Imagine, Inc. 1986. p. 90. (on the relatively typo-free "perfect issue")

983 "Inside Ackerman." *Famous Monsters of Filmland*. No. 57. Warren, September 1969. p. 3. (photo of Ackerman with artist Basil Gogos)

984 "Inside Ackerman." *Famous Monsters of Filmland*. No. 60. Warren, December 1969. (subheaded "Picture of Enthusiasm!")

985 "Inside Ackerman." *Famous Monsters of Filmland*. No. 61. Warren, January 1970.

986 "Inside Ackerman." *Famous Monsters of Filmland*. No. 62. Warren, February 1970.

987 "Inside Ackerman." *Famous Monsters of Filmland*. No. 63. Warren, March 1970.

988 "Inside Ackerman." *Graveyard Examiner: The Official Newsletter of the FJA/Famous Monsters Club*. Vol. 1. No. 1. Dynacomm, 1994. pp. 1–4.

989 "Inside Ackerman." *Graveyard Examiner: The Official Newsletter of the FJA/Famous Monsters Club*. Vol. 1. No. 2. Dynacomm, 1994.

990 "Inside Ackerman, Three Creepy People." *Famous Monsters of Filmland*. No. 59. Warren, November 1969.

991 "Inside Darkest Ackerman." *Famous Monsters of Filmland*. Vol. 5. No. 2. Whole No. 23. June 1963. p. 3.

992 "Inside Darkest Ackerman. *Famous Monsters of Filmland*. No. 26. Warren Publishing, Inc., January 1964.

993 "Inside Darkest Acula." *Famous Monsters of Filmland*. Vol. 3. No. 4. Whole No. 13. Philadelphia: Central Publications, Inc., August 1961. [pp. 40–44]; *Famous Monsters of Filmland 1965 Yearbook*. No. 3. Warren, 1965. (*The Incredible Shrinking Man*)

994 "Inside Darkest Acula." *Famous Monsters of Filmland*. Vol. 3. No. 6. Whole No. 15. Philadelphia: Central Publications, Inc., January 1962. [pp. 40–44]; *Famous Monsters of Filmland*. No. 42. Warren, January 1967. (*Invasion of the Body Snatchers*)

995 "Inside Darkest Acula." *Famous Monsters of Filmland*. No. 18. Philadelphia: Central Publications, Inc., July 1962. [pp. 26–33]; *Famous Monsters of Filmland Year Book/Fearbook*. New York: Warren Publishing Co., 1969. (on *The Amazing Colossal Man*.)

996 "Inside Darkest Acula." *Famous Monsters of Filmland*. No. 37. Warren, February 1966. (*Fiend Without a Face*)

997 "Inside Greenest Ackerman." *Famous Monsters of Filmland*. Vol. 5. No. 4. Whole No. 25. Warren Publishing, Inc., October 1963. p. 3.

998 "Inside the Monster." *Famous Monsters of Filmland*. No. 27. Warren Publishing, Inc., March 1964. p. 3.

999 "Interview: Catherine L. Moore." [As Jack Erman.] *Futurian War Digest*. Vol. 2. No. 1. October 1941.

1000 "Interview with Edgar Rice Burroughs." *Science Fiction Monthly.* No. 17. Melbourne, Australia: Atlas Publications Pty. Ltd., January 1957.

1001 "Into the Mothership." *Famous Monsters of Filmland.* No. 168. Warren, October 1980. (*Close Encounters of the Third Kind: The Special Edition*)

1002 "Introducing Imagination!" *Imagination!* Vol. 1. No. 1. October 1937. p. 12.

1003 "Introducing Perry Rhodan and His Electric Personality." *Perry Rhodan. No. 1. Enterprise Stardust.* K. H. Scheer & Walter Ernsting. New York: Ace Books, 1969, Ace, 1972, Ace, 1974.

1004 "Introducing the Author." *Imaginative Tales.* Vol. 3. No. 3. Ed. William L. Hamling. Greenleaf Publishing, May 1956. pp. 2, 131. (autobiographical remarks)

1005 "Introduction." *Best Science Fiction for 1973.* New York: Ace, 1973. pp. 9–15.

1006 "Introduction." *I, Vampire: Interviews with the Undead.* Stamford, CT: Longmeadow Press. 1995; Clemmons, NC: Renaissance E Books, 2001.

1007 "Introduction." *Metropolis.* Thea von Harbou. New York: Ace Books, 1963; 1975; as "Metropolis Ueber Alles." *Science Fiction Worlds of Forrest J Ackerman and Friends.* Reseda, CA: Powell Publications, 1969; *Adam.* July 1973; *Expanded Science Fiction Worlds of Forrest J Ackerman & Friends PLUS.* Rockville, MD: Sense of Wonder Press, 2002. (introduction to Thea von Harbou novel)

1008 "Introduction." *Science Fiction Worlds of Forrest J Ackerman and Friends.* Reseda, CA: Powell Publications, 1969. pp. 9–11.

1009 "Introduction." [With Jean Stine.] *Reel Future: The Stories That Inspired 16 Classic Science Fiction Movies.* Ed. with Jean Marie Stine. New York: Barnes & Noble Books, 1994; *Die Vergangenheit der Zukunft: Die Originalstories hinter den grossen Science-fiction-Filmen.* Nürnberg: Burgschmiet Verlag, 1998.

1010 "Introduction Just Call Me the Man with a Thousand Faces." *Famous Forry Fotos: Over 70 Years of AckerMemories.* Rockville, MD: Sense of Wonder Press, 2001.

1011 "Introduction: Pursuit to Mars." *Perry Rhodan. No. 16. Secret Barrier X.* W. W. Shols. New York: Ace Books, 1972. (introduces serialization of Garrett P. Serviss' *Edison's Conquest of Mars*)

1012 "Introduction-The Love and Lure of 'The Blind Spot.'" *The Blind Spot.* Hall, Austin and Homer Eon Flint. Philadelphia, PA: Prime Press, 1951; *Science Fiction Worlds of Forrest J Ackerman and Friends.* Reseda, CA: Powell Publications, 1969; New York: Ace Science Fiction Classic, 1976; *Expanded*

Science Fiction Worlds of Forrest J Ackerman & Friends PLUS. Rockville, MD: Sense of Wonder Press, 2002. (introduces work originally serialized in *Argosy* in 1921)

1013 "Introduction to an Unnamed Nondescript." [As Weaver Wright.] *Frontier.* Vol. 1. No. 2. Ed. Donn Brazier. Milwaukee, WI: September 1940.

1014 "Invasion of the Body Snatchers." *Famous Monsters of Filmland.* No. 151. Warren, March 1979. (1978 remake)

1015 "Invasion of the Saucer Men." *Famous Monsters of Filmland.* No. 38. Warren, April 1966. pp. 28–33; *Famous Monsters of Filmland 1969 Year Book/Fearbook.* New York: Warren Publishing Co., 1968; *Famous Monsters of Filmland 1970 Year Book/Fearbook.* Warren, 1969; *Warren Presents Movie Aliens Illustrated.* (*Warren Presents.* No. 4.) Warren, September 1979.

1016 "Invasion of the 2-Faced Monsters." *Famous Monsters of Filmland.* No. 28. Warren Publishing, Inc., May 1964. (photo mash-ups of horror film monsters)

1017 "Island of Lost Souls." *Forrest J Ackerman's Fantastic Movie Memories: Forrest Ackerman's Treasure Trove of Imagi-Movies.* Canoga Park, CA: New Media Books, 1985.

1018 "Island of Terror." *Famous Monsters of Filmland.* No. 42. Warren, January 1967.

1019 "It Can Happen Here!" *The Fort MacArthur Bulletin.* Friday 5 February 1943. p. 4-A.

1020 "It Conquered the World." *Monster World.* No. 4. Warren, June 1965.

1021 "It Grew." *Contact!* Ed. Dick & Leah Zeldes Smith for Ditto. (a.k.a. *Spirit of Things Past.* No. 4.) October 2001.

1022 "It Happened One Nite; or A Tale of Two Cities." *Glom.* No. 13. May 1949. (on a banquet held in honor of E. Everett Evans' first fiction sale)

1023 "It Lives by Night." *Famous Monsters of Filmland.* No. 111. Warren, October 1974.

1024 "It's Hare Raising!" *Monster World.* No. 3. Warren, April 1965. (Editorial)

1025 "It's Stfact." *Nova.* No. 3. Ed. Al Ashley. Winter 1943. p. 17. (science fiction trivia contributed by Ackerman, and fans Frank Robinson, Al Ashley, and Bob Tucker)

1026 "It's Utter Kaos." *Famous Monsters of Filmland.* No. 163. Warren, May 1980. (*The Nude Bomb*)

1027 "It's Written in the Stars." *Spacemen.* Vol. 2. No. 1. Whole No. 5. Philadelphia: Spacemen, Inc., October 1962. (Seattle's *A Journey to the Stars, Three Stooges in Orbit, The Night Crawlers* [released as *The Navy vs. the Night Monsters*], *The Day of the Triffids, Witch*, etc.) pp. 7–13.

1028 "Jack Williamson." *Gosh! Wow (Boy-oh-Boy)! Science Fiction*. New York: Bantam, 1982. pp. 23–25. (introduces Williamson's "Born of the Sun," reprints Ackerman's letter in the February 1934 *Astounding Stories*)

1029 "James Bond Meets Spectre: Fiend Number One." *Famous Monsters of Filmland*. No. 47. Warren, November 1967; *Famous Monsters of Filmland*. No. 101. Warren, September 1973.

1030 "James Whale, Frankenstein's Maker, Dead." *Science Fiction Times*. No. 274. (First July 1957 issue) p. 6.

1031 "Jaws of Moonraker." *Famous Monsters of Filmland*. No. 157. Warren, September 1979. (actor Richard Kiel)

1032 "Jaws 2." *Famous Monsters of Filmland*. No. 146. New York: Warren Publishing Co., August 1978.

1033 "Jesse James Meets Frankenstein's Daughter." *Monster World*. No. 8. Warren, May 1966.

1034 "Jewel-y Schwartz!" *Comic Book Marketplace*. Vol. 2. No. 52. Ed. Gary M. Carter. October 1997. p. 61. (Julius Schwartz)

1035 "John Flory." *Science Fiction Chronicle: The Monthly SF and Fantasy Newsmagazine*. Vol. 9. No. 6. Ed. Andrew I. Porter. March 1988. p. 12. (obituary)

1036 "Journey into Terror." *Famous Monsters of Filmland*. No. 152. Warren, April 1979. pp. 58–61. (amateur film)

1037 "Journey to the 7th Planet." *Famous Monsters of Filmland*. No. 43. Warren, March 1967; *Warren Presents Movie Aliens Illustrated*. (*Warren Presents*. No. 4.) Warren, September 1979.

1038 "Journey to the Seventh Planet." *Spacemen*. Vol. 2. No. 1. Whole No. 6. Philadelphia: Spacemen, Inc., January 1963; *Spacemen 1965 Yearbook*. Warren Publishing Co., 1964.

1039 "Jules Verne's Lost World." *Spacemen*. Vol. 1. No. 2. September 1961. Philadelphia: Spacemen, Inc., September 1961.

1040 "Just A-Monks Ourselves." [As Dr. Acula.] *Famous Monsters of Filmland*. No. 31. Warren Publishing Co., December 1964.

1041 "Just Around the Coroner." *Famous Monsters of Filmland*. Vol. 3. No. 3. Whole No. 12. Philadelphia: Central Publications, Inc., June 1961. [pp. 7–14.]

1042 "Just Imagine." *Famous Monsters of Filmland*. No. 81. Warren, December 1970.

1043 "Just Imagine." *Forrest J Ackerman Presents Mr. Monster's Movie Gold: A Treasure Trove of Imagi-Movies*. Ed. Hank Stine. Virginia Beach, VA: Donning Co. 1981. pp. 84–87.

1044 "Just Imagine." *Worlds of Tomorrow: The Amazing Universe of Science Fiction Art*. [With Brad Linaweaver.] Portland, OR: Collectors Press, 2004. pp. 15–17.

1045 "Kaleidoscope: When Worlds Kaleid." *Ackermanthology! 65 Astonishing, Rediscovered Sci-Fi Shorts*. Los Angeles, CA: General Publishing Group. 1997; *Ackermanthology: Millennium Edition 65 Astonishing, Rediscovered Sci-Fi Shorts*. Rockville, MD: Sense of Wonder Press, 2000.

1046 "Karloff in the Magic Castle." [As Paul Linden.] *Famous Monsters of Filmland*. No. 46. Warren, September 1967; *Famous Monsters of Filmland*. No. 56. July 1969; *Famous Monsters of Filmland*. No. 119. Warren, September 1975.

1047 "Karloff in the Magic Castle, Part 2." [As Paul Linden.] *Famous Monsters of Filmland*. No. 47. Warren, November 1967; *Famous Monsters of Filmland*. No. 56. Warren, July 1969; *Famous Monsters of Filmland*. No. 119. Warren, September 1975.

1048 "Karloff Revisited." *Famous Monsters of Filmland*. No. 109. Warren, August 1974.

1049 "Karloff Succumbs at 81." *Science Fiction Times*. No. 464. March 1969. pp. 1–4; *The Frankenscience Monster*. New York: Ace Publishing Corporation, 1969. pp. 12–15.

1050 "Karloff's Monster." *The Fantasy Fan*. Volume 2. No. 6. Whole No. 18. Ed. Charles D. Hornig. Elizabeth, NJ: Charles D. Hornig, February 1935; *The Fantasy Fan—The Fans' Own Magazine (September, 1933 — February, 1935; Vol. 1, Nos. 1–12; vol. 2, Nos. 13–18*. n.p., n.d Tacoma, WA[?]: Lance Thingmaker, 2010.

1051 "Keeping You Posted." *Forrest J Ackerman's Monsters & Imagi-Movies*. Ed. Robert V. Michelucci. Canoga Park, CA: New Media Pub. Co., 1985. pp. 49–54. (reproductions of classic film posters)

1052 "Kelly Freas Mugged." *Science Fiction Chronicle: The Monthly SF and Fantasy Newsmagazine*. Vol. 9. No. 8. Ed. Andrew I. Porter. May 1988. p. 6.

1053 "Kenneth Strickfaden 1897–1984." *Starlog*. No. 83. O'Quinn Studios, June 1984. p. 66.

1054 "The Kentucky Fried Movie." *Famous Monsters of Filmland*. No. 135. Warren, July 1977.

1055 "The King & I." *Famous Monsters of Filmland*. Vol. 5. No. 2. Whole No. No. 23. June 1963. [pp. 57–61]; *Famous Monsters of Filmland*. No. 56. July 1969; *The Frankenscience Monster*. New York:

Ace Publishing Corporation, 1969. pp. 152–155. (Ackerman's interview of Boris Karloff)

1056 "The King Is Gone" (Karloff Called to Death's Domain). *Famous Monsters of Filmland.* No. 56. July 1969. p. 3; *Forrest J Ackerman Famous Monster of Filmland #2.* Volume II (Issues #51–100). Universal City, CA: Hollywood Publishing Company, 1991. p. 29.

1057 "King Karloff Monarch of the Macabre." *Famous Monsters of Filmland.* No. 200. Orange, NJ: Dynacomm, May 1993. pp. 16–25.

1058 "King Karloff Remembered." *Forrest J Ackerman's Monster Land.* No. 1. Canoga Park, CA: New Media Publishing, Inc., December 1984. p. 6. (photo from *The Raven* with caption)

1059 "King Karloff Remembered." *Forrest J Ackerman's Monster Land.* No. 2. [Canoga Park, CA: New Media Pub. Co.], April 1985. p. 64. (captioned still of Boris Karloff as Dr. Scarabus in 1963 film *The Raven*)

1060 "King Kong Is Coming Back!" *Famous Monsters of Filmland.* Vol. 5. No. 3. Whole No. 24. Warren Publishing, Inc., August 1963. pp. 16–23; *Famous Monsters of Filmland.* No. 93. Warren, October 1972.

1061 "King Kong Kommercial." *Famous Monsters of Filmland.* No. 126. Warren, July 1976.

1062 "King Kong Koverage: Is It Spiderman? No! It's the Spider Scene!" *Mondo Cult.* No. 1. Ed. Jessie Lilley. Mondo Cult, Studio City, CA: 2005.

1063 "King Kong 1977." *Famous Monsters of Filmland.* No. 125. Warren, May 1976.

1064 "King Kong 1977." *Famous Monsters of Filmland.* No. 132. Warren, March 1977.

1065 "King of the Hill." *Famous Monsters of Filmland.* No. 202. No. Hollywood, CA: Dynacomm, Spring 1994. pp. 18–21. (introduction to Stephen King's 1961 story "The Killer")

1066 "King of the Lost Planet Rocketmen." *Spacemen.* Vol. 2. No. 3. Whole No. 7. Warren Publishing, Inc., September 1963.

1067 "Kong Men Die." *Famous Monsters of Filmland.* No. 100. Warren, August 1973. (Robert Armstrong & Merian C. Cooper)

1068 "Kong Turns Fifty." *Science Fiction Chronicle: The Monthly Science Fiction and Fantasy Newsmagazine.* Vol. 4. No. 11. Ed. Andrew Porter. August 1983. pp. 26–27.

1069 "Kongfidentially Yours." *Famous Monsters of Filmland.* No. 6. Philadelphia: Central Publications, Inc., February 1960. pp. 22–32; *Famous Monsters Yearbook.* No. 1. Summer-Fall 1962; *James Warren Presents the Best from Famous Monsters of Filmland.* New York: Paperback Library, 1964; *Famous Monsters 1968 Yearbook.* Warren, 1967; *Famous Monsters of Filmland.* Vol. 1. No. 4. Filmland Classics, May 2008. pp. 22–32. (replica edition)

1070 "Kong's King." *Forrest J Ackerman Presents Mr. Monster's Movie Gold: A Treasure Trove of Imagi-Movies.* Ed. Hank Stine. Virginia Beach, VA: Donning Co. 1981. pp. 88–93.

1071 "Kong's 'Mother' Dies." *Famous Monsters of Filmland.* No. 148. Warren, October 1978. (obituary for screenwriter Ruth Rose)

1072 "L. Ron Hubbard: Fond Remembrance — With Warts." *Science Fiction Chronicle: The Monthly Science Fiction and Fantasy Newsmagazine.* Vol. 7. No. 7. Ed. Andrew I. Porter. April 1986. p. 26.

1073 "The Lad of 1000 Faces: A Famous Filmonster Maker of the Future?" *Forrest J Ackerman's Monster Land.* No. 2. [Canoga Park, CA: New Media Pub. Co.], April 1985. pp. 58–59. (on the then 8-year-old David Mezz)

1074 "A Laff at My Expense." *Glom.* No. 7. May 1947. p. 4. (on the rejection of a client's story Ackerman sent to Christian publication *His* without knowing its nature)

1075 "Land of the Giants." *Famous Monsters of Filmland.* No. 55. Warren, May 1969.

1076 "Lang Is a Fan!" *Shangri L'Affaires.* No. 21. December 1944.

1077 "LASFS and the Denvention." *Shangri-La.* No. 2. Ed. Walter J. Daugherty. October 1940.

1078 "The Last Man on Earth Is Gone." *Famous Monsters of Filmland.* No. 113. Warren, January 1975. (obituary of Sidney Blackmer)

1079 "Last Minute Noose." [As "Far West Ackerman."] *Favorite Westerns of Filmland.* No. 1. Philadelphia: Central Publications, Inc., May 1960.

1080 "Last Minute Noose." [As "Far West Ackerman."] *Favorite Westerns of Filmland.* No. 2. Philadelphia: Central Publications, Inc., August 1960.

1081 "Last Minute Noose." [As "Far West Ackerman."] *Wildest Westerns.* No. 3. Philadelphia: Central Publications, Inc., October 1960.

1082 "Last Minute Noose." *Monster World.* No. 3. Warren, April 1965.

1083 "Last Minute Noose." (uncredited) *Wildest Westerns.* No. 4. Philadelphia: Central Publications, Inc., January 1961.

1084 "Last Minute Noose." (uncredited) *Wildest Westerns.* No. 5. Philadelphia: Central Publications, Inc., May 1961.

1085 "Last Minute Noose." (uncredited) *Wildest Westerns.* No. 6. Philadelphia: Central Publications, Inc., August 1961.

1086 "The Last Page." *Science Fiction Times.* No. 368. August 1961. (obituary of pulp writer Norvell W. Page)

1087 "Last Roundup." *Forrest J Ackerman's Fantastic Movie Memories: Forrest Ackerman's Treasure Trove of Imagi-Movies.* Canoga Park, CA: New Media Books, 1985.

1088 "The Last War." *Spacemen.* Vol. 2. No. 3. Whole No. 7. Warren Publishing, Inc., September 1963.

1089 "Late Scientificinema Flash." *Science Fiction Digest.* South Ozone Park, NY: Maurice Z. Ingher, October 1932.

1090 "L'cran a Quatre Dimensions." *Fiction.* France: June 1955. (guest review of Disneyland TV episode *Man in Space*)

1091 "The Legendary Lon." *Forrest J Ackerman Presents Mr. Monster's Movie Gold: A Treasure Trove of Imagi-Movies.* Ed. Hank Stine. Virginia Beach, VA: Donning Co. 1981. pp. 76–83.

1092 "Leo Margulies." *Luna Monthly.* No. 62. Ed. Ann F. Dietz. Oradell, NJ: February, 1976. pp. 12, 17. (Ackerman's eulogy for pulp publisher)

1093 "Lest I Forget..." *Amazing Forries: this is your life, Forrest J Ackerman.* Hollywood, CA: Metropolis Publications/Warren, 1976. p. 19. (continuing list of friends, supporters, influences)

1094 "Let Me Call You Swedeheart Forry Ackerman Does Stockholm." *Cult Movies.* No. 30. 1999. pp. 78–79.

1095 "Let's Not Get Gay." *The Alchemist.* Ed. Charles Hansen. Autumn 1946.

1096 "Letter from a Vampire." *Famous Monsters of Filmland.* Vol. 2. No. 7. Philadelphia: Central Publications, Inc., June 1960. pp. 46–49. (pun-laden missive from "Dr. Scalpela")

1097 "A Letter from Mr. Sci-Fi." *Spaceway Science Fiction.* Vol. 4. No. 1. Ed. William L. Crawford. CA: Fantasy Publishing Company, January 1969. (column)

1098 "A Letter from Mr. Sci-Fi." *Spaceway Science Fiction.* Vol. 4. No 2. Ed. William L. Crawford. CA: Fantasy Publishing Company, May/June. 1969.

1099 "A Letter from Mr. Sci-Fi." *Spaceway Science Fiction.* Vol. 4. No. 3. Ed. William L. Crawford. Fantasy Publishing Company, September-October 1969

1100 "A Letter from Mr. Sci-Fi." *Spaceway Science Fiction.* Vol. 5. No. 1. Ed. William L. Crawford. Fantasy Publishing Company, May-June 1970.

1101 "Letter to a Lycanthrope." *Famous Monsters of Filmland.* No. 99. Warren, July 1973.

1102 "Lt. Col. (Ret.) Oscar Garner Estes, Jr." *Science Fiction Chronicle: The Monthly Science Fiction and Fantasy Newsmagazine.* Vol. 8. No. 1. Ed. Andrew I. Porter. October 1986. p. 10.

1103 "Life Thief." *Famous Monsters of Filmland.* Vol. 1. No. 3. Philadelphia: Central Publications, Inc., April 1959. (*The 4-D Man*)

1104 "A Little Funtasy." *Forrest J Ackerman's Fantastic Movie Memories: Forrest Ackerman's Treasure Trove of Imagi-Movies.* Canoga Park, CA: New Media Books, 1985.

1105 "The Living Ghost." *Famous Monsters of Filmland.* No. 106. Warren, April 1974. (on actor John Agar prematurely announced as having died)

1106 "Lon Chaney." *Forrest J Ackerman's Monster Land.* No. 1. Canoga Park, CA: New Media Publishing, Inc., December 1984. p. 66. (two photographs of Chaney, Sr. with captions)

1107 "Lon Chaney Shall Not Die!" *Famous Monsters of Filmland.* Vol. 3. No. 5. Whole No. 14. Philadelphia: Central Publications, Inc., October 1961; *Famous Monsters of Filmland 1965 Yearbook.* No. 3. Warren, 1965. (photo from *London After Midnight*)

1108 "Lon Chaney Shall Not Die!" *Famous Monsters of Filmland.* Vol. 4. No. 1. Whole No. 16. Philadelphia: Central Publications, Inc., March 1962. [p. 48]; *Famous Monsters of Filmland.* No. 93. Warren, October 1972. (photo of Chaney Sr. "unmasked" sans make-up)

1109 "Lon Chaney Shall Not Die!" *Famous Monsters of Filmland.* No. 18. Philadelphia: Central Publications, Inc., July 1962; *Famous Monsters of Filmland 1965 Yearbook.* No. 3. Warren, 1965; *Famous Monsters of Filmland 1972 Fearbook.* Warren, 1971. (photo of Chaney from *The Road to Mandalay*)

1110 "Lon Chaney Shall Not Die!" *Forrest J Ackerman's Monster Land.* No. 2. [Canoga Park, CA: New Media Pub. Co.], April 1985. p. 66. (Chaney Sr. still from 1925 film *The Monster*)

1111 "Lon Chaney Shall Not Die." "*It's Alive! @85.*" Ed. Jeffrey Roberts & George Chastain. A MonsterBoom Special Publication, November 2001. p. 6.

1112 "Lon Chaney, Sr." *Famous Monsters of Filmland.* No. 102. Warren, October 1973.

1113 "Lon Chaney's 100th Birthday." *Fantasy Newsletter.* No. 59. Ed. Robert A. Collins. Boca Raton, FL: Florida Atlantic University, May 1983. p. 17.

1114 "Lon Is Gone." *Famous Monsters of Filmland.* No. 103. Warren, December 1973. p. 28. (obituary of Lon Chaney, Jr.)

1115 "London After Midnight, Part 1." [As Norris Chapnick and Ron Borst.] *Famous Monsters of Filmland.* No. 69. Warren, September 1970.

1116 "London After Midnight, Part 2." *Famous Monsters of Filmland.* No. 80. Warren, October 1970.

1117 "The Lone Stranger." *Famous Monsters of Filmland.* Vol. 4. No. 2. Whole No. 17. Philadelphia: Central Publications, Inc., May 1962. [pp. 21–25]; *Famous Monsters of Filmland 1965 Yearbook.* No. 3. Warren, 1965; *Famous Monsters of Filmland 1972 Yearbook.* Warren, 1971; *Famous Monsters of Filmland.* No. 105. Warren, March 1974. (actor Glenn Strange)

1118 "Long Live the King." *"It's Alive!@85"* Jeffrey Roberts & George Chastain. A MonsterBoom Special Publication, November 2001. p. 11. (memories of Karloff's recording *An Evening with Boris Karloff and His Friends*)

1119 "Look & Find Out." *Imagination!* Vol. 1. No. 1. October 1937. p. 16.

1120 "Look to the Future." *Spacemen.* Vol. 2. No. 3. Whole No. 7. Warren Publishing, Inc., September 1963.

1121 "The Lord of the Rings." *Famous Monsters of Filmland.* No. 151. Warren, March 1979. (Ralph Bakshi's 1978 animated film)

1122 "Lord of the Rings." *The Lord of the Rings: The Official Authorized Magazine of J. R. R. Tolkien's Classic Fantasy Epic.* A Warren Special Edition. Warren, 1979. pp. 6–43. (filmbook)

1123 "Lords of the Rotoscope." *The Lord of the Rings: The Official Authorized Magazine of J. R. R. Tolkien's Classic Fantasy Epic.* A Warren Special Edition. Warren, 1979. pp. 46–47.

1124 "The Lorre Story." *Famous Monsters of Filmland.* Vol. 4. No. 19. Philadelphia: Central Publications, Inc., September 1962; *Famous Monsters of Filmland 1965 Yearbook.* No. 3. Warren, 1965; *Famous Monsters of Filmland 1972 Yearbook.* Warren, 1971.

1125 "Los Angeles Beckons." *Pacificon News.* No. 1. March 1946. p. 6.

1126 "Los Angeles Fanzines." [As Weaver Wright.] *Shangri-La.* No. 12. CA: July 1949.

1127 "Lost Monster Movie Found." *Famous Monsters of Filmland.* No. 35. Warren, October 1965. pp. 20–21. (*Peer Gynt*)

1128 "Lost Planet." [As Geoffrey Giles with Walter Gillings.] *Fantasy.* No. 1. Ed. Walter Gillings. Temple Bar Pub. Co., December 1946. (Ackerman may have collaborated with Gillings on this piece)

1129 "The Lost World." *Famous Monsters of Filmland.* No. 183. Warren, May 1982.

1130 "Lou Barron." *Science Fiction Chronicle: The Monthly SF and Fantasy Newsmagazine.* Vol. 11. No. 4. Ed. Andrew I. Porter. January 1990. p. 8. (scorer of *Forbidden Planet*)

1131 "The Love & Lure of Lugosi." *Famous Monsters of Filmland.* No. 200. Orange, NJ: Dynacomm, May 1993. pp. 8–15.

1132 "Love at First Bite." *Famous Monsters of Filmland.* No. 154. Warren, June 1979. (preview)

1133 "Love Letters from My Fan Club." *Amazing Forries: this is your life, Forrest J Ackerman.* pp. 21–22. (criticism received and contretemps he was involved in)

1134 "Loveliest of Fiends." Famous Monsters of Filmland. No. 202. No. Hollywood, CA: Dynacomm, Spring 1994. pp. 36–38. (film *Innocent Blood*)

1135 "The Luckiest Boy in the World." *Famous Monsters of Filmland.* Vol. 3. No. 4. whole No. 13. Philadelphia: Central Publications, Inc., August 1961. [pp. 16–21.] (Monster fan Steve Mazin, then a neighbor of Ackerman)

1136 "Lucky 11." [With James Warren.] *Famous Monsters of Filmland.* Vol. 3. No. 2. Whole No. 11. Philadelphia: Central Publications, Inc., April 1961

1137 "Lugosi Lives Eternal." *Famous Monsters of Filmland.* No. 18. Philadelphia: Central Publications, Inc., July 1962. [pp. 13–14.]

1138 "Lugosi Lives Eternal." *Forrest J Ackerman's Monster Land.* No. 2. [Canoga Park, CA: New Media Pub. Co.], April 1985. p. 65. (still of Bela Lugosi from a 1920's stage performance)

1139 "Lugosi Lives Eternal." *"It's Alive!@85."* Ed. Jeffrey Roberts & George Chastain. A MonsterBoom Special Publication, November 2001. p. 5.

1140 "Lugosi Lives Infernal: Those Who Knew Bela Take Exception to Ed Wood Artistic 'Lie-Sense.'" *Famous Monsters of Filmland.* No. 205. N. Hollywood, CA: Dynacomm, December 1994. pp. 33–34.

1141 "Lugosi's Secret Terror." *Famous Monsters of Filmland.* Vol. 2. No. 9. November 1960; *James Warren Presents Son of Famous Monsters of Filmland.* New York: Paperback Library, 1965. [pp. 22–26.]

1142 "Luna Ill!" *Famous Monsters of Filmland.* No. 145. Warren, July 1978. (Carroll Borland)

1143 "Luna Lives!" *Famous Monsters of Filmland.* No. 149. Warren, November 1978.

1144 "Lurk Burke Lurk." *Famous Monsters of Filmland.* Vol. 4. No. 5. Whole No. 20. Philadelphia: Central Publications, Inc., November 1962. pp. 27, 29–32.

1145 "Lurking Ahead." *Famous Monsters of Filmland.* No. 62. Warren, February 1970.

1146 "Lurking Ahead." *Famous Monsters of Filmland*. No. 63. Warren, March 1970.

1147 "Lurking Ahead." *Monster World*. Vol. 1. No. 1. New York: Warren Publishing Co., November 1964.

1148 "Lurking Goreward." *Famous Monsters of Filmland*. No. 133. Warren, April 1977. (previews)

1149 "Macabre Messing in Deadly Blessing." *Famous Monsters of Filmland*. No. 177. Warren, September 1981. (preview)

1150 "The Mad Ghoul." *Famous Monsters of Filmland*. No. 180. Warren, January 1982.

1151 "Mad Labs: The Laboratory Story!" *Famous Monsters of Filmland*. Vol. 2. No. 7. Philadelphia: Central Publications, Inc., June 1960. [pp. 40–45]; "Boys Will Be Beasts." *James Warren Presents Famous Monsters of Filmland Strike Back!* New York: Paperback Library, 1965 (stills with captions of various mad scientist laboratories in films)

1152 "Madam Satan." [As Laurajean Ermayne.] *Tease!: The Magazine of Sexy Fun*. Ed. Greg Theakston. Marietta, GA: Pure Imagination Publishing, 1996. (on 1930 Cecil B. DeMille film)

1153 "The Maddest Doctor." *Monster World*. Vol. 1. No. 1. New York: Warren Publishing Co., November 1964; *Famous Monsters of Filmland 1971 Fearbook*. Warren, 1970; *Famous Monsters of Filmland*. No. 58. Warren, October 1969. (Lionel Atwill)

1154 "Madge's Prize Mss." No. 1. *Mikros*. No. 2. Ed. Russ Hodgkins. October 1938.

1155 "Madhouse." *Famous Monsters of Filmland*. No. 109. Warren, August 1974.

1156 "Maestro of Monsters." *Famous Monsters of Filmland*. No. 185. Warren, July 1982. (writer-producer Alex Gordon)

1157 "Magic Milestone." *Perry Rhodan. No. 100. Desert of Death's Domain*. Kurt Mahr. New York: Ace, August 1976.

1158 "The Maelstrom." *Perry Rhodan Special Release: Menace of Atomigeddon*. Kurt Mahr. / *Flight from Tarkihl*. Clark Darlton. New York: Ace, October 1977.

1159 "Make This Really a World Convention." *Philcon News*. No. 1. Ed. Robert A. Madle & Jack Agnew. February 1947. p. 4. (on the need for including international fans in the World Science Fiction Convention)

1160 "Making Monsters." *Famous Monsters of Filmland*. No. 31. Warren Publishing Co., December 1964. pp. 60–63.

1161 "Making Monsters the Professionals Show You How!" *Famous Monsters of Filmland*. No. 28. Warren Publishing, Inc., May 1964. pp. 67–69.

1162 "The Maltese Bippy." *Famous Monsters of Filmland*. No. 58. Warren, October 1969.

1163 "The Man Behind the Mask." *Fantasy Book*. Vol. 1. No. 1. Ed. Garret Ford. Fantasy Publishing Company, Inc. July 1947.

1164 "The Man Behind the Monster." [With Jack Taylor.] *The Frankenscience Monster*. New York: Ace Publishing Corporation, 1969. pp. 40–45.

1165 "A Man for All Seize-Ons." *Famous Monsters of Filmland*. No. 204. No. Hollywood, CA: Dynacomm, November 1994. pp. 36–41. (on Peter Cushing)

1166 "Man Made Monster." *Famous Monsters of Filmland*. No. 122. Warren, January 1976.

1167 "The Man of a Thousand Graces: FJA Remembers Vincent the Venerable." *Famous Monsters of Filmland*. No. 203. No. Hollywood, CA: Dynacomm, August/September 1994. pp. 8–9. [on Vincent Price]

1168 "The Man Who Killed the Fly Is Dead." *Famous Monsters of Filmland*. No. 39. Warren, June 1966. pp. 7–8. (Herbert Marshall)

1169 "The Man Who Lived Twice." *Glom*. No. 5. October 1946; *Fantastic Worlds*. [As Alden Lorraine.] Vol. 2. No. 2. Whole No. 6. Ed. Sam Sackett. Los Angeles, CA: Fantastic Worlds/S. J. Sackett, Spring 1954. (about author "Francis Flagg")

1170 "The Man Who Made the Monsters." *Famous Monsters of Filmland*. No. 207. N. Hollywood, CA: Dynacomm, March 1995. pp. 46–51.

1171 "The Man Who Made the Mummy Is No More." *Famous Monsters of Filmland*. No. 65. Warren, May 1970. (Karl Freund)

1172 "The Man with Nine Lives: Vincent Price 1911–1993." *Galaxy*. Vol. 1. No. 1. Ed. E. J. Gold. Penn Valley, CA: Institute for the Development of the Harmonious Human Being, Inc., Jan/Feb 1994. p. 44.

1173 "Maniac." *Famous Monsters of Filmland*. No. 172. Warren, April 1981. (preview)

1174 "The Maniacal Muppet Monsters." *Famous Monsters of Filmland*. No. 159. Warren, November 1979. (*The Muppet Movie*)

1175 "A Manimal Dies." *Famous Monsters of Filmland*. No. 150. Warren, January 1979. (strongman Joe Bonomo)

1176 "Manly P. Hall." *Science Fiction Chronicle: The Monthly SF and Fantasy Newsmagazine*. Vol. 12. No. 4. Ed. Andrew I. Porter. February 1991. p. 14. (Manly Palmer Hall obituary)

1177 "The Manster." *Famous Monsters of Filmland*. No. 28. May 1964. Warren Publishing, Inc., pp. 50–52; *Famous Monsters of Filmland*. No. 114. Warren, March 1975.

1178 "The Many Hands of Orlac." *Famous Monsters of Filmland*. No. 63. Warren, March 1970.

1179 "Many Harpy Returns." *Forrest J Ackerman's Monster Land*. No. 2. [Canoga Park, CA: New Media Pub. Co.], April 1985. p. 41.

1180 "The Mark of the Vampire" (part 1). *Famous Monsters of Filmland*. No. 61. Warren, January 1970.

1181 "The Mark of the Vampire" (part 2). *Famous Monsters of Filmland*. No. 62. Warren, February 1970.

1182 "Mark Patrick Carducci." *Science Fiction Chronicle*. Vol. 19. No. 1. October 1997. p. 22. (obituary)

1183 "The Martian Chronicles." *Famous Monsters of Filmland*. No. 160. Warren, January 1980. (preview of TV mini-series)

1184 "Mary Elizabeth 'Betty' Browder Perdue." *Science Fiction Chronicle: The Monthly SF and Fantasy Newsmagazine*. Vol. 9. No. 8. Ed. Andrew I. Porter. May 1988. p. 11. (obituary)

1185 "Mary's Amazing Monster." [With Donald F. Glut.] *Famous Monsters of Filmland*. No. 63. Warren, March 1970.

1186 "Mary's Monster Lives Again!" *Famous Monsters of Filmland*. No. 202. No. Hollywood, CA: Dynacomm, Spring 1994. pp. 9–11. (remainder of article is interview of Frank Darabont by Mark Patrick Carducci pp. 11–17.)

1187 "The Mask." *Famous Monsters of Filmland*. Vol. 4. No. 1. Whole No. 16. Philadelphia: Central Publications, Inc., March 1962. [pp. 35–39]; *Famous Monsters of Filmland*. No. 93. Warren, October 1972. (captioned stills from 1961 film)

1188 "The Mask of Fu Manchu!" *Famous Monsters of Filmland*. No. 65. Warren, May 1970.

1189 "The Masked Marvel of Monsterville." *Monster World*. No. 3. Warren, April 1965; *Famous Monsters of Filmland*. No. 86. Warren, September 1971. (Don Post, Sr.)

1190 "Masks of the Devil." *Forrest J Ackerman's Fantastic Movie Memories: Forrest Ackerman's Treasure Trove of Imagi-Movies*. Canoga Park, CA: New Media Books, 1985.

1191 "The Master Monster Maker." *Famous Monsters of Filmland*. No. 176. Warren, August 1981. (Terence Fisher)

1192 "Master Monster-Maker Mourned." *Famous Monsters of Filmland*. No. 55. Warren, May 1969. pp. 40–49. (obituary of film make-up artist Jack Pierce)

1193 "Master Monster Maker Winner in Hollywood." *Famous Monsters of Filmland*. No. 33. Warren, May 1965. pp. 16–19. (reader Val Warren)

1194 "Masters of Fantasy: A. Merritt — The Dwellers in the Mirage." *Famous Fantastic Mysteries*. Vol. 9. No. 1. Ed. Mary Gnaedinger. All-Fiction Field, Inc., October 1947. p. 97. (this and other items in the "Masters of Fantasy" series feature only the byline of illustrator Neil Austin, but evidence indicates they were written by Ackerman)

1195 "Masters of Fantasy: Algernon Blackwood — Pan's Gardener." *Famous Fantastic Mysteries*. Vol. 9. No. 4. Ed. Mary Gnaedinger. All-Fiction Field, Inc., April 1948. p. 121.

1196 "Masters of Fantasy: Arthur Machen: Inspirator of Lovecraft." *Famous Fantastic Mysteries*. Vol. 10. No. 2. Ed. Mary Gnaedinger. All-Fiction Field, Inc., December 1948. p. 12.

1197 "Masters of Fantasy: Clark Ashton Smith — The Star-Treader." *Famous Fantastic Mysteries*. Vol. 10. No. 6. Ed. Mary Gnaedinger. All-Fiction Field, Inc., August 1949. p. 109.

1198 "Masters of Fantasy: Dunsany — A True Lord of Fantasy." *Famous Fantastic Mysteries*. Vol. 10. No. 5. Ed. Mary Gnaedinger. All-Fiction Field, Inc., June 1949. p. 113.

1199 "Masters of Fantasy: Edgar Allan Poe — The Pit and the Pen — His Centenary." *Famous Fantastic Mysteries*. Vol. 11. No. 2. Ed. Mary Gnaedinger. All-Fiction Field, Inc., December 1949. p. 113.

1200 "Masters of Fantasy: Edgar Rice Burroughs: Tarzan! Barsoom! Pellucidar!" *Famous Fantastic Mysteries*. Vol. 10. No. 1. Ed. Mary Gnaedinger. All-Fiction Field, Inc., October 1948. p. 117.

1201 "Masters of Fantasy: Herbert George Wells — World Brain." *Famous Fantastic Mysteries*. Vol. 9. No. 5. Ed. Mary Gnaedinger. All-Fiction Field, Inc., June 1948. p. 101.

1202 "Masters of Fantasy: Howard Phillips Lovecraft — The Outsider." *Famous Fantastic Mysteries*. Vol. 8. No. 6. Ed. Mary Gnaedinger. All-Fiction Field, Inc., August 1947. p. 113.

1203 "Masters of Fantasy: John Taine — Reaper of the Rainbow." *Famous Fantastic Mysteries*. Vol. 10. No. 4. Ed. Mary Gnaedinger. All-Fiction Field, Inc., April 1949. p. 87.

1204 "Masters of Fantasy: M. P. Shiel — High Priest of Phantasy." *Famous Fantastic Mysteries*. Vol. 10. No. 3. Ed. Mary Gnaedinger. All-Fiction Field, Inc., February 1949. p. 90.

1205 "Masters of Fantasy: M. R. James — Ghost Writer Number One." *Famous Fantastic Mysteries*. Vol. 11. No. 4. Ed. Mary Gnaedinger. All-Fiction Field, Inc., April 1950. p. 113; [As "M. R. James-

Ghost Writer Number One."] *M. R. James Book of the Supernatural.* Ed. Peter Haining. London: Gollancz, 1975.

1206 "Masters of Fantasy: Olaf Stapledon — Odd John's Father." *Famous Fantastic Mysteries.* Vol. 11. No. 3. Ed. Mary Gnaedinger. All-Fiction Field, Inc., February 1950. p. 121.

1207 "Masters of Fantasy: Ray Bradbury — The October Man." (anonymous/uncredited) *Famous Fantastic Mysteries.* Vol. 11. No. 1. Ed. Mary Gnaedinger. All-Fiction Field, Inc., October 1949. p. 119.

1208 "Masters of Fantasy: Robert William Chambers — Maker of Moons." *Famous Fantastic Mysteries.* Vol. 9. No. 2. Ed. Mary Gnaedinger. All-Fiction Field, Inc., December 1947. p. 97.

1209 "Masters of Fantasy: Sydney Fowler Wright — Worlds of Wonder." *Famous Fantastic Mysteries.* Vol. 9. No. 3. Ed. Mary Gnaedinger. All-Fiction Field, Inc., February 1948. p. 113.

1210 "Masters of Fantasy: Stephen Vincent Benét." [With William Rose Benét.] *Famous Fantastic Mysteries.* Vol. 9. No. 6. Ed. Mary Gnaedinger. All-Fiction Field, Inc., August 1948. p. 113.

1211 "Matter of Life & Death.' *Famous Monsters of Filmland.* Vol. 3. No. 3. Whole No. 12. Philadelphia: Central Publications, Inc., June 1961. [pp. 32–33.] (on monster event staged by the University of California's Alpha Epsilon Pi Fraternity)

1212 "The Mausoleum." *Famous Monsters of Filmland.* No. 181. Warren, March 1982. (interview with Bobbie Bresee)

1213 "Max the Monster." *Famous Monsters of Filmland.* No. 38. Warren, April 1966. pp. 66–69.

1214 "Meet Austin Hall." *Science Fiction Digest.* Vol. 1. No. 10. Jamaica, NY: Conrad H. Ruppert, June 1933.

1215 "Meet Puckys Papas!" *Perry Rhodan. No. 14. Venus in Danger.* Kurt Mahr. New York: Ace, June 1972. 1974. (uncredited but likely by Ackerman)

1216 "Meet the Addams Family." *Monster World.* No. 9. New York: Warren, July 1966.

1217 "Memories of Imagi-Movies." *Forrest J Ackerman's Monsters & Imagi-Movies.* Ed. Robert V. Michelucci. Canoga Park, CA: New Media Pub. Co., 1985. pp. 26–39.

1218 "Menace from the Moon." *Spacemen.* Vol. 1. No. 1. Philadelphia, PA: Spacemen, Inc. July 1961. (*Battle in Outer Space*)

1219 "Metal Monsters." [As Maharba Merritt.] *Famous Monsters of Filmland.* Vol. 3. No. 3. Whole No. 12. Philadelphia: Central Publications, Inc., June 1961. [pp. 17–20]; *James Warren Presents Famous*

Monsters of Filmland Strike Back! New York: Paperback Library, 1965 (byline is a play on Abraham Merritt who authored *The Metal Monster*)

1220 "Meteor." *Famous Monsters of Filmland.* No. 160. Warren, January 1980. (filmbook)

1221 "Meteoriten." *Utopia-Grossband.* No. 22. Germany: 1955. (*Man in Space*)

1222 "Metropolis." *Spacemen.* Vol. 2. No. 1. Whole No. 6. Philadelphia: Spacemen, Inc., January 1963. (part 1 of filmbook)

1223 "Metropolis." *Spacemen.* Vol. 2. No. 3. Whole No. 7. Warren Publishing, Inc., September 1963. (part 2)

1224 "Metropolis." *Spacemen.* No. 8. June 1964. (part 3 of filmbook)

1225 "The Mexicreatures." *Famous Monsters of Filmland.* No. 29. July 1964. Warren Publishing, Inc., pp. 40–47. (monsters from Mexican-made films)

1226 "Mimsy Were the Mumbley-Pega Complains (Forrest) Ackerman." *Lethe.* No. 7. Ed. Jack Riggs. September 1948.

1227 "Mindwarp: An Infinity of Terror." *Famous Monsters of Filmland.* No. 176. Warren, August 1981. (preview of *Galaxy of Terror*)

1228 "Mir-Drac-Ulous Discovery." *Famous Monsters of Filmland.* No. 100. Warren, August 1973.

1229 "The Misery of the Wax Museum." *Famous Monsters of Filmland.* No. 182. Warren, April 1982.

1230 "Mr. Boo-kler." *Forrest J Ackerman's Monster Land.* No. 1. Canoga Park, CA: New Media Publishing, Inc., December 1984. pp. 22–24. (Ackerman interviews special effects artist and filmmaker John Carl Buechler)

1231 "Mr. Gimmick Is Gone." *Famous Monsters of Filmland.* No. 138. Warren, October 1977. (obituary of filmmaker William Castle)

1232 "Mister Monster." *Famous Monsters of Filmland.* No. 8. September 1960. pp. 23–30. includes "a complete list of Lon Chaney's film appearances" pp. 32–33; *James Warren Presents the Best from Famous Monsters of Filmland.* New York: Paperback Library, 1964; *Famous Monsters of Filmland Yearbook.* No. 2. 1964; *Famous Monsters of Filmland.* No. 69. Warren, September 1970. (Lon Chaney, Sr.)

1233 "Mr. Monster Remembered — Forrest J Ackerman remembers the death of Boris Karloff." *Fangoria.* No. 36. July 1984.

1234 "'Mr. Sci-Fi' Sets the Record Straight." *Starlog.* Vol. 8. No. 94. O'Quinn Studios, May 1985. pp. 34–35.

1235 "Mr. Special Effects Gone to the Forbidden Planet." *Famous Monsters of Filmland.* No. 147. Warren, September 1978. pp. 49–51. (obituary of special effects artist Arnold Gillespie)

1236 "Mixed Monsters fiendish foulups of creature features." *Famous Monsters of Filmland.* No. 34. Warren, August 1965. pp. 70–73; *Famous Monsters of Filmland 1971 Fearbook.* Warren, 1970. (correcting errors in past issues)

1237 "The Mole People." *Famous Monsters of Filmland.* No. 29. Warren Publishing, Inc., July 1964. pp. 62–67.

1238 "Monkey Business." *Forrest J Ackerman Presents Mr. Monster's Movie Gold: A Treasure Trove of Imagi-Movies.* Ed. Hank Stine. Virginia Beach, VA: Donning Co. 1981. pp. 94–103.

1239 "Monkey Shines." *Forrest J Ackerman's Monsters & Imagi-Movies.* Ed. Robert V. Michelucci. Canoga Park, CA: New Media Pub. Co., 1985. pp. 40–48. (photos and information on Charles Gemora and other actors who portrayed apes)

1240 "The Monster Eye a Lurk at Things to Come." *Famous Monsters of Filmland.* No. 31. Warren Publishing Co., December 1964. pp. 8–13.

1241 "Monster Kicks on Route 66." [With Steve Jochsberger.] *Famous Monsters of Filmland.* Vol. 4. No. 6. Whole No. 21. February 1963; *Famous Monsters of Filmland.* No. 93. Warren, October 1972.

1242 "The Monster Makers." *Famous Monsters of Filmland.* No. 29. Warren Publishing, Inc., July 1964. pp. 69–71. (part 2)

1243 "The Monster Man, Sire of Slan." *Monsters.* A. E. van Vogt. New York: Paperback Library, February 1965; *Science Fiction Monsters.* A. E. van Vogt. Pocket, September 1967; *Monsters.* A. E. van Vogt. Corgi, 1970; *Monsters.* A. E. van Vogt. Paperback Library, August 1970. (Introduction)

1244 "Monster Mix-Up." *Famous Monsters of Filmland.* No. 39. Warren, June 1966. pp. 47–48.

1245 "Monster Mix-Up." *Famous Monsters of Filmland.* No. 40. Warren, August 1966. pp. 4–7.

1246 "Monster Mix-Up." *Famous Monsters of Filmland.* No. 41. Warren, November 1966. pp. 62–65.

1247 "Monster Mix-Up." *Famous Monsters of Filmland.* No. 42. Warren, January 1967.

1248 "Monster Movie Madness." *Famous Monsters of Filmland.* No. 97. Warren, April 1973. [pp. 22–]; as "Monster Movie Marathon." *Famous Monsters of Filmland.* No. 188. New York: Warren Publishing Co., October 1982. pp. 54–; *Forrest J Ackerman Famous Monster of Filmland #2.* Volume II (Issues #51–100) Universal City, CA: Hollywood Publishing Company, 1991. pp. 70–72, 75–83, 85.

1249 "Monster on the Campus." *Famous Monsters of Filmland.* No. 31. Warren Publishing Co., December 1964. pp. 54–58. (1958 Universal film)

1250 "Monster Speaks." *Forrest J Ackerman's Fantastic Movie Memories: Forrest Ackerman's Treasure Trove of Imagi-Movies.* Canoga Park, CA: New Media Books, 1985. (short piece by Ackerman and fan letters re: *Mr. Monster's Movie Gold*)

1251 "The Monster That Challenged the World!" *Famous Monsters of Filmland.* No. 44. Warren, May 1967; *Famous Monsters of Filmland.* No. 84. Warren, June 1971.

1252 "The Monster Who Made a Man." *Famous Monsters of Filmland.* Vol. 1. No. 2. September 1958. [pp. 26–35.] (Boris Karloff); *James Warren Presents Son of Famous Monsters of Filmland.* New York: Paperback Library, 1965. (uncredited); *The Frankenscience Monster.* New York: Ace Publishing Corporation, 1969. pp. 104–114; *Forrest J Ackerman, Famous Monster of Filmland.* Pittsburgh, PA: Imagine, Inc. 1986. pp. 40–47. (with corrections/updates)

1253 "Monster World Salutes Sir Cedric Hardwicke!" *Monster World.* No. 9. New York: Warren, July 1966; as "Famous Monsters Salutes Sir Cedric Hardwicke." *Famous Monsters of Filmland.* No. 93. Warren, October 1972.

1254 "Monsterama." *Famous Monsters of Filmland.* No. 42. Warren, January 1967.

1255 "Monsterama." *Forrest J Ackerman's Monster Land.* No. 2. [Canoga Park, CA: New Media Pub. Co.], April 1985. pp. 60–61. (captioned stills and posters)

1256 "Monsterama: Rare Treats from the Arcane Archives of Karlon Torgosi." *Forrest J Ackerman's Monster Land.* No. 1. Canoga Park, CA: New Media Publishing, Inc., December 1984. pp. 43–44. (stills requested by fans)

1257 "Monsterbilia." *Rue Morgue Magazine.* No. 83. Toronto, Ontario: Marrs Media Inc., October 2008. p. 27.

1258 "Monstercon Masquerade Winners." *Famous Monsters of Filmland.* No. 120. Warren, October 1975. (1974 Famous Monsters Convention Costume Contest)

1259 "Monsterland U.S.A." *Famous Monsters of Filmland.* No. 32. Warren, March 1965. (*The Munsters*)

1260 "Monsterland's 25 Fearful Faces: Lucky Photo Finish Winners." *Forrest J Ackerman's Monster Land.* No. 3. Studio City, CA: New Media Pub. Co., June 1985. pp. 7–9.

1261 "Monsteriffic Movies of Tomorrow!" *Famous Monsters of Filmland*. No. 48. Warren, February 1968.

1262 "Monsters Are Badder Than Ever." *Famous Monsters of Filmland*. Vol. 1. No. 2. Philadelphia: Central Publications, Inc., September 1958. [pp. 9–17]; *James Warren Presents Famous Monsters of Filmland Strike Back!* New York: Paperback Library, 1965; *Forrest J Ackerman's Monsterama*. No. 1. Seattle, WA: Fantagraphics Books, May 1991. pp. 34–51

1263 "The Monsters Are Coming!" *Famous Monsters of Filmland*. No. 166. Warren, August 1980.

1264 "Monsters Are Good for You." *Famous Monsters of Filmland*. Vol. 1. No. 1. Philadelphia, PA: Central Publications, Inc., 1958; *Famous Monsters Yearbook*. No. 1. Summer-Fall 1962; *James Warren Presents the Best from Famous Monsters of Filmland*. New York: Paperback Library, 1964; *Famous Monsters of Filmland 1968 Yearbook*. Warren, 1967; *Forrest J Ackerman's Monsterama*. No. 1. Seattle, WA: Fantagraphics Books, May 1991. pp. 4–7.

1265 "Monsters from Japan." *Famous Monsters of Filmland*. No. 114. Warren, March 1975.

1266 "Monsters in Their Blood." *Famous Monsters of Filmland*. No. 121. Warren, December 1975. Warren, 1975. (family of Bela Lugosi)

1267 "Monsters Made Me." *Science Fiction Times*. No. 369. September 1961. pp. 24–26.

1268 "Monsters of Metropolis." *Famous Monsters of Filmland*. No. 31. Warren Publishing Co., December 1964. pp. 74–74. (film *Giant of Metropolis*)

1269 "Monsters of the World Unite!" *Famous Monsters of Filmland*. No. 112. Warren, December 1974. (announcement of the First Annual Famous Monsters Convention)

1270 "Monsters of Tomorrow." *Famous Monsters of Filmland*. Vol. 1. No. 3. Philadelphia: Central Publications, Inc., April 1959. (*Monster of Piedras Blancas* and Edward D. Wood Jr.'s *Night of the Ghouls*)

1271 "Monsters on the March." *Famous Monsters of Filmland*. No. 29. July 1964. Warren Publishing, Inc., pp. 9–14.

1272 "The Monster's Victim." *Monster World*. No. 8. Warren, May 1966.

1273 "Monsters Were His Meat!" *Famous Monsters of Filmland*. Vol. 3. No. 1. No. 10. Philadelphia: Central Publications, Inc., January 1961; *James Warren Presents Son of Famous Monsters of Filmland*. New York: Paperback Library, 1965.

1274 "A Monstrous Loss Death of the 'Little Giant.'" *Famous Monsters of Filmland*. No. 30. Warren Publishing Co., September 1964. pp. 13–21. (Peter Lorre)

1275 "Montana Monster Found in Lost World." *Famous Monsters of Filmland*. No. 36. Warren, December 1965. pp. 68–70; *Famous Monsters of Filmland 1971 Fearbook*. Warren, 1970.

1276 "Morgau-Lingvaj." [As Forest Gej Akerman???] *Science Fiction Fan*. Vol. 1. No. 1. Ed. Olon F. Wiggins. Denver, CO: July 1936.

1277 "The Most Horrible Frankenstein." *Famous Monsters of Filmland*. No. 28. Warren Publishing, Inc., May 1964. pp. 20–25.

1278 "Motel Hell." *Famous Monsters of Filmland*. No. 172. Warren, April 1981; *Warren Presents the Official Exclusive Horror Movie Yearbook 1981 Collector's Edition*. Warren, February 1981. (preview)

1279 "The Mouse-Beaver Strikes Again!" [As Forry Rhodan.] *Perry Rhodan. No. 13. The Immortal Unknown*. K. H. Scheer. New York: Ace, May 1972, 1974; London: Futura Publications, 1976.

1280 "The Mouth That Roared." *Famous Monsters of Filmland*. No. 105. Warren, March 1974. (obituary of Joe E. Brown)

1281 "Movie Memo." *The Fort MacArthur Bulletin*. Friday 5 February 1943. p. 1-A.

1282 "The Mummy That Came to Life." *Famous Monsters of Filmland*. Vol. 5. No. 4. Whole No. 25. Warren Publishing, Inc., October 1963. pp. 30–33. (on a short film *I Was a Teenage Mummy* by Ralph C. Bluemke)

1283 "The Mummy's Ghost." *Famous Monsters of Filmland*. No. 36. Warren, December 1965. pp. 24–34; *Famous Monsters of Filmland 1969 Year Book/Fearbook*. New York: Warren Publishing Co., 1968; *Famous Monsters of Filmland*. No. 188. New York: Warren Publishing Co., October 1982. pp. 24-.

1284 "Mummy's the Word." *Famous Monsters of Filmland*. Vol. 1. No. 4. August 1959. pp. 32–39; *Famous Monsters Yearbook*. No. 1. Summer-Fall 1962; *James Warren Presents the Best from Famous Monsters of Filmland*. New York: Paperback Library, 1964; *Famous Monsters 1968 Yearbook*. Warren, 1967; *Famous Monsters of Filmland*. Vol. 1. No. 4. Filmland Classics, May 2008. pp. 32–39. (replica edition)

1285 "The Mummy's Tomb, Part 1." *Famous Monsters of Filmland*. No. 82. Warren, February 1971. (filmbook)

1286 "The Mummy's Tomb, Part 2." *Famous Monsters of Filmland*. No. 83. Warren, April 1971.

1287 "Munster Go Home!" *Famous Monsters of Filmland*. No. 41. Warren, November 1966. pp. 52–57; *Famous Monsters of Filmland 1970 Year Book/Fearbook*. Warren, 1969.

1288 "Murders in the Rue Morgue." *Famous Monsters of Filmland.* No. 64. Warren, April 1970. (filmbook)

1289 "Murders in the Rue Morgue." *Famous Monsters of Filmland.* No. 94. Warren, November 1972. (1971 film version)

1290 "My Bloody Valentine Plus Happy Birthday to Me." *Famous Monsters of Filmland.* No. 182. Warren, April 1982.

1291 "My Brother." *Voice of the Imagi-Nation (VOM).* No. 39. Los Angeles, CA: Forrest J Ackerman, February 1945; *Amazing Forries: This is your Life, Forrest J Ackerman.* Hollywood, CA: Metropolis Publications, 1976. p. 27; *The Road to Veletrium.* No. 47. Yucca Valley, CA: James van Hise, October 2002. [obituary of Alden Ackerman with photo]

1292 "My 5 Favorite Fright Films." *Famous Monsters of Filmland.* No. 118. New York: Warren Publishing Co., August 1975. pp. 34–35.

1293 "My Prides..." *Amazing Forries: this is your life, Forrest J Ackerman.* Hollywood, CA: Metropolis Publications/Warren, 1976. p. 32.

1294 "My Science Fiction Collection." *The Fantasy Fan.* Vol. 1. No. 1. Ed. Charles D. Hornig. Elizabeth, NJ: Charles D. Hornig, September 1933. p. 8; *Yawning Vortex: The Tsathoggua Press Journal of Weird Fiction.* Vol. 1. No. 2. Ed. Perry M. Grayson. West Hills, CA: Tsathoggua Press, October 1994. pp. 19–20; *The Fantasy Fan—The Fans' Own Magazine (September, 1933–February, 1935; Vol. 1, Nos. 1–12; vol. 2, Nos. 13–18.* n.p., n.d Tacoma, WA[?]: Lance Thingmaker, 2010.

1295 "My Science Fiction Collection Part Two." *The Fantasy Fan.* Vol. 1. No. 2. Ed. Charles D. Hornig. Elizabeth, NJ: Charles D. Hornig, October 1933. p. 29; *Yawning Vortex: The Tsathoggua Press Journal of Weird Fiction.* Ed. Perry M. Grayson. Vol. 1. No. 2. West Hills, CA: Tsathoggua Press, October 1994. p. 20; *The Fantasy Fan—The Fans' Own Magazine (September, 1933–February, 1935; Vol. 1, Nos. 1–12; vol. 2, Nos. 13–18.* n.p., n.d Tacoma, WA[?]: Lance Thingmaker, 2010.

1296 "My Science Fiction Collection Part Three." *The Fantasy Fan.* Vol. 1. No. 3. Ed. Charles D. Hornig. Elizabeth, NJ: Charles D. Hornig, November 1933; *Yawning Vortex: The Tsathoggua Press Journal of Weird Fiction.* Vol. 1. No. 2. Ed. Perry M. Grayson. West Hills, CA: Tsathoggua Press, October 1994. p. 20; *The Fantasy Fan—The Fans' Own Magazine (September, 1933–February, 1935; Vol. 1, Nos. 1–12; vol. 2, Nos. 13–18.* n.p., n.d Tacoma, WA[?]: Lance Thingmaker, 2010.

1297 "My Science Fiction Collection Part Four." *The Fantasy Fan.* Vol. 1. No. 4. Ed. Charles D. Hornig. Elizabeth, NJ: Charles D. Hornig. De-cember 1933. p. 52; *Yawning Vortex: The Tsathoggua Press Journal of Weird Fiction.* Vol. 1. No. 2. Ed. Perry M. Grayson. West Hills, CA: Tsathoggua Press, October 1994. pp. 20–21; *The Fantasy Fan—The Fans' Own Magazine (September, 1933–February, 1935; Vol. 1, Nos. 1–12; vol. 2, Nos. 13–18.* n.p., n.d Tacoma, WA[?]: Lance Thingmaker, 2010.

1298 "My Science Fiction Collection Part Five." *The Fantasy Fan.* Vol. 1. No. 5. Elizabeth, NJ: Charles D. Hornig. January 1934; *Yawning Vortex: The Tsathoggua Press Journal of Weird Fiction.* Vol. 1. No. 2. Ed. Perry M. Grayson. West Hills, CA: Tsathoggua Press, October 1994. p. 21; *The Fantasy Fan—The Fans' Own Magazine (September, 1933–February, 1935; Vol. 1, Nos. 1–12; vol. 2, Nos. 13–18.* n.p., n.d Tacoma, WA[?]: Lance Thingmaker, 2010.

1299 "My Science Fiction Collection Part Six—Conclusion." *The Fantasy Fan.* Vol. 1. No. 6. Ed. Charles D. Hornig. Elizabeth, NJ: Charles D. Hornig, February 1934. p. 94; *Yawning Vortex: The Tsathoggua Press Journal of Weird Fiction.* Vol. 1. No. 2. Ed. Perry M. Grayson. West Hills, CA: Tsathoggua Press, October 1994. p. 21–22; *The Fantasy Fan—The Fans' Own Magazine (September, 1933–February, 1935; Vol. 1, Nos. 1–12; vol. 2, Nos. 13–18.* n.p., n.d Tacoma, WA[?]: Lance Thingmaker, 2010.

1300 "Mysterious Death." *Famous Monsters of Filmland.* No. 156. Warren, August 1979. (actor Victor Kilian)

1301 "The Mysterious Island." *Famous Monsters of Filmland.* No. 68. Warren, August 1970; *Famous Monsters of Filmland.* No. 137. Warren, September 1977. pp. 43–50.

1302 "Mystery of the Wax Museum." *Famous Monsters of Filmland.* No. 113. Warren, January 1975.

1303 "Mystery Photo Department." *Famous Monsters of Filmland.* Vol. 4. No. 1. Whole No. 16. Philadelphia: Central Publications, Inc., March 1962. [p. 40]

1304 "Never in a 1,000,000 Years." *Famous Monsters of Filmland.* No. 35. Warren, October 1965. p. 3. (Editorial)

1305 "News in General." *Science Fiction Times.* No. 313. (Second April 1959 issue)

1306 "News of the Month." (anonymous) *Other Worlds Science Stories.* Ed. Raymond A. Palmer. Clark Publishing Company, July 1950.

1307 "New Scientifilms." *The Time Traveller.* Vol. 1. No. 2. February 1932.

1308 "...The New Year of Monsters and How It's Groan." *Famous Monsters of Filmland.* Vol. 2. No. 1. Whole No. 6. Philadelphia: Central Publications, Inc., February 1960. pp. 9–19; *Famous Monsters of*

Filmland. Vol. 1. No. 4. Filmland Classics, May 2008. pp. 9–19. (replica edition)

1309 "New Year's Fanta-Film Fears." *Famous Monsters of Filmland.* No. 181. Warren, March 1982.

1310 "The New Year's New Fears." *Famous Monsters of Filmland.* No. 27. Warren Publishing, March 1964. pp. 6–19.

1311 "New Years, New Fears." *Famous Monsters of Filmland.* No. 172. Warren, April 1981.

1312 "Night of Dark Shadows." *Famous Monsters of Filmland.* No. 88. Warren, January 1972.

1313 "Night of the Blood Beast!" *Famous Monsters of Filmland.* No. 35. Warren, October 1965. pp. 31–37; *Famous Monsters of Filmland.* No. 119. Warren, September 1975; *Warren Presents Movie Aliens Illustrated.* (*Warren Presents.* No. 4.) Warren, September 1979.

1314 "1939 — Nycon I, New York City." Thokar, Greg. Ed. *Noreascon Three Souvenir Book.* Cambridge, MA: Massachusetts Convention Fandom, Inc., 1989. pp. 57–58.

1315 "1940—Chicon I, Chicago." Thokar, Greg. Ed. *Noreascon Three Souvenir Book.* Cambridge, MA: Massachusetts Convention Fandom, Inc., 1989. p. 68.

1316 "1941—Denvention I, Denver." Thokar, Greg. Ed. *Noreascon Three Souvenir Book.* Cambridge, MA: Massachusetts Convention Fandom, Inc., 1989. pp. 68–69.

1317 "1946 — Pacificon I, Los Angeles." Thokar, Greg. Ed. *Noreascon Three Souvenir Book.* Cambridge, MA: Massachusetts Convention Fandom, Inc., 1989. pp. 69–70.

1318 "1950— NORWESCON, Portland." Thokar, Greg. Ed. *Noreascon Three Souvenir Book.* Cambridge, MA: Massachusetts Convention Fandom, Inc., 1989. pp. 73–78.

1319 "1980's Nerve-Shattering Film Forecast." *Famous Monsters of Filmland.* No. 161. Warren, March 1980.

1320 "None Came Back, Except Ack; on Rocketship XM." *Fantasy Times.* No. 101. Ed. James V. Taurasi. March 1, 1950. p. 6.

1321 "Noose Reel: The Shape of Hangs to Come." *Famous Monsters of Filmland.* Vol. 4. No. 1. Whole No. 16. Philadelphia: Central Publications, Inc., March 1962. [pp. 6–8.]

1322 "Nosferatu!" *Famous Monsters of Filmland.* No. 153. Warren, May 1979.

1323 "Notes on Bob Olsen." *The Fantasy Fan.* Vol. 2. No. 1. Whole No. 13. Ed. Charles D. Hornig. Elizabeth, NJ: Charles D. Hornig, September 1934.

pp. 11, 15; *The Fantasy Fan—The Fans' Own Magazine* (September, 1933–February, 1935; *Vol. 1, Nos. 1–12; vol. 2, Nos. 13–18.* n.p., n.d Tacoma, WA[?]: Lance Thingmaker, 2010.

1324 "Now Dig This Skullduggery." *Famous Monsters of Filmland.* No. 69. Warren, September 1970.

1325 "Now Fear This!" *Famous Monsters of Filmland.* Vol. 5. No. 2. Whole No. No. 23. June 1963. pp. 10–17.

1326 "Now I Lay Me Down to Dream." *The Fantasite.* Vol. 1. No. 3. Ed. Phil Bronson. Hastings, MN: April 1941.

1327 "Now PONder This." *Glom.* No. 6. January 1947. p. 8. (on the Big Pond Fund)

1328 "Nude Gels." *Fantast.* No. 13. Ed. C. S. Youd, Doug Webster. April 1942.

1329 "The 'Nymph' O' Maniack." *Shangri-La.* January-February 1948; *Gosh! Wow (Boy-oh-Boy)! Science Fiction.* New York: Bantam, 1982. pp. 503–506; *Echoes of Valor II.* Ed. Karl Edward Wagner. Tor, 1989. pp. 92–10?. (hardcover); Tor, 1993. (trade paperback) [quotes from correspondence between Ackerman and Moore during the creation of "Nymph of Darkness"]

1330 "The Odd Genre." *If.* Vol. 6. No. 1. Ed. James L. Quinn. Buffalo, NY: Quinn Publishing Company, Inc., December 1955.

1331 "The Odd Genre." *If.* Vol. 6. No. 2. Ed. James L. Quinn. Buffalo, NY: Quinn Publishing Company, Inc., February 1956.

1332 "The Odd Genre." *If.* Vol. 6. No. 3. Ed. James L. Quinn. Buffalo, NY: Quinn Publishing Company, Inc., April 1956.

1333 "Of Fire and Felines: Jacques Tourneur, Dead." *Famous Monsters of Filmland.* No. 145. Warren, July 1978.

1334 "Of Men and Monsters." *Forrest J Ackerman Presents Mr. Monster's Movie Gold: A Treasure Trove of Imagi-Movies.* Ed. Hank Stine. Virginia Beach, VA: Donning Co. 1981. pp. 58–75.

1335 "The Old Dark House." *Famous Monsters of Filmland.* No. 66. Warren, June 1970.

1336 "Old Fantasy Films." *Alchemist.* Spring 1947. (*Just Imagine*); as "Just Imagine." *Perry Rhodan No. 64. The Ambassadors from Aurigel.* Kurt Mahr. New York: Ace, February 1975.

1337 "Old Fantasy Films." *Alchemist.* Vol. 2. No. 2. Winter 1947. (*Metropolis*); *Perry Rhodan. No. 75. Planet Topide, Please Reply!* Kurt Brand. New York: Ace, July 1975; ["Metropolis: A Fantasy Film Review"]; *Tales of the Time Travelers: Adventures of Forrest J Ackerman and Julius Schwartz.* Ed. John L.

Coker, III. Orlando, FL: Days of Wonder Publishers, 2009.

1338 "'Old' Kong Lives." *Famous Monsters of Filmland.* No. 132. Warren, March 1977.

1339 "Oldest Horror Actor Dies Ernest Thesiger: 1879–1961." *Famous Monsters of Filmland.* Vol. 3. No. 3. Whole No. 12. Philadelphia: Central Publications, Inc., June 1961. pp. 23–24.

1340 "Oliver Guest Speaker at World's First Class in SF Authorship." *Fantasy Times.* Vol. 7 No. 21. No. 165. November 1952. p. 6. (author Chad Oliver)

1341 "On Ray Cummings." *Fantasy Times.* No. 265. Ed. James V. Taurasi. 2 February 1957. pp. 1–2.

1342 "On the Fritz." *Fan-Dango.* Vol. 2. No. 2. Whole No. 6. Ed. Francis T. Laney. Los Angeles, Fall 1944. (Fritz Leiber, Jr.)

1343 "On the Screen." *Science Fiction News.* No. 11. Ed. Graham Stone. Sydney: July 1955.

1344 [on the wedding of Terry Carr and Miriam Dyches] [With Cynthia Goldstone.] *Fanac.* No. 33. 14 February 1959.

1345 "Once Around the Solar System." *Science-Fiction Plus.* Ed. Hugo Gernsback. Gernsback Publications, Inc. April 1953. [*Dream of the Stars*]

1346 "The One and Only Wendayne: A Bio in Brief of PR's Translator-in-Chief." *Perry Rhodan. No. 100. Desert of Death's Domain.* Kurt Mahr. New York: Ace, August 1976.

1347 "One Glorious Day." *Forrest J Ackerman Presents Mr. Monster's Movie Gold: A Treasure Trove of Imagi-Movies.* Ed. Hank Stine. Virginia Beach, VA: Donning Co. 1981. pp. 14–23. (information about and Ackerman's recollections of the 1922 film, incorporates synopsis and review of the film from *Representative Photoplays Analyzed*; a totally different piece from [Ackerman's Introduction to *The Collectors Guide to Monster Magazines*; see entry 2937])

1348 "150 Fantastic Films." *Famous Monsters of Filmland.* No. 150. Warren, January 1979. (previews)

1349 "The One Man Monster Show." *Famous Monsters of Filmland.* No. 200. Orange, NJ: Dynacomm, May 1993. pp. 26–. (Lon Chaney, Sr.)

1350 "Only 30 Chopping Days Left Until Halloween." [With James Warren and Phyllis Farkas.] *Famous Monsters of Filmland.* Vol. 2. No. 9. Philadelphia: Central Publications, Inc., November 1960. (first Gogos cover)

1351 "Onward Esperanto!" *Imagination!* Vol. 1. No. 1. October 1937. p. 8.

1352 "Onward Esperanto!" [As Erdstelulov.] *Imagination!* Vol. 1. No. 1. p. 13.

1353 "Onward Esperanto!" [As Erdstelulov.] *Imagination!* Vol. 1. No. 3. December 1937. p. 5.

1354 "Onward Esperanto!" [As Erdstelulov.] *Imagination!* Vol. 1. No. 4. January 1938.

1355 "Onward Esperanto!" [As Erdstelulov-Forsto.] *Imagination!* Vol. 1. No. 5. February 1938.

1356 "Onward Esperanto!" [As Erdstelulov.] *Imagination!* No. 7. April 1938. p. 5.

1357 "Onward Esperanto!" [As Erdstelulov.] *Imagination!* Vol. 1. No. 9. June 1938. p. 5.

1358 "Onward Esperanto!" [As Erdstelulov.] *Imagination!* Vol. 1. No. 10. July 1938.

1359 "Onward Esperanto!" [As Erdstelulov.] *Imagination!* Vol. 1. No. 11. August 1938. p. 7.

1360 "An Open Letter to Frank R. Paul (Deceased)." *Science Fiction Chronicle: The Monthly SF and Fantasy Newsmagazine.* Vol. 11. No. 7. Ed. Andrew I. Porter. April 1990. p. 31. (on the sale of an original Paul painting which enabled Ackerman to purchase a crypt in Forest Lawn)

1361 "Orbituary Department." *Spacemen.* Vol. 1. No. 1. Philadelphia, PA: Spacemen, Inc. July 1961.

1362 "Orbituary Department." *Spacemen.* Vol. 1. No. 2. September 1961. Philadelphia: Spacemen, Inc., September 1961.

1363 "Orbituary Department." *Spacemen.* Vol. 1. No. 3. Philadelphia: Spacemen, Inc., April 1962.

1364 "Orbituary Department." *Spacemen.* Vol. 2. No. 1. Whole No. 5. Philadelphia: Spacemen, Inc., October 1962. pp. 20–24.

1365 "Orbituary Department." *Spacemen.* Vol. 2. No. 3. Whole No. 7. Warren Publishing, Inc., September 1963.

1366 "Other Scare-Scores of King Karloff." *Famous Monsters of Filmland.* No. 44. Warren, May 1967.

1367 "Otto Kruger: Time Stops." *Famous Monsters of Filmland.* No. 113. Warren, January 1975. (obituary of Otto Kruger)

1368 "Our 5th Brrrthday!" *Famous Monsters of Filmland.* Vol. 5. No. 1. Whole No. 22. April 1963. p. 3. (editorial)

1369 "Our Man in West Berlin." *Science Fiction Chronicle: The Monthly SF and Fantasy Newsmagazine.* Vol. 6. No. 8. Ed. Andrew I. Porter. May 1985. p. 26. (on German screenings of *2010* and *Metropolis*)

1370 "Out of This World Convention." *Fantastic Universe.* Ed. Hans Stefan Santesson. New York: King-Size Publications, Inc., January 1957. (report on NyCon II)

1371 "Out of This World Monsters." *Famous Monsters of Filmland.* Vol. 1. No. 1. Philadelphia: Central Publications, Inc., 1958. pp. 38–43; *James Warren Presents the Best from Famous Monsters of Filmland.* New York: Paperback Library, 1964; *Famous Monsters of Filmland: Yearbook No. 2.* [1964] [Warren Publishing Co.], December 1963; *Famous Monsters of Filmland.* Vol. 1. No. 1. Filmland Classics, January 2008. pp. 38–43. (replica edition)

1372 "Outland." *Famous Monsters of Filmland.* No. 174. Warren, June 1981; *Film Fantasy Yearbook 1982 Collector's Edition.* Warren, March 1982. (preview)

1373 "Pacificon." *New Worlds.* Vol. 1. No. 2. Ed. John Carnell. London: Pendulum Publications, Ltd, October 1946.

1374 "Paging Perry Rhodan!" *Perry Rhodan. No. 14. Venus in Danger.* Kurt Mahr. New York: Ace, June 1972. 1974. (uncredited but likely by Ackerman)

1375 "The Panther Woman." *Famous Monsters of Filmland.* No. 169. Warren, November 1980. (obituary of actress Kathleen Burke)

1376 "Le 'Pap' de Tarzan Est un Grandpère: Une Intervue Exclusive avec l'Autor Mondfameuse par Forrest J Ackerman." *Glom.* No. 8. July 1947. (Edgar Rice Burroughs)

1377 "Paul W. Skeeters." *Locus: The Newspaper of the Science Fiction Field.* Vol. 16. No. 11. Whole No. 274. Ed. Charles N. Brown. Oakland, CA: November 1983. p. 26. (obituary)

1378 "Paul's Projector." *The Alchemist.* No. 2. March 1940.

1379 "A Peacelord Passes." *Perry Rhodan. No. 53. Spybot!* Clark Darlton. New York: Ace, September 1974.

1380 "Pen Names." *Amazing Forries: this is your life, Forrest J Ackerman.* Hollywood, CA: Metropolis Publications/Warren, 1976. p. 23.

1381 "People That Time Forgot." *Famous Monsters of Filmland.* No. 173. Warren, May 1981.

1382 "The Perils of Perrytonitis." *Perry Rhodan. No. 66. The Horror.* William Voltz. New York: Ace Books, 1975. (Stardust Editorial)

1383 "Perry Guest at Film Fest (Scientfilm World)." *Perry Rhodan. No. 23. Peril on Ice Planet.* Kurt Mahr. New York: Ace, April 1973.

1384 "Perry Rhodan & His Electronic Time Machine." [As Forry Rhodan.] *Perry Rhodan. No. 7. Fortress of the Six Moons.* K. H. Scheer. New York: Ace, September 1971, 1972, 1974.

1385 "Perry Rhodan's Right Hand Fan." *Perry Rhodan. No. 37. Epidemic Center: Aralon.* Clark Darlton. New York: Ace, January 1974.

1386 "The Perryscope." [As Forry Rhodan.] *Perry Rhodan. No. 6: The Secret of the Time Vault.* New York: Ace Books, 1971, 1972, 1974; London: Futura Publications, 1975.

1387 "The Perryscope." [As Forry Rhodan.] *Perry Rhodan. No. 7. Fortress of the Six Moons.* K. H. Scheer. New York: Ace, September 1971, 1972, 1974.

1388 "The Perryscope." [As Forry Rhodan.] *Perry Rhodan. No. 8. The Galactic Riddle.* Clark Darlton. New York: Ace, October 1971, 1972, 1974; London: Futura Publications, 1975.

1389 "The Perryscope." [As Forry Rhodan.] *Perry Rhodan. No. 9. Quest Through Space and Time.* Clark Darlton. New York: Ace, November 1971, 1974; London: Futura Publications, 1975.

1390 "The Perryscope." *Perry Rhodan: In the Center of the Galaxy.* Clark Darlton. New York: Ace, January 1978.

1391 "The Perryscope." *Perry Rhodan. No. 10. The Ghosts of Gol.* Kurt Mahr. New York: Ace, December 1971, 1972, 1974.

1392 "The Perryscope." *Perry Rhodan. No. 11. Planet of the Dying Sun.* Kurt Mahr. New York: Ace, February 1972, 1974.

1393 "The Perryscope." *Perry Rhodan. No. 12. Rebels of Tuglan.* Clark Darlton. New York: Ace, April 1972, 1974; London: Futura Publications, 1976.

1394 "The Perryscope." *Perry Rhodan. No. 13. The Immortal Unknown.* K. H. Scheer. New York: Ace, May 1972, 1974; London: Futura Publications, 1976.

1395 "The Perryscope." *Perry Rhodan. No. 14. Venus in Danger.* Kurt Mahr. New York: Ace, June 1972, 1974.

1396 "The Perryscope." *Perry Rhodan. No. 17. The Venus Trap.* Kurt Mahr. Ace, September, 1972.

1397 "The Perryscope." *Perry Rhodan. No. 18. Menace of the Mutant Master.* Kurt Mahr. New York: Ace Books, 1972.

1398 "The Perryscope." *Perry Rhodan. No. 20. The Thrall of Hypno.* New York: Ace, December 1972; London: Futura, 1976.

1399 "The Perryscope." *Perry Rhodan. No. 21. The Cosmic Decoy.* K. H. Scheer. New York: Ace, January 1973.

1400 "The Perryscope." *Perry Rhodan. No. 22. The Fleet of the Springers.* Kurt Mahr. New York: Ace Books, March 1973; London: Futura, 1977.

1401 "The Perryscope." *Perry Rhodan. No. 23. Peril on Ice Planet.* Kurt Mahr. New York: Ace, April 1973.

1402 "The Perryscope." *Perry Rhodan. No. 24. Infinity Flight.* Clark Darlton. New York: Ace, May 1973.

1403 "The Perryscope." *Perry Rhodan. No. 25. Snowman in Flames.* Clark Darlton. New York: Ace, June 1973.

1404 "The Perryscope." *Perry Rhodan. No. 26. Cosmic Traitor.* Kurt Brand. New York: Ace, July 1973.

1405 "The Perryscope." *Perry Rhodan. No. 27. Planet of the Gods.* Kurt Mahr. New York: Ace, August 1973; London: Futura Publications, 1977.

1406 "The Perryscope." *Perry Rhodan. No. 28. The Plague of Oblivion.* Clark Darlton. New York: Ace, August 1973; London: Futura, 1977.

1407 "The Perryscope." *Perry Rhodan. No. 29. A World Gone Mad.* Clark Darlton. New York: Ace, September 1973; London: Futura, 1977.

1408 "The Perryscope." *Perry Rhodan. No. 31. Realm of the Tri-Planets.* K. H. Scheer. New York: Ace, October 1973; London: Futura Publications, 1973.

1409 "The Perryscope." *Perry Rhodan. No. 32. Challenge of the Unknown.* Clark Darlton. New York: Ace. October 1973.

1410 "The Perryscope." *Perry Rhodan. No. 33. The Giant's Partner.* Clark Darlton. New York: Ace, November 1973.

1411 "The Perryscope." *Perry Rhodan No. 34. SOS: Spaceship Titan!* Kurt Brand. New York: Ace, November 1973; London: Orbit, 1978.

1412 "The Perryscope." *Perry Rhodan. No. 35. Beware the Microbots.* Kurt Mahr. New York: Ace, December 1973.

1413 "The Perryscope." *Perry Rhodan. No. 36. Man and Monster.* K. H. Scheer. New York: Ace, 1973.

1414 "The Perryscope." *Perry Rhodan. No. 39. The Silence of Gom.* Kurt Mahr. New York: Ace, February 1974.

1415 "The Perryscope." *Perry Rhodan. No. 40. Red Eye of Betelgeuse.* Clark Darlton. New York: Ace, February 1974.

1416 "The Perryscope." *Perry Rhodan. No. 41. The Earth Dies.* Clark Darlton. New York: Ace, March 1974.

1417 "The Perryscope." *Perry Rhodan. No. 42. Time's Lonely One.* K. H. Scheer. New York: Ace, March 1974.

1418 "The Perryscope." *Perry Rhodan. No. 43. Life Hunt.* Kurt Brand. New York: Ace, April 1974.

1419 "The Perryscope." *Perry Rhodan. No. 44. The Pseudo One.* Clark Darlton. New York: Ace, April 1974.

1420 "The Perryscope." *Perry Rhodan. No. 45. Unknown Sector: Milky Way.* Kurt Mahr. New York: Ace, May 1974.

1421 "The Perryscope." *Perry Rhodan. No. 46. Again Atlan!* K. H. Scheer. New York: Ace, May 1974.

1422 "The Perryscope." *Perry Rhodan. No. 47. Shadow of the Mutant Master.* Kurt Brand. New York: Ace, June 1974.

1423 "The Perryscope." *Perry Rhodan. No. 48. The Dead Live.* Clark Darlton. Ace, June 1974.

1424 "The Perryscope." *Perry Rhodan. No. 49. Solar Assassins.* Kurt Mahr. New York: Ace, July 1974.

1425 "The Perryscope." *Perry Rhodan. No. 50. Attack from the Unseen.* Clark Darlton. New York: Ace, July 1974.

1426 "The Perryscope." *Perry Rhodan. No. 51. Return from the Void.* Kurt Mahr. New York: Ace, August 1974.

1427 "The Perryscope." *Perry Rhodan. No. 52. Fortress Atlantis.* K. H. Scheer. New York: Ace, August 1974.

1428 "The Perryscope." *Perry Rhodan. No. 53. Spybot!* Clark Darlton. New York: Ace, September 1974.

1429 "The Perryscope." *Perry Rhodan. No. 54. The Blue Dwarfs.* Kurt Mahr. New York: Ace, September 1974.

1430 "The Perryscope." *Perry Rhodan. No. 55. The Micro-Techs.* Clark Darlton. New York: Ace, October 1974.

1431 "The Perryscope." *Perry Rhodan. No. 56. Prisoner of Time.* Clark Darlton. New York: Ace, October 1974.

1432 "The Perryscope." *Perry Rhodan. No. 57. A Touch of Eternity.* Clark Darlton. New York: Ace, November 1974.

1433 "The Perryscope." *Perry Rhodan. No. 58. The Guardians.* Kurt Mahr. New York: Ace, November 1974.

1434 "The Perryscope." *Perry Rhodan. No. 59. Interlude on Siliko 5.* Kurt Brand. New York: Ace, December 1974.

1435 "The Perryscope." *Perry Rhodan. No. 60. Dimension Search.* Clark Darlton. New York: Ace, December 1974.

1436 "The Perryscope." *Perry Rhodan. No. 62. The Last Days of Atlantis.* K. H. Scheer. New York: Ace, January 1975.

1437 "The Perryscope." *Perry Rhodan. No. 63. The Tigris Leaps.* Kurt Brand. New York: Ace, February 1975.

1438 "The Perryscope." *Perry Rhodan. No. 65. Renegades of the Future.* Kurt Mahr. New York: Ace, March 1975.

1439 "The Perryscope." *Perry Rhodan. No. 66. The Horror.* William Voltz. New York: Ace Books, 1975.

1440 "The Perryscope." Perry Rhodan. No. 67. Crimson Universe. K. H. Scheer. New York: Ace, April 1975.

1441 "The Perryscope." *Perry Rhodan. No. 68. Under the Stars of Druufon.* Clark Darlton. New York: Ace, April 1975.

1442 "The Perryscope." *Perry Rhodan. No. 69. The Bonds of Eternity.* Clark Darlton. New York: Ace, April 1975.

1443 "The Perryscope." *Perry Rhodan. No. 70. Thora's Sacrifice.* Kurt Brand. New York: Ace, April 1975.

1444 "The Perryscope." *Perry Rhodan. No. 71. The Atom Hell of Grautier.* Kurt Mahr. New York: Ace, May 1975.

1445 "The Perryscope." *Perry Rhodan. No. 72. Caves of the Druuffs.* Kurt Mahr. New York: Ace, May 1975.

1446 "The Perryscope." *Perry Rhodan. No. 73. Spaceship of Ancestors.* Clark Darlton. New York: Ace, June 1975.

1447 "The Perryscope." *Perry Rhodan. No. 74. Checkmate: Universe.* Clark Darlton. New York: Ace, July 1975.

1448 "The Perryscope." *Perry Rhodan. No. 75. Planet Topide, Please Reply!* Kurt Brand. New York: Ace, July 1975.

1449 "The Perryscope." *Perry Rhodan. No. 77. Conflict Center: Naator.* Clark Darlton. New York: Ace, August 1975.

1450 "The Perryscope." *Perry Rhodan. No. 78. Power Key.* K. H. Scheer. New York: Ace, September 1975.

1451 "The Perryscope." *Perry Rhodan. No. 79. The Sleepers.* William Voltz. New York: Ace, September 1975.

1452 "The Perryscope." *Perry Rhodan. No. 80. The Columbus Affair.* K. H. Scheer. New York: Ace, October 1975.

1453 "The Perryscope." *Perry Rhodan. No. 81. Pucky's Greatest Hour.* Kurt Brand. New York: Ace, October 1975.

1454 "The Perryscope." *Perry Rhodan. No. 82. Atlan in Danger.* Kurt Brand. New York: Ace, November 1975.

1455 "The Perryscope." *Perry Rhodan. No. 83. Ernst Ellert Returns!* Clark Darlton. New York: Ace, November 1975.

1456 "The Perryscope." *Perry Rhodan. No. 85. Enemy in the Dark.* Kurt Mahr. New York: Ace, December 1975.

1457 "The Perryscope." *Perry Rhodan. No. 86. Blazing Sun.* Clark Darlton. New York: Ace, January 1976.

1458 "The Perryscope." *Perry Rhodan. No. 87. The Starless Realm.* Clark Darlton. New York: Ace, January 1976.

1459 "The Perryscope." *Perry Rhodan. No. 89. Power's Price.* Kurt Brand. New York: Ace, February 1976.

1460 "The Perryscope." *Perry Rhodan. No. 90. Unleashed Powers.* Kurt Brand. New York: Ace, March 1976.

1461 "The Perryscope." *Perry Rhodan. No. 92. The Target Star.* Kurt Brand. New York: Ace, April 1976.

1462 "The Perryscope." *Perry Rhodan. No. 93. Vagabond of Space.* Clark Darlton. New York: Ace, April 1976.

1463 "The Perryscope." *Perry Rhodan. No. 94. Action: Division 3.* Kurt Mahr. New York: Ace, May 1976.

1464 "The Perryscope." *Perry Rhodan. No. 95. The Plasma Monster.* Kurt Brand. New York: Ace, May 1976.

1465 "The Perryscope." *Perry Rhodan. No. 96. Horn: Green.* William Voltz. New York: Ace, June 1976.

1466 "The Perryscope." *Perry Rhodan. No. 97. Phantom Fleet.* Clark Darlton. New York: Ace, June 1976.

1467 "The Perryscope." *Perry Rhodan. No. 98. The Idol from Passa.* Kurt Mahr. New York: Ace, July 1976.

1468 "The Perryscope." *Perry Rhodan. No. 99. The Blue System.* K. H. Scheer. New York: Ace, July 1976.

1469 "The Perryscope." *Perry Rhodan. No. 100. Desert of Death's Domain.* Kurt Mahr. New York: Ace, August 1976.

1470 "The Perryscope." *Perry Rhodan. No. 101. Blockade: Lepso.* Kurt Brand. New York: Ace, August 1976.

1471 "The Perryscope." *Perry Rhodan. No. 102. Spoor of the Antis.* William Voltz. New York: Ace, September 1976.

1472 "The Perryscope." *Perry Rhodan. No. 103. False Front.* Clark Darlton. New York: Ace, September 1976.

1473 "The Perryscope." *Perry Rhodan. No. 104. The Man with Two Faces.* Kurt Brand. New York: Ace, October 1976.

1474 "The Perryscope." *Perry Rhodan. No. 105. Wonderflower of Utik.* Kurt Mahr. New York: Ace, October 1976.

1475 "The Perryscope." *Perry Rhodan. No. 106. Caller from Eternity.* Kurt Brand. New York: Ace, December 1976.

1476 "The Perryscope." *Perry Rhodan. No. 107. The Emperor and the Monster.* William Voltz. New York: Ace, January 1977.

1477 "The Perryscope." *Perry Rhodan. No. 108. Duel Under the Double Sun.* K. H. Scheer. New York: Ace, February 1977.

1478 "The Perryscope." *Perry Rhodan. No. 109. The Stolen Spacefleet.* Clark Darlton. / *Perry Rhodan. No. 110. Sgt. Robot.* Kurt Mahr. New York: Ace Books, March 1977.

1479 "The Perryscope." *Perry Rhodan. No. 111. Seeds of Ruin.* William Voltz. / *Perry Rhodan No. 112. Planet Mechanica.* K. H. Scheer. New York: Ace, April 1977.

1480 "The Perryscope." *Perry Rhodan. No. 113. Heritage of the Lizard People.* Clark Darlton. / *Perry Rhodan. No. 114. Death's Demand.* Kurt Mahr. New York: Ace, May 1977.

1481 "The Perryscope." *Perry Rhodan. No. 115. Saboteurs in A-1.* Kurt Brand. / *Perry Rhodan. No. 116. The Psycho Duel.* William Voltz. New York: Ace, June 1977.

1482 "The Perryscope." *Perry Rhodan. No. 117. Savior of the Empire.* K. H. Scheer. / *Perry Rhodan. No. 118. The Shadows Attack.* Clark Darlton. New York: Ace, August 1977.

1483 "The Perryscope." *Perry Rhodan Special Release: Menace of Atomigeddon.* Kurt Mahr. / *Flight from Tarkihl.* Clark Darlton. New York: Ace, October 1977.

1484 "The Perryscope." *Perry Rhodan Special Release: Robot Threat: New York.* W. W. Shols. / *Pale Country Pursuit.* Hans Kneifel. New York: Ace, November 1977.

1485 "The Perryscope." *Perry Rhodan Special Release: The Wasp Men Attack & Spider Desert.* W. W. Shols and Ernst Vlcek. New York: Ace, September 1977.

1486 "The Perryscope." [With Wendayne Ackerman.] *Perry Rhodan. No. 61. Death Waits in Semispace.* Kurt Mahr. New York: Ace, January 1975.

1487 "Personalities." [As Kratano Kortague.] *Luna Monthly.* No. 47. Ed. Ann F. Dietz. Oradell, NJ: Summer 1973. p. 10.

1488 "Peter Grainger." *Luna Monthly.* No. 52. Ed. Franklin M. Dietz, Jr. Oradell, NJ: Frank Dietz & Ann Dietz, May 1974. p. 8. (obituary of fan and author)

1489 "Phantastiquestions & Ansrs Dept." *Imagination!* Vol. 1. No. 1. October 1937. p. 15.

1490 "Phantasy Preview Parade." *Famous Monsters of Filmland.* No. 176. Warren, August 1981.

1491 "The Phantom Lives." *Famous Monsters of Filmland.* No. 123. Warren, March 1976. (Count Dracula Society honors Lon Chaney, Sr.)

1492 "The Phantom of Lot 2." *Famous Monsters of Filmland.* No. 106. Warren, April 1974.

1493 "The Phantom of the Space Opera." *Spacemen.* Vol. 1. No. 2. September 1961. Philadelphia: Spacemen, Inc., September 1961; *Spacemen 1965 Yearbook.* Warren Publishing Co., 1964.

1494 "The Phantom Strikes Again." *Famous Monsters of Filmland.* Vol. 2. No. 9. November 1960. [pp. 34–44]; *Famous Monsters of Filmland.* No. 65. Warren, May 1970; *Famous Monsters of Filmland.* No. 188. New York: Warren Publishing Co., October 1982. [pp. 44–.] (filmbook of 1925 *The Phantom of the Opera*)

1495 "The Phantom's Last Fright." *Famous Monsters of Filmland.* No. 47. Warren, November 1967; *Famous Monsters of Filmland.* No. 101. Warren, September 1973. (Film Monsterdom mourns the Death of Claude Rains)

1496 "The Photofiles of FJA." *Forrest J Ackerman's Monsters & Imagi-Movies.* Ed. Robert V. Michelucci. Canoga Park, CA: New Media Pub. Co., 1985. pp. 26–27.

1497 "Philip Wylie." *Science Fiction Digest.* Vol. 2. No. 1. Jamaica, NY: Conrad H. Ruppert, September 1933. [author (1902–1971)]

1498 "Pickering Blows His Cool; The Great Scienti-Claus Robbery." *Degler!* No. 164. Ed. Andrew Porter. New York: 13 January 1967. (on a large-scale theft from Ackerman's collection)

1499 "Pierre Versins — An Appeal." *Luna Monthly.* No. 21. Ed. Ann F. Dietz. Oradell, NJ: February 1971. pp. 8–9. (describes work and collection of Versins, auction of items from Ackerman's collection to support same)

1500 "A Pioneer Passes." [As Forry Rhodan.] *Perry Rhodan. No. 9. Quest Through Space and Time.*

Clark Darlton. New York: Ace, November 1971, 1974; London: Futura Publications, 1975.

1501 "The Pit and the Pendulum." *Famous Monsters of Filmland*. Vol. 3. No. 5. Whole No. 14. Philadelphia: Central Publications, Inc., October 1961. [pp. 8–14]; *Famous Monsters of Filmland 1965 Yearbook. No. 3*. Warren, 1965; *Famous Monsters of Filmland*. No. 101. Warren, September 1973; *Famous Monsters of Filmland*. No. 110. Warren, September 1974. (on the Roger Corman film starring Vincent Price)

1502 "The Pitt ... and the Pendulum." *1975 Famous Monsters of Filmland Convention Book*. (actress Ingrid Pitt)

1503 "Poe Preview: Tales of Terror." *Famous Monsters of Filmland*. Vol. 4. No. 19. Philadelphia: Central Publications, Inc., September 1962; *Famous Monsters of Filmland 1965 Yearbook*. No. 3. Warren, 1965; *James Warren Presents Son of Famous Monsters of Filmland*. New York: Paperback Library, 1965; *Famous Monsters of Filmland 1972 Fearbook*. Warren, 1971.

1504 "Poe Script." *Gosh! Wow (Boy-oh-Boy)! Science Fiction*. New York: Bantam, 1982. p. 563.

1505 "Poetry." *Imagination!* Vol. 1. No. 1. October 1937. p. 13.

1506 "Poltergeist." *Famous Monsters of Filmland*. No. 185. Warren, July 1982.

1507 "Poster Parade." *Forrest J Ackerman's Fantastic Movie Memories: Forrest Ackerman's Treasure Trove of Imagi-Movies*. Canoga Park, CA: New Media Books, 1985.

1508 "Potpourri by 4e." *Futurian War Digest*. Vol. 1. No. 9. Ed. J. Michael Rosenblum. Leeds, UK: June 1941. [issue dedicated to Ackerman for his wartime aid to British fans]

1509 "The Pre-Historic Story." *Famous Monsters of Filmland*. Vol. 4. No. 19. Philadelphia: Central Publications, Inc., September 1962; *Famous Monsters of Filmland 1965 Yearbook. No. 3*. Warren, 1965; *Famous Monsters of Filmland 1972 Fearbook*. Warren, 1971; *Famous Monsters of Filmland*. No. 129. Warren, October 1976.

1510 "The Prehistoric Story, Part 2." *Famous Monsters of Filmland*. No. 63. Warren, March 1970.

1511 "The Pre-Historicons Leading Up to Famous Monsters Con, 1974." *Famous Monsters of Filmland Convention Book*. Warren/Phil Seuling, November 1974.

1512 "Presenting Famous Monsters First Annual Instant Monsters $2,500.00 Cash Prize Contest." *Famous Monsters of Filmland*. No. 31. Warren Publishing Co., December 1964. (announces monster photo paste-up contest) pp. 24–29.

1513 "Preview-'The Bride of Frankenstein.'" [With Ed Thomas.] *Fantasy Magazine*. Vol. 4. No. 6. Ed. Julius Schwartz. Jamaica, NY: May 1935.

1514 "Preview Things to Come." *Fantasy Magazine*. Vol. 6. No. 1. No. 35. Ed. Julius Schwartz. Jamaica, NY: January 1936.

1515 "Prince Sirki Summoned." *Forrest J Ackerman's Monsters & Imagi-Movies*. Ed. Robert V. Michelucci. Canoga Park, CA: New Media Pub. Co., 1985. pp. 16–25. (photos with captions of deceased stars and film personnel)

1516 "Prince Sirki Takes Dr. Jekyll & Mr. Hyde." *Famous Monsters of Filmland*. No. 120. Warren, October 1975. (obituary of actor Fredric March)

1517 "Prince Sirki Takes Joel McCrea." *Forrest J Ackerman's Monsterama*. No. 1. Seattle, WA: Fantagraphics Books, May 1991. p. 62. [actor Joel McCrea (1905–1990)]

1518 "Pvt. Ft. Mac'RC Chosen on Freddy Martin Show." *The Fort MacArthur Bulletin*. Friday 5 February 1943. p. 1-A.

1519 "Prozine Checklist for 1949." *Fantasy Advertiser*. Ed. Gus Wilmorth [& Roy Squires.] Glendale, CA: January 1950.

1520 "Public Vampire Number One." *Famous Monsters of Filmland*. Vol. 1. No. 2. Philadelphia: Central Publications, Inc., September 1958. [pp. 44–53]; *Famous Monsters of Filmland*. No. 92. Warren, September 1972; *Forrest J Ackerman's Monsterama*. No. 1. Seattle, WA: Fantagraphics Books, May 1991. pp. 52–61; as "The Terror from Transylvania." *A Book of Weird Tales*. (Ed. with Cliff Lawton) Burnley, Lancashire, England: Veevers and Hensman Ltd., n.d. Autumn 1960; *Famous Monsters of Filmland*. No. 124. Warren, April 1976. (Bela Lugosi)

1521 "Putting the Room to Sleep." *Tales of the Time Travelers: Adventures of Forrest J Ackerman and Julius Schwartz*. Ed. John L. Coker, III. Orlando, FL: Days of Wonder Publishers, 2009. (on a hypnosis session performed by L. Ron Hubbard)

1522 "The Quake of Things to Come." *Famous Monsters of Filmland*. No. 114. Warren, March 1975.

1523 "A Quarrel with Clark Ashton Smith." *The Fantasy Fan*. Vol. 1. No. 1. Ed. Charles D. Hornig. Elizabeth, NJ: Charles D. Hornig, September 1933; *The Boiling Point*. West Warwick, RI: Necronomicon Press, April 1985; *The Fantasy Fan—The Fans' Own Magazine (September, 1933–February, 1935; Vol. 1, Nos. 1–12; vol. 2, Nos. 13–18*. n.p., n.d Tacoma, WA[?]: Lance Thingmaker, 2010. (ignited the Ackerman-Smith-Lovecraft feud)

1524 "Quarterly Report." *Fantasy Advertiser*. Vol. 1. No. 6. Ed. Gus Wilmorth & Roy A. Squires. January 1947. (promoting the Fantasy Foundation)

1525 "Queen of Outer Space Unmasked." *Monster World*. No. 6. Warren, January 1966.

1526 "Quest for Fire." *Famous Monsters of Filmland*. No. 180. Warren, January 1982. (preview)

1527 "Questions & Answers." *Imagination!* Vol. 1. No. 3. December 1937. p. 5.

1528 "The Race to the Moon." *Marvel Science*. Vol. 3. No. 1. Ed. R. O. Erisman. New York: Stadium Publishing Corp., November 1950. (*Destination Moon*)

1529 "Radar Men from the Moon." *Spacemen*. Vol. 2. No. 1. Whole No. 5. Philadelphia: Spacemen, Inc., October 1962. pp. 14–19.

1530 "Radar Men from the Moon." *Spacemen*. Vol. 2. No. 1. Whole No. 6. Philadelphia: Spacemen, Inc., January 1963. (Part 2)

1531 "Radclyffe Hall." [As Laurajean Ermayne.] *Vice Versa*. Ed. Edythe Eyde [as "Lisa Ben"]. CA: November 1947. [writer Marguerite Radclyffe-Hall (1880–1943)]

1532 "Radio Fantasy." *Science Fiction Digest*. Vol. 1. No. 10. Jamaica, NY: Conrad H. Ruppert, June 1933.

1533 "Raiders of the Lost Ark." *Famous Monsters of Filmland*. No. 175. Warren, July 1981; *Film Fantasy Yearbook 1982 Collector's Edition*. Warren, March 1982. (preview)

1534 "Raiders of the Lost Ark." *Famous Monsters of Filmland*. No. 179. Warren, November 1981; *Film Fantasy Yearbook 1982 Collector's Edition*. Warren, March 1982. (photo essay)

1535 "Raiders of the Lost Ark." *Famous Monsters of Filmland*. No. 181. Warren, March 1982.

1536 "Rajah of Records." *The Fort MacArthur Bulletin*. Friday 5 February 1943. pp. 1-A–2-A. (on Captain Carl Oliver Ingman, illustrated by Will Gould)

1537 "Rare Treats!" *Famous Monsters of Filmland*. No. 111. Warren, October 1974.

1538 "Rare Treats!" *Famous Monsters of Filmland*. No. 113. Warren, January 1975.

1539 "Rare Treats!" *Famous Monsters of Filmland*. No. 114. Warren, March 1975.

1540 "Rare Treats!" *Famous Monsters of Filmland*. No. 115. Warren, April 1975.

1541 "Rare Treats." *Famous Monsters of Filmland*. No. 116. Warren, May 1975.

1542 "Rare Treats." *Famous Monsters of Filmland*. No. 117. Warren, July 1975.

1543 "Rare Treats!" *Famous Monsters of Filmland*. No. 118. New York: Warren Publishing Co., August 1975. pp. 36–39.

1544 "Rare Treats!" *Famous Monsters of Filmland*. No. 120. Warren, October 1975.

1545 "Rare Treats!" *Famous Monsters of Filmland*. No. 121. Warren, December 1975.

1546 "Rare Treats." *Famous Monsters of Filmland*. No. 125. Warren, May 1976.

1547 "Rare Treats." *Famous Monsters of Filmland*. No. 126. Warren, July 1976; *House of Horror*. No. 1. Warren, April 1978.

1548 "Rare Treats!" *Famous Monsters of Filmland*. No. 127. Warren, August 1976.

1549 "Rare Treats." *Famous Monsters of Filmland*. No. 128. Warren, September 1976.

1550 "Rare Treats." *Famous Monsters of Filmland*. No. 132. Warren, March 1977.

1551 "Rare Treats." *Famous Monsters of Filmland*. No. 135. Warren, July 1977.

1552 "Rare Treats." *Famous Monsters of Filmland*. No. 136. Warren, August 1977.

1553 "Rare Treats!" *Famous Monsters of Filmland*. No. 138. Warren, October 1977; *Famous Monsters of Filmland*. No. 168. Warren, October 1980.

1554 "Rare Treats." *Famous Monsters of Filmland*. No. 141. Warren, March 1978.

1555 "Rare Treats." *Famous Monsters of Filmland*. No. 145. Warren, July 1978.

1556 "Rare Treats." *Famous Monsters of Filmland*. No. 147. Warren, September 1978. pp. 64–67.

1557 "Rare Treats!" *Famous Monsters of Filmland*. No. 150. Warren, January 1979.

1558 "Rare Treats!" *Famous Monsters of Filmland*. No. 155. Warren, July 1979.

1559 "Rare Treats!" *Famous Monsters of Filmland*. No. 156. Warren, August 1979.

1560 "Rare Treats!" *Famous Monsters of Filmland*. No. 160. Warren, January 1980.

1561 "Rare Treats!" *Famous Monsters of Filmland*. No. 162. Warren, April 1980.

1562 "Rare Treats!" *Famous Monsters of Filmland*. No. 164. Warren, June 1980.

1563 "Rare Treats!" *Famous Monsters of Filmland*. No. 165. Warren, July 1980.

1564 "Rare Treats!" *Famous Monsters of Filmland*. No. 166. Warren, August 1980.

1565 "Rare Treats." *Famous Monsters of Filmland*. No. 171. Warren, March 1981.

1566 "Rare Treats." *Famous Monsters of Filmland*. No. 172. Warren, April 1981.

1567 "Rare Treats." *Famous Monsters of Filmland*. No. 173. Warren, May 1981.

1568 "Rare Treats." *Famous Monsters of Filmland.* No. 175. Warren, July 1981.

1569 "Rare Treats." *Famous Monsters of Filmland.* No. 176. Warren, August 1981.

1570 "Rare Treats." *Famous Monsters of Filmland.* No. 183. Warren, May 1982.

1571 "Rare Treats." *Famous Monsters of Filmland.* No. 184. Warren, June 1982.

1572 "Rare Treats." *Famous Monsters of Filmland.* No. 185. Warren, July 1982.

1573 "Rare Treats." *Famous Monsters of Filmland.* No. 186. Warren, August 1982.

1574 "Rare Treats." *Famous Monsters of Filmland.* No. 187. Warren, September 1982.

1575 "Rare Treats." *Famous Monsters of Filmland.* No. 189. November 1982.

1576 "Rare Treats." *Famous Monsters of Filmland.* No. 190. Warren, January 1983.

1577 "Rare Treats." *Forrest J Ackerman's Fantastic Movie Memories: Forrest Ackerman's Treasure Trove of Imagi-Movies.* Canoga Park, CA: New Media Books, 1985.

1578 "Re: Perry & Thora." *Perry Rhodan. No. 67. Crimson Universe.* K. H. Scheer. New York: Ace, April 1975.

1579 "Reach for Famous Monsters." [As Dr. Acula.] *Famous Monsters of Filmland.* No. 30. Warren Publishing Co., September 1964.

1580 "Read 'Em and Wonder." *The Buccaneer.* San Francisco, CA: Balboa High School, Wednesday, 7 June 1933. (phonetic brain teasers)

1581 "Readers' 'Youngest-Oldest' Contest Winners." *Famous Monsters of Filmland.* No. 100. Warren, August 1973

1582 "Reasons for Rhodan." *Perry Rhodan. No. 58. The Guardians.* Kurt Mahr. New York: Ace, November 1974.

1583 [Recipe] *It Came from the Kitchen: Monstrously Delicious Celebrity Recipes from Dracula, Frankenstein, the Wolf Man, Assorted Aliens and Beyond!* Geoff Issac and Gord Reid. BearManor Media, 2007.

1584 "Record-Setting SF Party." (uncredited) *Luna Monthly.* No. 52. Ed. Ann F. Dietz. Oradell, NJ: May 1974. pp. 6–7. (on a pre–Nebula Awards party held in the Ackermansion)

1585 "Remembrance of Things Past." *Locus: The Newspaper of the Science Fiction Field.* August 1981. p. 15. (captioned photograph of 100th LASFS meeting, on meeting of 16 original members in May 1981)

1586 "The Reptiles." *Monster World.* No. 10. Warren, September 1966.

1587 "Reputation." *Nova.* Ed. Al Ashley. November-December 1941.

1588 "Requiem for Richmond." *Famous Monsters of Filmland.* No. 107. Warren, May 1974.

1589 "Rest in Peace ... or Is It Pieces?" *Famous Monsters of Filmland.* No. 184. Warren, June 1982.

1590 "Retroactive Hugos." *The Gernsback Awards 1926.* Vol. 1. Los Angeles, CA: Triton Books, 1982; Holicong, PA: Wildside Press, 2003. pp. i–v. (describes his selection process, input he received from members of "First Fandom")

1591 "Retrospect: A Top 5 Genre Short Stories." *Touchpaper—The Science Fiction Newsletter of Polemics and Reviews.* No. 8. Ed. Tony Lee. Isle of Wight: Pigasus Press, 1998.

1592 "The Return of Bela Lugosi." *Famous Monsters of Filmland.* No. 100. Warren, August 1973. pp. 52–61; *Forrest J Ackerman Famous Monster of Filmland #2.* Volume II (Issues #51–100) Universal City, CA: Hollywood Publishing Company, 1991. pp. 98–107.

1593 "Return of the Blood Beast." *Famous Monsters of Filmland.* No. 37. Warren, February 1966. (part 2 of coverage in *Famous Monsters* No. 35)

1594 "Return of the Burn." *Famous Monsters of Filmland.* 1962. Vol. 3. No. 6. Whole No. 15. Philadelphia: Central Publications, Inc., January 1962. pp. 24–28.

1595 "The Return of Carry On, Monsters." *Famous Monsters of Filmland.* No. 38. Warren, April 1966. pp. 34–43.

1596 "The Return of Count Yorga." *Famous Monsters of Filmland.* No. 91. Warren, July 1972.

1597 "The Return of Frankenstein." *Famous Monsters of Filmland.* No. 30. Warren Publishing Co., September 1964. pp. 27–40. (*The Evil of Frankenstein.*)

1598 "The Return of Frankenstein." [As Paul Linden.] *Famous Monsters of Filmland.* No. 150. Warren, January 1979. pp. 46–51. (on amateur film in which Ackerman appeared)

1599 "The Return of Frankens-ten." *Famous Monsters of Filmland.* No. 26. Warren Publishing, Inc., January 1964. p. 57; *Famous Monsters of Filmland.* No. 110. Warren, September 1974; *Famous Monsters of Filmland.* No. 158. Warren, October 1979.

1600 "Return of Kong!" *Spacemen.* Vol. 2. No. 3. Whole No. 7. Warren Publishing, Inc., September 1963. pp. 52–56; *Famous Monsters of Filmland.* No. 51. Warren, August 1968; *Famous Monsters of Film-*

land. No. 114. Warren, March 1975; *Famous Monsters of Filmland.* No. 256. July/August 2011. (*King Kong vs. Godzilla*)

1601 "The Return of the Fly." *Famous Monsters of Filmland.* Vol. 1. No. 5. Philadelphia: Central Publications, Inc., November 1959. [pp. 34–40]; *Famous Monsters of Filmland 1965 Yearbook.* No. 3. Warren, 1965; *Famous Monsters of Filmland.* No. 36. Warren, December 1965. pp. 56–62.

1602 "Return of the Ghoul." *Famous Monsters of Filmland.* No. 113. Warren, January 1975.

1603 "Return of the Mexicreatures." *Famous Monsters of Filmland.* No. 31. Warren Publishing Co., December 1964. pp. 16–23. (further coverage of Mexican monster films)

1604 "Return of the Mexicreatures." *Famous Monsters of Filmland.* No. 33. Warren, May 1965. (Part 2)

1605 "Return of the Phantom." *Famous Monsters of Filmland.* Vol. 3. No. 1. No. 10. Philadelphia: Central Publications, Inc., January 1961; *Famous Monsters of Filmland 1965 Yearbook. No. 3.* Warren, 1965; *Famous Monsters of Filmland.* No. 47. Warren, November 1967.

1606 "Return of the Saucers." *Spacemen.* Vol. 1. No. 4. Philadelphia: Spacemen, Inc., July 1962. (*Earth vs. the Flying Saucers*)

1607 "Return of the Vampire." *Monster World.* No. 6. Warren, January 1966; *Famous Monsters of Filmland.* No. 45. Warren, July 1967; *Famous Monsters of Filmland.* No. 58. Warren, October 1969. (filmbook)

1608 "The Return of Things to Come." *Famous Monsters of Filmland.* 1962. Vol. 3. No. 6. Whole No. 15. Philadelphia: Central Publications, Inc., January 1962. pp. 7–12; as "The Return of the Return of Things to Come." *Famous Monsters of Filmland.* No. 80. Warren, October 1970.

1609 "The Revenge of the Creature from the Black Lagoon that Walks Among Us." *Famous Monsters of Filmland.* No. 5. November 1959. pp. 22–33; *Famous Monsters Yearbook.* No. 1. Summer-Fall 1962; *James Warren Presents The Best from Famous Monsters of Filmland.* New York: Paperback Library, 1964.

1610 "Revenge of the Zombies." *Monster World.* No. 6. Warren, January 1966; *Famous Monsters of Filmland.* No. 52. Warren, October 1968; *Famous Monsters of Filmland.* No. 128. Warren, September 1976.

1611 "The Rhodan Magnetic Digest." *Perry Rhodan.* No. 8. *The Galactic Riddle.* Clark Darlton. New York: Ace, October 1971, 1972, 1974; London: Futura Publications, 1975.

1612 "The Rhodanary (part 1)." *Perry Rhodan. No. 37. Epidemic Center: Aralon.* Clark Darlton. New York: Ace, January 1974.

1613 "The Rhodanary (part 2)." *Perry Rhodan. No. 38. Project: Earthsave.* Kurt Brand. New York: Ace, January 1974.

1614 "The Rhodanary." *Perry Rhodan. No. 39. The Silence of Gom.* Kurt Mahr. New York: Ace, February 1974.

1615 "The Rhodanary." *Perry Rhodan. No. 40. Red Eye of Betelgeuse.* Clark Darlton. New York: Ace, February 1974.

1616 "The Rhodanary." *Perry Rhodan. No. 41. The Earth Dies.* Clark Darlton. New York: Ace, March 1974.

1617 "The Rhodanary." *Perry Rhodan. No. 42. Time's Lonely One.* K. H. Scheer. New York: Ace, March 1974.

1618 "The Rhodanary." *Perry Rhodan. 43. Life Hunt.* Kurt Brand. New York: Ace, April 1974.

1619 "The Rhodanary." *Perry Rhodan. No. 44. The Pseudo One.* Clark Darlton. New York: Ace, April 1974.

1620 "The Rhodanary." *Perry Rhodan. No. 47. Shadow of the Mutant Master.* Kurt Brand. New York: Ace, June 1974.

1621 "The Rhodanary." *Perry Rhodan. No. 48. The Dead Live.* Clark Darlton. Ace, June 1974.

1622 "The Rhodanary." *Perry Rhodan. No. 49. Solar Assassins.* Kurt Mahr. New York: Ace, July 1974.

1623 "The Rhodanary." *Perry Rhodan. No. 50. Attack from the Unseen.* Clark Darlton. New York: Ace, July 1974.

1624 "The Rhodanary." *Perry Rhodan. 51. Return from the Void.* Kurt Mahr. New York: Ace, August 1974.

1625 "The Rhodanary." *Perry Rhodan. No. 52. Fortress Atlantis.* K. H. Scheer. New York: Ace, August 1974.

1626 "The Rhodanary." *Perry Rhodan. No. 53. Spybot!* Clark Darlton. New York: Ace, September 1974.

1627 "The Rhodanary." *Perry Rhodan. No. 55. The Micro-Techs.* Clark Darlton. New York: Ace, October 1974.

1628 "The Rhodanary." *Perry Rhodan. No. 56. Prisoner of Time.* Clark Darlton. New York: Ace, October 1974.

1629 "The Rhodanary." *Perry Rhodan. No. 57. A Touch of Eternity.* Clark Darlton. New York: Ace, November 1974.

1630 "The Rhodanary." *Perry Rhodan. No. 58. The Guardians.* Kurt Mahr. New York: Ace, November 1974.

1631 "The Rhodanary." *Perry Rhodan. No. 61. Death Waits in Semispace.* Kurt Mahr. New York: Ace, January 1975.

1632 "The Rhodanary." *Perry Rhodan. No. 63. The Tigris Leaps.* Kurt Brand. New York: Ace, February 1975.

1633 "The Rhodanary." *Perry Rhodan. No. 65. Renegades of the Future.* Kurt Mahr. New York: Ace, March 1975.

1634 "The Rhodanary." *Perry Rhodan. No. 66. The Horror.* William Voltz. New York: Ace Books, 1975.

1635 "The Rhodanary." *Perry Rhodan. No. 74. Checkmate: Universe.* Clark Darlton. New York: Ace, July 1975.

1636 "The Rhodanary." *Perry Rhodan. No. 75. Planet Topide, Please Reply!* Kurt Brand. New York: Ace, July 1975.

1637 "The Rhodanary." *Perry Rhodan. No. 76. Recruits for Arkon.* Clark Darlton. New York: Ace, August 1975.

1638 "The Rhodanary." *Perry Rhodan. No. 78. Power Key.* K. H. Scheer. New York: Ace, September 1975.

1639 "The Rhodanary." *Perry Rhodan. No. 80. The Columbus Affair.* K. H. Scheer. New York: Ace, October 1975.

1640 "The Rhodanary." *Perry Rhodan. No. 81. Pucky's Greatest Hour.* Kurt Brand. New York: Ace, October 1975.

1641 "Rhodan's Rebirth." [As Forry Rhodan.] *Perry Rhodan. No. 6: The Secret of the Time Vault.* New York: Ace Books, 1971, 1972, 1974; London : Futura Publications, 1975.

1642 "Rick Sneary." *Science Fiction Chronicle: The Monthly SF and Fantasy Newsmagazine.* Vol. 12. No. 4. Ed. Andrew I. Porter. February 1991. p. 14. (obituary of longtime fan)

1643 "R. I. P. (Reader In Peril!)" [as "Dr. Acula," revised by Ray Ferry] *Famous Monsters of Filmland.* No. 201. No. Hollywood, CA: Dynacomm, Fall 1993. [See: Ferry, pp. 266–267]

1644 "The Road Warrior." *Famous Monsters of Filmland.* No. 186. Warren, August 1982; *Film Fantasy Yearbook 1983 Collector's Edition.* Warren, March 1983. (preview)

1645 "The Robinson Gru-So Story." *Famous Monsters of Filmland.* No. 8. September 1960. [pp. 42–45.] (on Chris Robinson)

1646 "Robots, Aliens, Spacemen Battle in Star Wars." *Famous Monsters of Filmland.* No. 137. Warren, September 1977. pp. 57–61; *Famous Monsters of Filmland.* No. 158. Warren, October 1979.

1647 "The Rocketeer." *The Rocket.* Vol. 1. No. 1. Ed. Walt Daugherty. March 1940. (discusses authors involved with the American Rocket Association)

1648 "Rocketship X-M." *Imagination.* Ed. Raymond A. Palmer. Clark Publishing Company. October 1950.

1649 "Romain Gary." *Locus: The Newspaper of the Science Fiction Field.* Vol. 13. No. 12. Ed. Charles N. Brown. December 1980/January 1981. p. 28. (obituary)

1650 "Rosemarie Ernsting." *Science Fiction Chronicle: The Monthly SF and Fantasy Newsmagazine.* Vol. 8. No. 6. Ed. Andrew I. Porter. March 1987. p. 10. (wife of Perry Rhodan author Walter Ernsting)

1651 "Row, Row, Row Your 'Bot Gently Down the Time Stream." *Worlds of Tomorrow: The Amazing Universe of Science Fiction Art.* with Brad Linaweaver. Portland, OR: Collectors Press, 2004. pp. 55–56.

1652 "Run, Logan, Run." *Famous Monsters of Filmland.* No. 123. Warren, March 1976.

1653 "The Russian Chronicles: Two Weeks in the Soviet Union, with SF People." *Science Fiction Chronicle: The Monthly SF and Fantasy Newsmagazine.* Vol. 4. No. 1. Ed. Andrew Porter. New York: October 1982. pp. 9–10.

1654 "Saga of Shibano." *Science Fiction Times.* No. 459. October 1968. pp. 5, 8. (on Japanese fan Takumi Shibano's visit to Los Angeles)

1655 "St. George and the 7 Curses." *Famous Monsters of Filmland.* Vol. 3. No. 4. whole No. 13. Philadelphia: Central Publications, Inc., August 1961. [pp. 22–28]. [As "The Magic Sword."] *Famous Monsters of Filmland 1965 Yearbook.* No. 3. Warren, 1965; *Famous Monsters of Filmland.* No. 36. Warren, December 1965. pp. 14–22.

1656 "Sam the Simoleon Saver." Coker, John L. III. *Days of Wonder: Remembering Sam Moskowitz and Conrad H. Ruppert.* Orlando, FL: Days of Wonder Press, 1998. p. 8; *Tales of the Time Travelers: Adventures of Forrest J Ackerman and Julius Schwartz.* Ed. John L. Coker, III. Orlando, FL: Days of Wonder Publishers, 2009.

1657 "The Sapphic Cinema." [As Laurajean Ermayne.] *The Ladder.* Vol. 4. No. 7. San Francisco, CA: Daughters of Bilitis, 1960. (listing of films featuring lesbian themes)

1658 "Saturday the 14th." *Famous Monsters of Filmland.* No. 177. Warren, September 1981. (preview)

1659 "Saturn 3." *Famous Monsters of Filmland.* No. 164. Warren, June 1980; *Warren Presents the Official Exclusive Horror Movie Yearbook 1981 Collector's Edition.* Warren, February 1981.

1660 "Scanners." *Famous Monsters of Filmland.* No. 172. Warren, April 1981. (preview)

1661 "Scares, Scars & SPFX." *Famous Monsters of Filmland.* No. 187. Warren, September 1982.

1662 "Scene at S.F. Convention." *Science-Fiction Monthly.* No. 15. Melbourne, Australia: Atlas Publications Pty. Ltd., November 1956.

1663 "Scene on the Screen." *Science-Fiction Monthly.* No. 12. Melbourne, Australia: Atlas Publications Pty. Ltd., August 1956.

1664 "Scene on the Screen." *Science-Fiction Monthly.* No. 13. Melbourne, Australia: Atlas Publications Pty. Ltd., September 1956.

1665 "Scene on the Screen." *Science-Fiction Monthly.* No. 14. Melbourne, Australia: Atlas Publications Pty. Ltd., October 1956.

1666 "Scene on the Screen." *Science-Fiction Monthly.* No. 16. Melbourne, Australia: Atlas Publications Pty. Ltd., December 1956. (Bela Lugosi obituary)

1667 "Scene on the Screen." *Science Fiction Monthly.* No. 18. Melbourne, Australia: Atlas Publications Pty. Ltd., February 1957.

1668 "Schlock!" *Famous Monsters of Filmland.* No. 96. Warren, March 1973.

1669 "Science Fantasy: California." [As Norris Chapnick.] *Luna Monthly.* No. 8. Ed. Ann F. Dietz. Oradell, NJ: January 1970. pp. 4–5.

1670 "Science Fantasy: California II." [As Norris Chapnick.] *Luna Monthly.* No. 9. Ed. Ann F. Dietz. Oradell, NJ: February 1970. p. 4.

1671 "Science Fantasy: California." [As Norris Chapnick.] *Luna Monthly.* No. 10. Ed. Ann F. Dietz. Oradell, NJ: March 1970. pp. 4–5.

1672 "Science Fantasy Movie Review Supplement." *Scienti-Snaps.* Vol. 2. No. 3. Ed. Walter E. Marconette. Dayton, OH: Empress Publications, June 1939. (*F.P.I.*)

1673 "Science Fiction Fans Are Stub(born)." *FAN.* Ed. Walter J. Daugherty. July 1946. (for Pacificon)

1674 "Science Fiction Marquee: 1956." *The Science Fiction Yearbook 1957 Edition.* Ed. James V. Taurasi, Sr., Ray Van Houten and Frank Prieto. Paterson, NJ: Fandom House, 1957. pp. 18–19.

1675 "Science Fiction, Messenger of Light." *Fantasy Times.* No. 221. Ed. James V. Taurasi. April 2, 1955. pp. 3–5. (defending Walter Ernsting's German fanzine *Utopia*)

1676 "Science Fiction Serial." *Fantasy Magazine.* Vol. 4. No. 2. No. 26. Ed. Julius Schwartz. Jamaica, NY: Science Fiction Digest Company, October–November 1934.

1677 "The Scientelegram." *Science Fiction Digest.* Vol. 1. No. 1. South Ozone Park, NY: Maurice Z. Ingher, September 1932.

1678 "The Scientelegram." *Science Fiction Digest.* Vol. 1. No. 3. South Ozone Park, NY: Maurice Z. Ingher, November 1932.

1679 "SCIENTI-Claus on LA." *Shangri L'Affaires.* No. 34. December 1946. pp. 14–15.

1680 "Scientificinema News." *Science Fiction Digest.* South Ozone Park, NY: Maurice Z. Ingher, October 1932.

1681 "Scientificinematorially Speaking." *Fantasy Magazine.* Vol. 3. No. 1. Whole No. 19. Ed. Julius Schwartz. Jamaica, NY: Conrad H. Ruppert, March 1934.

1682 "Scientificinematorially Speaking." *Fantasy Magazine.* Vol. 3. No. 5. No. 23. Ed. Julius Schwartz. Jamaica, NY: Science Fiction Digest Company, July 1934. pp. 9, 11. [*The Young Diana,* etc.]

1683 "Scientificinematorially Speaking." *Fantasy Magazine.* Vol. 4. No. 1. No. 25. Ed. Julius Schwartz. Jamaica, NY: Science Fiction Digest Company, September 1934.

1684 "Scientificinematorially Speaking." *Fantasy Magazine.* Vol. 4 No. 4. Whole No. 28. Ed. Julius Schwartz. February/March 1935.

1685 "Scientificinematorially Speaking." *Fantasy Magazine.* Vol. 4. No. 6. Ed. Julius Schwartz. Jamaica, NY: May 1935.

1686 "Scientificinematorially Speaking." *Fantasy Magazine.* Vol. 5. No. 3. No. 33. Ed. Julius Schwartz. Jamaica, NY: August 1935.

1687 "Scientificinematorially Speaking." *Fantasy Magazine.* Vol. 5. No. 4. No. 34. Ed. Julius Schwartz. Jamaica, NY: September 1935.

1688 "Scientificinematorially Speaking." *Fantasy Magazine.* Vol. 6. No. 4. No. 38. Jamaica, NY: September 1936. (*Flash Gordon* serial)

1689 "Scientificinematorially Speaking." *Perry Rhodan. No. 32. Challenge of the Unknown.* Clark Darlton. New York: Ace. October 1973.

1690 "Scientificinematorially Speaking." *Science Fiction Digest.* Vol. 1. No. 10. Jamaica, NY: Conrad H. Ruppert, June 1933. (*Men Must Fight, Evolution*)

1691 "Scientificinematorially Speaking." *Science Fiction Digest.* Vol. 1. No. 11. Jamaica, NY: Conrad H. Ruppert, July 1933; as "Fritz Lang's Woman in the Moon." *Perry Rhodan. No. 31. Realm of the Tri-Planets.* New York: Ace, October 1973; London: Futura Publications, 1973. (Fritz Lang's *Frau im Mond* a.k.a. *By Rocket to the Moon*)

1692 "Scientificinematorially Speaking." *Science Fiction Digest.* Vol. 1. No. 12. Jamaica, NY: Conrad H. Ruppert, August 1933. (covers the German film *The Strange Case of Captain Ramper, King Kong*)

1693 "Scientificinematorially Speaking." *Science Fiction Digest.* Vol. 2. No. 3. Ed. Julius Schwartz. Jamaica, NY: Conrad H. Ruppert, October 1933.

1694 "Scientifilm, a Definition." *The Time Traveller.* Vol. 1. No. 7. August 1932.

1695 "Scientifilm Marquee." *Imagination Science Fiction.* Ed. William L. Hamling. Greenleaf Publishing Company, October 1955.

1696 "Scientifilm Marquee." *Imaginative Tales.* Ed. William L. Hamling. Greenleaf Publishing Company, January 1956.

1697 "Scientifilm Marquee." *Imaginative Tales.* Ed. William L. Hamling. Greenleaf Publishing Company, March 1956.

1698 "Scientifilm Marquee." *Imaginative Tales.* Vol. 3. No. 3. Ed. William L. Hamling. Greenleaf Publishing Company, May 1956. pp. 96–99.

1699 "Scientifilm Marquee." *Imaginative Tales.* Vol. 3. No. 4. Ed. William L. Hamling. Evanston, IL: Greenleaf Publishing, July 1956.

1700 "Scientifilm Marquee." *Imaginative Tales.* Ed. William L. Hamling. Greenleaf Publishing, September 1956.

1701 "Scientifilm Marquee." *Imaginative Tales.* Ed. William L. Hamling. Greenleaf Publishing, November 1956.

1702 "Scientifilm Marquee." *Imaginative Tales.* Ed. William L. Hamling. Greenleaf Publishing, January 1957.

1703 "Scientifilm Marquee." *Imaginative Tales.* Ed. William L. Hamling. Greenleaf Publishing, March 1957.

1704 "Scientifilm Marquee." *Imaginative Tales.* Ed. William L. Hamling. Greenleaf Publishing, May 1957.

1705 "Scientifilm Marquee." *Imaginative Tales.* Ed. William L. Hamling. Greenleaf Publishing, July 1957.

1706 "Scientifilm Marquee." *Imaginative Tales.* Ed. William L. Hamling. Greenleaf Publishing, September 1957.

1707 "Scientifilm Marquee." *Imaginative Tales.* Ed. William L. Hamling. Greenleaf Publishing, November 1957.

1708 "Scientifilm Marquee." *Imaginative Tales.* Ed. William L. Hamling. Greenleaf Publishing, January 1958.

1709 "Scientifilm Marquee." *Imaginative Tales.* Ed. William L. Hamling. Greenleaf Publishing, March 1958.

1710 "Scientifilm Marquee." *Imaginative Tales.* Ed. William L. Hamling. Greenleaf Publishing, May 1958.

1711 "Scientifilm Marquee." *Space Travel.* Ed. William L. Hamling. IL: Greenleaf Publishing Company, July 1958.

1712 "Scientifilm Marquee." *Space Travel.* Ed. William L. Hamling. IL: Greenleaf Publishing Company, September 1958.

1713 "Scientifilm Mystery Solved." (anonymous) *Fantasy News.* Ed. James V. Taurasi. New York: 18 August 1940.

1714 "Scientifilm News." *The Time Traveller.* Vol. 1. No. 6. July 1932.

1715 "Scientifilm News." *The Time Traveller.* Vol. 1. No. 8. September 1932.

1716 "The Scientifilm Parade." [As Spencer Strong.] *Fantasy Times.* Vol. 8. No. 16. No. 184. August 1953. p. 4. ("Chad Oliver's *Astounding* Story 'The Edge of Forever' Has Been Sold to Television. Another Ackerman Deal.")

1717 "The Scientifilm Parade." [As Weaver Wright.] *Fantasy Times.* December 1951.

1718 "The Scientifilm Parade. " *Fantasy Times.* No. 148. (2nd February 1952 issue)

1719 "The Scientifilm Parade." *Fantasy Times.* (1st May 1952 issue).

1720 "The Scientifilm Parade." *Fantasy Times.* (2nd May 1952 issue).

1721 "Scientifilm Parade" *Spaceway.* Ed. William L. Crawford. Fantasy Publishing Co., Inc., June 1955.

1722 "Scientifilm Parade." *Spaceway.* (UK) Vol. 1. No. 2. Ed. William L. Crawford. Regular Publications Ltd. February 1954.

1723 "Scientifilm Parade." *Spaceway.* (UK) Vol. 1. No. 4. Ed. William L. Crawford. Regular Publications Ltd. 1956.

1724 "Scientifilm Parade." *Spaceway Stories of the Future.* Vol. 1. No. 1. CA: Fantasy Publishing. February 1954. (*Project Moonbase, Donovan's Brain, War of the Worlds*); (section on *Project Moonbase*) *Perry Rhodan. No. 57. A Touch of Eternity.* Clark Darlton. New York: Ace, November 1974.

1725 "Scientifilm Parade." *Spaceway Stories of the Future.* Vol. 1. No. 3. CA: Fantasy Publishing,

April 1954; *Spaceway*. (UK) Vol. 1. No. 3. Ed. William L. Crawford. Regular Publications Ltd., April 1954. (*Riders to the stars*)

1726 "Scientifilm Parade." *Spaceway Stories of the Future*. Vol. 2. No. 1. CA: Fantasy Publishing, June 1954.

1727 "Scientifilm Parade." *Spaceway Stories of the Future*. Vol. 2. No. 2. CA: Fantasy Publishing, December 1954.

1728 "Scientifilm Parade." *Spaceway Stories of the Future*. Vol. 2. No. 3. CA: Fantasy Publishing, February 1955. (*This Island Earth*)

1729 "Scientifilm Previews." *Nebula Science Fiction*. No. 2. Ed. Peter Hamilton. Glasgow: Crownpoint Publications, Spring 1953.

1730 "Scientifilm Previews." *Nebula Science Fiction*. No. 3. Ed. Peter Hamilton. Glasgow: Crownpoint Publications, Summer 1953. (*The War of the Worlds*)

1731 "Scientifilm Previews." *Nebula Science Fiction*. No. 4. Vol. 1. No. 4. Glasgow: Crownpoint Publications, Autumn 1953.

1732 "Scientifilm Previews." *Nebula Science Fiction*. No. 5. Vol. 2. No. 1. Glasgow: Crownpoint Publications, September 1953.

1733 "Scientifilm Previews." *Nebula Science Fiction*. No. 6. Vol. 2. No. 2. Glasgow: Crownpoint Publications, December 1953.

1734 "Scientifilm Previews." *Nebula Science Fiction*. Vol. 2. No. 3. Whole No. 7. Ed. Peter Hamilton. Glasgow: Crownpoint Publications, February 1954.

1735 "Scientifilm Previews." *Nebula Science Fiction*. No. 8. Glasgow: Crownpoint Publications, Peter Hamilton. Vol. 2. No. 3. April 1954.

1736 "Scientifilm Previews." *Nebula Science Fiction*. No. 10. Glasgow: Peter Hamilton. October 1954; as "Killers from Space." *Perry Rhodan No. 34. SOS: Spaceship Titan!* Kurt Brand. New York: Ace, November 1973; London: Orbit, 1978.

1737 "Scientifilm Previews." *Nebula Science Fiction*. No. 11. Glasgow: Peter Hamilton. December 1954.

1738 "Scientifilm Previews." *Nebula Science Fiction*. No. 12. Glasgow: Peter Hamilton. April 1955.

1739 "Scientifilm Previews." *Nebula Science Fiction*. No. 13. Glasgow: Peter Hamilton. September 1955. (Edward D. Wood, Jr.'s *Bride of the Atom* a.k.a. *Bride of the Monster*)

1740 "Scientifilm Previews." *Nebula Science Fiction*. No. 14. Glasgow: Peter Hamilton. November 1955. (*Invasion of the Body Snatchers*, *The Beast with 1,000,000 Eyes*)

1741 "Scientifilm Previews." *Nebula Science Fiction*. No. 15. Glasgow: Peter Hamilton. January 1956.

1742 "Scientifilm Previews." *Nebula Science Fiction*. No. 16. Ed. Peter Hamilton. Glasgow, March 1956. (*The Phantom from 10,000 Leagues*, *Tarantula*)

1743 "Scientifilm Previews." *Nebula Science Fiction*. No. 17. Ed. Peter Hamilton. Glasgow, July 1956.

1744 "Scientifilm Previews." *Nebula Science Fiction*. No. 19. Ed. Peter Hamilton. Glasgow, December 1956.

1745 "Scientifilm Previews." *Nebula Science Fiction*. No. 20. Ed. Peter Hamilton, Glasgow: March 1957.

1746 "Scientifilm Previews." *Nebula Science Fiction*. No. 21. Ed. Peter Hamilton. Glasgow: May 1957.

1747 "Scientifilm Previews." *Nebula Science Fiction*. No. 22. Ed. Peter Hamilton. Glasgow: July 1957.

1748 "Scientifilm Previews." *Nebula Science Fiction*. No. 23. Ed. Peter Hamilton. Glasgow: August 1957.

1749 "Scientifilm Previews." *Nebula Science Fiction*. No. 24. Ed. Peter Hamilton. Glasgow, September 1957. (reviews of *Invasion of the Saucer-Men*, *The Monster That Challenged the World*, *The Vampire*); (section on) "The Invasion of the Saucer-Men." *Perry Rhodan. No. 62. The Last Days of Atlantis*. K. H. Scheer. New York: Ace, January 1975.

1750 "Scientifilm Previews." *Nebula Science Fiction*. No. 25. Ed. Peter Hamilton. Glasgow, October 1957.

1751 "Scientifilm Previews." *Nebula Science Fiction*. No. 26. Ed. Peter Hamilton. Glasgow, January 1958.

1752 "Scientifilm Previews." *Nebula Science Fiction*. No. 27. Ed. Peter Hamilton. Glasgow, February 1958.

1753 "Scientifilm Previews." *Nebula Science Fiction*. No. 28. Ed. Peter Hamilton. Glasgow, March 1958.

1754 "Scientifilm Previews." *Nebula Science Fiction*. No. 29. Ed. Peter Hamilton. Glasgow, April 1958.

1755 "Scientifilm Previews." *Nebula Science Fiction*. No. 30. Ed. Peter Hamilton. Glasgow, May 1958.

1756 "Scientifilm Previews." *Nebula Science Fiction*. No. 31. Ed. Peter Hamilton. Glasgow, June 1958.

1757 "Scientifilm Previews." *Nebula Science Fiction*. No. 33. Ed. Peter Hamilton. Glasgow, August 1958.

1758 "Scientifilm Previews." *Nebula Science Fiction.* No. 34. Ed. Peter Hamilton. Glasgow, September 1958.

1759 "Scientifilm Previews." *Nebula Science Fiction.* No. 35. Ed. Peter Hamilton. Glasgow, October 1958.

1760 "Scientifilm Previews." *Nebula Science Fiction.* No. 36. Ed. Peter Hamilton. Glasgow, November 1958. (reviews of *The Blob, I Married a Monster from Outer Space, Earth vs. The Spider, Teenage Caveman, How to Make a Monster*); (section on) "The Blob." *Perry Rhodan. No. 61. Death Waits in Semispace.* Kurt Mahr. New York: Ace, January 1975.

1761 "Scientifilm Previews." *Nebula Science Fiction.* No. 37. Ed. Peter Hamilton. Glasgow, December 1958.

1762 "Scientifilm Previews." *Nebula Science Fiction.* No. 38. Ed. Peter Hamilton. Glasgow, January 1959.

1763 "Scientifilm Realm." *Odyssey.* Vol. 1. No. 2. Ed. Roger Elwood. Summer 1976. New York: Gambi Publications, 1976.

1764 "Scientifilm Searchlight." *Flying Saucers from Other Worlds.* Ed. Raymond A. Palmer. Evanston, IL: Palmer Publications, Inc., July 1957.

1765 "Scientifilm Searchlight." *Other Worlds Science Stories.* No. 21. Ed. Raymond A. Palmer. Evanston, IL: Palmer Publications, Inc., March 1957. (photo of Ackerman on cover)

1766 "Scientifilm Snap." *Science Fiction Digest.* Vol. 1. No. 9. Jamaica, NY: Conrad H. Ruppert, May 1933.

1767 "Scientifilm Snapshots." *Fantasy Magazine.* Vol. 2. No. 5. No. 17. Ed. Julius Schwartz. Jamaica, NY: Conrad H. Ruppert, January 1934.

1768 "Scientifilm Snapshots." *Fantasy Magazine.* Vol. 3. No. 2. No. 20. Ed. Julius Schwartz. Jamaica, NY: Conrad H. Ruppert, April 1934.

1769 "Scientifilm Snapshots." *Fantasy Magazine.* Vol. 3. No. 4. No. 22. Ed. Julius Schwartz. Jamaica, NY: Conrad H. Ruppert, June 1934.

1770 "Scientifilm Snapshots." *Fantasy Magazine.* Vol. 3. No. 6. No. 24. Ed. Julius Schwartz. Jamaica, NY: Science Fiction Digest Company, August 1934.

1771 "Scientifilm Snapshots." *Fantasy Magazine.* Vol. 4. No. 2. No. 26. Ed. Julius Schwartz. Jamaica, NY: Science Fiction Digest Company, October-November 1934.

1772 "Scientifilm Snapshots." *Fantasy Magazine.* Vol. 4. No. 3. No. 27. Ed. Julius Schwartz. Jamaica, NY: Science Fiction Digest Company, December 1934/January 1935.

1773 "Scientifilm Snapshots." *Fantasy Magazine.* Vol. 4. No. 6. Ed. Julius Schwartz. Jamaica, NY: May 1935.

1774 "Scientifilm Snapshots." *Fantasy Magazine.* Vol. 5. No. 1. No. 31. Ed. Julius Schwartz. Jamaica, NY: June 1935.

1775 "Scientifilm Snapshots." *Fantasy Magazine.* Vol. 5. No. 2. No. 32. Ed. Julius Schwartz. Jamaica, NY: July 1935. (also review of *The Return of Peter Grimm*)

1776 "Scientifilm Snapshots." *Fantasy Magazine.* Vol. 5. No. 3. No. 33. Ed. Julius Schwartz. Jamaica, NY: August 1935.

1777 "Scientifilm Snapshots." *Fantasy Magazine.* Vol. 5. No. 4. No. 34. Ed. Julius Schwartz. Jamaica, NY: September 1935.

1778 "Scientifilm Snapshots." *Fantasy Magazine.* Vol. 6. No. 1. No. 35. Ed. Julius Schwartz. Jamaica, NY: January 1936.

1779 "Scientifilm Snapshots." *Fantasy Magazine.* Vol. 6. No. 2. No. 36. Ed. Julius Schwartz. Jamaica, NY: March 1936.

1780 "Scientifilm Snapshots." *Fantasy Magazine.* Vol. 6. No. 3. Ed. Julius Schwartz. Jamaica, NY: June 1936.

1781 "Scientifilm Snapshots." *Science Fiction Digest.* Vol. 2. No. 2. Ed. Julius Schwartz. Jamaica, NY: Conrad H. Ruppert, October 1933. (covers *Bride of Frankenstein* [then called *The Return of Frankenstein*], *Island of Lost Souls, L'Atlantide*; *King of the Jungle,* etc.)

1782 "Scientifilm Snapshots." *Science Fiction Digest.* Vol. 2. No. 3. Ed. Julius Schwartz. Jamaica, NY: Conrad H. Ruppert, November 1933.

1783 "Scientifilm Special." *Science Fiction Digest.* Vol. 2. No. 3. October 1933. (*The Invisible Man*)

1784 "The Scientifilm Story." *A Reference Guide to American Science Fiction Films. Volume 1.* [With A. W. Strickland.] Bloomington, IN: T.I.S. Publications Division, 1981. p. vii. (Ackerman's foreword)

1785 "Scientifilm Synopses." *The Time Traveller.* Vol. 1. No. 4. April-May 1932. (*The Last Man on Earth*)

1786 "Scientifilm Synopses." *The Time Traveller.* Vol. 1. No. 5. June 1932. (*High Treason*)

1787 "Scientifilm Synopses." *The Time Traveller.* Vol. 1. No. 6. July 1932. (*Aelita*)

1788 "Scientifilm Synopses." *The Time Traveller.* Vol. 1. No. 7. August 1932. (*A Message from Mars*)

1789 "Scientifilm Synopses." *The Time Traveller.* Vol. 1. No. 8. September 1932. (*The Cabinet of Dr. Caligari*)

1790 "Scientifilm Theme Songs." *Fantasy Magazine.* Vol. 2. No. 6. Ed. Julius Schwartz. Jamaica, NY: Conrad H. Ruppert, February 1934.

1791 "Scientifilm World." *Perry Rhodan. No. 6: The Secret of the Time Vault.* New York: Ace Books, 1971, 1972, 1974; London : Futura Publications, 1975.

1792 "Scientifilm World." *Perry Rhodan. No. 7. Fortress of the Six Moons.* K. H. Scheer. New York: Ace, September 1971, 1972, 1974.

1793 "Scientifilm World." *Perry Rhodan. No. 8. The Galactic Riddle.* Clark Darlton. New York: Ace, October 1971, 1972, 1974; London: Futura Publications, 1975.

1794 "Scientifilm World." *Perry Rhodan. No. 9. Quest Through Space and Time.* Clark Darlton. New York: Ace, November 1971, 1974; London: Futura Publications, 1975.

1795 "Scientifilm World." *Perry Rhodan. No. 10. The Ghosts of Gol.* Kurt Mahr. New York: Ace, December 1971, 1972, 1974.

1796 "Scientifilm World." *Perry Rhodan. No. 11. Planet of the Dying Sun.* Kurt Mahr. New York: Ace, February 1972, 1974.

1797 "Scientifilm World." *Perry Rhodan. No. 12. Rebels of Tuglan.* Clark Darlton. New York: Ace, April 1972, 1974; London Futura Publications, 1976.

1798 "Scientifilm World." *Perry Rhodan. No. 13. The Immortal Unknown.* K. H. Scheer. New York: Ace, May 1972, 1974; London: Futura Publications, 1976.

1799 "Scientifilm World." *Perry Rhodan. No. 14. Venus in Danger.* Kurt Mahr. New York: Ace, June 1972. 1974.

1800 "Scientifilm World." *Perry Rhodan. No. 15. Escape to Venus.* Clark Darlton. New York: Ace, July 1972; 1974.

1801 "Scientifilm World." *Perry Rhodan. No. 16. Secret Barrier X.* W. W. Shols. New York: Ace Books, 1972.

1802 "Scientifilm World." *Perry Rhodan. No. 17. The Venus Trap.* Kurt Mahr. Ace, September, 1972.

1803 "Scientifilm World." *Perry Rhodan. No. 18. Menace of the Mutant Master.* Kurt Mahr. New York: Ace Books, 1972.

1804 "Scientifilm World." *Perry Rhodan. No. 19. Mutants vs. Mutants.* Clark Darlton. New York: Ace, November 1972; London: Futura, 1976.

1805 "Scientifilm World." *Perry Rhodan. No. 20. The Thrall of Hypno.* Clark Darlton. New York: Ace, December 1972; London: Futura, 1976.

1806 "Scientifilm World: The End of the World." *Science Fiction Digest?*?? [1931]; *Perry Rhodan.*

No. 66. The Horror. William Voltz. New York: Ace Books, 1975.

1807 "Scientifilmaticorrespondence." *Glom.* No. 6. January 1947.

1808 "Scientifilms." *Fantasy Magazine.* Vol. 6. No. 3. Ed. Julius Schwartz. Jamaica, NY: June 1936. (*Condemned to Live, The Man Who Changed His Mind* (a.k.a. *The Man Who Lived Again*), *The Witch of Timbuctu* [released as *The Devil-Doll*] and *Trapped by Television*)

1809 "The Scientifilms." *Science Fiction Digest.* Vol. 1. No. 6. South Ozone Park, NY: Maurice Z. Ingher, February 1933. (*Our Heavenly Bodies, The Golem, The Sky Splitter*)

1810 "The Scientifilms." *Science Fiction Digest.* Vol. 1. No. 7. South Ozone Park, NY: Maurice Z. Ingher, March 1933. (*Metropolis, Betty Boop's Ups and Downs, Radio-Mania*)

1811 "The Scientifilms." *Science Fiction Digest.* Vol. 1. No. 9. Jamaica, NY: Conrad H. Ruppert, May 1933. (*Along the Moon Beam Trail, The Stellar Express, Colonel Heeza Liar*)

1812 "Scientifilms." *The Time Traveller.* Vol. 1. No. 1. January 1932. p. 1. (the oft-cited list of "Scientifilms"— supposedly the first such compiled — by Ackerman including *Dracula*, etc.)

1813 "Scientifilms and the Silver (Dollar) Screen." *SFWA Bulletin.* Vol. 2. No. 2. April 1966. pp. 10–11.

1814 "Scientifilms Never Seen." *Fantasy Magazine.* Vol. 4. No. 6. Ed. Julius Schwartz. Jamaica, NY: May 1935.

1815 "Sci-Fi Flashes." *Etherline.* No. 64. Ed. Ian J. Crozier. Australia: 195-

1816 "Sci-Fi Flashes." *Etherline.* No. 65. Ed. Ian J. Crozier. Australia: 1956[?]

1817 "Sci-Fi Flashes." *Etherline.* No. 71. Ed. Ian J. Crozier. Australia: 195-

1818 "The Sci-Fi Guy: Forrest J Ackerman." *Lunacon '74* program book. (list of accomplishments)

1819 "Sci-Fi Is My Beat." *Offbeat Magazine.* Vol. 1. No. 6. Ed. Raymond Lee. Encino, CA: Defilee Pub, 1959; *Tales of the Time Travelers: Adventures of Forrest J Ackerman and Julius Schwartz.* Ed. John L. Coker, III. Orlando, FL: Days of Wonder Publishers, 2009.

1820 "Sci-Fi Knowledge Comes to College." [As Forry Rhodan.] *Perry Rhodan. No. 12. Rebels of Tuglan. Clark Darlton.* New York: Ace, April 1972, 1974.

1821 "Sci-Fi Meets Die-Fi." *Famous Monsters of Filmland.* No. 128. Warren, September 1976.

1822 "Sci-Fi Scene: L.A." *Fanac.* No. 28. Ed. Terry Carr and Ron Ellik. 28 October 1958.

1823 "Sci-Fi Scene: L.A." *Fanac.* No. 29. 16 November 1958.

1824 "Sci-Fi Scene: L.A." *Fanac.* No. 30. Ed. Terry Carr and Ron Ellik. 5 December 1958.

1825 "Sci-Fi Scene: L.A." *Fanac.* No. 31. Ed. Terry Carr and Ron Ellik. 18 December 1958. (column) [E. E. Evans funeral]

1826 "Sci-Fi Scene: L.A." *Fanac.* No. 33. Ed. Terry Carr and Ron Ellik. 14February 1959.

1827 "Sci-Fi Scene: L.A." *Fanac.* No. 34. Ed. Terry Carr and Ron Ellik. 24 February 1959.

1828 "Sci-Fi Scene: L.A." *Fanac.* No. 36. Ed. Terry Carr and Ron Ellik. 4 April 1959. (column)

1829 "Sci-Fi Scene: L.A." *Fanac.* No. 40. Ed. Terry Carr and Ron Ellik. 9 June 1959.

1830 "Sci-Fi Scene: L.A." *Fanac.* No. 71. Ed. Walter Breen. 28 January 1961.

1831 "Scream and Scream Again." *Famous Monsters of Filmland.* No. 90. Warren, May 1972.

1832 "The Scream Test." *Famous Monsters of Filmland.* Vol. 1. No. 1. Philadelphia: Central Publications, Inc., 1958. pp. 52–57; *James Warren Presents the Best from Famous Monsters of Filmland.* New York: Paperback Library, 1964; *Famous Monsters Yearbook.* No. 1. Summer-Fall 1962; *Famous Monsters 1968 Yearbook.* Warren, 1967; *Famous Monsters of Filmland.* Vol. 1. No. 1. Filmland Classics, January 2008. pp. 52–57. (replica edition)

1833 "Screaming Mimi." [As Dr. Acula.] *Famous Monsters of Filmland.* No. 28. Warren Publishing, Inc., May 1964.

1834 "Screamoscope Is Here!" *After Hours.* Vol. 1. No. 4. Ed. James Warren, Jay Publishing Co., Inc. 1957; *Pure Images.* No. 3. Ed. Greg Theakston. New York: Pure Imagination, 1991.

1835 "Screams on the Shiver Screen." *Famous Monsters of Filmland.* No. 177. Warren, September 1981.

1836 "2nd Fantastic Amateur Make-Up Contest!" *Famous Monsters of Filmland.* No. 36. Warren, December 1965. pp. 40–41; *Monster World.* No. 6. Warren, January 1966.

1837 "The Secret of the Mystery Pair." *Famous Monsters of Filmland.* No. 120. Warren, October 1975.

1838 "The Secret That Dr. Jeckyll Couldn't Hide." *Famous Monsters of Filmland.* Vol. 3. No. 2. Whole No. 11. Philadelphia: Central Publications, Inc., April 1961. [pp. 32–39.]

1839 "Senior Day." [As Ione Lee Hurd.] *The Buccaneer.* San Francisco, CA: Balboa High School, Friday 31 March 1933. (on a "miscellaneous dress" day held at the school)

1840 "The Seven Faces of Dr. Lao." *Famous Monsters of Filmland.* No. 29. Warren Publishing, Inc., July 1964. pp. 53–56; *Famous Monsters of Filmland.* No. 65. Warren, May 1970.

1841 "'Seymour' Nevermore." *Famous Monsters of Filmland.* No. 120. Warren, October 1975. (obituary of actor Larry Vincent)

1842 "The Shadows Lengthen ... and Life Ends." *Famous Monsters of Filmland.* No. 105. Warren, March 1974. (obituary of Glenn Strange)

1843 "Shadows of Yesteryear." *Forrest J Ackerman's Fantastic Movie Memories: Forrest Ackerman's Treasure Trove of Imagi-Movies.* Canoga Park, CA: New Media Books, 1985.

1844 "The Shake of Things to Come." *Famous Monsters of Filmland.* Vol. 2. No. 7. Philadelphia: Central Publications, Inc., June 1960. pp. 9–18.

1845 "The Shake of Things to Come." *Famous Monsters of Filmland.* No. 107. Warren, May 1974.

1846 "Shape of Screams to Come!" *Famous Monsters of Filmland.* No. 60. Warren, December 1969.

1847 "Shape of Space to Come." *Spacemen.* Vol. 1. No. 1. Philadelphia, PA: Spacemen, Inc., July 1961.

1848 "The Shape of Stings to Come!" *Famous Monsters of Filmland.* No. 40. Warren, August 1966. pp. 32–35.

1849 "The Shape of Things Ahead." *Famous Monsters of Filmland.* Vol. 4. No. 19. Philadelphia: Central Publications, Inc., September 1962; as "The Shape of Things Gone By." *Famous Monsters of Filmland.* No. 49. Warren, May 1968.

1850 "The Shape of Things That Came." *Worlds of Tomorrow: The Amazing Universe of Science Fiction Art.* with Brad Linaweaver. Portland, OR: Collectors Press, 2004. pp. 8–9.

1851 "The Shape of Things to Come." *Famous Monsters of Filmland.* Vol. 1. No. 2. Philadelphia: Central Publications, Inc., September 1958. [pp. 19–25.]

1852 "The Shape of Things to Come." *Famous Monsters of Filmland.* Vol. 1. No. 3. Philadelphia: Central Publications, Inc., April 1959; *Famous Monsters of Filmland 1969 Year Book/Fearbook.* New York: Warren Publishing Co., 1968.

1853 "The Shape of Things to Come." *Famous Monsters of Filmland.* No. 53. Warren, January 1969.

1854 "The Shape of Things to Come." *Famous Monsters of Filmland.* No. 169. Warren, November 1980.

1855 "Shape of Wings to Come." *Spacemen.* Vol. 1. No. 4. Philadelphia: Spacemen, Inc., July 1962.

1856 "The Shapes of Things to Come." *Famous Monsters of Filmland.* No. 152. Warren, April 1979. pp. 38–44.

1857 "The Shapes of Things to Come." *Forrest J Ackerman's Monsters & Imagi-Movies.* Ed. Robert V. Michelucci. Canoga Park, CA: New Media Pub. Co., 1985. pp. 12–13.

1858 "Shazam." *Famous Monsters of Filmland.* No. 101. Warren, September 1973. (actor Tom Tyler who starred in *The Adventures of Captain Marvel* movie serial)

1859 "The She Creature." *Monster World.* No. 3. Warren, April 1965; *Famous Monsters of Filmland.* No. 40. Warren, August 1966. pp. 48–57; *Famous Monsters of Filmland 1970 Year Book/Fearbook.* Warren, 1969; *Famous Monsters of Filmland.* No. 87. Warren, November 1971.

1860 "'She' Dies." *Famous Monsters of Filmland.* No. 171. Warren, March 1981. (obituary of actress Helen Gahagan Douglas)

1861 "Shedding Some Light on *The Black Hole.*" *Famous Monsters of Filmland.* No. 161. Warren, March 1980.

1862 "The Shining." *Famous Monsters of Filmland.* No. 167. Warren, September 1980; *Warren Presents the Official Exclusive Horror Movie Yearbook 1981 Collector's Edition.* Warren, February 1981. (preview)

1863 "The Ship of Things to Come." *Famous Monsters of Filmland.* Vol. 2. No. 9. November 1960. [pp. 9–18.]

1864 "The Ship of Things to Come." *Famous Monsters of Filmland.* No. 175. Warren, July 1981.

1865 "The Ship of Things to Come." *Perry Rhodan.* No. 7. Fortress of the Six Moons. K. H. Scheer. New York: Ace, September 1971, 1972, 1974.

1866 "The Ship of Things to Come." *Perry Rhodan.* No. 8. The Galactic Riddle. Clark Darlton. New York: Ace, October 1971, 1972, 1974; London: Futura Publications, 1975.

1867 "The Ship of Things to Come." *Perry Rhodan.* No. 10. The Ghosts of Gol. Kurt Mahr. New York: Ace, December 1971, 1972, 1974.

1868 "The Ship of Things to Come." *Perry Rhodan.* No. 11. Planet of the Dying Sun. Kurt Mahr. New York: Ace, February 1972, 1974.

1869 "The Ship of Things to Come." *Perry Rhodan.* No. 12. Rebels of Tuglan. Clark Darlton. New York: Ace, April 1972, 1974; London Futura Publications, 1976.

1870 "The Ship of Things to Come." *Perry Rhodan.* No. 13. The Immortal Unknown. K. H. Scheer. New York: Ace, May 1972, 1974; London: Futura Publications, 1976.

1871 "The Ship of Things to Come." *Perry Rhodan.* No. 14. Venus in Danger. Kurt Mahr. New York: Ace, June 1972. 1974.

1872 "The Ship of Things to Come." *Perry Rhodan.* No. 15. Escape to Venus. Clark Darlton. New York: Ace, July 1972; 1974.

1873 "The Ship of Things to Come." *Perry Rhodan No. 16. Secret Barrier X.* W. W. Shols. New York: August 1972; 1974.

1874 "The Ship of Things to Come." *Perry Rhodan.* No. 18. Menace of the Mutant Master. Kurt Mahr. New York: Ace Books, 1972.

1875 "The Ship of Things to Come." *Perry Rhodan.* No. 20. The Thrall of Hypno. Clark Darlton. New York: Ace, December 1972; London: Futura, 1976.

1876 "The Ship of Things to Come." *Perry Rhodan.* No. 21. The Cosmic Decoy. K. H. Scheer. New York: Ace, January 1973.

1877 "The Ship of Things to Come." *Perry Rhodan.* No. 22. The Fleet of the Springers. Kurt Mahr. New York: Ace Books, March 1973; London: Futura, 1977.

1878 "The Ship of Things to Come." *Perry Rhodan.* No. 23. Peril on Ice Planet. Kurt Mahr. New York: Ace, April 1973.

1879 "The Ship of Things to Come." *Perry Rhodan.* No. 24. Infinity Flight. Clark Darlton. New York: Ace, May 1973.

1880 "The Ship of Things to Come." *Perry Rhodan.* No. 28. The Plague of Oblivion. Clark Darlton. New York: Ace, August 1973; London: Futura, 1977.

1881 "The Ship of Things to Come." *Perry Rhodan.* No. 30. To Arkon! Kurt Mahr. New York: Ace, September 1973.

1882 "The Ship of Things to Come." *Perry Rhodan.* No. 31. Realm of the Tri-Planets. K. H. Scheer. New York: Ace, October 1973; London: Futura Publications, 1973.

1883 "The Ship of Things to Come." *Perry Rhodan.* No. 32. Challenge of the Unknown. Clark Darlton. New York: Ace. October 1973.

1884 "The Ship of Things to Come." *Perry Rhodan.* No. 33. The Giant's Partner. Clark Darlton. New York: Ace, November 1973.

1885 "The Ship of Things to Come." *Perry Rhodan No. 34. SOS: Spaceship Titan!* Kurt Brand. New York: Ace, November 1973; London: Orbit, 1978.

1886 "The Ship of Things to Come." *Perry Rhodan. No. 35. Beware the Microbots.* Kurt Mahr. New York: Ace, December 1973.

1887 "The Ship of Things to Come." *Perry Rhodan. No. 36. Man and Monster.* K. H. Scheer. New York: Ace, 1973.

1888 "The Ship of Things to Come." *Perry Rhodan. No. 37. Epidemic Center: Aralon.* Clark Darlton. New York: Ace, January 1974.

1889 "The Ship of Things to Come." *Perry Rhodan. No. 39. The Silence of Gom.* Kurt Mahr. New York: Ace, February 1974.

1890 "The Ship of Things to Come." *Perry Rhodan. No. 40. Red Eye of Betelgeuse.* Clark Darlton. New York: Ace, February 1974.

1891 "The Ship of Things to Come." *Perry Rhodan. No. 41. The Earth Dies.* Clark Darlton. New York: Ace, March 1974.

1892 "The Ship of Things to Come." *Perry Rhodan. No. 42. Time's Lonely One.* K. H. Scheer. New York: Ace, March 1974.

1893 "The Ship of Things to Come." *Perry Rhodan. No. 43. Life Hunt.* Kurt Brand. New York: Ace, April 1974.

1894 "The Ship of Things to Come." *Perry Rhodan. No. 44. The Pseudo One.* Clark Darlton. New York: Ace, April 1974.

1895 "The Ship of Things to Come." *Perry Rhodan. No. 46. Again Atlan!* K. H. Scheer. New York: Ace, May 1974.

1896 "The Ship of Things to Come." *Perry Rhodan. No. 47. Shadow of the Mutant Master.* Kurt Brand. New York: Ace, June 1974.

1897 "The Ship of Things to Come." *Perry Rhodan. No. 48. The Dead Live.* Clark Darlton. New York: Ace, June 1974.

1898 "The Ship of Things to Come." *Perry Rhodan. No. 49. Solar Assassins.* Kurt Mahr. New York: Ace, July 1974.

1899 "The Ship of Things to Come." *Perry Rhodan. No. 50. Attack from the Unseen.* Clark Darlton. New York: Ace, July 1974.

1900 "The Ship of Things to Come." *Perry Rhodan. No. 52. Fortress Atlantis.* K. H. Scheer. New York: Ace, August 1974.

1901 "The Ship of Things to Come." *Perry Rhodan. No. 53. Spybot!* Clark Darlton. New York: Ace, September 1974.

1902 "The Ship of Things to Come." *Perry Rhodan. No. 54. The Blue Dwarfs.* Kurt Mahr. New York: Ace, September 1974.

1903 "The Ship of Things to Come." *Perry Rhodan. No. 55. The Micro-Techs.* Clark Darlton. New York: Ace, October 1974.

1904 "The Ship of Things to Come." *Perry Rhodan. No. 56. Prisoner of Time.* Clark Darlton. New York: Ace, October 1974.

1905 "The Ship of Things to Come." *Perry Rhodan. No. 57. A Touch of Eternity.* Clark Darlton. New York: Ace, November 1974.

1906 "The Ship of Things to Come." *Perry Rhodan. No. 58. The Guardians.* Kurt Mahr. New York: Ace, November 1974.

1907 "The Ship of Things to Come." *Perry Rhodan. No. 59. Interlude on Siliko 5.* Kurt Brand. New York: Ace, December 1974.

1908 "The Ship of Things to Come." *Perry Rhodan. No. 60. Dimension Search.* Clark Darlton. New York: Ace, December 1974.

1909 "The Ship of Things to Come." *Perry Rhodan. No. 61. Death Waits in Semispace.* Kurt Mahr. New York: Ace, January 1975.

1910 "The Ship of Things to Come." *Perry Rhodan. No. 63. The Tigris Leaps.* Kurt Brand. New York: Ace, February 1975.

1911 "The Ship of Things to Come." *Perry Rhodan No. 64. The Ambassadors from Aurigel.* Kurt Mahr. New York: Ace, February 1975.

1912 "The Ship of Things to Come." *Perry Rhodan. No. 66. The Horror.* William Voltz. New York: Ace Books, 1975.

1913 "The Ship of Things to Come." *Perry Rhodan. No. 69. The Bonds of Eternity.* Clark Darlton. New York: Ace, April 1975.

1914 "The Ship of Things to Come." *Perry Rhodan. No. 70. Thora's Sacrifice.* Kurt Brand. New York: Ace, April 1975.

1915 "The Ship of Things to Come." *Perry Rhodan. No. 71. The Atom Hell of Grautier.* Kurt Mahr. New York: Ace, May 1975.

1916 "The Ship of Things to Come." *Perry Rhodan. No. 72. Caves of the Druuffs.* Kurt Mahr. New York: Ace, May 1975.

1917 "The Ship of Things to Come." *Perry Rhodan. No. 73. Spaceship of Ancestors.* Clark Darlton. New York: Ace, June 1975.

1918 "The Ship of Things to Come." *Perry Rhodan. No. 74. Checkmate: Universe.* Clark Darlton. New York: Ace, July 1975.

1919 "The Ship of Things to Come." *Perry Rhodan. No. 75. Planet Topide, Please Reply!* Kurt Brand. New York: Ace, July 1975.

1920 "The Ship of Things to Come." *Perry Rhodan. No. 76. Recruits for Arkon.* Clark Darlton. New York: Ace, August 1975.

1921 "The Ship of Things to Come." *Perry Rhodan. No. 77. Conflict Center: Naator.* Clark Darlton. New York: Ace, August 1975.

1922 "The Ship of Things to Come." *Perry Rhodan. No. 78. Power Key.* K. H. Scheer. New York: Ace, September 1975.

1923 "The Ship of Things to Come." *Perry Rhodan. No. 79. The Sleepers.* William Voltz. New York: Ace, September 1975.

1924 "The Ship of Things to Come." *Perry Rhodan. No. 80. The Columbus Affair.* K. H. Scheer. New York: Ace, October 1975.

1925 "The Ship of Things to Come." *Perry Rhodan. No. 81. Pucky's Greatest Hour.* Kurt Brand. New York: Ace, October 1975.

1926 "The Ship of Things to Come." *Perry Rhodan. No. 82. Atlan in Danger.* Kurt Brand. New York: Ace, November 1975.

1927 "The Ship of Things to Come." *Perry Rhodan. No. 83. Ernst Ellert Returns!* Clark Darlton. New York: Ace, November 1975.

1928 "The Ship of Things to Come." *Perry Rhodan. No. 84. Secret Mission: Moluk.* William Voltz. New York: Ace, December 1975.

1929 "The Ship of Things to Come." *Perry Rhodan. No. 85. Enemy in the Dark.* Kurt Mahr. New York: Ace, December 1975.

1930 "The Ship of Things to Come." *Perry Rhodan. No. 86. Blazing Sun.* Clark Darlton. New York: Ace, January 1976.

1931 "The Ship of Things to Come." *Perry Rhodan. No. 87. The Starless Realm.* Clark Darlton. New York: Ace, January 1976.

1932 "The Ship of Things to Come." *Perry Rhodan. No. 88. The Mystery of the Anti.* K. H. Scheer. New York: Ace, February 1976.

1933 "The Ship of Things to Come." *Perry Rhodan. No. 89. Power's Price.* Kurt Brand. New York: Ace, February 1976.

1934 "The Ship of Things to Come." *Perry Rhodan. No. 90. Unleashed Powers.* Kurt Brand. New York: Ace, March 1976.

1935 "The Ship of Things to Come." *Perry Rhodan. No. 91. Friend to Mankind.* Kurt Brand. New York: Ace, March 1976.

1936 "The Ship of Things to Come." *Perry Rhodan. No. 92. The Target Star.* Kurt Brand. New York: Ace, April 1976.

1937 "The Ship of Things to Come." *Perry Rhodan. No. 93. Vagabond of Space.* Clark Darlton. New York: Ace, April 1976.

1938 "The Ship of Things to Come." *Perry Rhodan. No. 94. Action: Division 3.* Kurt Mahr. New York: Ace, May 1976.

1939 "The Ship of Things to Come." *Perry Rhodan. No. 95. The Plasma Monster.* Kurt Brand. New York: Ace, May 1976.

1940 "The Ship of Things to Come." *Perry Rhodan. No. 96. Horn: Green.* William Voltz. New York: Ace, June 1976.

1941 "The Ship of Things to Come." *Perry Rhodan. No. 97. Phantom Fleet.* Clark Darlton. New York: Ace, June 1976.

1942 "The Ship of Things to Come." *Perry Rhodan. No. 98. The Idol from Passa.* Kurt Mahr. New York: Ace, July 1976.

1943 "The Ship of Things to Come." *Perry Rhodan. No. 99. The Blue System.* K. H. Scheer. New York: Ace, July 1976.

1944 "The Ship of Things to Come." *Perry Rhodan. No. 100. Desert of Death's Domain.* Kurt Mahr. New York: Ace, August 1976.

1945 "The Ship of Things to Come." *Perry Rhodan. No. 101. Blockade: Lepso.* Kurt Brand. New York: Ace, August 1976.

1946 "The Ship of Things to Come." *Perry Rhodan. No. 102. Spoor of the Antis.* William Voltz. New York: Ace, September 1976.

1947 "The Ship of Things to Come." *Perry Rhodan. No. 103. False Front.* Clark Darlton. New York: Ace, September 1976.

1948 "The Ship of Things to Come." *Perry Rhodan. No. 104. The Man with Two Faces.* Kurt Brand. New York: Ace, October 1976.

1949 "The Ship of Things to Come." *Perry Rhodan. No. 105. Wonderflower of Utik.* Kurt Mahr. New York: Ace, October 1976.

1950 "The Ship of Things to Come." *Perry Rhodan. No. 106. Caller from Eternity.* Kurt Brand. New York: Ace, December 1976.

1951 "The Ship of Things to Come." *Perry Rhodan. No. 107. The Emperor and the Monster.* William Voltz. New York: Ace, January 1977.

1952 "The Ship of Things to Come." *Perry Rhodan. No. 108. Duel Under the Double Sun.* K. H. Scheer. New York: Ace, February 1977.

1953 "The Ship of Things to Come." *Perry Rhodan. No. 109. The Stolen Spacefleet.* Clark Darlton. New York: Ace Books, March 1977.

1954 "The Ship of Things to Come." *Perry Rhodan. No. 110. Sgt. Robot.* Kurt Mahr. New York: Ace Books, March 1977.

1955 "The Ship of Things to Come." *Perry Rhodan. No. 111. Seeds of Ruin.* William Voltz. / *Perry Rhodan No. 112. Planet Mechanica.* K. H. Scheer. New York: Ace, April 1977.

1956 "The Ship of Things to Come." *Perry Rhodan. No. 113. Heritage of the Lizard People.* Clark Darlton. / *Perry Rhodan. No. 114. Death's Demand.* Kurt Mahr. New York: Ace, May 1977.

1957 "The Ship of Things to Come." *Perry Rhodan. No. 115. Saboteurs in A-1.* Kurt Brand. / *Perry Rhodan. No. 116. The Psycho Duel.* William Voltz. New York: Ace, June 1977.

1958 "Ship of Things to Come." *Spacemen.* Vol. 1. No. 3. Philadelphia: Spacemen, Inc., April 1962.

1959 "Shock of a Lifetime Ackermonster Dismayed." *Fangoria.* No. 25. February 1983. pp. 31–33. (Ackerman further addresses the circumstances surrounding his departure from *Famous Monsters*; his unused "Acksclusive The Editorial FM Wouldn't Print" "Shock of a Lifetime" is included on p. 33.)

1960 "The Shock of Things to Come." [As Dr. Acula.] *Famous Monsters of Filmland.* Vol. 1. No. 4. Philadelphia: Central Publications, Inc., August 1959. pp. 9–27; *Forrest J Ackerman's Monsterama.* No. 2. Seattle, WA: Fantagraphics Books, Spring 1992. pp. 6–25; *Famous Monsters of Filmland.* Vol. 1. No. 4. Filmland Classics, May 2008. pp. 9–27. (replica edition)

1961 "The Shock of Things to Come." [As Dr. Acula.] *Famous Monsters of Filmland.* No. 36. Warren, December 1965. pp. 6–9.

1962 "The Shock of Things to Come." *Famous Monsters of Filmland.* No. 167. Warren, September 1980.

1963 "The Shock of Things to Come." *Forrest J Ackerman's Monsterama.* No. 2. Seattle, WA: Fantagraphics Books, Spring 1992. pp. 6–25.

1964 "Shock Shorts." *Amazing Forries: this is your life, Forrest J Ackerman.* Hollywood, CA: Metropolis Publications/Warren, 1976. p. 30.

1965 "Shock Treatment." *Famous Monsters of Filmland.* No. 179. Warren, November 1981. (preview)

1966 "The Shop of Things to Come." *Famous Monsters of Filmland.* Vol. 3. No. 4. whole No. 13. Philadelphia: Central Publications, Inc., August 1961. [pp. 8–13, 62–68.]

1967 "The Shop of Things to Come." *Forrest J Ackerman Presents Mr. Monster's Movie Gold: A Treasure Trove of Imagi-Movies.* Ed. Hank Stine. Virginia Beach, VA: Donning Co. 1981. pp. 199–201.

1968 "Sic Transit Gloria Monday." *Canadian Fandom.* No. 5. Ed. Beak Taylor. November 1943.

1969 "Sidereal Cruises." *Glom.* No. 3. February 1946. p. 3. (review of 1942 French film)

1970 "Sight for Sore Eyes." *Famous Monsters of Filmland.* Vol. 4. No. 5. Whole No. 20. Philadelphia: Central Publications, Inc., November 1962. pp. 7–12.

1971 "Sign of the Times." *Forrest J Ackerman's Fantastic Movie Memories: Forrest Ackerman's Treasure Trove of Imagi-Movies.* Canoga Park, CA: New Media Books, 1985.

1972 "Sinbad Strikes Again!" *Famous Monsters of Filmland.* No. 136. Warren, August 1977. (*Sinbad and the Eye of the Tiger*)

1973 "6 Monsters for the Price of One!" *Monster World.* Vol. 1. No. 1. New York: Warren Publishing Co., November 1964; *Famous Monsters of Filmland.* No. 90. Warren, May 1972; *Famous Monsters of Filmland.* No. 137. Warren, September 1977. pp. 31–38. (*The Black Sleep*)

1974 "Six Startling Scientifilms." *Science Fiction Digest.* Vol. 2. No. 4. Ed. Julius Schwartz. Jamaica, NY: Conrad H. Ruppert, December 1933. (*F.P.1., Death Takes a Holiday, When Worlds Collide, Son of Kong, The Invisible Man, A Trip to Mars*)

1975 "The Skull." *Famous Monsters of Filmland.* No. 37. Warren, February 1966; *Famous Monsters of Filmland 1971 Fearbook.* Warren, 1970.

1976 "Sky-Fi & Skeery Stuff." *Famous Monsters of Filmland.* No. 144. Warren, June 1978.

1977 "Skywalker Meets Stella Star!" *Famous Monsters of Filmland.* No. 170. Warren, January 1981. pp. 26–29. (on the 7th Annual Sci-Fi Academy Awards)

1978 "Slay It Again, Sam." *Famous Monsters of Filmland.* No. 142. Warren, April 1978. (Samuel Z. Arkoff)

1979 "Sleuth Is Stranger Than Fiction." *The Gorgon.* Ed. Stanley Mullin. Vol. 1. No. 5. Denver, CO: November 1947.

1980 "Smile If You ... Call Him Monster!" *Monster World.* No. 7. Warren, March 1966; *Famous Monsters of Filmland.* No. 58. Warren, October 1969; *Famous Monsters of Filmland.* No. 91. Warren, July 1972.

1981 "A Snapshot Scientifilm Preview." *Science Fiction Digest.* South Ozone Park, NY: Maurice Z. Ingher, December 1932. (*King Kong*)

1982 "A Snapshot Scientifilm Preview." *Science Fiction Digest*. Vol. 1. No. 6. South Ozone Park, NY: Maurice Z. Ingher, February 1933. (*The Island of Lost Souls*)

1983 "Snoops & Scoops." *Cult Movies*. No. 27. 1998. p. 76.

1984 "Snoops & Scoops." *Cult Movies*. No. 28. 1999. p. 64.

1985 "Something New — Choose Your News!" *Tympani*. Vol. 1. No. 17. Ed. Robert Stein and Redd Boggs. December 1947. (on the firing of Charles Burbee as Shangri-L'Affaires editor)

1986 "Son of Fear-Jerkers." *Famous Monsters of Filmland*. No. 89. Warren, March 1972.

1987 "Son of Frankenstein." *Monster World*. No. 7. Warren, March 1966; *Famous Monsters of Filmland*. No. 52. Warren, October 1968. (filmbook)

1988 "Son of Jaws Meets Daughter of Exorcist." *Famous Monsters of Filmland*. No. 123. Warren, March 1976. (previews)

1989 "Son of Kong." [As Weaver Wright.] *Famous Monsters of Filmland*. No. 200. Orange, NJ: Dynacomm, May 1993. pp. 40–47. (Harryhausen)

1990 "Son of Kong." *Famous Monsters of Filmland*. Vol. 4. No. 5. Whole No. 20. Philadelphia: Central Publications, Inc., November 1962. pp. 34–40. (part 1 of a piece on Ray Harryhausen)

1991 "Son of Kong." *Famous Monsters of Filmland*. Vol. 4. No. 6. Whole No. 21. February 1963. (continuation)

1992 "Son of Kong." *Famous Monsters of Filmland*. No. 109. Warren, August 1974. (filmbook)

1993 "Son of Kong." (part 3) *Famous Monsters of Filmland*. Vol. 5. No. 2. Whole No. No. 23. June 1963. pp. 46–53; *Famous Monsters of Filmland*. No. 93. Warren, October 1972.

1994 "Son of Mad Labs." *Famous Monsters of Filmland*. Vol. 3. No. 1. No. 10. Philadelphia: Central Publications, Inc., January 1961.

1995 "Son of Max Factor the Alien Factor." *Famous Monsters of Filmland*. No. 143. Warren, May 1978. pp. 32–35. (preview)

1996 "Son of Mister Monster." *Famous Monsters of Filmland*. Vol. 3. No. 2. Whole No. 11. Philadelphia: Central Publications, Inc., April 1961. [pp. 16–23]; *Famous Monsters of Filmland: Yearbook No. 2*. [1964] Warren Publishing Co., December 1963; *James Warren Presents the Best from Famous Monsters of Filmland*. New York: Paperback Library, 1964. (Lon Chaney, Jr.)

1997 "Son of Mister Monster." *Famous Monsters of Filmland*. No. 200. Orange, NJ: Dynacomm, May 1993. pp. 34–39. (Lon Chaney, Jr.)

1998 "Son of Movie Monster Marathon." *Famous Monsters of Filmland*. No. 107. Warren, May 1974.

1999 "Son of 1,000,000 B.C." *Famous Monsters of Filmland*. No. 39. Warren, June 1966. pp. 4–6.

2000 "Son of Salem's Lot." *Famous Monsters of Filmland*. No. 166. Warren, August 1980.

2001 "Son of Science Fiction Week." [As Forry Rhodan.] *Perry Rhodan*. No. 17. *The Venus Trap*. Kurt Mahr. Ace, September, 1972.

2002 "Son of Teatempestpot." *Perry Rhodan*. No. 28. *The Plague of Oblivion*. Clark Darlton. New York: Ace, August 1973; London: Futura, 1977.

2003 "Son of Wax Museum." *Monster World*. No. 4. Warren, June 1965.

2004 "Soul of a Monster, Heart of a Marshmallow." *Famous Monsters of Filmland*. No. 103. Warren, December 1973. (obituary of George Macready)

2005 "The Sound of Music." (Stardust Editorial) *Perry Rhodan*. No. 54. *The Blue Dwarfs*. Kurt Mahr. New York: Ace, September 1974.

2006 "The Sound of Terror." *Famous Monsters of Filmland*. No. 126. Warren, July 1976. (obituary of composer Bernard Herrmann)

2007 "The Southern California Scene." [As Morris Chapnick.] *Luna Monthly*. No. 2. Ed. Ann F. Dietz. Oradell, NJ: July 1969. pp. 7–8, 28. [byline notes "Fisher Trentworth is on vacation"]

2008 "The Southern California Scene." ("as seen by" Fisher Trentworth) *Luna Monthly*. No. 21. Ed. Ann F. Dietz. Oradell, NJ: February 1971. p. 10.

2009 "The Southern California Scene LATELY IN L. A." [As Fisher Trentworth.] *Luna Monthly*. No. 51. Ed. Ann F. Dietz. Oradell, NJ: Spring 1974. pp. 6–7.

2010 "Space Fans of the World Unite!" *Spacemen*. Vol. 2. No. 1. Whole No. 5. Philadelphia: Spacemen, Inc., October 1962. p. 3. (inviting readers to the 20th World Science Fiction Convention)

2011 "The Space Film Telescoop." *Spacemen*. Vol. 1. No. 2. September 1961. Philadelphia: Spacemen, Inc., September 1961.

2012 "Space Monsterama." *Spacemen*. Vol. 1. No. 1. Philadelphia, PA: Spacemen, Inc. July 1961; as "The Movies Look at Other Worlds and Other Aliens." *Warren Presents Movie Aliens Illustrated*. (*Warren Presents*. No. 4.) Warren, September 1979.

2013 "Space Screen." *Spacemen*. No. 8. June 1964. (previews)

2014 "Spacemen of Distinction #1." *Spacemen*. Vol. 1. No. 4. Philadelphia: Spacemen, Inc., July 1962.

2015 "Spacemen of Distinction #2." *Spacemen.* Vol. 2. No. 1. Whole No. 5. Philadelphia: Spacemen, Inc., October 1962. p. 25. (Exeter from *This Island Earth*)

2016 "Spacial Coverage." *Spacemen.* Vol. 2. No. 1. Whole No. 5. Philadelphia: Spacemen, Inc., October 1962. (covers of SF books and magazines) pp. 28–33.

2017 "Speaking of Monsters." *Famous Monsters of Filmland.* No. 66. Warren, June 1970.

2018 "Speaking of Monsters: A Feast Fit for a Beast." *Famous Monsters of Filmland.* No. 90. Warren, May 1972.

2019 "Speaking of Monsters: A Rick Baker Monsterpiece." *Famous Monsters of Filmland.* No. 151. Warren, March 1979.

2020 "Speaking of Monsters: A Shot in the (H)arm!" *Famous Monsters of Filmland.* No. 186. Warren, August 1982.

2021 "Speaking of Monsters: A Smashing Issue!" *Famous Monsters of Filmland.* No. 104. Warren, January 1974.

2022 "Speaking of Monsters: Ackermonster Meets Wolfman." *Famous Monsters of Filmland.* No. 96. Warren, March 1973.

2023 "Speaking of Monsters: Alien's Twin?" *Famous Monsters of Filmland.* No. 157. Warren, September 1979. p. 3. (Editorial)

2024 "Speaking of Monsters: Beauty and the Best." *Famous Monsters of Filmland.* No. 176. Warren, August 1981.

2025 "Speaking of Monsters: Big Al." *Famous Monsters of Filmland.* No. 125. Warren, May 1976.

2026 "Speaking of Monsters: Big Head Son of Bigfoot." *Famous Monsters of Filmland.* No. 152. Warren, April 1979. p. 3.

2027 "Speaking of Monsters: Big Hit!" *Famous Monsters of Filmland.* No. 105. Warren, March 1974.

2028 "Speaking of Monsters: Children of the Bite!" *Famous Monsters of Filmland.* No. 97. Warren, April 1973.

2029 "Speaking of Monsters: Comb and Get It!" *Famous Monsters of Filmland.* No. 170. Warren, January 1981. p. 3.

2030 "Speaking of Monsters: Creatures Fit for a King!" *Famous Monsters of Filmland.* No. 108. Warren, July 1974.

2031 "Speaking of Monsters: Creepy Crawly!" *Famous Monsters of Filmland.* No. 146. New York: Warren Publishing Co., August 1978.

2032 "Speaking of Monsters: Crown Prints." *Famous Monsters of Filmland.* No. 134. Warren, May 1977.

2033 "Speaking of Monsters: 'Cut.'" *Famous Monsters of Filmland.* No. 124. Warren, April 1976.

2034 "Speaking of Monsters: Darn Tootin'!" *Famous Monsters of Filmland.* No. 156. Warren, August 1979.

2035 "Speaking of Monsters: Darth Shadows." *Famous Monsters of Filmland.* No. 163. Warren, May 1980.

2036 "Speaking of Monsters: Dr. Ackle & Sister Hyde." *Famous Monsters of Filmland.* No. 139. Warren, December 1977.

2037 "Speaking of Monsters: Dr. Jeckyll & Sister Steel." *Famous Monsters of Filmland.* No. 153. Warren, May 1979.

2038 "Speaking of Monsters: Don't Make This Dino Sore!" *Famous Monsters of Filmland.* No. 154. Warren, June 1979.

2039 "Speaking of Monsters: Drink Deep!" *Famous Monsters of Filmland.* No. 112. Warren, December 1974.

2040 "Speaking of Monsters: Eye Opener." *Famous Monsters of Filmland.* No. 133. Warren, April 1977.

2041 "Speaking of Monsters: Famous First!" *Famous Monsters of Filmland.* No. 173. Warren, May 1981.

2042 "Speaking of Monsters: Fang-tastic Issue! 'Tomb Much' Cry Fans!" *Famous Monsters of Filmland.* No. 130. Warren, December 1976.

2043 "Speaking of Monsters: Fiendly Persuasion." *Famous Monsters of Filmland.* No. 80. Warren, October 1970. [editorial explains the jump in numbering]

2044 "Speaking of Monsters: Fiery Stories." *Famous Monsters of Filmland.* No. 174. Warren, June 1981.

2045 "Speaking of Monsters: Finger Lickin' Good." *Famous Monsters of Filmland.* No. 145. Warren, July 1978.

2046 "Speaking of Monsters: FM Is Hot!" *Famous Monsters of Filmland.* No. 115. Warren, April 1975.

2047 "Speaking of Monsters: FM on Friday the 13th." *Famous Monsters of Filmland.* No. 167. Warren, September 1980.

2048 "Speaking of Monsters: Frankenstein 1980." *Famous Monsters of Filmland.* No. 168. Warren, October 1980.

2049 "Speaking of Monsters: Frankenstein's Bride Meets The Invisible Man." *Famous Monsters of Filmland.* No. 189. November 1982.

2050 "Speaking of Monsters: Fright On!" *Famous Monsters of Filmland.* No. 91. Warren, July 1972.

2051 "Speaking of Monsters: From Shampoo to Real Boo!" *Famous Monsters of Filmland.* No. 185. Warren, July 1982.

2052 "Speaking of Monsters: Ghoulden Awardees." *Famous Monsters of Filmland.* No. 164. Warren, June 1980.

2053 "Speaking of Monsters: Gotcha Buffalo'ed." *Famous Monsters of Filmland.* No. 148. Warren, October 1978.

2054 "Speaking of Monsters: Guaranteed Eye-Popping!" *Famous Monsters of Filmland.* No. 106. Warren, April 1974.

2055 "Speaking of Monsters: Hammer Strikes Again." *Famous Monsters of Filmland.* No. 123. Warren, March 1976.

2056 "Speaking of Monsters: Happy Thanks-Carving." *Famous Monsters of Filmland.* No. 180. Warren, January 1982.

2057 "Speaking of Monsters: Have a Cool Yule with a Ghoul in This Horrific Holiday Issue!" *Famous Monsters of Filmland.* No. 89. Warren March 1972.

2058 "Speaking of Monsters: Hear Now Evil See Now Evil!" *Famous Monsters of Filmland.* No. 120. Warren, October 1975.

2059 "Speaking of Monsters: Here's Blood in Your Eye." *Famous Monsters of Filmland.* No. 172. Warren, April 1981.

2060 "Speaking of Monsters: Here's Lurking at You, Kid!" *Famous Monsters of Filmland.* No. 166. Warren, August 1980.

2061 "Speaking of Monsters: Hold the Phone!" *Famous Monsters of Filmland.* No. 165. Warren, July 1980.

2062 "Speaking of Monsters: Hotline to Horror." *Famous Monsters of Filmland.* No. 95. Warren, January 1973.

2063 "Speaking of Monsters: Hottest Issue Yet! Fahrenheit 450!." *Famous Monsters of Filmland.* No. 107. Warren, May 1974.

2064 "Speaking of Monsters: How Does This Grab You?" *Famous Monsters of Filmland.* No. 93. Warren, October 1972. p. 3.

2065 "Speaking of Monsters: Inside Godzilla." *Famous Monsters of Filmland.* No. 114. Warren, March 1975. (Japanese monsters)

2066 "Speaking of Monsters: It's a Scream!" *Famous Monsters of Filmland.* No. 137. Warren, September 1977. (Editorial)

2067 "Speaking of Monsters: Just Imagine." *Famous Monsters of Filmland.* No. 68. Warren, August 1970.

2068 "Speaking of Monsters: King Karloff & Legendary Lugosi." *Famous Monsters of Filmland.* No. 178. Warren, October 1981.

2069 "Speaking of Monsters: King Korn." *Famous Monsters of Filmland.* No. 122. Warren, January 1976.

2070 "Speaking of Monsters: Last Respects and Final Farewells to ... Lon Chaney Jr." *Famous Monsters of Filmland.* No. 103. December 1973.

2071 "Speaking of Monsters: Logan's Fun." *Famous Monsters of Filmland.* No. 143. Warren, May 1978. p. 3.

2072 "Speaking of Monsters: M_ _Worry?" *Famous Monsters of Filmland.* No. 111. Warren, October 1974.

2073 "Speaking of Monsters: Marrow Christmas!" *Famous Monsters of Filmland.* No. 161. Warren, March 1980.

2074 "Speaking of Monsters: Meet the Monsters." *Famous Monsters of Filmland.* No. 87. Warren, November 1971.

2075 "Speaking of Monsters: Meet Your Creature." *Famous Monsters of Filmland.* No. 136. Warren, August 1977.

2076 "Speaking of Monsters: Merry Xmas from Mighty Joe Claus." *Famous Monsters of Filmland.* No. 150. Warren, January 1979.

2077 "Speaking of Monsters: Moby Shark Bites Again." *Famous Monsters of Filmland.* No. 121. December 1975. Warren, 1975.

2078 "Speaking of Monsters: Music, Monster, Please." *Famous Monsters of Filmland.* No. 131. Warren, January 1977.

2079 "Speaking of Monsters: No Jolting Around!" *Famous Monsters of Filmland.* No. 188. New York: Warren Publishing Co., October 1982.

2080 "Speaking of Monsters: Out of This Swirl! Son of Monster Mash." *Famous Monsters of Filmland.* No. 109. Warren, August 1974.

2081 "Speaking of Monsters: Planet of the Oops!" *Famous Monsters of Filmland.* No. 98. Warren, May 1973.

2082 "Speaking of Monsters: Population Hexplosion." *Famous Monsters of Filmland.* No. 83. Warren, April 1971.

2083 "Speaking of Monsters: Pretty Snaky!" *Famous Monsters of Filmland*. No. 117. Warren, July 1975.

2084 "Speaking of Monsters: Rebecca of Sunnybrook Farm." *Famous Monsters of Filmland*. No. 119. Warren, September 1975.

2085 "Speaking of Monsters: Robby Dick." *Famous Monsters of Filmland*. No. 135. Warren, July 1977. p. 3.

2086 "Speaking of Monsters: Salem's Lot Was Hellish Hot." *Famous Monsters of Filmland*. No. 183. Warren, May 1982.

2087 "Speaking of Monsters: Santa Claws Strieks Again!" *Famous Monsters of Filmland*. No. 113. Warren, January 1975.

2088 "Speaking of Monsters: Santa Claws' Surprises." *Famous Monsters of Filmland*. No. 141. Warren, March 1978.

2089 "Speaking of Monsters: Scare Stare." *Famous Monsters of Filmland*. No. 138. Warren, October 1977.

2090 "Speaking of Monsters: Scarred to Death." *Famous Monsters of Filmland*. No. 169. Warren, November 1980.

2091 "Speaking of Monsters: She's Beautiful She's Engaged!" *Famous Monsters of Filmland*. No. 155. Warren, July 1979.

2092 "Speaking of Monsters: Shrieking of Monsters." *Famous Monsters of Filmland*. No. 171. Warren, March 1981.

2093 "Speaking of Monsters: Slime on His Hands." *Famous Monsters of Filmland*. No. 162. Warren, April 1980.

2094 "Speaking of Monsters: Somebody Stole My Gal(axy)." *Famous Monsters of Filmland*. No. 149. Warren, November 1978.

2095 "Speaking of Monsters: Sheer Horror." *Famous Monsters of Filmland*. No. 160. Warren, January 1980.

2096 "Speaking of Monsters: Super Chick!" *Famous Monsters of Filmland*. No. 116. Warren, May 1975.

2097 "Speaking of Monsters: Thanks Graving." *Famous Monsters of Filmland*. No. 82. Warren, February 1971.

2098 "Speaking of Monsters: The Beast with Grin." *Famous Monsters of Filmland*. No. 187. Warren, September 1982.

2099 "Speaking of Monsters: The Big Bang." *Famous Monsters of Filmland*. No. 175. Warren, July 1981.

2100 "Speaking of Monsters: The Bride Wore Fright." *Famous Monsters of Filmland*. No. 184. Warren, June 1982.

2101 "Speaking of Monsters: The Cabinet of Dr. Killer-Gory." *Famous Monsters of Filmland*. No. 129. Warren, October 1976.

2102 "Speaking of Monsters: The Eyes Have It." *Famous Monsters of Filmland*. No. 177. Warren, September 1981.

2103 "Speaking of Monsters: The Fourth of Ghoul Lie!" *Famous Monsters of Filmland*. No. 86. Warren, September 1971.

2104 "Speaking of Monsters: The Mask of Acker-Manchu." *Famous Monsters of Filmland*. No. 65. Warren, May 1970.

2105 "Speaking of Monsters: The Necks Voice You Hear..." *Famous Monsters of Filmland*. No. 144. Warren, June 1978.

2106 "Speaking of Monsters: The Ogre & The Organ." *Famous Monsters of Filmland*. No. 126. Warren, July 1976.

2107 "Speaking of Monsters: The Phantom Lives Again." *Famous Monsters of Filmland*. No. 69. Warren, September 1970.

2108 "Speaking of Monsters: The Price Is Writhe!" *Famous Monsters of Filmland*. No. 127. Warren, August 1976.

2109 "Speaking of Monsters: The Return of Dracula." *Famous Monsters of Filmland*. No. 92. Warren, September 1972.

2110 "Speaking of Monsters: They're Beautiful! They're Engaged!" *Famous Monsters of Filmland*. No. 99. Warren, July 1973.

2111 "Speaking of Monsters: Timber!" *Famous Monsters of Filmland*. No. 179. Warren, November 1981.

2112 "Speaking of Monsters: Tooth or Kong-Sequences." *Famous Monsters of Filmland*. No. 128. Warren, September 1976.

2113 "Speaking of Monsters: Tree's a Crowd." *Famous Monsters of Filmland*. No. 181. Warren, March 1982.

2114 "Speaking of Monsters: Truck or Treat." *Famous Monsters of Filmland*. No. 81. Warren, December 1970.

2115 "Speaking of Monsters: Ugly Roomer." *Famous Monsters of Filmland*. No. 140. Warren, January 1978.

2116 "Speaking of Monsters: Undying Monsters Karloff Lugosi." *Famous Monsters of Filmland*. No. 64. Warren, April 1970.

2117 "Speaking of Monsters: Up at Bat!" *Famous Monsters of Filmland*. No. 158. Warren, October 1979.

2118 "Speaking of Monsters: Wake up to Famous Monsters!" *Famous Monsters of Filmland*. No. 101. Warren, September 1973.

2119 "Speaking of Monsters: Wax Enthusiastic!" *Famous Monsters of Filmland*. No. 159. Warren, November 1979.

2120 "Speaking of Monsters: Weird Delighted to See You Again!" *Famous Monsters of Filmland*. No. 110. Warren, September 1974.

2121 "Speaking of Monsters: Welcome..." *Famous Monsters of Filmland*. No. 102. Warren, October 1973.

2122 "Speaking of Monsters: What's Alien Ya?" *Famous Monsters of Filmland*. No. 142. Warren, April 1978.

2123 "Speaking of Monsters: What's Your Hangup?" *Famous Monsters of Filmland*. No. 147. Warren, September 1978. p. 3.

2124 "Speaking of Monsters: Who's Afraid of the Big Black Cat?." *Famous Monsters of Filmland*. No. 67. Warren, July 1970.

2125 "Speaking of Monsters: Who's the Ugliest of Them All?" *Famous Monsters of Filmland*. No. 94. Warren, November 1972. p. 3. (Editorial)

2126 "Speaking of Monsters: Wolf This Issue Down!" *Famous Monsters of Filmland*. No. 118. New York: Warren Publishing Co., August 1975. p. 3.

2127 "Speaking of Monsters: You Can't See the Trees for the Forrest." *Famous Monsters of Filmland*. No. 132. Warren, March 1977.

2128 "Speaking of Monsters: You're Invited!" *Famous Monsters of Filmland*. No. 182. Warren, April 1982.

2129 "Special Effects." *Famous Monsters of Filmland Star Wars Spectacular*. Warren Publishing Co., October 1977.

2130 [Special Feature.] *Specula*. No. 1. Ed. Arthur L. Joquel, II. January 1941. (on Austin Hall)

2131 "Special Guest on Telecast." *Spacemen*. Vol. 2. No. 3. Whole No. 7. Warren Publishing, Inc., September 1963. (Ackerman's appearance on *The Jack Barry Show*)

2132 "Special Message from Igor." [As Igor.] *Famous Monsters of Filmland*. Vol. 1. No. 2. Philadelphia: Central Publications, Inc., September 1958. p. 66. (inviting readers' letters and subscriptions, offers prizes)

2133 "Spieling with Spielberg: The Extra(ordinary) Extra Terrestrial Talks to FJAM." *Forrest J Ackerman's Monster Land*. No. 1. Canoga Park, CA: New Media Publishing, Inc., December 1984. pp. 51–52, 61; as "Spieling with Spielberg — A Close Encounter with an E(xtraordinary) T(alent)." *Enterprise Incidents SF Movieland*. No. 28. Ed. James van Hise. Studio City, CA: New Media Publishing, Inc. April 1985. pp. 10–13. (brief interview touches on Spielberg's favorite genre films, then-upcoming film *The Goonies* and *Amazing Stories* TV series, reprint slightly altered)

2134 "SSSSSSSS." *Famous Monsters of Filmland*. No. 104. January 1974.

2135 "The Stamp of Zod." *Famous Monsters of Filmland*. No. 178. Warren, October 1981; *Film Fantasy Yearbook 1982 Collector's Edition*. Warren, March 1982. (Terence Stamp interview)

2136 "Stanton A Coblentz." *Science Fiction Chronicle: The Monthly SF and Fantasy Newsmagazine*. Vol. 4. No. 2. Ed. Andrew Porter. November 1982. p. 6. (obituary for SF writer [1896–1982])

2137 "Stapledon's Search for Sol-Mates Proves Hot Stuff" *Philcon Memory Book*. 1947. (*Tympani*)

2138 "A Star Is Born." *An Illustrated History of Heidi Saha: Fantasy Fandom's Famous Femme*. New York: Warren Publishing Co., 1973.

2139 "A Star Is Unborn." *Monsterscene*. No. 8. Lombard, IL: Gogo Entertainment Group, Inc., Summer 1996. pp. 5–11. (Ackerman's cameo roles)

2140 "The Star Sinister." *Lon of 1000 Faces*. Beverly Hills, CA and Pangbourne, Bershire, England: Morrison, Raven-Hill Co., 1983. 286 pp; Rockville, MD: Sense of Wonder Press, 2003. (Introduction)

2141 "Star Trek, the Emotion and Action Picture." [As Kert Kamdois.] *Famous Monsters of Filmland*. No. 161. Warren, March 1980.

2142 "Star Trek, 23rd Century Style." *Famous Monsters of Filmland*. No. 145. Warren, July 1978. (*Star Trek: The Motion Picture*)

2143 "Star Wares." *Famous Monsters of Filmland*. No. 141. Warren, March 1978.

2144 "Star Wars Soars." *Famous Monsters of Filmland*. No. 140. Warren, January 1978.

2145 "Star Wars: The Empire Strikes Back." *Famous Monsters of Filmland*. No. 167. Warren, September 1980.

2146 "Star Wars Two!" *Famous Monsters of Filmland*. No. 145. Warren, July 1978.

2147 "Stardust Editorial." *Perry Rhodan. No. 30. To Arkon!* Kurt Mahr. New York: Ace, September 1973.

2148 "Stardust Editorial." *Perry Rhodan. No. 50. Attack from the Unseen.* Clark Darlton. New York: Ace, July 1974.

2149 "Stardust Editorial." *Perry Rhodan. 51. Return from the Void.* Kurt Mahr. New York: Ace, August 1974. (Ackerman's response to a letter from reader Lou Perkins which is quoted in full)

2150 "Stardust Editorial." [With Keith Harris.] *Perry Rhodan. No. 52. Fortress Atlantis.* K. H. Scheer. New York: Ace, August 1974.

2151 "Stardust Gate Editorial." [With Elizabeth Konig.] *Perry Rhodan. No. 29. A World Gone Mad.* Clark Darlton. New York: Ace, September 1973; London: Futura, 1977.

2152 "Stardust Malady Lingers On." *The Fort MacArthur Bulletin.* Friday 5 February 1943. p. 1-A. (on a "Pvt. Saul Freehafer")

2153 "Stardust Meloday." [As Forry Rhodan.] *Perry Rhodan. No. 11. Planet of the Dying Sun.* Kurt Mahr. New York: Ace, February 1972, 1974.

2154 "Stark Trek!" *Famous Monsters of Filmland.* No. 64. Warren, April 1970; *Famous Monsters of Filmland.* No. 142. Warren, April 1978.

2155 "Starship Invasions." *Famous Monsters of Filmland.* No. 142. Warren, April 1978.

2156 "Station EBC." *Shangri L'Affaires.* No. 33. Ed. Charles Burbee. October 1946.

2157 "Steven Jochsberger." *Science Fiction Chronicle: The Monthly SF and Fantasy Newsmagazine.* Vol. 11. No. 4. Ed. Andrew I. Porter. January 1990. p. 10. (film archivist)

2158 "STFUN." *Shangri L'Affaires.* Ed. Len Moffatt. No. 15. November 1949. pp. 4–5.

2159 "Stick Out Your Tongue." *Shangri-La.* No. 10. January 1949.

2160 "The Stone Men Strike!" *Famous Monsters of Filmland.* No. 34. Warren, August 1965. pp. 38–41. (*Hercules Against the Moon Men*)

2161 "Stop Thief!" *Famous Monsters of Filmland.* 1962. Vol. 3. No. 6. Whole No. 15. Philadelphia: Central Publications, Inc., January 1962. [p. 3.] (theft of robot film stills from James Warren's briefcase)

2162 "Story Scientifilmatic." *Science Fiction Digest.* Vol. 1. No. 12. Jamaica, NY: Conrad H. Ruppert, August 1933.

2163 "Strange Things Are Coming." *Famous Monsters of Filmland.* No. 52. Warren, October 1968.

2164 "Such Men Are Dangerous, Especially If They're Born in Lugos, Hungary!" *Famous Monsters of Filmland.* No. 112. Warren, December 1974.

2165 "A Super Birthday." *Famous Monsters of Filmland.* No. 148. Warren, October 1978.

2166 "Super Monsters Invade Super Markets." *Famous Monsters of Filmland.* No. 38. Warren, April

1966. pp. 46–51. (Ackerman and Tor Johnson appearances to promote Don Post Studios)

2167 "The Super Movie for the Superfan — Superman." *Famous Monsters of Filmland.* No. 151. Warren, March 1979.

2168 ["Super Science Satire." *Science Fiction — The Advance Guard of Future Civilization.* Vol. 1. No. 2. Ed. Jerome Siegel. Cleveland, OH: November 1932.]

2169 "Super Space." *Spacemen.* Vol. 1. No. 4. Philadelphia: Spacemen, Inc., July 1962. (*The Mask of Fu Manchu*)

2170 "The Super Space." *Spacemen.* Vol. 2. No. 1. Whole No. 5. Philadelphia: Spacemen, Inc., October 1962. pp. 26–27. (*Things to Come*)

2171 "The Super Space." *Spacemen.* Vol. 2. No. 1. Whole No. 6. Philadelphia: Spacemen, Inc., January 1963. (*Frau im Mond*)

2172 "The Super Space." *Spacemen.* Vol. 2. No. 3. Whole No. 7. Warren Publishing, Inc., September 1963. (*The Time Machine*)

2173 "Superman 2." *Famous Monsters of Filmland.* No. 175. Warren, July 1981; *Film Fantasy Yearbook 1982 Collector's Edition.* Warren, March 1982. (preview)

2174 "Superman III." *Famous Monsters of Filmland.* No. 190. Warren, January 1983. (interview with actor Marc McClure) pp. 26–28.

2175 "Supernatural Lee." *Monster World.* No. 7. Warren, March 1966. (Christopher Lee)

2176 "Surf Terror." *Monster World.* No. 10. Warren, September 1966.

2177 "T. O'Conor Sloane." *Gosh! Wow (Boy-oh-Boy)! Science Fiction.* New York: Bantam, 1982. pp. 165–166. (1930's *Amazing Stories* editor Sloane's original introduction to Meek's "Futility")

2178 "Tales from the Crypt." *Famous Monsters of Filmland.* No. 91. Warren, July 1972. (1972 Amicus film)

2179 "Tales of Frankenstein." *Famous Monsters of Filmland.* No. 69. Warren, September 1970; *Famous Monsters of Filmland.* No. 138. Warren, October 1977.

2180 "Tales That Witness Madness!" *Famous Monsters of Filmland.* No. 106. Warren, April 1974. (preview)

2181 "Tape of Things to Come." *Famous Monsters of Filmland.* No. 18. Philadelphia: Central Publications, Inc., July 1962. [pp. 7–12.]

2182 "Tarantula." *Monster World.* No. 6. Warren, January 1966; *Famous Monsters of Filmland.* No.

50. July 1968. New York: Warren Publishing Co., 1968.

2183 "Tarzan le Bien Aimé." (Tarzan the Well-Loved) *V.* Vol. 48. Special No. 200. Summer 1948; as "Tarzan and the Golden Loin." *Science Fiction Worlds of Forrest J Ackerman and Friends.* Reseda, CA: Powell Publications, 1969; *Expanded Science Fiction Worlds of Forrest J Ackerman & Friends PLUS.* Rockville, MD: Sense of Wonder Press. 2002.

2184 "Tarzan Strips Forever (Not an interview with Edgar Rice Burbee)." [With Tigrina.] *Shangri L'Affaires.* Ed. Charles Burbee. No. 33. October 1946.

2185 "Teatempestpot." [As Forry Rhodan with Charles A. Crayne.] *Perry Rhodan. No. 22. The Fleet of the Springers.* Kurt Mahr. New York: Ace, March 1973; London: Futura, 1977.

2186 "Terri E[llen Merritt-]Pinckard 1930–2004." *Locus.* Vol. 54. No. 5. Whole No. 532. Ed. Charles N. Brown. May 2005. (obituary)

2187 "Terrible Terror from Tuscon." *Famous Monsters of Filmland.* No. 32. Warren, March 1965. (fan film)

2188 "The Terror Trail." *Famous Monsters of Filmland.* No. 186. Warren, August 1982.

2189 "Terror Vision." *Famous Monsters of Filmland.* Vol. 1. No. 2. Philadelphia: Central Publications, Inc., September 1958. pp. 56–62. (TV horror hosts)

2190 "Terrors of the Man-Eating Plants." *Famous Monsters of Filmland.* No. 60. Warren, December 1969.

2191 "Terrors of the Time Machine." *Famous Monsters of Filmland.* No. 6. February 1960. pp. 38–44; *Famous Monsters of Filmland: Yearbook No. 2.* [1964] Warren Publishing Co., December 1963; *James Warren Presents Son of Famous Monsters of Filmland.* New York: Paperback Library, 1965; *Famous Monsters of Filmland.* No. 110. Warren, September 1974; *Famous Monsters of Filmland.* Vol. 1. No. 4. Filmland Classics, May 2008. pp. 38–44. (replica edition)

2192 "Terrorscope on Tomorrow." *Famous Monsters of Filmland.* No. 51. Warren, August 1968.

2193 "The Thing." *Famous Monsters of Filmland.* No. 185. Warren, July 1982. (preview of John Carpenter's remake)

2194 "They Said It Couldn't Be Done." [With James Warren as Dr. Acula & his zombies.] *Famous Monsters of Filmland.* Vol. 1. No. 4. Philadelphia: Central Publications, Inc., August 1959. p. 3; *James Warren Presents Famous Monsters of Filmland Strike Back!* New York: Paperback Library, 1965; *Forrest J*

Ackerman's Monsterama. No. 2. Seattle, WA: Fantagraphics Books, Spring 1992. p. 27; *Famous Monsters of Filmland.* Vol. 1. No. 4. Filmland Classics, May 2008. p. 3. (replica edition)

2195 "They Scared the _____ Out of Me." *Forrest J Ackerman Presents Mr. Monster's Movie Gold: A Treasure Trove of Imagi-Movies.* Ed. Hank Stine. Virginia Beach, VA: Donning Co. 1981. pp. 42–57.

2196 "They'll Leach You Alive." *Famous Monsters of Filmland.* No. 32. Warren, March 1965. (*Mr. Sardonicus*)

2197 "They'll Make Your Heart Pound: Michael Carreras and Hammer Films." *1975 Famous Monsters of Filmland Convention Book; Famous Monsters of Filmland.* No. 123. Warren/Phil Seuling, March 1976.

2198 "The Thing with 2 Heads." *Famous Monsters of Filmland.* No. 98. Warren, May 1973.

2199 "Things I'll Never Know." *The Buccaneer.* San Francisco, CA: Balboa High School, Wednesday, 7 June 1933. (good-natured ribbing of some of Ackerman's fellow classmates)

2200 "Things My Teachers Taught Me (That I Don't Believe)." *Amazing Forries: this is your life, Forrest J Ackerman.* Hollywood, CA: Metropolis Publications/Warren, 1976. p. 26.

2201 "Things That Have Warmed the Cockles of My Heart." *Amazing Forries: this is your life, Forrest J Ackerman.* Hollywood, CA: Metropolis Publications/Warren, 1976. pp. 24–25.

2202 "13 Faces of Frankenstein." *Famous Monsters of Filmland.* No. 39. Warren, June 1966. pp. 58–60. (Willis O'Brien sketches for King Kong/Frankenstein project, text on p. 60)

2203 "13 O'Clock." [With James Warren.] *Famous Monsters of Filmland.* Vol. 3. No. 4. whole No. 13. Philadelphia: Central Publications, Inc., August 1961. pp. 2–3.

2204 "13 Years of Chills + Thrills." *Famous Monsters of Filmland 1971 Fearbook.* Warren, 1970.

2205 "This." *Imagination!* Vol. 1. No. 1. Los Angeles: Forrest J Ackerman, October 1937. p. 2.

2206 "Those Special Effects! Battlestar Galactica." *Famous Monsters of Filmland.* No. 151. Warren, March 1979.

2207 "3 Current Chillers." *Famous Monsters of Filmland.* Vol. 3. No. 1. No. 10. Philadelphia: Central Publications, Inc., January 1961.

2208 "3 Days in Rhodania." *Perry Rhodan Special Release: The Crystal Prince.* K. H. Scheer. / *War of the Ghosts.* Clark Darlton. New York: Ace, December 1977.

2209 "3E+4E = MANY MEMOR*EEE*S." *Food for Demons: The E. Everett Evans Memorial Volume.* San Diego, CA: Shroud Publishers, 1971. pp. 59–60. (appreciation for Evans story "The Martian and the Vampire")

2210 "Three More Deaths!" *Science Fiction Times.* No. 297. (Second July 1958 issue) (R. DeWitt Miller, Robert Albert De Pina, "Death of a Knanve" [Francis Towner Laney])

2211 "Three New Mags, Coming." *Fantasy Review.* Vol. 1. No. 4. Ed. Walter Gillings. Ilford, Essex, UK: Aug-Sep 1947.

2212 "A Thrilling Scene ... Relived from The Mummy's Hand." *Famous Monsters of Filmland.* No. 31. Warren Publishing Co., December 1964. pp. 14–15.

2213 "Through Time and Space with Forry Ackerman" (Part 1). *Mimosa.* No. 16. Ed. Rich and Nicki Lynch. Gaithersburg, MD: December 1994. pp. 4–6. (autobiographical column)

2214 "Through Time and Space with Forry Ackerman" (Part 2). *Mimosa.* No. 17. Ed. Rich and Nicki Lynch. Gaithersburg, MD: October 1995. pp. 32–33.

2215 "Through Time and Space with Forry Ackerman" (Part 3). *Mimosa.* No. 18. Ed. Rich and Nicki Lynch. Gaithersburg, MD: May 1996. pp. 22–24.

2216 "Through Time and Space with Forry Ackerman" (Part 4). *Mimosa.* No. 19. Gaithersburg, MD: November 1996.

2217 "Through Time and Space with Forry Ackerman" (Part 5). *Mimosa.* No. 20. Gaithersburg, MD: May 1997.

2218 "Through Time and Space with Forry Ackerman" (Part 6). *Mimosa.* No. 21. Gaithersburg, MD: December 1997.

2219 "Through Time and Space with Forry Ackerman" (Part 7). *Mimosa.* No. 22. Gaithersburg, MD: June 1998.

2220 "Through Time and Space with Forry Ackerman" (Part 8). *Mimosa.* No. 23. Gaithersburg, MD: January 1999.

2221 "Through Time and Space with Forry Ackerman" (Part 9). *Mimosa.* 24. Gaithersburg, MD: August 1999.

2222 "Through Time and Space with Forry Ackerman" (Part 10). *Mimosa.* 25. Gaithersburg, MD: April 2000.

2223 "Through Time and Space with Forry Ackerman" (Part 11). *Mimosa.* 26. Gaithersburg, MD: December 2000.

2224 "Through Time and Space with Forry Ackerman" (Part 12). *Mimosa.* 27. Gaithersburg, MD: December 2001. pp. 41–42.

2225 "Thru Space & Time with Donovan's Brain." *Spacemen.* Vol. 2. No. 1. Whole No. 6. Philadelphia: Spacemen, Inc., January 1963. (Curt Siodmak)

2226 "Time After Time." *Famous Monsters of Filmland.* No. 159. Warren, November 1979. (preview)

2227 "The Time Bandits." *Famous Monsters of Filmland.* No. 181. Warren, March 1982. (preview)

2228 "The Time Chronicles." *Famous Monsters of Filmland.* No. 156. Warren, August 1979.

2229 "Time Flies ... and So Does Forry Rhodan." *Perry Rhodan.* No. 82. *Atlan in Danger.* Kurt Brand. New York: Ace, November 1975.

2230 "Time for Space." *Spacemen.* Vol. 2. No. 1. Whole No. 6. Philadelphia: Spacemen, Inc., January 1963.

2231 "The Time Tatler." *Science Fiction Digest.* Vol. 1. No. 3. South Ozone Park, NY: Maurice Z. Ingher, November 1932. (column)

2232 "The Time Tatler." *Science Fiction Digest.* South Ozone Park, NY: Maurice Z. Ingher, December 1932.

2233 "The Time Tatler." *Science Fiction Digest.* South Ozone Park, NY: Maurice Z. Ingher, February 1933.

2234 "The Time Tatler." *Science Fiction Digest.* Vol. 1. No. 7. South Ozone Park, NY: Maurice Z. Ingher, March 1933.

2235 "The Time Tatler." *Science Fiction Digest.* Vol. 1. No. 9. Jamaica, NY: Conrad H. Ruppert, May 1933.

2236 "The Time Tatler." *Science Fiction Digest.* Vol. 1. No. 11. Jamaica, NY: Conrad H. Ruppert, July 1933.

2237 "Time Traveler #1." *Famous Monsters of Filmland.* No. 68. Warren, August 1970.

2238 "The Time Travelers." *Monster World.* Vol. 1. No. 2. New York: Warren, January 1965; *Famous Monsters of Filmland.* No. 130. Warren, December 1976. (preview)

2239 "Time Vault Tales: The Fifth Candle." *Famous Monsters of Filmland.* No. 203. No. Hollywood, CA: Dynacomm, August/September 1994. p. 20. (introduction to 1939 story by "Cyril Mand")

2240 "To All Those Who Cared for Wendayne Ackerman." *Science Fiction Chronicle: The Monthly SF and Fantasy Newsmagazine.* Vol. 11. No. 8. Ed. Andrew I. Porter. May 1990. pp. 35–37.

2241 "To Kill a Mocking Bat." *Famous Monsters of Filmland*. No. 36. Warren, December 1965. pp. 42–53. (a transcript of Ackerman's August 1963 appearance on *The Joe Franklin Show* interspersed with full-page photos of classic monsters. See entry 2863)

2242 "To-marrow's Trailers." *Famous Monsters of Filmland*. No. 26. Warren Publishing, Inc., January 1964. pp. 10–15.

2243 "To Mars and Back in 14 Days." *Fantasy Advertiser*. Vol. 4. No. 2. Ed. Roy A. Squires. Glendale, CA: May 1950.

2244 "The Tomb Machine." *Famous Monsters of Filmland*. Vol. 3. No. 1. No. 10. Philadelphia: Central Publications, Inc., January 1961.

2245 "Tomb-Morrows Movies." *Famous Monsters of Filmland*. Vol. 5. No. 3. Whole No. 24. Warren Publishing, Inc., August 1963. pp. 9–14.

2246 "Tongue of Tomorrow." *Science Fiction Fan*. Vol. 1. No. 1. Ed. Olon F. Wiggins. Denver, CO: July 1936.

2247 "A Top 10 Science Fiction Novels." *The Zone and Premonitions*. No. 7. Ed. Tony Lee. Arreton, Isle of Wight: Pigasus Press, Winter 1998/99.

2248 "Topper's Last Trip." *Famous Monsters of Filmland*. No. 98. Warren, May 1973. (Leo G. Carroll)

2249 "Tour of the Universe." *Famous Monsters of Filmland*. No. 170. Warren, January 1981. pp. 6–11. (on Universal Studios tour)

2250 ["Tourist Trap." (As Gabbeaux Legrand.) *Famous Monsters of Filmland*. No. 156. Warren, August 1979. (filmbook)]

2251 "Tragedy of 1958." *The Science Fiction Times*. No. 288. February 1958. (obituary of Henry Kuttner)

2252 "Training for Space." *Spacemen*. Vol. 1. No. 3. Philadelphia: Spacemen, Inc., April 1962.

2253 "The Transformation." *The Gorgon*. Vol. 1. No. 2. Ed. Stanley Mullin. Denver, CO: May 1947.

2254 "Treasured Tales from the Time Vault an Ackerman Archival Recovery 'Out Around Rigel' by Robert H. Wilson." *Perry Rhodan*. *No. 67: Crimson Universe*. New York: Ace, 1975; *Gosh! Wow (Boy-oh-Boy)! Science Fiction*. New York: Bantam, 1982. pp. 1–3. (Ackerman's introduction to this story, first published in *Astounding Stories*, December 1931)

2255 [Tribute Page] *First Australian Science Fiction Convention*. Ed. Nick Solntseff. Australia: Nick Solntseff, 22 March 1952.

2256 "A Tribute to Ray Bradbury-Part One." *Creation Comix Magazine*. Ed. Bob Schreck. Creation Comix Conventions, Inc. 1983. (Ackerman's remarks at a Ray Bradbury Roast)

2257 "Trivia Trix: More Than Just the Usual Questions and Answers: The Shape of Things That Never Came: FJA Recollects a Lexicon of Lost and Unmade Imagi-Movies from Decades Past." *Filmfax: The Magazine of Unusual Film & Television*. No. 8. Oct./Nov. 1987. pp. 19–21.

2258 "Truck or Treat." [With James Warren and Phyllis Farkas and the Skeleton Crew.] *Famous Monsters of Filmland*. Vol. 1. No. 5. Philadelphia: Central Publications, Inc., November 1959. p. 3. (Editorial)

2259 "TV Means Terrifying Monsters." *Famous Monsters of Filmland*. Vol. 1. No. 1. Philadelphia: Central Publications, Inc., 1958. pp. 58–65; *Famous Monsters of Filmland*. Vol. 1. No. 1. Filmland Classics, January 2008. pp. 58–65 (replica edition)

2260 "20th Anniversary Intl SF Film Festival." *Science Fiction Chronicle: The Monthly SF and Fantasy Newsmagazine*. Vol. 4. No. 4. January 1983. pp. 16, 18. (on the "Festival Internazionale del Film di Fantascienza" for which Ackerman served on the jury)

2261 "20th SF Film Fest and 9th Annual Awards." *Famous Monsters of Filmland*. No. 189. November 1982.

2262 "Twice Told Tales." [As Weaver Wright.] *Imagination! The Fanmag of the Future with a Future!* Vol. 1. No. 12. Los Angeles: Los Angeles Chapter — Science-Fiction Association, September 1938. p. 8.

2263 "Two on a Guillotine." *Famous Monsters of Filmland*. No. 32. Warren, March 1965. (1965 film)

2264 "2000 Years of Science Fiction." [As Geoffrey Giles with Walter Gillings.] *Science-Fantasy*. Vol. 1. No. 2. Ed. Walter Gillings. Nova Publications Ltd., Winter 1950.

2265 "Two Westmores Die." *Famous Monsters of Filmland*. No. 107. Warren, May 1974. (Bud and Wally Westmore)

2266 "TWS's Plans." *Imagination!* Vol. 1. No. 1. October 1937. p. 5. (Thrilling Wonder Stories)

2267 "Universal Languages." *Fantasy Magazine*. Vol. 4. No. 4. Whole No. 28. Ed. Julius Schwartz. February/March 1935.

2268 "Universal's Classic Frankenstein." *The Frankenstein File*. Ed. Peter Haining. London: New English Library, 1977. pp. 34–51. (synopsis of 1931 film)

2269 "The Unnerving Night Stalker." *Famous Monsters of Filmland*. No. 95. Warren, January 1973; *Famous Monsters of Filmland*. No. 147. Warren, September 1978.

2270 "untitled Introduction." *Souvenir Book of Mr. Science Fiction's Fantasy Museum*. New York: Kodansha, 1978. pp. 1–2.

2271 "untitled introduction to Edward D. Wood. Jr.'s 'Gemeni.'" *Famous Monsters of Filmland*. No. 201. No. Hollywood, CA: Dynacomm, Fall 1993. p. 14.

2272 ["Untitled Notes."] [As F.J.A.] *The Time Traveller*. Science Fiction's First Fan Magazine. Vol. 1. No. 9. Ed. Allen Glasser. Winter 1933. p. 2.

2273 "untitled piece on John W. Campbell, Jr." *Famous Monsters of Filmland*. Vol. 3. No. 3. Whole No. 12. Philadelphia: Central Publications, Inc., June 1961. [p. 41] (accompanies the first installment of the condensed reprint of Campbell's "Who Goes there?," the basis for the motion picture *The Thing from Another World*)

2274 "untitled tribute to Peter Cushing." *Scarlet Street*. No. 16. Ed. Richard Valley. 1994. p. 23.

2275 "untitled tribute to Vincent Price." *Scarlet Street*. No. 13. Ed. Richard Valley. 1993. p. 28.

2276 "Der Utopische Film in Hollywood." *Utopia Sonderband*. No. 1. Rastatt, Baden, Germany: Erich Pabel Verlag, 1956.

2277 "Der Utopische Film in Hollywood." *Utopia Sonderband*. No. 2. Rastatt, Baden, Germany: Erich Pabel Verlag, 1956.

2278 "The V-Bomb." *Marvel Science*. Vol. 3. No. 1. Ed. R. O. Erisman. New York: Stadium Publishing Corp., November 1950.

2279 "The Vampire and the Ballerina." *Famous Monsters of Filmland*. No. 46. Warren, September 1967.

2280 "Vampire Circus." *Famous Monsters of Filmland*. No. 106. Warren, April 1974.

2281 "The Vampire Lovers." *Famous Monsters of Filmland*. No. 90. Warren, May 1972; *1975 Famous Monsters of Filmland Convention Book*. Warren/Phil Seuling, 1975.

2282 "Vampirella and I." *Vampirella: 25th Anniversary Special*. New York: Harris Comics, October 1996.

2283 "Vampires 3." *Famous Monsters of Filmland*. No. 41. Warren, November 1966. pp. 22–23; *Famous Monsters of Filmland 1970 Year Book/Fearbook*. Warren, 1969.

2284 "Vampires 3." *Famous Monsters of Filmland*. No. 172. Warren, April 1981. (previews; different from previous entry)

2285 "Vampi's Feary Tales." *Vampirella*. No. 3. Warren, January 1970. p. 1. (*Queen of Outer Space*)

2286 "Van Vogt, Ackerman Win Italian Hugos." *Science Fiction Chronicle*. Vol. 2. No. 10. Ed. Andrew

Porter. July 1981. p. 4. (brief news piece accompanied by photo of Ackerman holding award)

2287 "The Vault of Horror." *Famous Monsters of Filmland*. No. 104. January 1974.

2288 "Vernell Coriell." *Science Fiction Chronicle: The Monthly SF and Fantasy Newsmagazine*. Vol. 8. No. 6. Ed. Andrew I. Porter. March 1987. p. 8. (obituary of Edgar Rice Burroughs aficionado and founder of The Burroughs Bibliophiles)

2289 "Versins Museum Expands." *Science Fiction Chronicle*. Vol. 2. No. 10. Ed. Andrew Porter. July 1981. p. 12. (collector Pierre Versins)

2290 "Vibrant Statistics." *Forrest J Ackerman Presents Mr. Monster's Movie Gold: A Treasure Trove of Imagi-Movies*. Ed. Hank Stine. Virginia Beach, VA: Donning Co. 1981. pp. 205.

2291 "'Vicarion' Author Passes." *Science Fiction Times*. No. 305. (December 1958 issue) (obituary of Henry Gardner Hunting)

2292 "Village of the Giants." *Famous Monsters of Filmland*. No. 37. Warren, February 1966; *Famous Monsters of Filmland*. No. 110. Warren, September 1974.

2293 "Vincent the Invincible." [With Roger Elwood.] *Famous Monsters of Filmland*. Vol. 5. No. 4. Whole No. 25. Warren Publishing, Inc., October 1963. pp. 14–19. (Vincent Price)

2294 "Virgil D. Smith." *Science Fiction Chronicle: The Monthly SF and Fantasy Newsmagazine*. Vol. 8. No. 10. Ed. Andrew I. Porter. July 1987. p. 18. (fan, son of Myrtle R. Douglas)

2295 "Visiting Bob Olsen's." *The Time Traveller*. Vol. 1. No. 1. January 1932.

2296 "Vital Message." *Perry Rhodan Special Release: The Crystal Prince*. K. H. Scheer. / *War of the Ghosts*. Clark Darlton. New York: Ace, December 1977.

2297 "Voyage of the Space Eagle" *Spacemen*. Vol. 1. No. 1. Philadelphia, PA: Spacemen, Inc. July 1961. (*12 to the Moon*)

2298 "Walt Liebscher." *Science Fiction Chronicle: The Monthly SF and Fantasy Newsmagazine*. Vol. 6. No. 7. Ed. Andrew I. Porter. April 1985. p. 8. (obituary of longtime fan)

2299 "Walter J. Daugherty." *Bay-Con Program Book*. August 1968.

2300 "War of the Words." *Amazing Forries: this is your life, Forrest J Ackerman*. Hollywood, CA: Metropolis Publications/Warren, 1976. pp. 12–13. (Ackerman's favorite sayings and phrases)

2301 "Ward of the Rings." *The Lord of the Rings: The Official Authorized Magazine of J. R. R.*

Tolkien's Classic Fantasy Epic. A Warren Special Edition. Warren, 1979. pp. 44–45. (about J. R. R. Tolkien)

2302 "Warlords of Atlantis." *Famous Monsters of Filmland.* No. 151. Warren, March 1979. (preview)

2303 "Warning! Monsters & May-Hem Ahead!" *Famous Monsters of Filmland.* No. 208. No. Hollywood, CA: Dynacomm, May 1995. p. 3.

2304 "Warriors of the Ring: The Cast of Characters of Lord of the Rings." *The Lord of the Rings: The Official Authorized Magazine of J. R. R. Tolkien's Classic Fantasy Epic.* A Warren Special Edition. Warren, 1979. pp. 4–5.

2305 "Watch Out for 3-D!" *Famous Monsters of Filmland.* No. 184. Warren, June 1982.

2306 "Way Down South — on B'way." [As "Dr. Ac's Dawter."] *Imagination!* Vol. 1. No. 11. August 1938. p. 12.

2307 "Way Out West"— Fantascience Flashes. *Imagination!* Vol. 1. No. 1. October 1937. p. 7.

2308 "We Gotta Protect the Kiddies." [As Helen Urban.] *Sex & Censorship Magazine.* Volume 1. No. 2. San Francisco, CA: Mid-Tower Publishing. Corp. 1958.

2309 "We Have a Hunch You're About to Be Haunted." *Famous Monsters of Filmland.* No. 33. Warren, May 1965. (Editorial)

2310 "We Laughed All the Way to the Morgue." *Famous Monsters of Filmland.* No. 100. Warren, August 1973; *Forrest J Ackerman Famous Monster of Filmland #2.* Volume II (Issues #51–100) Universal City, CA: Hollywood Publishing Company, 1991. pp. 92–96.

2311 "Week-end magazine." *Fantasy Times.* No. 245. April 2, 1956. p. 5.

2312 "Week-End Magazine." *Fantasy Times.* No. 262. (First January 1957 issue) [checklist of science fiction story reprints in *The New York Post* updated from the list in *Fantasy Times* No. 245.]

2313 "Weekend Magazine: A Checklist of New York Post Science Fiction." *Fantasy Times.* No. 223. May 2, 1955. p. 5.

2314 "WeinbauManuscript: Dawn of Flame." *Spaceways.* Vol. 3. No. 1. Whole No. 17. Ed. Harry Warner, Jr. December 1940; *Remembrance of Things Past. VIII: A Selection from the pages of Spaceways.* Ed. Bill Evans. Mt. Rainier, MD: A Weltschmerz Production, August 1962. p. 130.

2315 "Weird Award." *Famous Monsters of Filmland.* Vol. 4. No. 5. Whole No. 20. Philadelphia: Central Publications, Inc., November 1962. p. 3. (photo with caption of James Warren presenting Famous Monsters Magazine Producers Award to film producer James H. Nicholson)

2316 "Welcome Back, Monster Lovers." *Famous Monsters of Filmland.* No. 200. Orange, NJ: Dynacomm, May 1993. p. 3.

2317 "Welcome Back, Monster Lovers!" *Famous Monsters of Filmland.* No. 251. Ed. Jessie Lilley and Michael Heisler. Movieland Classics, LLC., July 2010.

2318 "Welcome, Monster Lovers." *Famous Monsters of Filmland.* Vol. 1. No. 1. Philadelphia: Central Publications, Inc., 1958; *Famous Monsters Yearbook.* No. 1. Summer-Fall 1962; *Famous Monsters 1968 Yearbook.* Warren, 1967; *Famous Monsters of Filmland.* Vol. 1. No. 1. Filmland Classics, January 2008.

2319 "Welcome, Monster Lovers." *Forrest J Ackerman's Monster Land.* No. 1. Canoga Park, CA: New Media Publishing, Inc., December 1984. pp. 3–4. [Editorial, different from that of *Famous Monsters of Filmland* No. 1., etc.]

2320 "Welcome to Metropolis." *Cult Movies.* No. 26. 1998. p. 4.

2321 "Welcome to the World's Newest Magazine." *Spacemen.* Vol. 1. No. 1. Philadelphia, PA: Spacemen, Inc. July 1961; as "Welcome to Spacemen 1965 Yearbook." *Spacemen 1965 Yearbook.* Warren Publishing Co., 1964.

2322 "Welcome to 'Tomoro.'" *Science-Fiction Classics: The Stories That Morphed into Movies.* New York: TV Books Inc., 1999.

2323 "Wells of Wisdom." [As "Mary Wollenheim Stonecraft as told to FJA."] *Eclipse.* Vol. 1. No. 1. Ed. Richard J. Kuhn. February 1941; *FMZ Digest.* Vol. 1. No. 1. February-March 1941.

2324 "We're Back for Another Count!" *James Warren Presents Son of Famous Monsters of Filmland.* New York: Paperback Library, 1965. (uncredited)

2325 "The Werewolf Dies in London." *Famous Monsters of Filmland.* No. 136. Warren, August 1977. (obituary of actor Henry Hull)

2326 "Werewolf in a Girls' Dormitory." *Famous Monsters of Filmland.* No. 34. Warren, August 1965. pp. 18–22. (1961 film *Ghoul in a Girl's Dormitory*)

2327 "Werewolf in Monsterland." *Famous Monsters of Filmland.* No. 30. Warren Publishing Co., September 1964. pp. 51–63.

2328 "Werewolf of London." *Famous Monsters of Filmland.* Vol. 5. No. 3. Whole No. 24. August 1963. Warren Publishing, Inc., pp. 50–56; *Famous Monsters of Filmland.* No. 41. Warren, November 1966. pp. 37–51; *Famous Monsters of Filmland.* No. 86. Warren, September 1971.

2329 "Werewolves of the World Unite in The Howling." *Famous Monsters of Filmland*. No. 174. Warren, June 1981; *Film Fantasy Yearbook 1982 Collector's Edition*. Warren, March 1982.

2330 "The Westercon X Saga: $5,000 Spent at the Bar, Con Winds Up Over $200 in the Red!" *Science Fiction Times*. No. 277. August 1957. pp. 3–4. (account of July 1957 science fiction convention)

2331 "We've Lost Bud." *Famous Monsters of Filmland*. No. 112. Warren, December 1974. (obituary of Bud Abbott)

2332 "What Gives at This Convention? Explained by Forrest J Ackerman." *Pacificon News*. No. 1. March 1946. p. 5.

2333 "What Kind of Monster Reads FM?" *Famous Monsters of Filmland*. No. 32. March 1965. (Editorial)

2334 "What Mad Universe?" [As Forry Rhodan.] *Perry Rhodan. No. 15. Escape to Venus*. Clark Darlton. New York: Ace, July 1972; 1974.

2335 "What Makes Luna Tick?" *Famous Monsters of Filmland*. No. 39. Warren, June 1966. pp. 38–45; *Famous Monsters of Filmland*. No. 59. November 1969. (interview with actress Carroll Borland)

2336 "What's Bruin?" *Shangri-La*. Vol. 19. April 1950.

2337 "What's Grue for '82." *Famous Monsters of Filmland*. No. 180. Warren, January 1982.

2338 "When Boris Karloff Died." *Famous Monsters of Filmland*. No. 153. Warren, May 1979. pp. 48–55. (contains material by Gordon Shriver and Ronald N. Waite)

2339 "When Dracula Invaded England." *Famous Monsters of Filmland*. No. 35. Warren, October 1965. pp. 6–12; *Famous Monsters of Filmland*. No. 68. Warren, August 1970; *Famous Monsters of Filmland*. No. 129. Warren, October 1976.

2340 "When Frighthood Was in Flower." *Science Fiction Worlds of Forrest J Ackerman and Friends*. Reseda, CA: Powell Publications, 1969; *Expanded Science Fiction Worlds of Forrest J Ackerman & Friends PLUS*. Rockville, MD: Sense of Wonder Press. 2002.

2341 "When the Devil Commands." *The Frankenscience Monster*. New York: Ace Publishing Corporation, 1969. pp. 101–104.

2342 "White Christmas." *The Fort MacArthur Bulletin*. 24 December 1945; *Glom*. No. 3. February 1946. p. 2.

2343 "White Zombie." *Famous Monsters of Filmland*. No. 38. Warren, April 1966. pp. 16–21; *Famous Monsters of Filmland*. No. 60. Warren, December 1969.

2344 "Whither Ackermankind?" *Novae Terrae*. Vol. 1. No. 9. Ed. Maurice K. Hanson and Dennis A. Jacques. Nuneaton, UK: Nuneaton Science Fiction League, December 1936. pp. 4–7. (response to criticism)

2345 "Who Calls? A Telefunnyarn by Operator 4e." *Le Zombie*. Volume 5. No. 1. Whole No. 48. Ed. Bob Tucker. Bloomington, IL: July-August 1941. (on a phone call from fan Art Widner)

2346 "Whollyweird, Call the World! Conned in Canada In Dutch in Holland." *Cult Movies*. No. 24. 1997. p. 69.

2347 "The Whollyweird Reporter." *Cult Movies*. No. 20. 1996. p. 34.

2348 "Why Christopher Lee Is Mad at Me (William Shatner too)." *Famous Monsters of Filmland*. No. 157. Warren, September 1979.

2349 "Why I Collect Science Fiction." *Xenophile*. No. 20. Ed. Nils Hardin. St. Louis, MO: January 1976. p. 5. (contribution to survey; see entry 2934.)

2350 "Why I Left Famous Monsters." *Stoner's Monster Mayhem*. No. 9. Ed. Richard Stoner. July 2000.

2351 "Why We Might Have Another World War!" [As Alden Lorraine.] *Marvel Science*. Vol. 3. No. 1. Ed. R. O. Erisman. New York: Stadium Publishing Corp., November 1950.

2352 "Wild Munster Coach." *Monster World*. No. 4. Warren, June 1965.

2353 "Will Color Kill Fantascience Films?" *Science-Fantasy Correspondent*. Vol. 1. No. 2. Ed. Willis Conover, Jr. Cambridge, MD and Belleville, NJ: Science-Fantasy Correspondent, January-February 1937.

2354 "Will the Real Count Dracula Please Arise and Be Counted." *Famous Monsters of Filmland*. No. 82. Warren, February 1971.

2355 "William L. Crawford." *Science Fiction Chronicle: The Monthly SF and Fantasy Newsmagazine*. Vol. 5. No. 7. Ed. Andrew I. Porter. April 1984. p. 6. (obituary for early fan and publisher)

2356 "Wings of Tomorrow." *Spacemen*. Vol. 1. No. 2. September 1961. Philadelphia: Spacemen, Inc., September 1961.

2357 "Wings Over the World" *Famous Monsters of Filmland*. Vol. 4. No. 19. Philadelphia: Central Publications, Inc., September 1962; *Famous Monsters of Filmland*. No. 49. Warren, May 1968; *Famous Monsters of Filmland*. No. 114. Warren, March 1975.

2358 "Wings Over the WorldCon." *Imaginative Tales*. Ed. William L. Hamling. IL: Greenleaf Publishing Company, March 1958. (report on LonCon

I, the 15th World Science Fiction Convention held in London)

2359 "The Winter, Spring, Summer and Fall of the House of Usher!" *Famous Monsters of Filmland.* Vol. 2. No. 9. November 1960. pp. 28–32; *Famous Monsters of Filmland: Yearbook No. 2.* [1964] Warren Publishing Co., December 1963.

2360 "With a Song in My Heart for You. Across 17 Lustrums of Wonder with 4e." *"It's Alive!@85."* Ed. Jeffrey Roberts & George Chastain. A Monster-Boom Special Publication, November 2001. pp. 2–4.

2361 "Without Warning." *Famous Monsters of Filmland.* No. 171. Warren, March 1981; *Warren Presents the Official Exclusive Horror Movie Yearbook 1981 Collector's Edition.* Warren, February 1981. (preview)

2362 "The Wizard of Ahs!" *Famous Monsters of Filmland.* No. 201. No. Hollywood, CA: Dynacomm, Fall 1993. pp. 56–63.

2363 "Wolfen!" *Famous Monsters of Filmland.* No. 179. Warren, November 1981; *Film Fantasy Yearbook 1982 Collector's Edition.* Warren, March 1982. (preview)

2364 "Wonders of the Ackermuseum." [As Paul Linden.] *Forrest J Ackerman's Monster Land.* No. 1. Canoga Park, CA: New Media Publishing, Inc., December 1984. pp. 25–26.

2365 "The World at Bay." *Science-Fiction Plus.* Vol. 1. No. 3. Ed. Hugo Gernsback. (Sam Moskowitz) Gernsback Publications, Inc., May 1953. (*The Magnetic Monster*)

2366 "The World Goes Bats." *Famous Monsters of Filmland.* No. 154. Warren, June 1979.

2367 "World Newsfax." *Science Fiction Times.* No. 303 (First November 1958 issue) p. 2. (planned film version of *The Time Machine* proposed by Benedict Bogeaus to star Joseph Cotten)

2368 "World Newsfax." *Science Fiction Times.* No. 313. (Second April 1959 issue) (news column)

2369 "The Worst Thing I Ever Did." *Amazing Forries: this is your life, Forrest J Ackerman.* Hollywood, CA: Metropolis Publications/Warren, 1976. p. 15. (coinage of "sci-fi")

2370 "The Wrath of Khan!" *Famous Monsters of Filmland.* No. 185. Warren, July 1982. (preview)

2371 "Yesteryear's Tomorrows." *Forrest J Ackerman's Fantastic Movie Memories: Forrest Ackerman's Treasure Trove of Imagi-Movies.* Canoga Park, CA: New Media Books, 1985.

2372 "You Dashed for It." *Famous Monsters of Filmland.* Vol. 4. No. 6. Whole No. 21. February 1963. (Editorial)

2373 "You Itched for It!" *Famous Monsters of Filmland.* No. 6. February 1960. pp. 46–49; *Famous Monsters of Filmland.* No. 93. Warren, October 1972; *Famous Monsters of Filmland.* Vol. 1. No. 4. Filmland Classics, May 2008. pp. 46–49. (replica edition) (humorous alterations and captions for horror film stills)

2374 "You Take the Cake Harpy Birthday." *Famous Monsters of Filmland.* No. 147. Warren, September 1978. p. 63.

2375 "Young Frankenstein." *Famous Monsters of Filmland.* No. 111. Warren, October 1974.

2376 "You're Stuck!" *James Warren Presents the Best from Famous Monsters of Filmland.* New York: Paperback Library, 1964.

2377 "Zaentz Preserve Us!" *The Lord of the Rings: The Official Authorized Magazine of J. R. R. Tolkien's Classic Fantasy Epic.* A Warren Special Edition. Warren, 1979. pp. 46–47. (on Saul Zaentz)

2378 "Zap! Zoom!! Flash!!! Flash Gordon Lives Again!" *Famous Monsters of Filmland.* No. 170. Warren, January 1981. pp. 30–36. (on De Laurentiis film)

2379 "Zardoz." *Famous Monsters of Filmland.* No. 111. Warren, October 1974. (1974 John Boorman film)

2380 "Zombie ... Bites the Big Apple." *Famous Monsters of Filmland.* No. 169. Warren, November 1980. (Lucio Fulci's *Zombie* a.k.a. *Zombi 2*, etc.)

Online Writings

2381 "Forry Person #1 Calling the World!" <http://web.archive.org/web/20001011100655/http://www.best.com/~4forry/fmoftalk.htm> (on why he resigned from the revived *Famous Monsters*)

2382 "4SJ's Sci-Fi Kaleidoscope." (undated) No. 1. <http://www.scifi.com/pulp/4SJ/no1>

2383 "4SJ's Sci-Fi Kaleidoscope." 20 March 1996. No. 2. <http://www.scifi.com/pulp/4SJ/no2>

2384 "4SJ's Sci-Fi Kaleidoscope." 3 April 1996. No. 3. <http://www.scifi.com/pulp/4SJ/no3>

2385 "4SJ's Sci-Fi Kaleidoscope." 17 April 1996. No. 4. <http://www.scifi.com/pulp/4SJ/no4>

2386 "4SJ's Sci-Fi Kaleidoscope." 1 May 1996. No. 5.

2387 "4SJ's Sci-Fi Kaleidoscope." 15 May 1996. No. 6. <http://www.scifi.com/pulp/4SJ/no5>

2388 "4SJ's Sci-Fi Kaleidoscope." 29 May 1996. No. 7. <http://www.scifi.com/pulp/4SJ/no6>

2389 "4SJ's Sci-Fi Kaleidoscope." 12 June 1996. No. 8. <http://www.scifi.com/pulp/4SJ/no7>

2390 "4SJ's Sci-Fi Kaleidoscope." 26 June 1996. No. 9. <http://www.scifi.com/pulp/4SJ/no8>

2391 "4SJ's Sci-Fi Kaleidoscope." 10 July 1996. No. 10. [misnumbered 9 on the site] <http://www.scifi.com/pulp/4SJ/no9>

2392 "4SJ's Sci-Fi Kaleidoscope." 24 July 1996. No. 11. <http://www.scifi.com/pulp/4SJ/no11/>

2393 "4SJ's Sci-Fi Kaleidoscope." 7 August 1996. No. 12. <http://www.scifi.com/pulp/4SJ/no12/>

2394 "4SJ's Sci-Fi Kaleidoscope." 21 August 1996. No. 13. <http://www.scifi.com/pulp/4SJ/no13/>

2395 "4SJ's Sci-Fi Kaleidoscope." 18 September 1996. No. 14. <http://www.scifi.com/pulp/4SJ/no14/>

2396 "4SJ's Sci-Fi Kaleidoscope." 2 October 1996. No. 15. <http://www.scifi.com/pulp/4SJ/no15/>

2397 "4SJ's Sci-Fi Kaleidoscope." 16 October 1996. No. 16. <http://www.scifi.com/pulp/4SJ/no16/>

2398 "4SJ's Sci-Fi Kaleidoscope." 30 October 1996. No. 17. <http://www.scifi.com/pulp/4SJ/>

2399 "4SJ's Sci-Fi Kaleidoscope." 27 November 1996. No. 18. <http://www.scifi.com/pulp/4SJ/>

2400 "4SJ's Sci-Fi Kaleidoscope." 25 December 1996. No. 19. <http://www.scifi.com/pulp/4SJ/>

2401 "4SJ's Sci-Fi Kaleidoscope." 22 January 1997. No. 20. <http://www.scifi.com/pulp/4SJ/>

2402 "4SJ's Sci-Fi Kaleidoscope." 26 February 1997. No. 21. <http://www.scifi.com/pulp/4SJ/>

2403 "4SJ's Sci-Fi Kaleidoscope." 19 March 1997. No. 22. <http://www.scifi.com/pulp/4SJ/>

2404 "4SJ's Sci-Fi Kaleidoscope." 16 April 1997. No. 23. <http://www.scifi.com/pulp/4SJ/>

2405 "4SJ's Sci-Fi Kaleidoscope." 28 May 1997 No. 23. (misnumbered; formerly at <www.scifi.com/pulp/4SJ/>)

2406 "4SJ's Sci-Fi Kaleidoscope." 2 July 1997 No. 25. <http://www.scifi.com/pulp/4SJ/>

2407 "4SJ's Sci-Fi Kaleidoscope." 30 July 1997. No. 26. <http://www.scifi.com/pulp/4SJ/>

2408 "If I Had My Life to Live Over Again." <http://web.archive.org/web/20001010230617/http://www.best.com/~4forry/brain1.htm>

2409 "Posbi Invasion Introduction: The Road to Rhodania." <http://www.perry-rhodan-usa.com/posbiintro> (Ackerman's foreword to an unpublished *Perry Rhodan* volume)

2410 "21st Century Bradbury." <http://www.best.com/~4forry/> (account of Ackerman's grandfather's involvement with Bradbury Building)

Poetry/Verse

2411 "The ABC's of Aliens, Beasts and Creatures." [As Weaver Wright with Sharon Keeran.] *Famous Monsters of Filmland.* No. 42. Warren, January 1967; *Famous Monsters of Filmland 1970 Year Book/Fearbook.* Warren, 1969; *Famous Monsters of Filmland.* No. 88. Warren, January 1972.

2412 "Alden." *The Pirate and Other Poems: By a Valedictorian.* Rochester, MI: The Pretentious Press, 1990.

2413 "'Andhow' the Magician." *The Buccaneer.* San Francisco, CA: Balboa High School, Friday 19 May 1933.

2414 "Aprés Mot." Outlandi: an objet of obscurious vision ... [satyrical, satirical, and such poems] A Virgin Forrest Publication, prepared at the Sign of the Green Fansions — for FAPA (Fantasy Amateur Press Association), 10 October 1944.

2415 "Bloody Jip." *The Pirate and Other Poems: By a Valedictorian.* Rochester, MI: The Pretentious Press, 1990.

2416 "The Community Chest." *The Pirate and Other Poems: By a Valedictorian.* Rochester, MI: The Pretentious Press, 1990.

2417 "Congoretulations." *Fangoria.* No. 100. Ed. Anthony Timpone. New York: O'Quinn Studios, March 1991. p. 5.

2418 "Happy Birthday." *The Pirate and Other Poems: By a Valedictorian.* Rochester, MI: The Pretentious Press, 1990.

2419 "Help!" *The Pirate and Other Poems: By a Valedictorian.* Rochester, MI: The Pretentious Press, 1990.

2420 "In Remembrance Peter Lorre." *Famous Monsters of Filmland.* No. 29. July 1964; *Forrest J Ackerman, Famous Monster of Filmland.* Pittsburgh, PA: Imagine, Inc. 1986. p. 120.

2421 "Los Angeles." *The Pirate and Other Poems: By a Valedictorian.* Rochester, MI: The Pretentious Press, 1990.

2422 "Mars." *The Pirate and Other Poems: By a Valedictorian.* Rochester, MI: The Pretentious Press, 1990.

2423 "Missing You." *The Pirate and Other Poems: By a Valedictorian.* Rochester, MI: The Pretentious Press, 1990.

2424 "Oh, Zombie, Oh!" [As "Dr. Ackula."] *Spaceways.* Vol. 2. No. 8. Whole No. 16. Ed. Harry B. Warner, Jr. October 1940. p. 25.

2425 "The Pirate." *The Pirate and Other Poems: By a Valedictorian.* Rochester, MI: The Pretentious Press, 1990.

2426 "Resumé of Rays." *Unusual Stories*. Ed. William L. Crawford. Everett, PA: Fantasy Publishers, May 1935; *Perry Rhodan. No. 53. Spybot!* New York: Ace, September 1974; *Rainbow Fantasia: 35 Spectrumatic Tales of Wonder*. Ed. Forrest J Ackerman. Rockville, MD: Sense of Wonder Press, 2001.

2427 "San Francisco." *The Pirate and Other Poems: By a Valedictorian*. Rochester, MI: The Pretentious Press, 1990.

2428 "Stef Gets in Your Eyes." [As Weaver Wright.] *Gargoyle*. December 1940.

2429 "The Storm." *The Pirate and Other Poems: By a Valedictorian*. Rochester, MI: The Pretentious Press, 1990.

2430 "The Turkey." *The Pirate and Other Poems: By a Valedictorian*. Rochester, MI: The Pretentious Press, 1990.

2431 [untitled limerick] *Vampirella*. No. 75. Warren, January 1979). p. 4.

2432 (untitled poem) [As Koyle Chapeque.] *Famous Monsters of Filmland*. No. 12. June 1961. [pseudonym is a play on Karel Capek, author of *R.U.R* (*Rossum's Universal Robots*)]

Reviews

2433 "ACK Reviews Visiak." *The Gorgon*. Vol. 1. No. 4. Ed. Stanley Mullin. Denver, CO: September 1947. (E. H. Visiak)

2434 "And the Darkness Falls." [Ed. Boris Karloff.] *Horror: 100 Best Books*. Ed. Stephen Jones and Kim Newman. London: Xanadu, 1988; New York: Carroll & Graf, 1988; 1990; 1998.

2435 "An Appraisal of 'The Fox Woman.'" *Neophyte*. Ed. William Rotsler. January 1948. (A. Merritt)

2436 "Atoms at Eve." *Macabre*. Vol. 1. No. 1. Ed. Don Hutchinson & Jack Doherty. Toronto: March 1948. pp. 15–16. [review of story "To This End" by Y. Edith Fried/e/o?]

2437 "The Big Eye." Max Ehrlich. [As Weaver Wright.] *Marvel Science Stories*. Vol. 3. No. 1. Ed. Robert O. Erisman. New York: Stadium Publishing Corporation, November 1950.

2438 "The Blind Spot." [Austin Hall and Homer Eon Flint.] [As Weaver Wright.] *Astounding Science Fiction*. Vol. 46. No. 1. Ed. John W. Campbell, Jr. New York: Street & Smith Publications, Inc., September 1951. [p. 124.]

2439 [Book reviews] (some as Weaver Wright) *Fantasy Advertiser*. Vol. 4. No. 1. Los Angeles: March 1950. (works by Isaac Asimov and Murray Leinster)

2440 "The Cosmic Geoids and One Other." [John Taine.] *Astounding Science Fiction*. Vol. 46. No. 5. Ed. John W. Campbell, Jr. New York: Street & Smith Publications, Inc., January 1951. [pp. 74–(75?)]

2441 "Curiouser and Curiouser." [As Geoffrey Giles with Walter Gillings.] *Fantasy Review*. Vol. 1. No. 6. Ed. Walter Gillings. Ilford, Essex, UK: Dec. 1947-Jan. 1948. p. 12. (review of *At Close of Eve: an Anthology of New Curious Stories*.)

2442 "The Dark Other." [Stanley G. Weinbaum.] *Other Worlds Science Stories*. Vol. 2. No. 4. Whole No. 8. Ed. Raymond A. Palmer. Evanston, IL: Clark Publishing Co., November 1950.

2443 "Day of the Triffids." [John Wyndham.] *Astounding Science Fiction*. Vol. 47. No. 6. Ed. John W. Campbell, Jr. New York: Street & Smith Publications, Inc. August 1951.

2444 "Deliver Me from Eva." [Paul Bailey.] *Horror: 100 Best Books*. Ed. Stephen Jones, Kim Newman. London: Xanadu, 1988; New York: Carroll & Graf, 1988; 1990; 1998.

2445 "Deliver Me from Eva." [Paul Bailey.] *Vampire*. No. 9. Ed. Joseph Kennedy. June 1947. ("Bookshelf Browsings" department)

2446 "Dr. Keller Again." [As Weaver Wright.] *The Arkham Sampler*. Vol. 2. No. 1. Ed. August Derleth. Sauk City, WI: Arkham House, Winter 1949; *Arkham House Sampler (1948–1949)*. Sauk City, WI: Arkham House/The August Derleth Society, 2010. (Gernsback era science fiction author Dr. David H. Keller [1880–1966])

2447 "Dream Come True." *Dream Quest*. Vol. 1. No. 1. Ed. Don Wilson. July 1947. (review of 1924 film *Waxworks*)

2448 "The Eosian Records." *Fantasy Review*. Vol. 3. No. 14. Ed. Walter Gillings. Ilford, Essex, UK: Apr.-May 1949. (review of John Taine's *The Cosmic Geoids and One Other*.)

2449 "Fear and Typewriter in the Sky." [L. Ron Hubbard.] *Astounding Science Fiction*. Vol. 47. No. 6. Ed. John W. Campbell, Jr. New York: Street & Smith Publications, Inc., August 1951.

2450 "Fort Without Theories." *Fantasy Review*. Ed. Walter Gillings. Volume 1. No. 4. Aug-Sep 1947. p. 15. (review of R. DeWitt Miller's *Forgotten Mysteries*)

2451 "Heinlein's Space Manual." *Fantasy Review*. Vol. 3. No. 13. Ed. Walter Gillings. Ilford, Essex, UK: Feb.-Mar. 1949. pp. 21–22. (review of Robert A. Heinlein's *Space Cadet*)

2452 "The House That Stood Still." [A. E. van Vogt.] [As Weaver Wright.] *Astounding Science Fic-*

tion. Vol. 47. No. 6. Ed. John W. Campbell, Jr. Street & Smith Publications, Inc., April 1951. p. 135.

2453 "Invasion of the Saucer-Men." *Science Fiction Times.* No. 274. (First July 1957 issue) p. 5.

2454 "Keller in Capitals." [As Weaver Wright.] *Fantasy Review.* Vol. 3. No. 13. Ed. Walter Gillings. Ilford, Essex, UK: Feb.-Mar. 1949. pp. 21–22. (review of David H. Keller, M.D.'s *The Solitary Hunters and the Abyss*)

2455 "Kinsmen of the Dragon." [Stanley Mullen.] [As Weaver Wright.] *Astounding Science Fiction.* Vol. 47. No. 6. Ed. John W. Campbell, Jr. New York: Street & Smith Publications, Inc. August 1951. [p. 141.]

2456 "Light a Last Candle." [As Geoffrey Giles with Walter Gillings.] *Vision of Tomorrow.* Vol. 1. No. 9. Ed. Philip Harbottle & Ronald E. Graham., June 1970. (review of book by Vincent King)

2457 "The Mantle of Merritt." [As Geoffrey Giles with Walter Gillings.] *Fantasy Review.* Vol. 2. No. 10. Ed. Walter Gillings. Ilford, Essex, UK: Aug.-Sep. 1948. p. 11. [review of *The Black Wheel* by A. Merritt and Hannes Bok (New Collectors' Group, 1947).]

2458 "Mars Is — Hell." *Planet Stories.* Vol. 4. No. 9. Ed. Jerome Bixby. New York: Love Romances Co., Inc., November 1950. p. 3; as "Rocketship X-M." *Perry Rhodan. No. 70. Thora's Sacrifice.* Kurt Brand. New York: Ace, April 1975; *Martianthology: An Ackermanthology of Sense of Wonder Stories.* Rockville, MD: Sense of Wonder Press, 2003. (review of *Rocketship X-M*)

2459 "Movie Review." *Tympany.* Ed. Bob Stein & Redd Boggs. 26 May 1947. (Swedish film *The Girl and the Devil*)

2460 "Nineteen Eighty-Four." [George Orwell.] *Marvel Science Stories.* Vol. 3. No. 1. Ed. Robert O. Erisman. New York: Stadium Publishing Corporation, November 1950.

2461 "Peril to Our Planet." *Tyrann.* No. 7. Ed. Henry Ebel and Norbert Hirschhorn. 1953??? (*War of the Worlds* film review)

2462 "Play Review: '2001.'" [As Allis Kerlay.] *Imagination!* Vol. 1. No. 6. Los Angeles: March 1938.

2463 "Play Review: 'The Living Lie.'" [As Namrckca J Tscrrof.] *Imagination!* No. 7. Los Angeles: April 1938. pp. 9–10.

2464 "The Poor Man's Necronomicon — 'Pilgrims' Through Print Shop and Bindery." *Tympany.* No. 13.(?) Ed. Robert L. Stein & Redd Boggs. 1 September 1947. (review of J. O. Bailey's *Pilgrims Through Space and Time: Trends and Patterns in Scientific and Utopian Fiction*)

2465 "Radio Review: '1994.'" [As Weaver Wright.] *Imagination!* Vol. 1. No. 5. Los Angeles: February 1938. p. 8.

2466 "Red Planet." [Robert A. Heinlein.] [As Weaver Wright.] *Other Worlds Science Stories.* Vol. 2. No. 2. Whole No. 6. Ed. Raymond A. Palmer. Evanston, IL: Clark Publishing Co., September 1950.

2467 "REVIEW: About Books: All on One Shelf." [as Geoffrey Giles (with Walter Gillings).] *Fantasy Review.* Vol. 3. No. 15. Ed. Walter Gillings. Ilford, Essex, UK: Summer 1949. pp. 17–19.

2468 "Review-Conquered Power." [As Jack Erman.] *Imagination!* Vol. 1. No. 5. Los Angeles: February 1938.

2469 "Review: *Logan's Run*." [William F. Nolan and George Clayton Johnson.] *Fantastic.* Vol. 17. No. 6. Ed. Harry Harrison. Flushing, NY: Ultimate Publishing Co. Inc., August 1968.

2470 [review of "Dr. Cyclops"] *Astonishing Stories.* Vol. 1. No. 3. Ed. Frederik Pohl. Chicago, IL: Fictioneers, Inc. June 1940.

2471 "Review: *Solitary Hunters and the Abyss*" [David H. Keller.] [As Weaver Wright.] *The Arkham Sampler.* Vol. 2. No. 1. Ed. August Derleth. Sauk City, WI: Arkham House, Winter 1949; *Arkham House Sampler (1948–1949).* Sauk City, WI: Arkham House/The August Derleth Society, 2010.

2472 "The Road to the Stars." [As Geoffrey Giles with Walter Gillings.] *Science-Fantasy.* Vol. 1. No. 1. Nova Publications Ltd., Summer 1950.

2473 "Science Fiction, Horror & Fantasy Film and Television Credits." [Harris M. Lentz, III.] *Science Fiction Review.* No. 84. Ed. Richard E. Geis. Spring 1984. p. 17.

2474 "The Ship of Ishtar." [A. Merritt.] [As Alden Lorraine.] *Astounding Science Fiction.* Vol. 47. No. 6. Ed. John W. Campbell, Jr. New York: Street & Smith Publications, Inc., January 1950.

2475 "Sixth Column." [Robert A. Heinlein.] *Other Worlds Science Stories.* Vol. 2. No. 2. Whole No. 6. Ed. Raymond A. Palmer. Evanston, IL: Clark Publishing Co., September 1950.

2476 "Slave New World." *Science-Fantasy Review.* Vol. 3. No. 16. Ed. Walter Gillings. Ilford, Essex, UK: Autumn 1949. pp. 22–23. (George Orwell's *Nineteen Eighty-Four.*)

2477 "Space Cadet." [Robert A. Heinlein.] *Other Worlds Science Stories.* Ed. Raymond A. Palmer. Vol. 1. No. 4. Evanston, IL: Clark Publishing Co., May 1950.

2478 "Starship Troopers." *Cult Movies.* No. 29. 1999. p. 67. (film review)

2479 "The 31st of February." [Nelson S. Bond.] *Astounding Science Fiction*. Vol. 45. No. 4. Ed. John W. Campbell, Jr. New York: Street & Smith Publications, Inc., June 1950. [p. 100.]

2480 "The 31st of February." [Nelson S. Bond.] *Other Worlds Science Stories*. Vol. 2. No. 1. Whole No. 5. Ed. Raymond A. Palmer. Evanston, IL: Clark Publishing Co., July 1950.

2481 "The Toymaker." [Raymond F. Jones.] *Astounding Science Fiction*. Vol. 48. No. 1. Ed. John W. Campbell, Jr. New York: Street & Smith Publications, Inc., September 1951. [pp. 125–126?]

2482 "Triton." [L. Ron Hubbard] [As Weaver Wright.] *Astounding Science Fiction*. Vol. 44. No. 6. Ed. John W. Campbell, Jr. New York: Street & Smith Publications, Inc., February 1950.

2483 "Twenty Years of Fillers." [as Geoffrey Giles (with Walter Gillings).] *Fantasy Review*. Vol. 3. No. 15. Ed. Walter Gillings. Ilford, Essex, UK: Summer 1949. p. 27. (review of August Derleth collection *Not Long for This World*)

2484 "The World Below." [S. Fowler Wright.] *Marvel Science Stories*. Vol. 3. No. 1. Ed. Robert O. Erisman. New York: Stadium Publishing Corporation, November 1950.

2485 "Worlds of Wonder." [Olaf Stapledon.] *Other Worlds Science Stories*. Vol. 1. No. 4. Ed. Raymond A. Palmer. Evanston, IL: Clark Publishing Co., May 1950.

SCREENPLAYS

2486 "Filmgore." [With Ken Dixon.] Director: Ken Dixon. Wizard Video/Force Video, 1983.

2487 "Frankenstein from Space." [As Weaver Wright with Budd Bankson.] *Famous Monsters of Filmland*. No. 3. April 1959; *Forrest J Ackerman's Monsterama*. No. 2. Seattle, WA: Fantagraphics Books, Spring 1992. pp. 29–30. (film treatment)

2488 "The Horror Hall of Fame: A Monster Salute." Braverman Productions Inc. Rothman/Wohl Productions, 1974. Director: Charles Braverman. (uncredited, credited as technical advisor)

2489 "Lugosi, The Forgotten King." MPI Home Video, 1985. Directors: Mark S. Gilman Jr., Dave Stuckey. (uncredited)

2490 "Mad Monster Party?" (Len Korobkin and Harvey Kurtzman, story by Arthur Rankin Jr.) Director: Jules Bass 1967. (uncredited)

2491 "Metropolis II." Director: Paul Hasse. (black & white short film, a winning entry in the 7th Annual Kodak Teenage Movie Contest)

2492 "Monster of Metropolis." ca. 1963.

2493 "Monsters of the Moon." September 1940. (film scenario accompanied by stills prepared for Chicon I, the Second World Science Fiction Convention) [reprinted 1953 with Ray Heinz and Mike Frisby???]

2494 "My Lovely Monster." Sender Freies Berlin (SFB)/Westdeutscher Rundfunk (WDR)/XenonFilm, 1990. Director: Michael Bergmann. (additional dialogue)

2495 "Siegfried Saves Metropolis" ("Shooting Script For First Annual Amateur Home Movie Contest" sponsored by "Famous Monsters of Filmland") Warren Publishing Co., 1961. [one version produced by Paul Davids]

2496 "Son of Siegfried."

2497 "Twin of Frankenstein." Warren Publishing Company, 1963. 30 pp. Warren Publishing Co., 1961. ("Shooting Script for First Annual Amateur Home Movie Contest" sponsored by *Famous Monsters of Filmland*)

2498 "The Wizard of Mars." Director: David L. Hewitt. (additional dialogue [for John Carradine])

COMICS

2499 "Down to Earth!" *Vampirella*. No. 2. New York: Warren, November 1969; *Vampirella: Silver Anniversary Collection*. No. 3. (Good Girl Edition) March 1997; *Vampirella: The Crimson Chronicles*. No. 1. Harris Publications, 2004; *Vampirella: Crimson Chronicles Maximum*. Harris Publications, 2008; *Vampirella Archives Volume 1*. Runnemede, NJ: Dynamite Entertainment, 2010/2011. [Pencils: Mike Royer]

2500 "Just Imagine: Jeanie." *Questar: Science Fiction/Fantasy Adventure*. No. 4. Ed. William G. Wilson, Jr. Pittsburgh, PA: MW Communications, August 1979. pp. 31–40. [illustrated by James Warhola]

2501 "Just Imagine: Jeanie." *Questar: Science Fiction/Fantasy Adventure*. No. 5. Ed. William G. Wilson, Jr. Ed. William G. Wilson, Jr. November 1979. James Warhola (art)

2502 "Just Imagine: Jeanie." *Questar: Science Fiction/Fantasy Adventure*. No. 6. Ed. William G. Wilson, Jr. February 1980.

2503 "Just Imagine: Jeanie." *Questar: Science Fiction/Fantasy Adventure*. Vol. 1. No. 4. Whole No. 8. Ed. William G. Wilson, Jr. August 1980. pp. 53–58. [illustrated by Harold Schuler, Ackerman receives "created by" credit]

2504 "Just Imagine: Jeanie Chapter Five: Discovery." *Questar: Science Fiction/Fantasy Adventure.* Vol. 3. No. 2. Whole No. 10. Ed. William G. Wilson, Jr. Pittsburgh, PA: MW Communications, December 1980. pp. 49–53. [Script: John Nubbin, Pencils: Mike Grell]

2505 "Just Imagine: Jeanie Chapter Seven: Interlude." *Questar: Science Fiction/Fantasy Adventure.* Vol. 3. No. 4. Whole No. 12. Ed. William G. Wilson, Jr. Pittsburgh, PA: MW Communications, June 1981. pp. 30–34. [Script: John Nubbin, Pencils: Ron Frenz] (Ackerman no longer credited as creator)

2506 "Just Imagine: Jeanie Chapter Six: Pause in a Dry and Deadly Place." *Questar: Science Fiction/ Fantasy Adventure.* Vol. 3. No. 3. Whole No. 11. Ed. William G. Wilson, Jr. Pittsburgh, PA: MW Communications, February 1981. pp. 51–58. [Script: John Nubbin, Pencils: Mike Grell]

2507 *Monster Matinee Celebrating Monster Movies of the Thirties & Forties!* No. 1. Chaos Classic Monsters, October 1997. [Pencils: Kyle Hotz.]

2508 *Monster Matinee. No. 2.: Celebrating Monster Movies of the Fifties!* Chaos Classic Monsters, October 1997.

2509 "Run for Your Wife." [As Jack Erman with Richard Carnell.] *Vampirella.* No. 4. New York: Warren, April 1970; *Vampirella Archives Volume 1.* Runnemede, NJ: Dynamite Entertainment, 2010/ 2011.

2510 "Twin of Frankenstein." (comic strip story credited to Ackerman) *Tales of Horror.* No. 1. 1960. (monster fanzine) Chip Gnam (pencils) Bob Madden (inking)

2511 ["Vampirella and the Alien Amazon." *Vampirella.* No. 81. Warren, September 1979. Art/ Pencils: Pablo Marcos. (most sources credit William DuBay for script)]

2512 "Vampirella of Draculon." *Vampirella.* No. 1. New York: Warren, September 1969; *Hyde-25.* No. 0. Harris Comics, April 1995. (reprint); *Vampirella.* No. 1. Harris Publications, Oct. 2001. [1969 Commemorative Special]; *Vampirella: The Crimson Chronicles.* No. 1. Harris Publications, 2004; *Vampirella: Crimson Chronicles Maximum.* Harris Publications, 2008; *Vampirella Archives Volume 1.* Runnemede, NJ: Dynamite Entertainment, 2010/ 2011. [this is the "origin" story of the character written by Ackerman and originally drawn by Tom Sutton (1937–2002)]

2513 "Vampirella of Drakulon." *Vampirella: 25th Anniversary Special.* Harris Comics, October 1996. (re-drawn by Mark Texeira from Ackerman's script)

2514 "Venus Amazons." (Vampi's Feary Tales: Queen of Outer Space!) *Vampirella.* No. 3. New York: Warren, January 1970; *Vampirella: The Crimson Chronicles.* No. 1. Harris Publications, 2004; *Vampirella Archives Volume 1.* Runnemede, NJ: Dynamite Entertainment, 2010/2011. [Art/Pencils: Dick Piscopo]

CALENDARS

2515 *Amazing Stories from the Collection of Forrest J Ackerman.* Landmark General Corp, 1991.

2516 *Famous Monsters 1992 Coverart Calendar.* Raygen Entertainment, 1991.

2517 *The Horror Collection of Forrest J Ackerman 1990 Calendar.*

TRADING CARDS

2518 *The Ackermonster's Cardiacards! Classic Monster Movie Lobby Cards.* Vol. 1–45.

2519 [*Famous Monsters of Filmland.* Rosan, 1963. (these 64 trading cards did not contain any text or material by Ackerman and are only included for their associational value)]

2520 *Forrest J Ackerman's Classicards!* Dynacomm, 1992. (45 card set, reproductions of magazine covers)

2521 *Mr. Sci-Fi's Scientifiction Cards!* Raygen Entertainment. 1991.

WORKS TRANSLATED BY ACKERMAN

2522 "In 2112." J. U. Giesy and Junius B. Smith. *The Cavalier.* 10 August 1912; *International Science Fiction.* Vol. 1. No. 2. Ed. Frederik Pohl. New York: Galaxy Publishing Corporation, June 1968. (Esperanto translation by Ackerman)

2523 "Pressure Cruise." Andrei Gorbovski. *Perry Rhodan.* No. 58. The Guardians. Kurt Mahr. New York: Ace, November 1974. (translated by Ackerman with Norbert F. Novotny)

PUBLISHED LETTERS

2524 *Air Wonder Stories.* Vol. 1. No. 11. Ed. Hugo Gernsback. New York: Stellar Publications, May 1930.

2525 *Amazing Detective Tales.* Vol. 1. No. 9. Mt. Morris, IL: Techni-Craft Publishing Corp., September 1930.

2526 *Amazing Stories.* Vol. 6. No. 10. Ed. T. O'Conor Sloane. Teck Publishing Corp., January 1932; "Poor Amazing Gets It!" *The Fantastic Pulps.* Peter Haining. UK: Gollancz, 1975; New York: St. Martin's Press, 1976; Vintage Books, 1976.

2527 *Amazing Stories.* Vol. 6. No. 11. Ed. T. O'Conor Sloane. Dunnellen, NJ: Teck Publishing Corp., February 1932.

2528 *Amazing Stories.* Vol. 6. No. 12. Ed. T. O'Conor Sloane. Dunnellen, NJ: Teck Publishing Corp., March 1932.

2529 *Amazing Stories.* Vol. 7. No. 11. Ed. T. O'Conor Sloane. Dunnellen, NJ: Teck Publications, Inc., February 1933.

2530 *Amazing Stories.* Vol. 8. No 1. Ed. T. O'Conor Sloane. Dunnellen, NJ: Teck Publications, Inc., April 1933.

2531 *Amazing Stories.* Vol. 8. No 4. Ed. T. O'Conor Sloane. Dunnellen, NJ: Teck Publications, Inc., July 1933.

2532 *Amazing Stories.* Vol. 8. No. 7. Ed. T. O'Conor Sloane. Dunnellen, NJ: Teck Publications, Inc., November 1933.

2533 *Amazing Stories.* Vol. 8. No. 12. Ed. T. O'Conor Sloane. Dunnellen, NJ: Teck Publications, Inc., March 1934.

2534 *Amphipoxi.* No. 8. 1968. Ed. Billy H. Pettit. The Hague, Netherlands. (Letter pertains to early fanzines)

2535 *Astonishing Stories.* Vol. 1. No. 1. Ed. Frederik Pohl. (uncredited). Chicago: Fictioneers, February 1940.

2536 *Astonishing Stories.* Vol. 1. No. 3. Chicago: Fictioneers, June 1940.

2537 *Astounding Science Fiction.* Vol. 37. No. 3. Ed. John W. Campbell, Jr. New York: Street & Smith Publications, Inc., May 1946.

2538 *Astounding Stories.* Vol. 11. No. 2. Ed. Harry Bates. New York: Clayton Magazines, Inc., November 1932.

2539 *Astounding Stories.* Vol. 12. No. 4. Ed. F. Orlin Tremaine. New York: Street & Smith Publications, Inc., December 1933.

2540 *Astounding Stories.* Vol. 12. No. 6. Ed. F. Orlin Tremaine. New York: Street & Smith Publications, Inc. February 1934; *Gosh! Wow! (Boy-oh-Boy)! Science Fiction.* New York: Bantam, 1982. pp. 23–25.

2541 *Astounding Stories.* Vol. 14. No. 2. Ed. F. Orlin Tremaine. New York: Street & Smith Publications, Inc. October 1934.

2542 *Astounding Stories.* Vol. 14. No. 5. Ed. F. Orlin Tremaine. New York: Street & Smith Publications, Inc. January 1935.

2543 *Astounding Stories.* Vol. 15. No. 5. Ed. F. Orlin Tremaine. New York: Street & Smith Publications, Inc. July 1935.

2544 *Astounding Stories.* Vol. 15. No. 6. Ed. F. Orlin Tremaine. New York: Street & Smith Publications, Inc. August 1935.

2545 *Astounding Stories.* Vol. 8. No. 1. Ed. Harry Bates. New York: Clayton Magazines, Inc., October 1931. [As Stone T. Farmington.]

2546 *Astounding Stories.* Vol. 8. No. 2. Ed. Harry Bates. New York: Clayton Magazines, Inc., November 1931.

2547 *Astounding Stories.* Vol. 9. No. 1. Ed. Harry Bates. New York: Clayton Magazines, Inc., January 1932.

2548 *Astounding Stories.* Vol. 10. No. 1. Ed. Harry Bates. New York: Clayton Magazines, Inc., April 1932.

2549 *Astounding Stories.* Vol. 9. No. 3. Ed. Harry Bates. New York: Clayton Magazines, Inc., March 1932.

2550 *Astounding Stories of Super-Science.* Vol. 2. No. 2. Ed. Harry Bates. New York: Publishers' Fiscal Corporation, May 1930. [headed "Likes Interplanetary Stories" by editors]

2551 *Astounding Stories of Super-Science.* Vol. 4. No. 2. Ed. Harry Bates. Publishers' Fiscal Corporation, November 1930. [headed "Not One Poor Story Yet" by editors (signed Forrest James Ackerman)]

2552 *Astounding Stories of Super-Science.* Vol. 4. No. 3. Ed. Harry Bates. Reader's Guild, Inc., December 1930.

2553 *Astounding Stories of Super-Science.* Vol. 5. No. 1. Ed. Harry Bates. Readers' Guild, Inc., January 1931. [asking for stories by Ed Earl Repp, headed "A Request" by editors]

2554 *Astounding Stories of Super-Science.* Vol. 6. No. 1. Ed. Harry Bates. April 1931. [headed "I Do; I Don't."]

2555 *Astounding Stories of Super-Science.* Vol. 6. No. 3. Ed. Harry Bates. New York: Clayton Magazines, Inc., June 1931.

2556 [*Astounding Stories of Super-Science.* Vol. 7. No. 1. Ed. Harry Bates. New York: Clayton Magazines, Inc., July 1931.]???

2557 *Astounding Stories of Super-Science.* Vol. 7. No. 2. Ed. Harry Bates. New York: Clayton Magazines, Inc., August 1931.

2558 *Brooklyn Daily Eagle.* Brooklyn, NY: 8 November 1931. (to "Aunt Jean" in the Junior Eagle section)

2559 "Copy of a Letter from a Fan (Age 15) to the Producer of 'King Kong.'" *Glom.* No. 9. October 1947; *Shangri-La.* June 1949; *Forrest J Ackerman Presents Mr. Monster's Movie Gold: A Treasure Trove of Imagi-Movies.* Ed. Hank Stine. Virginia Beach, VA: Donning Co. 1981. pp. 88–89. (11 October 1932 letter from Ackerman to Merian C. Cooper)

2560 *Cult Movies.* No. 7. 1992. p. 5.

2561 "Dear Mr. Wellman." *Glom.* No. 6. January 1947. p. 6. (8 December 1946 letter from Ackerman to filmmaker William A. Wellman)

2562 *Degler!* No. 167. Ed. Andrew Porter. New York: 3 February 1967. pp. 3–4. (on fan Stephen Pickering)

2563 *Famous Fantastic Mysteries.* Ed. Mary Gnaedinger. Vol. 9. No. 4. All-Fiction Field, Inc., April 1948. p. 123. [As Weaver Wright.]

2564 *Famous Fantastic Mysteries.* Vol. 7. No. 5. Ed. Mary Gnaedinger. All-Fiction Field, Inc., August 1946. p. 8. [As Weaver Wright.]

2565 *Famous Fantastic Mysteries.* Vol. 8. No. 4. Ed. Mary Gnaedinger. All-Fiction Field, Inc., April 1947. pp. 119–120. [As Weaver Wright.]

2566 *Famous Fantastic Mysteries.* Vol. 8. No. 6. Ed. Mary Gnaedinger. All-Fiction Field, Inc., August 1947. p. 122.

2567 *Famous Fantastic Mysteries.* Vol. 9. No. 5. Ed. Mary Gnaedinger. All-Fiction Field, Inc., June 1948.

2568 *Fan-atic.* No. 2. Ed. Charles Heling. March 1941.

2569 *Fandom Speaks — Free Speech.* Ed. Jack Clements & Rex Ward. January 1948.

2570 *The Fantasite.* Vol. 1. No. 3. Ed. Phil Bronson. Hastings, MN: April 1941.

2571 *Fantast.* No. 13. Ed. C. S. Youd, Doug Webster. April 1942.

2572 *The Fantasy Fan.* Vol. 1. No. 2. Ed. Charles D. Hornig. Elizabeth, NJ: Charles D. Hornig, October 1933; *The Boiling Point.* West Warwick, RI: Necronomicon Press, April 1985; *The Fantasy Fan — The Fans' Own Magazine (September, 1933–February, 1935; Vol. 1, Nos. 1–12; vol. 2, Nos. 13–18.* n.p., n.d Tacoma, WA[?]: Lance Thingmaker, 2010.

2573 *The Fantasy Fan.* Vol. 1. No. 4. Ed. Charles D. Hornig. Elizabeth, NJ: Charles D. Hornig. December 1933; *The Boiling Point.* West Warwick, RI: Necronomicon Press, April 1985; *The Fantasy Fan —*

The Fans' Own Magazine (September, 1933–February, 1935; Vol. 1, Nos. 1–12; vol. 2, Nos. 13–18. n.p., n.d Tacoma, WA[?]: Lance Thingmaker, 2010.

2574 *The Fantasy Fan.* Vol. 1. No. 5. Elizabeth, NJ: Charles D. Hornig. January 1934; *The Boiling Point.* West Warwick, RI: Necronomicon Press, April 1985; *The Fantasy Fan — The Fans' Own Magazine (September, 1933–February, 1935; Vol. 1, Nos. 1–12; vol. 2, Nos. 13–18.* n.p., n.d Tacoma, WA[?]: Lance Thingmaker, 2010.

2575 *Fantasy Times.* No. 189. (1st November 1953 issue) [response to literary agent Scott Meredith]

2576 *Futurian War Digest.* Vol. 2. No. 6. Whole No. 18. Ed. J. Michael Rosenblum. Leeds, UK: March 1942.

2577 *Infinity Science Fiction.* Vol. 1. No. 2. Ed. Larry T. Shaw. Royal Publications, Inc., February 1956.

2578 "Letter from a Vampire." *Famous Monsters of Filmland.* No. 7. June 1960. pp. 46–49. (pun-laden missive from "Dr. Scalpela")

2579 [Letter from Ackerman to Bela Lugosi. 27 December 1954.] Rhodes, Gary Don and Richard Sheffield. *Bela Lugosi: Dreams and Nightmares.* Narberth, PA: Collectables, 2007.

2580 *Locus: The Newspaper of the Science Fiction Field.* No. 232. April 1980.

2581 *Locus: The Newspaper of the Science Fiction Field.* No. 237. September 1980. (on Donald F. Glut's receipt of the Galaxy Award)

2582 *Locus: The Newspaper of the Science Fiction Field.* No. 242. March 1981. p. 14. (regarding author Kris Neville)

2583 *Locus: The Newspaper of the Science Fiction Field.* No. 250. November 1981.

2584 *Locus: The Newspaper of the Science Fiction Field.* Vol. 15. No. 4. Whole No. 255. Ed. Charles N. Brown. Oakland, CA: Locus Publications, April 1982. p. 12.

2585 *Locus.* Vol. 24. No. 5. Whole No. 352. Ed. Charles N. Brown. Oakland, CA: Locus Publications, May 1990. p. 61.

2586 *Locus.* Vol. 37. No. 2. Whole No. 427. Ed. Charles N. Brown. Oakland, CA: Locus Publications, August 1996. p. 66.

2587 *Locus.* Vol. 40. No. 5. Whole No. 448. Ed. Charles N. Brown. Oakland, CA: Locus Publications, May 1998. p. 59.

2588 *Locus.* Vol. 42. No. 5. Whole No. 460. Ed. Charles N. Brown. Oakland, CA: Locus Publications, May 1999. p. 70.

2589 *Locus.* Vol. 45. No. 6. Whole No. 479. Ed. Charles N. Brown. Oakland, CA: Locus Publications, December 2000. p. 74.

2590 *Locus.* Vol. 46. No. 2. Whole No. 481. Ed. Charles N. Brown. Oakland, CA: Locus Publications, February 2001. p. 76.

2591 *Locus.* Vol. 48. No. 1. Whole No. 492. Ed. Charles N. Brown. Oakland, CA: Locus Publications, January 2002. p. 79.

2592 *Locus.* Vol. 50. No. 2. Whole No. 505. Ed. Charles N. Brown. Oakland, CA: Locus Publications, February 2003. p. 88.

2593 *Lore.* No. 5. Ed. Jerry Page. April 1966. p. 55. (on Richard Tooker and "Garret Ford")

2594 *Lore.* No. 5. Ed. Jerry Page. April 1966. pp. 55–56. (on "Garret Ford")

2595 *Lore.* No. 5. Ed. Jerry Page. April 1966. p. 58 [As "Captain Dracula."] [on pulp titles]

2596 "Mr. Filmonster Lives." *Horrorfan.* Vol. 1. No. 2. New York: GCR Publishing, Summer 1989. p. 4.

2597 "A New Method of Evaluation." *Science Wonder Quarterly.* Vol. 1. No. 1. Ed. Hugo Gernsback. Mt. Morris, IL: Stellar Publishing Corporation, Fall 1929. p. 136; *Amazing Forries: this is your life, Forrest J Ackerman.* Hollywood, CA: Metropolis Publications, 1976. p. 11; *Gosh! Wow (Boy-oh-Boy)! Science Fiction.* New York: Bantam, 1982. pp. xvii–xviii; *Futures Past.* No. 4. Ed. Jim Emerson. Convoy, OH: April 1994. p. 27.

2598 *Novae Terrae.* Vol. 1. No. 6. Ed. Maurice K. Hanson and Dennis A. Jacques. Nuneaton, UK: Nuneaton Science Fiction League, August 1936. p. 9.

2599 *Novae Terrae.* Ed. Maurice K. Hanson. December 1938.

2600 *Nuz from Home.* Vol. 1. No. 14. Ed. Walter Dunkelberger. Fargo, ND: 1943.

2601 "Open Letter." *Fantasy Times.* No. 191. (1st December 1953 issue)

2602 "An Open Letter to Frank R. Paul (Deceased)." *Science Fiction Chronicle: The Monthly SF and Fantasy Newsmagazine.* Vol. 11. No. 7. Ed. Andrew I. Porter. April 1990. p. 31. (on the sale of an original Paul painting which enabled Ackerman to purchase a crypt in Forest Lawn)

2603 *Planet Stories.* Vol. 1. No. 3. Ed. Malcolm Reiss. New York: Love Romances, Summer 1940.

2604 *The Planeteer.* Ed. James Blish & William Miller, Jr. Vol. 1. Whole No. 5. March 1936. p. 12; (1971 reprint enclosed with) *Canticles from Labowitz.* No. 7. Ed. Gary H. Labowitz. Norristown, PA: Canticle Press, 1971.

2605 *Playboy.* Vol. 1. No. 11. Ed. Hugh M. Hefner. Chicago: HMH Pub. Co., October 1954.

2606 *Real Fact Comics.* No. 3. New York: National Comics Publications, Inc., July-August 1946. (You Tell Us! letters column)

2607 *Science Fiction Chronicle.* Vol. 2. No. 9. Ed. Andrew Porter. June 1981. pp. 18–19. (concerns monies owed/due clients and heirs, seeking whereabouts of same)

2608 *Science Fiction Chronicle: The Monthly Science Fiction and Fantasy Newsmagazine.* Vol. 4. No. 9. Ed. Andrew Porter. June 1983. p. 12. (refutes that he and A. E. van Vogt were the principals behind Triton Books)

2609 *Science Fiction Chronicle: The Monthly Science Fiction and Fantasy Newsmagazine.* Vol. 5. No. 11. Ed. Andrew I. Porter. August 1984. pp. 14, 16. (clarifying his role in a revival of *Weird Tales* magazine)

2610 *Science Fiction Chronicle: The Monthly Science Fiction and Fantasy Newsmagazine.* Vol. 7. No. 1. Ed. Andrew I. Porter. October 1985. p. 20. (pointing out that he and Wendayne were present at a World SF Writers Meeting covered in the previous issue)

2611 *Science Fiction Chronicle: The Monthly Science Fiction and Fantasy Newsmagazine.* Vol. 7. No. 5. Ed. Andrew I. Porter. February 1986. p. 16. (seeking short story title)

2612 *Science Fiction Chronicle: The Monthly Science Fiction and Fantasy Newsmagazine.* Vol. 7. No. 11. Ed. Andrew I. Porter. August 1986. pp. 26, 28. (items he believed to be missing from his collection, one of which was later offered in the Guernsey's auction)

2613 *Science Fiction Chronicle: The Monthly Science Fiction and Fantasy Newsmagazine.* Vol. 8. No. 1. Ed. Andrew I. Porter. October 1986. p. 20. (reports he has found one of the items he reported missing, announces banquet in honor of his sixty years as a fan)

2614 *Science Fiction Chronicle: The Monthly Science Fiction and Fantasy Newsmagazine.* Vol. 8. No. 4. Ed. Andrew I. Porter. January 1987. pp. 18–19. (on a joke leveled at him while presenting the Big Heart Award at the WorldCon)

2615 *Science Fiction Chronicle: The Monthly SF and Fantasy Newsmagazine.* Vol. 9. No. 2. Ed. Andrew I. Porter. November 1987. p. 24. (clarifying how much of his collection would be auctioned)

2616 *Science Fiction Chronicle: The Monthly SF and Fantasy Newsmagazine.* Vol. 9. No. 8. Ed. Andrew I. Porter. May 1988. pp. 22, 29. (on the Guernsey's auction)

2617 *Science Fiction Chronicle: The Monthly SF and Fantasy Newsmagazine.* Vol. 11. No. 7. Ed. Andrew I. Porter. April 1990. p. 24. (on Robert A. Heinlein's supposed use of "sci-fi" before him, later disproved)

2618 *Science Fiction Review.* Vol. 5. No. 2. Whole No. 17. Ed. Richard E. Geis. May 1976. p. 34.

2619 *Science Fiction Review.* Vol. 8. No. 3. Whole No. 31. Ed. Richard E. Geis. Portland, OR: May 1979. p. 21. (refuting claims of misogyny on the part of Hugo Gernsback)

2620 *Science Fiction Review.* No. 54. Ed. Richard E. Geis. Portland, OR: Richard E. Geis, Spring 1985. pp. 20–21.

2621 *Science Fiction Review.* No. 56. Ed. Richard E. Geis. Portland, OR: Richard E. Geis, Fall 1985. pp. 35–36.

2622 *Science Wonder Quarterly.* Vol. 1. No. 2. Ed. Hugo Gernsback. Mt. Morris, IL: Stellar Publishing Corporation, Winter 1930.

2623 *Science Wonder Quarterly.* Vol. 1. No. 3. Ed. Hugo Gernsback. Mt. Morris, IL: Stellar Publishing Corporation, Spring 1930.

2624 *The Scream Factory.* No. 15. The Deadline Publications, Autumn 1994.

2625 *Slant.* No. 3. Ed. Walter A. Willis. Spring 1950. p. 22.

2626 *Stardust.* Vol. 1. No. 3. Ed. William Lawrence Hamling. Chicago: August 1940. [As Weaver Wright.]

2627 *Startling Stories.* Vol. 28. No. 1. Ed. Samuel Mines. Kokomo, IN: Better Publications, Inc., November 1952. p. 128.

2628 *Stirring Science Stories.* Vol. 1. No. 1. Ed. Donald A. Wollheim. Holyoke, MA: Albing Publications, February 1941. [With Morojo.]

2629 *Stirring Science Stories.* Vol. 1. No. 3. Ed. Donald A. Wollheim. Holyoke, MA: Albing Publications, June 1941.

2630 *Strange Stories.* Vol. 1. No. 2. New York: Better Publications, Inc., April 1939. [As Weaver Wright.]

2631 *Strange Tales of Mystery and Terror.* Vol. 2. No. 1. Ed. Harry Bates. New York: Clayton Magazines, Inc., June 1932.

2632 *Strange Tales of Mystery and Terror.* Vol. 2. No. 3. Ed. Harry Bates. New York: Clayton Magazines, Inc., October 1932.

2633 *Sun Spots.* No. 20. Ed. Gerry de la Ree. October 1941. p. 9. (signed "4E Ackerman")

2634 *Super Science Stories.* Vol. 5. No. 1. Ed. Ejler Jakobsson. New York: Fictioneers; Toronto: Fictioneers, January 1949.

2635 *Thrilling Wonder Stories.* Vol. 9. No. 1. Ed. Mort Weisinger. New York: Better Publications, February 1937. pp. 126, 128.

2636 *Vampirella.* No. 75. New York: Warren, January 1979. p. 4. (limerick)

2637 *Weird Tales.* Vol. 26. No. 5. Ed. Farnsworth Wright. Chicago: Popular Fiction Publishing Co., Inc. November 1935.

2638 *Weird Tales.* Vol. 35. No. 2. Ed. Farnsworth Wright. New York: March 1940. [As Weaver Wright.]

2639 *Weird Tales.* Vol. 35. No. 9. Ed. Dorothy McIlwraith. New York: May 1941. [As Weaver Wright.]

2640 "Where Did You Put Those Papers?" *Science Fiction Studies.* No. 40. Volume 13. Part 3. November 1986.

2641 *Wonder Stories.* Vol. 2. No. 12. Ed. Hugo Gernsback. Mt. Morris, IL: Stellar Publishing Corporation, May 1931. pp. 1493, 1485.

2642 *Wonder Stories.* Vol. 3. No. 1. Ed. Hugo Gernsback. Mt. Morris, IL: Stellar Publishing Corporation, June 1931. pp. 136–137. (Letter commenting on the April 1931 issue)

2643 *Wonder Stories.* Vol. 3. No. 6. Ed. Hugo Gernsback. Mt. Morris, IL: Stellar Publishing Corporation, November 1931. p. 806.

2644 *Wonder Stories.* Vol. 3. No. 7. Ed. Hugo Gernsback. Mt. Morris, IL: Stellar Publishing Corporation, December 1931.

2645 *Wonder Stories.* Vol. 3. No. 9. Mt. Morris, IL: Stellar Publishing Corporation, February 1932.

2646 *Wonder Stories.* Vol. 4. No. 12. Ed. Hugo Gernsback. Mt. Morris, IL: Stellar Publishing Corporation, May 1933.

2647 *Wonder Stories.* Vol. 5. No. 2. Ed. Hugo Gernsback. Mt. Morris, IL: Stellar Publishing Corporation, August 1933.

2648 *Wonder Stories.* Vol. 5. No. 3. Ed. Hugo Gernsback. Mt. Morris, IL: Stellar Publishing Corporation, October 1933.

2649 *Wonder Stories.* Vol. 5. No. 6. Ed. Charles D. Hornig. Springfield, MA: Continental Publications, Inc., January 1934.

2650 *Wonder Stories.* Vol. 5. No. 8. Ed. Charles D. Hornig. Springfield, MA: Continental Publications, Inc., March 1934.

2651 *Wonder Stories.* Vol. 6. No. 1. Ed. Charles D. Hornig. Springfield, MA: Continental Publications, Inc., June 1934.

2652 *Wonder Stories.* Vol. 6. No. 7. Ed. Charles D. Hornig. Springfield, MA: Continental Publications, Inc., December 1934.

2653 [*Wonder Stories.* Vol. 6. No. 8. Springfield, MA: Continental Publications, Inc., January 1935.??]

2654 *Wonder Stories.* Vol. 6. No. 11. Ed. Charles D. Hornig. Springfield, MA: Continental Publications, Inc., April 1935; *Gosh! Wow (Boy-oh-Boy)! Science Fiction.* New York: Bantam, 1982. pp. 447–450.

2655 *Wonder Stories.* Vol. 7. No. 8. Ed. Charles D. Hornig. Springfield, MA: Continental Publishing, April 1936.

2656 *Wonder Stories Quarterly.* Vol. 1. No. 4. Ed. Hugo Gernsback. Mt. Morris, IL: Stellar Publishing Corporation, Summer 1930.

2657 *Wonder Stories Quarterly.* Vol. 2. No. 1. Ed. Hugo Gernsback. Mt. Morris, IL: Stellar Publishing Corporation, Fall 1930.

2658 *Wonder Stories Quarterly.* Vol. 2. No. 2. Ed. Hugo Gernsback. Mt. Morris, IL: Stellar Publishing Corporation, Winter 1931.

2659 *Wonder Stories Quarterly.* Vol. 2. No. 3. Ed. Hugo Gernsback. Mt. Morris, IL: Stellar Publishing Corporation, Spring 1931.

2660 *Wonder Stories Quarterly.* Vol. 3. No. 1. Ed. Hugo Gernsback. Mt. Morris, IL: Stellar Publishing Corporation, Fall 1931.

2661 *Writer's Digest.* Cincinnati: Writer's Digest, November 1947.

2662 *Yandro.* No. 125. Ed. Robert Coulson. June 1963.

2663 *Le Zombie.* No. 24. Ed. Bob Tucker. 24 February 1940. p. 3. (on Ackerman's resignation from the Science Fiction League "Signed Feb. 10, 1940")

CIRCULARIZED LETTERS

2664 "Forrest J Ackerman's 2000 A. D. Commemorative Message. (1 January 2000)" [AOL posting]; *Tales of the Time Travelers: Adventures of Forrest J Ackerman and Julius Schwartz.* Ed. John L. Coker, III. Orlando, FL: Days of Wonder Publishers, 2009.

2665 "In Contemplation of My Inevitable Demise." <http://www.aintitcool.com/node/39346>; *Tales of the Time Travelers: Adventures of Forrest J Ackerman and Julius Schwartz.* Ed. John L. Coker, III. Orlando, FL: Days of Wonder Publishers, 2009. (letter circularized by Ackerman on AOL, dated Mother's Day, 2003)

2666 "A Letter Regarding a Heart Attack on My 50th Birthday (1966)." *Tales of the Time Travelers:*

Adventures of Forrest J Ackerman and Julius Schwartz. Ed. John L. Coker, III. Orlando, FL: Days of Wonder Publishers, 2009.

2667 "Moonday Tribute (July 1969)." *Luna Monthly.* No. 4. Ed. Ann F. Dietz. Oradell, NJ: September 1969; [as "A Moonday Tribute (July, 1969)."] *Tales of the Time Travelers: Adventures of Forrest J Ackerman and Julius Schwartz.* Ed. John L. Coker, III. Orlando, FL: Days of Wonder Publishers, 2009.

2668 "Open Letter to the Sci Fi and Fantasy World." *Locus.* Vol. 14. No. 4. Whole No. 244. May 1981. p. 21.

2669 "Wee Bonnie Barker R.I.P." 14 August 1988. (tribute to Wendayne's Chihuahua)

SPEECHES

2670 "Another Part of the Forrest. (Dragon* Con, Atlanta, GA (June 1997)." *Tales of the Time Travelers: Adventures of Forrest J Ackerman and Julius Schwartz.* Ed. John L. Coker, III. Orlando, FL: Days of Wonder Publishers, 2009.

2671 "Down Memory Lane. RiverCon XIX, Louisville, KY (July 30, 1994)." *Tangent.* Vol. 3. No. 3. Whole No. 14. Jan-Mar 1996; *Tales of the Time Travelers: Adventures of Forrest J Ackerman and Julius Schwartz.* Ed. John L. Coker, III. Orlando, FL: Days of Wonder Publishers, 2009.

2672 "A Fan of Many Firsts — Fan Guest of Hornor speech RiverCon XIX, First Fandom Reunion, Louisville, KY (July 30, 1994)." *Tales of the Time Travelers: Adventures of Forrest J Ackerman and Julius Schwartz.* Ed. John L. Coker, III. Orlando, FL: Days of Wonder Publishers, 2009. (speech given by Ackerman at convention)

2673 "Graduation Speech June 19th, 1929." *The Pirate and Other Poems: By a Valedictorian.* Rochester, MI: The Pretentious Press, 1990.

2674 "Hair-Raising Tales from Horrorwood (Dragon*Con, Atlanta, GA (June 1997)." *Tales of the Time Travelers: Adventures of Forrest J Ackerman and Julius Schwartz.* Ed. John L. Coker, III. Orlando, FL: Days of Wonder Publishers, 2009.

2675 "My Life Inside a Time Machine. (World Science Fiction Convention, Anaheim, CA 2006)." *Tales of the Time Travelers: Adventures of Forrest J Ackerman and Julius Schwartz.* Ed. John L. Coker, III. Orlando, FL: Days of Wonder Publishers, 2009.

2676 "A Tale from the Time Vault: A Tribute to Raymond Z. Gallun. (I-Con 14, Long Island, NY (April 1995)." *Tales of the Time Travelers: Adventures of Forrest J Ackerman and Julius Schwartz.* Ed. John

L. Coker, III. Orlando, FL: Days of Wonder Publishers, 2009.

DISCOGRAPHY

Albums

2677 *An Evening with Boris Karloff and His Friends.* Decca DL 4833. (script with Milt Larsen and Verne Langdon)

2678 *Forrest J Ackerman presents Music for Robots.* Frank Coe. Hollywood, CA: Science Fiction Records, 196– [Side One: "The Tin Age Story." (18 min.) narrated and acted by Ackerman. Side Two: "Tobor the Backward Robot," "Lever, Come Back to Me," "The Transistor's Sister," "When Rossum played Possum," "The anti-rust twist."]

2679 *Mr. Monster Waits in Heaven for a Letter to an Angel.* (read by Princess Catherine Oxenberg, unreleased[?] reading of Ackerman' short story)

2680 *Noreascon Awards Banquet.* NESFA: 1971. (double LP contains Ackerman's remarks at the affair)

Liner Notes

2681 *Doctor Druid's Haunted Séance.* Verne Langdon. Electric Lemon Record Co.— Stereo #PLP-1909 1973; The Orchard, 2008. (Liner notes by Ackerman; jacket art by Ron Cobb. "Featuring ERIK at the Paris Opera Pipe Organ")

2682 *Gonna Roll the Bones/In the Witch's Tent.* [As read by Fritz Leiber.] Alternate World Recordings, Inc. 1976. (praises Leiber's distinctive delivery)

2683 *John Carradine: Poe with Pipes.* [Stereo #PLP-1918] Hollywood, CA: Electric Lemon, 1975. (Liner Ackerman, jacket art by Ron Cobb; album of Poe verse read by actor Carradine)

2684 *"The Monster Who Made a Man." An Evening with Boris Karloff and His Friends.* Decca DL [7]4833.

2685 *The Phantom of the Organ.* Verne Langdon. Hollywood, CA: Electric Lemon Records, 1973; *Amazing Forries: this is your life, Forrest J Ackerman.* p. 18; *The Phantom of the Organ/The Vampyre at the Harpsichord.* Studio City, CA: Electric Lemon Record Co., 2000. (re-issue on CD)

2686 *The Vampyre at the Harpsichord.* Hollywood, CA: Electric Lemon, 1974. Stereo #PLP-1916 1974. (Liner notes by Ackerman, jacket art by Ron Cobb.)

FILMOGRAPHY

Film Roles

2687 *The Aftermath.* The Nautilus Film Company, 1982. The Curator Director: Steve Barkett.

2688 *Amazon Women on the Moon.* (a.k.a. *Cheeseburger Film Sandwich*). Universal Pictures, 1987. sequence directed by Robert K. Weiss.

2689 *Attack of the 60 Foot Centerfolds.* American Independent Productions/Concorde-New Horizons, 1995. Dracula statue. Director: Fred Olen Ray.

2690 *Beverly Hills Cop III.* Paramount Pictures, 1994. Bar Patron (uncredited) Director: John Landis.

2691 *Bikini Drive-In.* American Independent Productions, 1995. Man with Insect Repellent. Director: Fred Olen Ray.

2692 *The Boneyard Collection.* Irena Belle Films, 2006. Dr. Acula. Director: Edward L. Plumb.

2693 *Ceremony.* Trident Releasing, 1994. Sylvia's father. Director: Joe Castro.

2694 *Chicon 62.* 1962. Director: Donald F. Glut. (footage of Ackerman's visit to Glut's home)

2695 *The Creep.* 2001. The Host. Director: Mark Del Rio.

2696 *Curse of the Queerwolf.* Pirromount Productions, 1988. Mr. Richardson. Director: Mark Pirro.

2697 *David "The Rock" Nelson's Mummy Returns.* (a.k.a. *The Mummy's Mad Mayhem*) Director: David "The Rock" Nelson.

2698 *Dead Alive* (a.k.a. *Braindead*). WingNut Films, 1992. Forry. Director: Peter Jackson.

2699 *The Dead Undead.* Signature Entertainment, 2010. Wheelchair ZomVamp. Directors: Matthew R. Anderson, Edward Conna.

2700 *The Demon Monster from Outer Space.* 200–. Director: David "The Rock" Nelson.

2701 *Devil Ant.* 1999. Director: David "The Rock" Nelson.

2702 *Devil Ant 2.* 2002. Director: David "The Rock" Nelson.

2703 *Dinosaur Valley Girls.* Frontline Entertainment Group, 1996. Acker-Man on the street. Director: Donald F. Glut.

2704 *The Double-D Avenger.* William Winckler Productions, 2001. Museum Caretaker. Director: William Winckler.

2705 *Dracula vs. Frankenstein.* Independent International Pictures (I-I), 1971. Dr. Beaumont Director: Al Adamson.

2706 *Equinox.* 1970. (uncredited voice on tape recorder [in short film version? *The Equinox ... A Journey into the Supernatural*]) Director: Jack Woods and (uncredited) Dennis Muren. [expanded from short film directed by Muren, the original version featuring Ackerman's voice is included on the Criterion Collection DVD release]

2707 *Evil Spawn.* American Independent Productions, 1987. Pool Man. Directors: Kenneth J. Hall, Ted Newsom and Fred Olen Ray. (uncredited)

2708 *The Farmer's Daughter.* RKO Radio Pictures, 1947. Audience Extra at Finley Rally (uncredited) Director: H. C. Potter.

2709 *Frankenstein and Me.* France Film/Téléfilm Canada, 1996. Priest. Director: Robert Tinnell.

2710 *Frankenstein Stalks.* 2000. Director: David "The Rock" Nelson.

2711 *Frost.* Atlantis Media/Frost/Gladstone Mediaservice, 2004. Director: Dominik Alber.

2712 *Future War.* Cine Excel Entertainment/Silver Screen International, 1997. Park Victim. Director: Anthony Doublin.

2713 *The Genie.* Director: Dale Frey/Al Lewis. Unicorn Productions, 1957.

2714 *Graceland.* "Signs of Life." Director: Robert Sexton. 2004. (music video)

2715 *Hard to Die* (a.k.a. *Tower of Terror, Sorority House Massacre 3*). 1990. Dr. Ed Newton. Director: Jim Wynorski.

2716 *Hey, Rookie.* Columbia Pictures Corporation, 1944. "Sgt. Ack-Ack" (uncredited) Director: Charles Barton.

2717 *Hollywood Boulevard.* New World Pictures, 1976. party guest Directors: Allan Arkush and Joe Dante.

2718 *The Homestretch.* Twentieth Century–Fox Film Corporation, 1947. Director: H. Bruce Humberstone.

2719 *The Howling.* AVCO Embassy Pictures, 1981. Bookstore Customer (uncredited) Director: Joe Dante.

2720 *I Was a Teenage Mummy.* Director: Ralph C. Bluemke. 1962. A Square-One Production/Jerall Films/Top Quality Video, 1995. (Ackerman narrated video release)

2721 *Innocent Blood.* Warner Bros. Pictures, 1992. Stolen Car Man. Director: John Landis.

2722 *Into the Night.* Universal Pictures, 1985. [Behind the stars in a coffee shop scene] Director: John Landis.

2723 *It Came from Alpha Centauri.* Director: Jim Hollander. (8mm) ca. 1962.

2724 *The Kentucky Fried Movie.* United Film Distribution Company (UFDC), 1977. Jurist Director: John Landis.

2725 *King Kong.* Paramount Pictures/Dino De Laurentiis Company, 1976. Fleeing Extra in Crowd (uncredited) Director: John Guillermin.

2726 *The Laughing Dead.* 1989. Corpse #1. Director: Somtow Sucharitkul.

2727 *Letter to an Angel.* 1996. Director: Ron Ford.

2728 *Michael Jackson's Thriller.* Optimum Productions, 1983; *Michael Jackson: Number Ones.* 2003. "Man in cinema" (reprisal of *Schlock* role) Director: John Landis.

2729 *Miss Werewolf.* 2001. Director: David "The Rock" Nelson.

2730 *Monster Tales.* 2002. Director: David "The Rock" Nelson.

2731 *My Lovely Monster.* Sender Freies Berlin (SFB)/Westdeutscher Rundfunk (WDR)/Xenon-Film, 1990. The Master. Director: Michael Bergmann.

2732 *My Mom's a Werewolf.* Hairy Productions, 1989. Boris Faroff (uncredited). Director: Michael Fischa.

2733 *The Naked Monster.* Heidelberg Films, 2005. Flustered Man. Directors: Wayne Berwick, Ted Newsom. (recut of 1985 film *Attack of the B-Movie Monster*)

2734 *Nudist Colony of the Dead.* Pirromount Productions, 1991. Judge Rhinehole. Director: Mark Pirro.

2735 *Oscar.* Silver Screen Partners IV/Touchstone Pictures, 1991. Wedding Guest (uncredited[?]) Director: John Landis.

2736 *Polish Vampire: Behind the Fangs.* Pirromount Pictures, 2001. Narrator. Director: Mark Pirro (video short)

2737 *The Power.* Metro-Goldwyn-Mayer (MGM), 1968. (uncredited, cameo role "Delegate A. C. Fogbottom," excised) Director: Byron Haskin.

2738 *Pumpkinman.* 2003?/2004. Director: David "The Rock" Nelson.

2739 *Queen of Blood.* (a.k.a. *Planet of Blood*) American International Pictures (AIP), 1966. Dr. Faraday's aide Director: Curtis Harrington.

2740 *Red Velvet.* Ulalume Films, 2009. [As Himself.] Director: Bruce Dickson.

2741 *The Return of the Frankenstein Monster.* Blind Hermit Productions, 1976. The Monster. Director: Walter J. Daugherty. (amateur short)

2742 *Return of the Living Dead Part II* (a.k.a. *Revenge of the Living Dead*). Greenfox, 1988. Harvey Kramer (Special Zombie). Director: Ken Wiederhorn.

2743 *Robocop 2.* Orion Pictures Corporation/Tobor Productions, 1990. Director: Irvin Kershner. (scene with Ackerman from *Queen of Blood* seen on TV screen during store robbery)

2744 *SadoMannequin.* Popgun Productions Inc., 2001. Dr. Acula. Director: Jim Torres. (short film)

2745 *Scalps.* 21st Century Film Corporation, 1983. Professor Fisher Trentworth Director: Fred Olen Ray.

2746 *Scarlet Moon.* Visual Experience Productions/NY: Troma Team Video, 2006. The General. Director: Warren F. Disbrow. [Ackerman's role shot in 1999]

2747 *Schlock* (a.k.a. *The Banana Monster*) Gazotskie Productions/Jack H. Harris Enterprises, 1971. "Man in cinema." Director John Landis.

2748 *The Scorned.* Creative Light Entertainment/DHG Productions, 2005. Man In Wheelchair (uncredited) Director: Robert Kubilos (made-for-TV)

2749 *Second Unit.* Road House Films Inc., 2011. Scary Old Man. Directors: Ian Johnston, Michael MacDonald.

2750 *Skinned Deep.* Center Ring Entertainment, 2004. Forrey. Director: Gabriel Bartalos.

2751 *That Little Monster.* Ottermole Moving Picture Company, 1994. Edward Van Groan. Director: Paul Bunnell.

2752 *The Time Travelers.* American International Pictures (AIP), 1964. Square-frame Technician #3. Director: Ib Melchior.

2753 *Transylvania Twist.* Concord Productions Inc., 1989. Funeral Director. Director: Jim Wynorski.

2754 *Tyran the Terrible.* 1962. (8mm short) Director: Jim Hollander.

2755 *The Vampire Hunters Club.* Doodle Barnett Productions/Irena Belle Films, 2001. Forry. Director: Donald F. Glut. [short film]

2756 *Vampirella.* Concorde–New Horizons/Showtime Networks/Sunset Films International, 1996. Club Patron (uncredited) Director: Jim Wynorski.

2757 *Werewolf & the Witch.* 2007. Director: David "The Rock" Nelson.

2758 *The Winner's Circle.* Twentieth Century–Fox Film Corporation, 1948. Man in Crowd (uncredited) Director: Felix E. Feist

2759 *The Wizard of Speed and Time.* Medusa Produzione/Rochambeau, 1988. Mustached Man at Garage Sale. Director: Mike Jittlov.

Unreleased

2760 *The Conquest of Mars.* (disintegrated by Martian death ray) Director: Stephen C. Wathen. (8mm feature length amateur film adaptation of Garrett P. Serviss' *Edison's Conquest of Mars* filmed between 1965–1972, sequel to *The War of the Worlds*)

2761 *The Lucifer Chest.*

2762 *Monster Invasion.*

2763 *Open Season.*

2764 *Secret Invasion.*

2765 *Serge of Power.*

2766 *Space Ninja.*

2767 *Turkeys in Outer Space.*

2768 *Way Out West.* (amateur short film)

Documentary Appearances

2769 *Ackerman on Bradbury.* Urban Archipelago Films, 2006. Director: Roger Lay, Jr.

2770 *American Scary.* Director: John E. Hudgens. POOB Productions/Z-Team Productions, 2006.

2771 *Attack of the 50 Foot Monster Mania.* Van Ness Films, 1999.

2772 *Big, Fat and Tacky: A Trip to Karloffornia.* Director: Fred Anderson. Fredzilla Film, 2003. (documentary short)

2773 *Biography — Bela Lugosi: Hollywood's Dark Prince.* Director: Kevin Burns. Van Ness Films, Inc./Twentieth Television/Arts and Entertainment Network, 1995.

2774 *Biography — Boris Karloff: The Gentle Monster.* Director: Kevin Burns. Twentieth Television/Arts and Entertainment Network, 1995.

2775 *Biography — Lon Chaney Jr.: Son of a Thousand Faces.* Director: Kevin Burns. Twentieth Television/Arts and Entertainment Network, 1995.

2776 *Charles Beaumont: The Short Life of Twilight Zone's Magic Man.* Director: Jason V. Brock. JaSunni Productions, 2010.

2777 *Chiller: 3 Days of Peace, Love & GORE.* Director: Brian Belefant. A Film by Michael Di Certo and Russell Maggio/A Kilroy Sees Stars and RM Digital Services Production, 2001.

2778 *Cult Movies TV.* Episode 1. Hollywood, CA: Cult Movies, 199–. [With Brad Linaweaver.]

2779 *Dinosaur Movies.* Director: Donald F. Glut. Popcorn Pictures, 1993.

2780 *The Dream Pioneers.* Princeton, NJ: Films for the Humanities, 2002, 2004.

2781 *Drive-In Madness!* Imagine Inc., 1987. Director: Tim Ferrante. (Screen Scaries)

2782 *E! Mysteries & Scandals: Lon Chaney Sr. and Jr.* E! Entertainment Television, 2000.

2783 *The Eyes of Fritz Lang.* All Day Entertainment/Image Entertainment, 2000. (featurette extra on *The 1,000 Eyes of Dr. Mabuse* DVD)

2784 *Fangoria's Weekend of Horrors.* Directors: Mike Hadley and Kerry O'Quinn. O'Quinn Productions/Starlog Video, 1986.

2785 *50th Anniversary Brunch Noreascon Three Videotape.* Massachusetts Convention Fandom, Incorporated, 1989. (Ackerman speaks among other personalities in celebration of the 50th anniversary of the World Science Fiction Convention)

2786 *Finding the Future: A Science Fiction Conversation.* Director: Casey Moore. Anomalous Entertainment LLC, 2004.

2787 *Flying Saucers Over Hollywood: The 'Plan 9' Companion.* Director: Mark Patrick Carducci. Atomic Pictures, 1992. (Video)

2788 *Forrest J Ackerman's Amazing Worlds of Science Fiction & Fantasy.* Forrest J Ackerman; Ray Ferry. Orange, NJ: Dynacomm Video, 1992. (VHS videotape)

2789 *Forrest J Ackerman's Hooray for Horrorwood!* Orange, NJ: Big Tomato Productions/Dynacomm Video, 1990.

2790 *Forrest J Ackerman's 35th Anniversary Famous Monsters of Filmland Horror, Sci-Fi & Fantasy World Convention.* Director: Ray Ferry. Dynacomm, 1993. (VHS Video)

2791 *Frazetta: Painting with Fire.* Director: Lance Laspina. Cinemachine/Dark Kingdom Inc./ Razor Digital Entertainment. Beverly Hills, CA: Razor Digital Entertainment, 2004.

2792 *Goolians: A Docu-Comedy.* Directors: Daniel Roebuck, Deverill Weekes, Wally Wingert. Ink & Paint (Firm); Archie Comic Publications, Inc; Entertainment Rights, 2006. [interview]

2793 *Great Books: Frankenstein.* The Learning Channel (TLC), 1993/9.

2794 *H. G. Wells: The Father of Science Fiction.* Paramount Home Entertainment/Sparkhill Production. (DVD extra for 2005 Special Collector's Edition release of 1953's *The War of the Worlds*)

2795 *Heartstoppers: Horror at the Movies.* Directors: Steve Purcell and Neil Steinberg. Riverstreet Productions, 1992. (TV)

2796 *The History of the SF Film.* Director: Thys Ockersen. Vrijzinnig Protestantse Radio Omroep (VPRO), 1982.

2797 *Hollywood Dinosaur Chronicles.* Director: James Forsher. Rhino Home Video, 1987. (VHS videotape)

2798 *Hollywood Goes Ape!* Director: Donald F. Glut. Popcorn Pictures, 1994.

2799 *Hollywood Rated "R."* Directors: Dominique Cazenave, Doug Headline. Kalamazoo International, 1997.

2800 *In Search of the True Story of Frankenstein.* (BBC)

2801 *Into the Zone: The Story of the Cacophony Society.* Director: Jon Alloway. 2011.

2802 *It's Alive: The True Story of Frankenstein.* Director: Richard Brown. A&E Television Networks, 1994. (TV special)

2803 *Jack Parsons: Jet Propelled Antichrist.* Director: Daniel Zuckerbrot. Reel Time Images, 2008.

2804 *Jules Verne & Walt Disney: Explorers of the Imagination.* Writer/Director: David J. Skal. Buena Vista Home Entertainment, 2003.

2805 *Keepers of the Frame.* Director: Mark McLaughlin. Mount Pilot Productions, 1999.

2806 *The Life After Death Project.* Director: Paul Davids. 2011.

2807 *Lon Chaney: A Thousand Faces.* Director: Kevin Brownlow. Photoplay Productions/Turner Classic Movies, 2000.

2808 *Look, Up in the Sky: The Amazing Story of Superman.* Director: Kevin Burns. Bad Hat Harry Productions/Prometheus Entertainment, 2006.

2809 *Lugosi, the Forgotten King.* MPI Home Video, 1985. Host/Narrator. Directors: Mark S. Gilman Jr., Dave Stuckey.

2810 *The Making of 'The Double-D Avenger.'* Director: William Winckler. William Winckler Productions, 2004.

2811 *Masters of Fantasy: Hollywood Horror Legends.* Sci-Fi Channel/Dick Crew Productions, Inc., 1996.

2812 *Midnight Madness—The History of Horror, Sci-Fi and Fantasy Films.* Midnight Marquee, 2011. (Ackerman's comments from Fanex events)

2813 *Mr. Science Fiction's Fantastic Universe.* Directed and Produced by Forrest J Ackerman and Jimmie Pitts. Burbank, CA: Vampire Video, 1987. [Video]

2814 *Monsterama: Basil Gogos.* Director: Daniel Roebuck. Prometheus Entertainment, 2004. (TV)

2815 *Monsterama: The Ackermonster.* Director: Daniel Roebuck. Prometheus Entertainment, 2004. (TV)

2816 *My Life with Count Dracula.* Hungry Jackal Productions, 2003. Director: Dustin Lance Black. (documentary on Dr. Donald A. Reed)

2817 *My Lucille.* (music video for B. B. King song) audience member Director: John Landis. [part of B. B. King *Into the Night* documentary which Landis co-directed with Jeff Okun]

2818 *My Memoirs of 4SJ — Famous Monster of Horrorwood Karloffornia.* Director: Bill "Drac" Edwards.

2819 *Norwegian Actresses in Hollywood.* Directors: Oyvind Asbjornsen and Niels Petter Solberg. Asbjørnsen & Co., 2003. (TV)

2820 *Ray Harryhausen: The Early Years Collection.* Sparkhill Production, 2005.

2821 *The Real Frankenstein: An Untold Story.* ABC/Kane Productions, 1995.

2822 *Rewind America.* Inner Vision Films, 2001.

2823 *Ringers: Lord of the Fans.* Director: Carlene Cordova. Planet BB Entertainment, 2005.

2824 *Schlock! The Secret History of American Movies.* Director: Ray Greene. Pathfinder Pictures, 2001.

2825 *Science Fiction Films.* University of Kansas, 1971. (Ackerman lectures on various productions and personnel)

2826 *The Sci-Fi Boys.* Writer/Director: Paul Davids. Yellow Hat Productions/Universal Studios Home Entertainment, 2006.

2827 *The Sci-Fi Files 2: Spaceships and Aliens.* Director: Peter Swain. A Satel Doc production in association with the Learning Channel, Canal +, Docstar and NHK/WinStar Home Entertainment/ Fox Lorber Associates, 1998.

2828 *Secret Lives: L. Ron Hubbard.* Director: Jill Robinson. 3BM Television, 1997. (TV)

2829 *Secret World of Superfans.* Director: Sam Okun. Sam Okun Productions, 2008.

2830 *Sex, Death & The Hollywood Mystique.* Director: Larry Wessel. WesselMania, 1999.

2831 *Shock Cinema Vol. 2.* 1991.

2832 *Sleazemania III: The Good, the Bad and the Sleazy.* Rhino Home Video, 1986. Johnny Legend. Ackerman seen in test footage from Fred Olen Ray's unfinished *Beach Blanket Bloodbath* [IMDB has this as a segment of *Sleazemania Strikes Back*]

2833 *Spine Tingler! The William Castle Story.* Director: Jeffrey Schwarz. Automat Pictures/Spine Tingler/Sony Pictures Home Entertainment, 2007.

2834 *The Texas Chainsaw Massacre: A Family Portrait.* 1988. Director: Brad Shellady. (Ackerman appears over the credits discussing the original 1974 film)

2835 *To the Galaxy and Beyond with Mark Hamill.* Director: Kevin Burns. Arts and Entertainment Network, 1997. (a.k.a. *Hollywood Aliens & Monsters*)

2836 *To the Moon and Beyond.* (PBS special on Apollo 11 25th anniversary)

2837 *The Truth About Science Fiction.* A Weller/ Grossman production for History Channel; Arts and Entertainment Network. New Video Group, 1999.

2838 *The Undying Monsters!* Director: Robert Leininger. 2006. (documentary short)

2839 *Universal Horror.* Director: Kevin Brownlow. Photoplay Productions/Universal TV, 1998. (TV)

2840 *Vampira: The Movie.* VAMP Productions, 2006. Director: Kevin Sean Michaels.

2841 *Visions from the Edge: The Art of Science Fiction.* Director: Michael MacDonald. 3097225 Nova Scotia, 2005. (TV special)

2842 *Visiting ... with Huell Howser.* Huell Howser Productions, 2000. (video tour of the Glendower Ackermansion)

2843 *The Witch's Dungeon: 40 Years of Chills.* Director: Dennis Vincent. Colorbox Studios, 2006.

2844 *Working with a Master: John Landis.* Director: Frank H. Woodward. Crest Digital, 2006.

2845 *Worldcon '96.* Triage Entertainment, 1996. (broadcast on the Sci-Fi Channel)

Documentaries About

2846 *The AckerMonster Chronicles!* Director: Jason Brock. JaSunni Productions, 2012.

2847 *Famous Monster: Forrest J Ackerman.* Director: Michael MacDonald. Writer: Ian Johnston Road House Films Inc., 2007.

2848 *Monsterama: The Ackermonster.* Director: Daniel Roebuck. Writer: Brian Anthony Prometheus Entertainment, 2004. (TV)

TV/Talk Show Appearances

2849 *The Antigravity Room.* YTV/Sci-Fi Channel, March 3, 1997. (a whirlwind tour of the Ackermansion)

2850 *Art Linkletter's House Party. / The Linkletter Show.*

2851 *Behind the Screen with John Burke.* AMC, 29 October 2000.

2852 *Bob Wilkins Creature Features.* (1970's)

2853 *CBS Eye on People.*

2854 *Chiller Cinema: The King of Bad Movies.* 2001.

2855 *Confidential File* [hosted by Paul Coates, 1950's] (Ackerman substituted as guest for Aldous Huxley)

2856 *Dead Beat Video Magazine.* Directors: Anthony C. Ferrante and Rod Reed. Postmortem Video, 1990.

2857 *Down Memory Lane.*

2858 *Eye on LA.*

2859 *Good Morning, America.*

2860 *Homes.* (New Zealand, 1991)

2861 *The Horror Hall of Fame.* Director: Ron de Moraes. (Ackerman received "Grimmy" award on-camera)

2862 *The Jack Barry Show.*

2863 *The Joe Franklin Show.* 27 August 1963. (a transcript appears in "To Kill a Mocking Bat." See entry 2241.)

2864 *The Joe Pyne Show.* [With Dr. Donald A. Reed.]

2865 *Just for the Record.* Beyond International Group, 1988. (Australia)

2866 *Magic Mirror.* Denmark, 1996.

2867 *Merv Griffin.* 15 March 1971. (alongside Vincent Price, John Carradine, Don Post, Glenn Strange, and Frank Gorshin, discussed in *Mr. Monster's Movie Gold* p. 198)

2868 *Merv Griffin Show.* ca. 1982. (seen displaying items from his collection to Griffin and guest actor Barry Bostwick)

2869 *Michaels' Movie Madness.* Dream World Productions, 1988.

2870 *The Mike Douglas Show.* October 1975

2871 *My Hollywood.* Cinemax, 1999.

2872 *Only in Hollywood.* Peter Jones Productions, Inc.

2873 *Prisoners of Gravity:* "Fans." TVOntario, aired 8 October 1992.

2874 *Professor Griffin's Midnight Shadow Show.* "Professor Bruno Lampini" (voice only)

2875 *Sci-Fi Buzz.* Dick Crew Productions, 1994–97. (various episodes covered "Son of Famous Monsters Convention," the Glendower Ackermansion, Ackerman's 80th birthday, etc.)

2876 *Starstruck.* Alien. Aired: 9 June 1979. Director: Al Viola. (TV pilot)

2877 *To Tell the Truth.* Goodson-Todman Productions, 1969.

2878 *The Tomorrow Show: Coast to Coast.* 7 November 1975. (Ackerman guested with actor Peter Cushing and Leonard Wolf) [a transcript appeared in *Famous Monsters of Filmland* No. 133. See entry 484]

2879 *Two on the Town.*

2880 WLWT Cincinnati. September 1949. (early locally televised coverage of the 7th World science Fiction Convention)

2881 *You Asked for It.*

2882 *You Bet Your Life.* 1992/93. (Bill Cosby-hosted game show)

MATERIAL IN BOOKS BY OTHERS

2883 "A. E. 'Slan' Vogt." *The John W. Campbell Letters with Isaac Asimov and A. E. van Vogt, Volume 2.* Ed. Perry A. Chapdelaine, Sr., Tony Chapdelaine, and George Hay. Franklin, TN: AC Projects, 1993.

2884 "About the Author." *The Far-Out Worlds of A. E. van Vogt.* New York: Ace, 1968; 1970; as *The Worlds of A. E. van Vogt.* A. E. van Vogt. New York: Ace, 1974; New English Library, 1974; 1975.

2885 "Afterword." *Reference Guide to Fantastic Films: Science Fiction, Fantasy, and Horror, Volume 1: A–F.* Walt Lee. Los Angeles: Chelsea-Lee Books, 1972; *Children of the Night.* No. 1. Ed. Derek Jensen. Prairie Village, KS: 1975.

2886 "Afterword: A Brush with Genius." *From the Pen of Paul: The Fantastic Images of Frank R. Paul.* Ed. Stephen D. Korshak. Orlando, FL: Shasta/Phoenix, 2009; *Frank R. Paul: Father of Science Fiction Art.* New York: Castle Books, 2010. pp. 125–126. (includes a 22 November 1960 letter from Paul to Ackerman)

2887 "Afterword: Imagi-Movie Memories 1922–1968." *Graven Images: The Best of Horror, Fantasy, and Science-Fiction Film Art from the Collection of Ronald V. Borst.* [Ronald V. Borst; Keith Burns; Leith Adams; Margaret A. Borst] New York: Grove Press, 1992. pp. 229–233; Tokyo Kokusho Kanko-kai, 1992; 1997; *Immagini Sepolta.* Rome: Fanuccu Editoire, 1993; *Idoles del Cine de Terror.* Spanish Ediciones B, March 1994.

2888 ["C. L. Moore." Perret, Patti. *The Faces of Science Fiction: Intimate Portraits of the Men and Women Who Shape the Way We Look at the Future.* New York: Bluejay Books, 1984.] (Ackerman ghosted this piece for the then-ailing Moore)

2889 "Can You Ever Forgive Me, Hannes?" *The Hannes Bok Memorial Showcase of Fantasy Art.* Ed. Emil Petaja. San Francisco, SISU Publishers. 1974.

2890 [contribution] *Atlantean Chronicles.* Henry M. Eichner. Alhambra, CA: Fantasy Publishing Company, Inc., 1971.

2891 [contribution] *The Future Focus Book of Lists II: The Sequel.* Future Focus Science Fiction Specialties, 1987.

2892 "David A. Kyle." Coker, John L. Ed. *A Gathering to Honor Forrest J Ackerman Presented by David A. Kyle and Friends.* Orlando, FL: Days of Wonder Publishers, 2006. (Ackerman tribute to longtime friend and fellow fan)

2893 "DEATH TAKES A HELL-A-DAY." [As "Dr. Acula."] Edward D. Wood. *Orgy of the Dead.* San Diego, CA: Greenleaf Classics, 1966. (short stories by Wood "Night of the Banshee," "Final Curtain," "The Day the Mummies Danced" novelization of Wood film accompanied by stills)

2894 "A Decade of Decay and Decadence." *The Collector's Guide to Monster, Science Fiction, and Fantasy Film Magazines.* Bob Michelucci. Pittsburgh, PA: Imagine, 1988.

2895 "Donovan's Brainstorm." *Forrest J Ackerman Presents Donovan's Brain.* Curt Siodmak. Mill Valley, CA: Pulpless.com, 1999.

2896 "Earthquake! Earthquake!" *Forrest J Ackerman Presents This Island Earth.* Raymond F. Jones. Mill Valley, CA: Pulpless.com, 1999. (Introduction)

2897 "Edmond Hamilton: The Word-Saver." *Weird Heroes Volume 6.* Ed. Byron Preiss. New York: Pyramid, 1977. pp. 142–

2898 "Eerie Memories." *Eerie Archives.* Volume 1. Ed. Shawna Gore. Milwaukie, OR: Dark Horse Comics, 2009. pp. 4–5.

2899 "Epilogue." *Tomart's Price Guide to Horror Movie Collectibles.* Nathan Hanneman and Aaron Crowell. Dayton, OH: Tomart Publications, 2003.

2900 "Foreweird[:] Lobby as Hobby Cards." *Color Collector's Guide: Horror, Science Fiction, Fantasy: Movie Poster and Lobby Cards Magazine.* No. 1. Ed. Robert Brosch. Allen Park, MI: Archival Photography, 1990.

2901 [Foreword] *The Amazing, Colossal Book of Horror Trivia: Everything You Always Wanted to Know About Scary Movies but Were Afraid to Ask.* Jonathan Malcolm Lampley, Ken Beck & Jim Clark. Nashville, TN: Cumberland House Publishing. 1999.

2902 "Foreword." *David A. Kyle: A Life of Science Fiction Ideas and Dreams.* Ed. John L. Coker, III. Orlando, FL: Days of Wonder Publishers, 2006. pp. 12–16.

2903 "Foreword!" [*A Forbidden Look Inside The*] *House of Ackerman: A Photographic Tour of the Legendary Ackermansion.* Al Astrella, James Greene. Baltimore: Midnight Marquee Press, 2010.

2904 "Foreword." *Gothica/Erotica, or, Of Sex and Horror. Deadly After Dark.* Jeff Gelb, Michael Garrett, Ed. 1994.

2905 "Foreword." *London After Midnight. A Lost Film Reconstructed.* Philip J. Riley. New York: Cornwall Books, 1985; as *London After Midnight— A Reconstruction.* Duncan, OK: BearManor Media, 2011. [an earlier version was announced under the title *London after Midnight Revisited* and imprint of London: Metropolis Books, 1981 in which Ackerman was to be credited as co-author with Philip J. Riley but apparently never printed]

2906 "Foreword." *MagicImage Filmbooks presents Frankenstein.* Ed. Philip J. Riley. Abesecon, NJ: MagicImage Filmbooks, 1989. (Screenplay to the 1931 film by Garrett Ford and Francis Edwards Faragoh)

2907 "Foreword." *MagicImage Filmbooks Presents the Bride of Frankenstein.* Ed. Philip J. Riley. Abesecon, NJ: MagicImage Filmbooks, 1989.

2908 "Foreword." *Monster Magazine & Fanzine Collector's Guide.* No. 2. Michael W. Pierce and John M. Ballentine. P&B Publishing, 2000.

2909 "Foreword." *Monsters: A Celebration of the Classics from Universal Studios.* Roy Milano; Editor-Jennifer Osborne. New York: Random House/Del Rey, 2006.

2910 "Foreword." *Science Fiction, Horror and Fantasy Film and Television Credits.* Harris M. Lentz. Jefferson, NC: McFarland and Company, Inc. 1983.

2911 "Foreword." *The Sunken World: A Romance of Atlantis.* Stanton A. Coblentz. Los Angeles, CA: Fantasy Publishing Co. Inc. (F.P.C.I.), 1948.

2912 "Foreword." *Ultra Low Budget Movie Making.* Mark Pirro. Van Nuys, CA: Pirromount, 1994.

2913 "Foreword." *Xombie: Dead on Arrival.* James Farr. Ed. Cindi Rice. Studio City, CA: Xombie, 2007. (Graphic Novel)

2914 "Forrest J Ackerman." Perret, Patti. *The Faces of Science Fiction: Intimate Portraits of the Men and Women Who Shape the Way We Look at the Future.* New York: Bluejay Books, 1984; *Mr. Monster.* Las Vegas: Alan White, 2009. p. 2.

2915 "Forryword." *Directed by Jack Arnold.* Dana M. Reemes. Jefferson, NC: McFarland, 1988.

2916 "Forry-word." *Forrest J Ackerman's the Anthology of the Living Dead.* Ed. J. Travis Grundon and L. B. Goddard. Antelope, CA: Black Bed Sheet Books/Diverse Media, 2009.

2917 "Forry-Word — Behind the Celebr-8-Ball." *Famous Monsters Chronicles.* Ed. Dennis Daniel with Jim Knusch. [Co-editors: Greg Theakston, Bill Warren] Albany, NY: FantaCo Enterprises, 1991. p. 7.

2918 "The Genesis of an Invisible Venusienne: Afterword to 'Nymph of Darkness.'" *Echoes of Valor II.* Ed. Karl Edward Wagner. New York: Tor, 1989; *Ackermanthology! 65 Astonishing, Rediscovered Sci-Fi Shorts,* Los Angeles. CA: General Publishing Group. 1997; *Ackermanthology: Millennium Edition 65 Astonishing, Rediscovered Sci-Fi Shorts.* Rockville, MD: Sense of Wonder Press, 2000.

2919 "I Loved You, Bill: Afterword." *The Work of William F. Temple: An Annotated Bibliography & Guide.* Mike Ashley. San Bernardino, CA: Borgo Press, 1994.

2920 "I Never Met a Luna Mutant I Did Not Like." *MagicImage Filmbooks presents This Island Earth.* Ed. Philip J. Riley. Absecon, NJ: MagicImage Filmbooks, 1990. (Preface)

2921 "If This Goes On — And It Did!" *If This Goes On.* Ed. Charles Nuetzel. Beverly Hills, CA: Book Company of America, 1965; *Après ... La Guerre Atomique.* Verviers: Gérard, 1970. (Introduction)

2922 "The Impossible Dream?" *The Collectors Guide to Monster Magazines.* Ed. Bob Michelucci. Pittsburgh, PA: Dick Zdinak Associates, 1977. p. 115. (on film-related items Ackerman was lacking for his collection)

2923 "Introduction." *Color Collectors Guide No. 1.* Michigan Archival Photography, 1989.

2924 "Introduction." *Deliver Me from Eva.* Paul Bailey. Lakewood, CO: Millipede Press, 2007.

2925 "Introduction." *The Fires of Pele: Mark Twain's Legendary Lost Journal.* Ed. Paul Davids and Hollace Davids. Los Angeles, CA: Pictorial Legends, 1986.

2926 "Introduction." *Forrest J Ackerman Presents Hauser's Memory.* Curt Siodmak. Mill Valley, CA: Pulpless.com, 1999.

2927 "Introduction." *Forrest J. Ackerman presents Invasion of Mars — Sequel to War of the Worlds.* Garrett P. Serviss. Resada, CA: Powell Publications. 1969. [retitling of Serviss novel *Edison's Conquest of Mars*]

2928 "Introduction." *Images of Tomorrow.* Charles Nuetzel. CA: Powell Publications. 1969.

2929 "Introduction." *The Legend of Hammer Horror.* Hajime Ishida. Osaka, Japan: Castle Company Ltd., 1995.

2930 "Introduction." *Monsterrific Jokes, Puzzles, Puns & Riddles.* David J. Marchant. Lulu Press, 2006.

2931 "Introduction." *Nightmare Theatre.* Robert Marrero. Key West, FL: RGM Publications, 1986.

2932 "Introduction." *Stardrift and Other Fantastic Flotsam.* Emil Petaja. Alhambra, CA: Fantasy Publishing Company, 1971.

2933 "Introduction." *Two Dozen Dragon Eggs.* Donald A. Wollheim. Reseda, CA: Powell Books. 1969.

2934 "Introduction by FJA — The Man Who Collected Himself." *Fantasy Magazine Index.* Delbert W. Winans. Baltimore, MD: Delbert W. Winans, March 1977. pp. 4–6. (introduction incorporates portions of Ackerman's contribution to article "Why I Collect Science Fiction" [see entry 2349]; publication indexing contents of monster magazines)

2935 "Introduction Imagi-Movie Marathon." *Vintage Monster Movies.* Robert Marrero. Key West, FL: Fantasma Books, 1993.

2936 "Introduction: Monster Mosaic." *The Essential Monster Movie Guide: A Century of Creature Features on Film, TV, and Video.* Stephen Graham Jones. London: Titan Books, 1999; Billboard Books, 2000. pp. 6–20.

2937 "Introduction: One Glorious Day." *The Collectors Guide to Monster Magazines.* Ed. Bob Michelucci. Pittsburgh, PA: Dick Zdinak Associates, 1977. pp. 8–9. (dated 13 July 1977)

2938 "Introduction: The Queen of Blood." *Queen of Blood.* Charles Nuetzel. San Diego, CA: Greenleaf Classics, 1966; *e*I*.* Vol. 4. No. 2. Whole No. 19. Ed. Earl Kemp. April 2005. (novelization of Curtis Harrington film accompanied by stills)

2939 "Introduction to 'While You're Up.'" *The Avram Davidson Treasury.* Avram Davidson. New York: Tor, 1998. p. 409.

2940 "Introduction-Arty facts." Weist, Jerry, Ed. *Original Comic Art: Identification and Price Guide.* Avon Books. 1992; *The Comic Art Price Guide Second Edition with Pulp, Underground Comix, and Monster Magazine Price Guides.* Gloucester, MA: Arcturian Books/Krause Publications, 2000. (Ackerman listed as "Contributor and advisor")

2941 "Just Imagine!" *Perry Rhodan. No. 1800.* Universal City, CA: Vector Enterprises, 1997.

2942 "My Friend, the Monster." *The Frankenstein Legend: A Tribute to Mary Shelley and Boris Karloff.* Donald F. Glut. Metuchen, NJ: Scarecrow Press, 1973. (Introduction)

2943 "Of Beans and Rice." *Edgar Rice Burroughs: The Man Who Created Tarzan.* Irwin Porges. Provo, UT: Brigham Young University Press, 1975; London: New English Library [etc.], 1976; New York: Ballantine Books, 1976.

2944 "Preface." *Confiction Souvenir Book.* Ed. Johan-Martijn Flaton. Confiction, 1990.

2945 "Preface." *Science-Fiction Classics: The Stories That Morphed into Movies.* New York: TV Books Inc., 1999.

2946 "The Reel Dracula's Daughter." *Countess Dracula: A Novel.* Carroll Borland. Absecon, NJ: MagicImage FilmBooks, 1994. (Foreword)

2947 "Ten Best." *Golden Horrors: An Illustrated Critical Filmography of Terror Cinema, 1931–1939.* Bryan Senn. Jefferson, NC: McFarland, 1996; 2006. p. 489.

2948 "Tomb Swift: An Introduction (of Sorts)." Crowther, Peter & Kramer, Edward E., Eds. *Tombs.* New York: White Wolf Publishers, 1994.

2949 (untitled piece on John Landis) Vallan, Giulia D'Agnolo. *John Landis.* Milwaukie, OR: M Press, 2008.

2950 "The Van Who Sold the Future." *Reflections of A. E. Van Vogt.* Lakemont, GA: Fictioneer Books Ltd. 1975. pp. 7–9. (Introduction)

2951 "When Pulp Art Was in Flower." Lesser, Robert. *Pulp Art: Original Paintings: Original Cover Paintings for the Great American Pulp Magazines.* New York: Gramercy Books. 1997.

2952 "A Word from Our Founder." Riley, Philip J. Ed *MagicImage Filmbooks Presents This Island Earth.* Absecon, NJ: MagicImage Filmbooks, 1990.

EDITED WORKS

Periodicals

Amateur Publications/Fanzines

2953 *Ackermaniac Presents Hoffmania.* 1941.

2954 *Baroque Bagatales Brobdingnagian.* 1938. (autograph pamphlet sold at the First National Science Fiction Convention) [Immortal Storm, p. 145]

2955 *The BiWeekly Transmission Science Fact and Science Fantasy Newsmagazine.* (ca. 1979)

2956 *Black and White.* Ed. Ackerman and Jack Speer. Nova Press, Summer 1944.

2957 *By-4e.* June 1941.

2958 *The Damn Denventioneer Thing.* [As 4SJ Ackerman with T. Bruce Yerke.] (bound into *The Denventioneer*)

2959 *The Denventioneer Voice of the Imagi-Nation.* [With Morojo.] (bound into *The Denventioneer*)

2960 *The Discovery of the Future.* (Speech delivered by Guest of Honor Robert A. Heinlein at 3rd World Science Fiction Convention), Denver, Independence Day, 1941. Recorded on Discs by Walter J. Daugherty. Los Angeles: A Novacious Publication, 1941. (Limited First Edition of 200 copies followed by a 100-copy reprint)

2961 *E.-T.* 1941. (portfolio of extraterrestrial beings drawn by Ackerman's grandfather George Wyman)

2962 *FantaSnide.* December 1943.

2963 *Fantasticonglomeration.* No. 1. March 1945-No. 2. July 1945. (continued as *Glom*)

2964 *The Fantasy Foundation: Bulletin Number One: A Checklist of Fantasy Magazines.* Los Angeles: The Fantasy Foundation, 1946. (material by Ackerman and other fans)

2965 *Get Them Out on Time (The Mailings, That Is).* Ed. with Charles E. Burbee. Los Angeles: 194- 1 p. (on Burbee's bid for Official Editor and Ackerman's for Secretary-Treasurer of the Fantasy Amateur Press Association)

2966 *Glom.* No. 3.–No. 13. February 1946-May 1949.

2967 *Guteto.* Vol. 1. No. 1. June 1941. (Fantasy Amateur Press Association fanzine edited with Morojo; in Esperanto)

2968 *Imagi-Music.* No. 1. January-February 1942-No. 2. Spring 1943.

2969 *Imagination!* Vol. 1. No. 1. October 1937-Vol. 1. No. 12. September 1938.

2970 *In Memoriam H. G. Wells.* Ed. Ackerman and Arthur Louis Joquel, II. Los Angeles, CA: 1946. (cover photograph of Wells, 14 August 1946 *New York Times* obituary, Wells Bibliography, etc.)

2971 *The Madman of Mars.* No. 1. March 1942-No. 4. March 1943.

2972 *Metalo-Mag.* March 1943. (fanzine printed on a dogtag)

2973 *The Meteor.* No. 1. ca. 1931.-No. 4. San Francisco: 15 May 1931. [by the fourth number this was edited by James H. Nicholson]

2974 *Metropolis.* July 1939. 8 pp. (publication for First World Science Fiction Convention)

2975 *1940 Yearbook of Science, Fantasy and Weird Fiction.* Los Angeles, CA: An Imag-Index Publication, 1940. 36 pp. (compiled by Franklyn H. Brady, and A. Ross Kuntz, with assistance from Melvin S. Dolmatz and Ackerman)

2976 *1961 Famous Monsters Convention Book.*

2977 *Novacious.* No. 1. December 1938.-No. 7. Dec. 1940? Ed. Forrest J Ackerman & Morojo (Myrtle R. Douglas).

2978 *Novaj Horizontoj.* Autumn 1939. [With Morojo.]

2979 *Polaris: Paul Freehafer the Good Die Young.* [As by Forry Ackerman and friends.] April 1944. 3 pp. [fanzine tribute to well-liked fan Paul Robinson Freehafer, (1916–1944)]

2980 *Presenting Adam Singlesheet.* Fall 1944.

2981 *Rahuun Ta-Ka or Revenge.* No. 1. June 1943–No. 2. September 1943; *Outlandi: an objet of obscurious vision. [satyrical, satirical, and such poems]* Los Angeles: A Virgin Forrest Publication, prepared at the Sign of the Green Fansions — for FAPA (Fantasy Amateur Press Association), 10 October 1944. (sequel to *Madman of Mars*)

2982 *Report on the 1961 Festivention, A Message from the Future!* (Forry Ackerman, 1944)

2983 [*Rocketship X-M* newsletter May 1950]

2984 *Science Fiction: Hobby or Duty?* No. 1. Spring 1941/June 1941.

2985 *Shangri-La.* No. 14. October 1949. (Editor)

2986 *Shangri-L'Affairres.* No. 4. Forrest J Ackerman/Arthur L. Joquel for the LASFS (Los Angeles Science Fantasy Society): July 1942.

2987 *Special Delivery.* (Ackerman & Morojo, 1944?)

2988 *Staplecon.* No. 1. 1943.

2989 *S-TF News.* ca. 1931. [According to the Pavlat-Evans Index this ran "about 8 issues" Pavlat, 117]

2990 *Stf Stickers Stationery Suchstuffery.* A Novacious Publication, 1940. 5 pp.

2991 *Voice of Imagi-Nation.* (VOM) No. 1. January 1939–No. 50. July 1947.

2992 *Vombozine.* July 1946. (contribution to *Combozine* produced for the PacifiCon)

Newspapers

2993 *The Fort MacArthur Bulletin.* 1942–1945.

Professionally Published Periodicals

2994 *Close Encounters of the Third Kind.* New York: Warren Publishing, January 1978. (Official Authorized Edition)

2995 *Dracula '79.* (*Warren Presents.* No. 5.) Warren, September 1979. (Senior Editor)

2996 *Famous Monsters of Filmland.* Vol. 1. No. 1. February 1958.-No. 190. January 1983.

2997 *Famous Monsters of Filmland.* No. 200. Orange, NJ: Dynacomm, May 1993.-No. 210. No. Hollywood, CA: Dynacomm, Nov./Dec. 1995. [credited as "editor & writer"]

2998 *Famous Monsters of Filmland 1972 Fearbook.* Warren, 1971.

2999 *Famous Monsters Star Wars Spectacular.* Warren Publishing Co., October 1977.

3000 *Film Fantasy Yearbook 1982 Collector's Edition.* Warren, March 1982.

3001 *Film Fantasy Yearbook 1983 Collector's Edition.* Warren, March 1983.

3002 *Forrest J Ackerman's Monster Land.* Vol. 1. No. 1. Canoga Park, CA: New Media Publishing, Inc., December 1984. [February 1985 on cover]-*Monsterland.* No. 10. New Media Publishing, Inc. June 1986.

3003 *Forrest J Ackerman's Monsterama.* No. 1. May 1991-No. 2. Seattle, WA: Fantagraphics Books, Spring 1992.

3004 *House of Horror.* No. 1. Warren, April 1978.

3005 *The Lord of the Rings: The Official Authorized Magazine of J. R. R. Tolkien's Classic Fantasy Epic.* A Warren Special Edition. New York: Warren Pub. 1979.

3006 *Screen Thrills.* Vol. 1. No. 1. New York: Warren, June 1962. (contributing editor)

3007 *Warren Presents the Official Exclusive Horror Movie Yearbook 1981 Collector's Edition.* Warren, February 1981.

3008 *Wonderama Annual 1993 — First Issue, Forgotten Futures.* New York: Pure Imagination, 1993. (intended as an annual publication)

Perry Rhodan *Books*

Translated from German by Wendayne Ackerman with assistance from Sig Wahrman, Stuart J. Byrne, Dwight R. Decker, et al., the series also presented short story reprints and original vignettes. Additionally Wendayne Ackerman is listed as Editor for Nos. 1–4. Ackerman is credited as Managing Editor with Donald A. Wollheim listed as Editor for Nos. 7–10, Frederik Pohl for Nos. 14–18 and Pat LoBrutto for Nos. 59–118 and the Special Releases. Nos. 109–118 were double editions bound together.

3009 1: *Enterprise Stardust.* K. H. Scheer & Walter Ernsting. New York: Ace, 1969.

3010 2: *The Radiant Dome.* K. H. Scheer and Walter Ernsting. New York: Ace, 1969.

3011 3: *Galactic Alarm.* Kurt Mahr and W. W. Shols. New York: Ace, 1969.

3012 4: *Invasion from Space.* Walter Ernsting and Kurt Mahr. New York: Ace, 1970.

3013 5: *The Vega Sector.* K. H. Scheer and Kurt Mahr. New York: Ace, 1970.

3014 6: *The Secret of the Time Vault*. Clark Darlton. New York: Ace, 1970.

3015 7: *Fortress of the Six Moons*. K. H. Scheer. New York: Ace, 1970.

3016 8: *The Galactic Riddle*. Clark Darlton. New York: Ace, October 1971, 1972, 1974; London: Futura Publications, 1975.

3017 9: *Quest Through Space and Time*. Clark Darlton. New York: Ace, November 1971, 1974; London: Futura Publications, 1975.

3018 10: *The Ghosts of Gol*. Kurt Mahr. New York: Ace, December 1971, 1972, 1974.

3019 11: *Planet of the Dying Sun*. Kurt Mahr. New York: Ace, February 1972, 1974.

3020 12: *Rebels of Tuglan*. Clark Darlton. New York: Ace, April 1972, 1974; London Futura Publications, 1976.

3021 13: *The Immortal Unknown*. K. H. Scheer. New York: Ace, May 1972, 1974; London: Futura Publications, 1976.

3022 14: *Venus in Danger*. Kurt Mahr. New York: Ace, June 1972. 1974.

3023 15: *Escape to Venus*. Clark Darlton. New York: Ace, July 1972; 1974.

3024 16: *Secret Barrier X*. W. W. Shols. New York: Ace Books, 1972.

3025 17: *The Venus Trap*. Kurt Mahr. New York: Ace, September, 1972.

3026 18: *Menace of the Mutant Master*. Kurt Mahr. New York: Ace Books, 1972.

3027 19: *Mutants vs. Mutants*. Clark Darlton. New York: Ace, November 1972; London: Futura, 1976.

3028 20: *The Thrall of Hypno*. Clark Darlton. New York: Ace, December 1972; London: Futura, 1976.

3029 21: *The Cosmic Decoy*. K. H. Scheer. New York: Ace, January 1973.

3030 22: *The Fleet of the Springers*. Kurt Mahr. New York: Ace Books, March 1973; London: Futura, 1977.

3031 23: *Peril on Ice Planet*. Kurt Mahr. New York: Ace, April 1973.

3032 24: *Infinity Flight*. Clark Darlton. New York: Ace, May 1973.

3033 25: *Snowman in Flames*. Clark Darlton. New York: Ace, June 1973.

3034 26: *Cosmic Traitor*. Kurt Brand. New York: Ace, July 1973.

3035 27: *Planet of the Gods*. Kurt Mahr. New York: Ace, August 1973; London: Futura Publications, 1977.

3036 28: *The Plague of Oblivion*. Clark Darlton. New York: Ace, August 1973; London: Futura, 1977.

3037 29: *A World Gone Mad*. Clark Darlton. New York: Ace, September 1973; London: Futura, 1977.

3038 30: *To Arkon!* Kurt Mahr. New York: Ace, September 1973.

3039 31: *Realm of the Tri-Planets*. New York: Ace, October 1973; London: Futura Publications, 1973.

3040 32: *Challenge of the Unknown*. Clark Darlton. New York: Ace. October 1973.

3041 33: *The Giant's Partner*. Clark Darlton. New York: Ace, November 1973.

3042 34: *SOS: Spaceship Titan!* Kurt Brand. New York: Ace, November 1973; London: Orbit, 1978.

3043 35: *Beware the Microbots*. Kurt Mahr. New York: Ace, December 1973.

3044 36: *Man and Monster*. K. H. Scheer. New York: Ace, 1973.

3045 37: *Epidemic Center: Aralon*. Clark Darlton. New York: Ace, January 1974.

3046 38: *Project: Earthsave*. Kurt Brand. New York: Ace, January 1974.

3047 39: *The Silence of Gom*. Kurt Mahr. New York: Ace, February 1974.

3048 40: *Red Eye of Betelgeuse*. Clark Darlton. New York: Ace, February 1974.

3049 41: *The Earth Dies*. Clark Darlton. New York: Ace, March 1974.

3050 42: *Time's Lonely One*. K. H. Scheer. New York: Ace, March 1974.

3051 43: *Life Hunt*. Kurt Brand. New York: Ace, April 1974.

3052 44: *The Pseudo One*. Clark Darlton. New York: Ace, April 1974.

3053 45: *Unknown Sector: Milky Way*. Kurt Mahr. New York: Ace, May 1974.

3054 46: *Again Atlan!* K. H. Scheer. New York: Ace, May 1974.

3055 47: *Shadow of the Mutant Master*. Kurt Brand. New York: Ace, June 1974.

3056 48: *The Dead Live*. Clark Darlton. Ace, June 1974.

3057 49: *Solar Assassins*. Kurt Mahr. New York: Ace, July 1974.

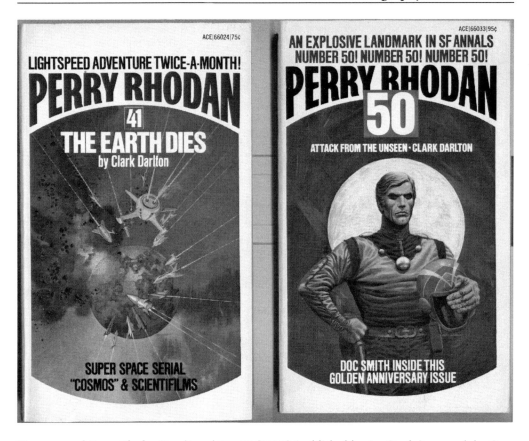

The covers of *Perry Rhodan* No. 41 and No. 50 [3058] (published by Ace Books), artwork by Gray Morrow.

3058 50: *Attack from the Unseen.* Clark Darlton. New York: Ace, July 1974.

3059 51: *Return from the Void.* Kurt Mahr. New York: Ace, August 1974.

3060 52: *Fortress Atlantis.* K. H. Scheer. New York: Ace, August 1974.

3061 53: *Spybot!* Clark Darlton. New York: Ace, September 1974.

3062 54: *The Blue Dwarfs.* Kurt Mahr. New York: Ace, September 1974.

3063 55: *The Micro-Techs.* Clark Darlton. New York: Ace, October 1974.

3064 56: *Prisoner of Time.* Clark Darlton. New York: Ace, October 1974.

3065 57: *A Touch of Eternity.* Clark Darlton. New York: Ace, November 1974.

3066 58: *The Guardians.* Kurt Mahr. New York: Ace, November 1974.

3067 59: *Interlude on Siliko 5.* Kurt Brand. New York: Ace, December 1974.

3068 60: *Dimension Search.* Clark Darlton. New York: Ace, December 1974.

3069 61: *Death Waits in Semispace.* Kurt Mahr. New York: Ace, January 1974.

3070 62: *The Last Days of Atlantis.* K. H. Scheer. New York: Ace, January 1975.

3071 63: *The Tigris Leaps.* Kurt Brand. New York: Ace, February 1975.

3072 64: *The Ambassadors from Aurigel.* Kurt Mahr. New York: Ace, February 1975.

3073 65: *Renegades of the Future.* Kurt Mahr. New York: Ace, March 1975.

3074 66: *The Horror.* William Voltz. New York: Ace Books, 1975.

3075 67: *Crimson Universe.* K. H. Scheer. New York: Ace, April 1975.

3076 68: *Under the Stars of Druufon.* Clark Darlton. New York: Ace, April 1975.

3077 69: *The Bonds of Eternity.* Clark Darlton. New York: Ace, April 1975.

3078 70: *Thora's Sacrifice*. Kurt Brand. New York: Ace, April 1975.

3079 71: *The Atom Hell of Grautier*. Kurt Mahr. New York: Ace, May 1975.

3080 72: *Caves of the Druuffs*. Kurt Mahr. New York: Ace, May 1975.

3081 73: *Spaceship of Ancestors*. Clark Darlton. New York: Ace, June 1975.

3082 74: *Checkmate: Universe*. Clark Darlton. New York: Ace, July 1975.

3083 75: *Planet Topide, Please Reply!* Kurt Brand. New York: Ace, July 1975.

3084 76: *Recruits for Arkon*. Clark Darlton. New York: Ace, August 1975.

3085 77: *Conflict Center: Naator*. Clark Darlton. New York: Ace, August 1975.

3086 78: *Power Key*. K. H. Scheer. New York: Ace, September 1975.

3087 79: *The Sleepers*. William Voltz. New York: Ace, September 1975.

3088 80: *The Columbus Affair*. K. H. Scheer. New York: Ace, October 1975.

3089 81: *Pucky's Greatest Hour*. Kurt Brand. New York: Ace, October 1975.

3090 82: *Atlan in Danger*. Kurt Brand. New York: Ace, November 1975.

3091 83: *Ernst Ellert Returns!* Clark Darlton. New York: Ace, November 1975.

3092 84: *Secret Mission: Moluk*. William Voltz. New York: Ace, December 1975.

3093 85: *Enemy in the Dark*. Kurt Mahr. New York: Ace, December 1975.

3094 86: *Blazing Sun*. Clark Darlton. New York: Ace, January 1976.

3095 87: *The Starless Realm*. Clark Darlton. New York: Ace, January 1976.

3096 88: *The Mystery of the Anti*. K. H. Scheer. New York: Ace, February 1976.

3097 89: *Power's Price*. Kurt Brand. New York: Ace, February 1976.

3098 90: *Unleashed Powers*. Kurt Brand. New York: Ace, March 1976.

3099 91: *Friend to Mankind*. Kurt Brand. New York: Ace, March 1976.

3100 92: *The Target Star*. Kurt Brand. New York: Ace, April 1976.

3101 93: *Vagabond of Space*. Clark Darlton. New York: Ace, April 1976.

3102 94: *Action: Division 3*. Kurt Mahr. New York: Ace, May 1976.

3103 95: *The Plasma Monster*. Kurt Brand. New York: Ace, May 1976.

3104 96: *Horn: Green*. William Voltz . New York: Ace, June 1976.

3105 97: *Phantom Fleet*. Clark Darlton. New York: Ace, June 1976.

3106 98: *The Idol from Passa*. Kurt Mahr. New York: Ace, July 1976.

3107 99: *The Blue System*. K. H. Scheer. New York: Ace, July 1976.

3108 100: *Desert of Death's Domain*. Kurt Mahr. New York: Ace, August 1976.

3109 101: *Blockade: Lepso*. Kurt Brand. New York: Ace, August 1976.

3110 102: *Spoor of the Antis*. William Voltz. New York: Ace, September 1976.

3111 103: *False Front*. Clark Darlton. New York: Ace, September 1976.

3112 104: *The Man with Two Faces*. Kurt Brand. New York: Ace, October 1976.

3113 105: *Wonderflower of Utik*. Kurt Mahr. New York: Ace, October 1976.

3114 106: *Caller from Eternity*. Kurt Brand. New York: Ace, December 1976.

3115 107: *The Emperor and the Monster*. William Voltz. New York: Ace, January 1977.

3116 108: *Duel Under the Double Sun*. K. H. Scheer. New York: Ace, February 1977.

3117 109: *The Stolen Spacefleet*. Clark Darlton. New York: Ace Books, March 1977.

3118 110: *Sgt. Robot*. Kurt Mahr. New York: Ace Books, March 1977.

3119 111: *Seeds of Ruin*. William Voltz. New York: Ace, April 1977.

3120 112: *Planet Mechanica*. K. H. Scheer. New York: Ace, April 1977.

3121 113: *Heritage of the Lizard People*. Clark Darlton. New York: Ace, May 1977.

3122 114: *Death's Demand*. Kurt Mahr. New York: Ace, May 1977.

3123 115: *Saboteurs in A-1*. Kurt Brand. New York: Ace, June 1977.

3124 116: *The Psycho Duel*. William Voltz. New York: Ace, June 1977.

3125 117: *Savior of the Empire*. K. H. Scheer. New York: Ace, August 1977.

3126 118: *The Shadows Attack.* Clark Darlton. New York: Ace, August 1977.

3127 119. *Between Galaxies.* Kurt Mahr. Van Nuys, CA: Master Publications, 1978.

3128 120. *Killers from Hyperspace.* William Voltz. Van Nuys, CA: Master Publications, October 1978.

3129 121. *Atom Fire on Mechanica.* Clark Darlton. Van Nuys, CA: Master Publications, October 1978.

3130 122. *Volunteers for Frago.* Kurt Brand. Van Nuys, CA: Master Publications, October 1978.

3131 123. *The Fortress in Time.* Kurt Mahr. Van Nuys, CA: Master Publications, October 1978.

3132 124. *The Sinister Power.* Kurt Brand. Van Nuys, CA: Master Publications, October 1978.

3133 125. *Robots, Bombs, and Mutants.* William Voltz. Van Nuys, CA: Master Publications, January 1979.

3134 126. *The Guns of Everblack.* K. H. Scheer. Van Nuys, CA: Master Publications, January 1979.

3135 127. *Sentinels of Solitude.* Clark Darlton. Van Nuys, CA: Master Publications, January 1979.

3136 128. *The Beasts Below.* Kurt Mahr. Van Nuys, CA: Master Publications, January 1979.

3137 129. *Blitzkrieg Galactica.* Kurt Brand. Van Nuys, CA: Master Publications, January 1979.

3138 130. *Peril Unlimited.* Kurt Brand. Van Nuys, CA: Master Publications, January 1979.

3139 131. *World Without Mercy.* William Voltz. Van Nuys, CA: Master Publications, January 1979.

3140 132. *Deadmen Shouldn't Die.* Clark Darlton. Van Nuys, CA: Master Publications, April 1979.

3141 133. *Station of the Invisibles.* Kurt Mahr. Van Nuys, CA: Master Publications, April 1979.

3142 134. *Agents of Destruction.* Kurt Brand. Van Nuys, CA: Master Publications, April 1979.

3143 135. *Humans Keep Out!* William Voltz. Van Nuys, CA: Master Publications, April 1979.

3144 136. *The Robot Invitation.* K.H. Scheer. Van Nuys, CA: Master Publications, April 1979.

3145 137. *Phantom Horde.* Clark Darlton; Stuart J Byrne; David Zlotky. [with *Star Man* Nos. 1–5.] Clark Darlton, Kurt Brand. Van Nuys, CA: Master Publications, July 1979.

3146 *Perry Rhodan: In the Center of the Galaxy.* Clark Darlton. New York: Ace, January 1978.

3147 *Perry Rhodan Special Release: Menace of Atomigeddon.* Kurt Mahr. / *Flight from Tarkihl.* Clark Darlton. New York: Ace, October 1977.

3148 *Perry Rhodan Special Release: Robot Threat: New York.* W. W. Shols. / *Pale Country Pursuit.* Hans Kneifel. New York: Ace, November 1977.

3149 *Perry Rhodan Special Release: The Crystal Prince.* K. H. Scheer. / *War of the Ghosts.* Clark Darlton. New York: Ace, December 1977.

3150 *Perry Rhodan Special Release: The Wasp Men Attack & Spider Desert.* W. W. Shols and Ernst Vlcek. New York: Ace, September 1977.

LOST OR UNPUBLISHED WORKS

Fiction

3151 "All Hail, Hillary!"

3152 "The Day Porn Died."

3153 "Fire from the Skies." *The Buccaneer.* (Ackerman may have misremembered a piece which appeared under a different title)

3154 "Generation of Vapors."

3155 "The Man Who Lived His Wife Over Again."

3156 "The Man Who Murdered Music."

3157 "A Myth Is as Good as a Mile." [With Robert Bloch; mentioned in afterword to Ackerman's Powell paperback collection *Science Fiction Worlds of Forrest J Ackerman*, p. 222.]

3158 "Perpetual Motion." (handwritten short story [seen in *Hooray For Horrorwood!* documentary])

3159 "SIMULACRUMS XXX."

3160 "The Woman Who Destroyed Hollywood's Heritage."

Nonfiction

3161 "Forrest J Ackerman #1 Everything." [As Paul Linden.]

3162 "My Life in a Time Machine." 2001.

FOREIGN TRANSLATIONS

Fiction

3163 "La Fatala Ekrigardo." ["The Fatal Glance"] *Heroldo de Esperanto.* Holland. [date unknown] (Esperanto publication of short story)

3164 "Den Obesvarade Frågan." ["The Mute Question"(?)] *Häpna!* Ed. Karl G. Kindberg. Jönköping, Finland: Kindberg & Söner, 3/maj 1954.

Nonfiction

3165 "L'Autuer, Tel Qu'il Se Voit." ["The Author, Such as He Sees Himself."] *V.* 59. Ed. Georges-H. Gallet. SOTEPE ["Société Technique de Presse et d'Edition"], 1959. (V Séléctions été 59.)

3166 "Ces Amours de Monstres! Pin-Up Surprise." *V.* 59. Ed. Georges-H. Gallet. SOTEPE ["Société Technique de Presse et d'Edition"], 1959. (V Séléctions été 59.) (Ackerman's photographs of a female model)

Books

3167 *Galleria degli Orrori: 100 Anni di Cinema Fantastico Attraverso i Manifesti della Collezione Ferrari.* [With Andrea Ferrari.] Lugano, Italy: Galleria Gottardo/Capelli, 1995.

3168 *Las Mejores Historias de Horror.* Barcelona: Editorial Bruguera, 1969; 1971; 1972; 1973; 1974; 1975. (Ackerman-edited anthology of horror short stories)

3169 Úžasné Příběhy: Antologie Klasické Americké Sci-fi. (*Amazing Stories: Anthology of Classic Sci-Fi*) Praha: Asociace fanoušků Science Fiction (AFSF), 1992. [shortened softcover Czech Language version of *Gosh! Wow (Boy-oh-Boy)! Science Fiction.*]

3170 *Die Vergangenheit der Zukunft: Die Originalstories hinter den grossen Science-fiction-Filmen.* Nürnberg: Burgschmiet Verlag, 1998. (German translation of *Reel Future: The Stories That Inspired 16 Classic Science Fiction Movies*)

Periodicals

3171 *Famosos "Monsters" del Cine.* No. 1. Barcelona: Garbo Editorial, April 1975.

3172 *Famosos "Monsters" del Cine.* No. 2. Barcelona: Garbo Editorial, May 1975.

3173 *Famosos "Monsters" del Cine.* No. 3. Barcelona: Garbo Editorial, June 1975.

3174 *Famosos "Monsters" del Cine.* No. 4. Barcelona: Garbo Editorial, July 1975.

3175 *Famosos "Monsters" del Cine.* No. 5. Barcelona: Garbo Editorial, August/September 1975.

3176 *Famosos "Monsters" del Cine.* No. 6. Barcelona: Garbo Editorial, October 1975.

3177 *Famosos "Monsters" del Cine.* No. 7. Barcelona: Garbo Editorial, November 1975.

3178 *Famosos "Monsters" del Cine.* No. 8. Barcelona: Garbo Editorial, December 1975.

3179 *Famosos "Monsters" del Cine.* No. 9. Barcelona: Garbo Editorial, January 1976.

3180 *Famosos "Monsters" del Cine.* No. 10. Barcelona: Garbo Editorial, February 1976.

3181 *Famosos "Monsters" del Cine.* No. 11. Barcelona: Garbo Editorial, March 1976.

3182 *Famosos "Monsters" del Cine.* No. 12. Barcelona: Garbo Editorial, April 1976.

3183 *Famosos "Monsters" del Cine.* No. 13. Barcelona: Garbo Editorial, May 1976.

3184 *Famosos "Monsters" del Cine.* No. 14. Barcelona: Garbo Editorial, June 1976.

3185 *Famosos "Monsters" del Cine.* No. 15. Barcelona: Garbo Editorial, July 1976.

3186 *Famosos "Monsters" del Cine.* No. 16. Barcelona: Garbo Editorial, August 1976.

3187 *Famosos "Monsters" del Cine.* No. 17. Barcelona: Garbo Editorial, September 1976.

3188 *Famosos "Monsters" del Cine.* No. 18. Barcelona: Garbo Editorial, October 1976.

3189 *Famosos "Monsters" del Cine.* No. 19. Barcelona: Garbo Editorial, November 1976.

3190 *Famosos "Monsters" del Cine.* No. 20. Barcelona: Garbo Editorial, December 1976.

3191 *Famosos "Monsters" del Cine.* No. 21. Barcelona: Garbo Editorial, January 1977.

3192 *Famosos "Monsters" del Cine.* No. 22. Barcelona: Garbo Editorial, February 1977.

3193 *Famosos "Monsters" del Cine.* No. 23. Barcelona: Garbo Editorial, March 1977.

3194 *Famosos "Monsters" del Cine.* No. 24. Barcelona: Garbo Editorial, April 1977.

INTERVIEWS

3195 Ackerman, Forrest J. "To Kill a Mocking Bat." *Famous Monsters of Filmland.* No. 36. December 1965. pp. 42–53; *Famous Monsters of Filmland 1971 Fearbook.* Warren, 1970. (transcript of interview of Ackerman from *Joe Franklin Show*; see entry 2863).

3196 Adams, Carol & Douglas Buchanan. "Collectors: An Interview with Forrest J Ackerman." *Bedside, Bathtub & Armchair Companion to Frankenstein.* New York: Continuum, 2007. [pp. 190-?]

3197 Adams, Ron. "Give This Kid Anything He Wants!" *MonsterMad.* No. 1. Ed. George Chastain. Morgantown, WV: July 1997. pp. 8–11.

3198 Anderson, Philip. "Forrest J Ackerman — Legendary Sci-Fi/Fantasy Historian and Afficianado." 23 July 2000— Comic Con International — San Diego, CA KAOS2000 <http://www.kaos2000. net/interviews/forrestackerman/>

3199 Atkins, Rick. "The Ghoulden Boy Strikes Again." *Let's Scare 'Em!: Grand Interviews and a Filmography of Horrific Proportions, 1930–1961.* Jefferson, NC: McFarland & Co., 1997. pp. 149–176.

3200 Austin, A. J. "Interview: Forrest J. Ackerman." *Thrust.* Ed. D. Douglas Fratz. MD: Thrust Publications, Summer 1989. pp. 19–20.

3201 Bembaron, Jeffrey Mark. "Interview. A Visit with the King of Eerie." *Synn Watch: The Magazine of Esoteric Entertainment.* Longwood, FL: Paragon Publications. 1999. pp. 17–20.

3202 Berry, Mark. "Forrest Ackerman." *Bizarre Magazine.* 2007.

3203 Berry, Mark. "The King of Fangdom." *SFX Magazine.* No. 137. Ed. Dave Bradley. Bath, UK: Future Publishing Ltd UK, December 2005. pp. 54–56.

3204 Blass, Terry. "One Famous Monster of an Interview." *Chiller Theatre.* Vol. 1. No. 5. Ed. Kevin Clement. Rutherford, NJ: Chiller Theatre, Inc. 1996. (Interview portion titled "Forrest J Ackerman the Oh-Punner of the Way Out!")

3205 Brunas, John & Michael, et al. "Zack and Ack Are Back." *Scarlet Street: The Magazine of Mystery and Horror.* No. 4. Ed. Richard Valley. Fall 1991. pp. 56–58. [article credited to John & Michael Brunas, Jessie Lilley, Richard Valley and Tom Weaver]

3206 Copner, Michael & Coco Kiyonaga. "Nights of Futures Past: An Intimate Interview: Forrest J Ackerman." *Cult Movies.* No. 37. January 2001. pp. 58–61.

3207 Corupe, Paul. "Famous Monster." *Rue Morgue Magazine.* No. 83. Toronto, Ontario: Marrs Media Inc., October 2008. pp. 18–20, 25–25, 28. (interview portion)

3208 Daniel, Dennis and Chas. Balun. "Ask Ackerman: Deep Red interviews the Famous Monster(man)." *Deep Red Magazine.* No. 3. Ed. Chas Balun. Albany, NY: FantaCo Enterprises, June 1988. pp. 57–61.

3209 Decker, Sean J. "Mr. Monster." <http://www.horroronline.com/db/A/interview_with_forrest_j._ackerman/index.html>

3210 Dorf, Shel. "Up from Fandom." *Comics Buyers Guide.* No. 909. Iola, WI: Krause Publications, 14 April 1991. p. 46.

3211 Druktenis, Dennis J. "The Ackermonster, Forrest J Ackerman." *Scary Monsters.* No. 3. Highwood, IL: Dennis Druktenis Publishing & Mail Order, Inc., June 1992. pp. 12–15, 22. (Issue dedicated to Ackerman and *Famous Monsters of Filmland*, four pages with an article and an interview, including photos)

3212 Elliot, Dr. Jeffrey M. "Take me home, little boy..." *Questar: Science Fiction/Fantasy Adventure.* Vol. 2. No. 3. Whole No. 7. Ed. William G. Wilson, Jr. Pittsburgh, PA: MW Communications, June 1980. pp. 45–47, 61–63.

3213 Elliott, Elton T. "The Ackerman Interview." *Science Fiction Review.* Vol. 7. No. 4. Whole No. 27. Ed. Richard E. Geis. Portland, OR: Sept. 1978. p. 46. (addenda to previous interview, re: *Perry Rhodan*)

3214 Elliott, Elton T. "Interview with Forrest J. Ackerman." *Science Fiction Review.* No. 25. Ed. Richard E. Geis. Portland, OR: May 1978. p. 94.

3215 Enfantino, Peter. Interview. *The Scream Factory.* Vol. 1. No. 1. Brooks, Clifford, Peter Enfantino and Joe Lopez, Eds. San Jose, CA: The Deadline Publications, Winter 1988.

3216 Etchison, Dennis. "Presenting! The Amazing! Ackermonster!" *Cavalier.* Vol. 17. No. 8. Ed. Robert J. Shea. Los Angeles, CA: Arizill Publishing Co., June 1967. pp. 56–57, 59, 80–81.

3217 Fisher, Gary. "An Interview with Forrest J Ackerman." 1997. <http://www.armchair.com/warp/ackerman.html>

3218 Gilbert, Elizabeth. "My Favorite Martian." *GQ: Gentlemen's Quarterly.* March 2001. Vol. 7. No. 1. Issue 3. p. 330.

3219 Gourlay, Jack. "Filmfax Hall of Fame: The Most Memorable Hollywood Personalities Lon Chaney, Jr. Part Two." *Filmfax.* No. 21. July 1990. (Ackerman is one of several interviewees, his comments run on pp. 70–71.)

3220 Graham, Craig. "Interview: Ray Bradbury and Forrest J Ackerman." *Futuria Fantasia.* Ray Bradbury. Los Angeles: Graham, 2007.

3221 Grant, Ed. "Forry's a Jolly Good Fellow Famous Monsters of Filmland Founder Forrest J Ackerman as Told to Ed Grant." *The Phantom of the Movies' VideoScope.* No. 24. Ocean Grove, NJ: Phan-Media, Inc. Fall 1997. (October/December 1997). pp. 40–41.

3222 Grayson, Perry M. "At the Castle of the Effjay of Akkamin an Interview with Forrest J Ackerman Conducted by Perry Grayson." *Yawning Vortex: The Tsathoggua Press Journal of Weird Fiction.* Ed. Perry M. Grayson. Vol. 1. No. 2. West Hills, CA: Tsathoggua Press, October 1994. pp. 14–19.

3223 Gudino, Rod. "Forrest J Ackerman Trouble in Monsterland." *Rue Morgue*. No. 21. Marrs Media Inc. May/June 2001. pp. 14–15.

3224 Harris, Lee. "Uncle Forry: First and Last Fan." *Cult Movies*. No. 11. 1994. pp. 26–28.

3225 Harris, Michael. "FJA in London." *Monsters Incorporated*. No. 27. UK: 1965. pp. 11–13.

3226 Hatcher, Lint. "Enter: The Ackermansion." *Wonder*. No. 7. Atlanta, GA: Lint Hatcher, 1993. pp. 24–26.

3227 Hatcher, Lint, and Rod Bennett. "Inside Darkest Ackerman or Forrest J Ackerman the Best *Fiend* a Kid Ever Had!" *Wonder*. No. 7. Atlanta, GA: Lint Hatcher, 1993. pp. 4–11, 52–53.

3228 [Interview] *Buyer's Guide For Comic Fandom*. No. 183. Ed. Alan Light. Dyna Pubs Enterprises, 20 May 1977. (newsprint adzine)

3229 [Interview] *The Dark Side: The Magazine of the Macabre and Fantastic*. No. 138. April/May 2009.

3230 [Interview] *Previews*. Vol. VII. No. 7. Diamond, July 1997.

3231 Jablonski, Dustin "Doc Monster." "The Maniacal Adventures of ... Dustin Jablonski (a.k.a. Dr. Monster)." *Stoner's Monster Mayhem*. No. 1. Ed. Richard Stoner. Winter 1995. pp. 12–13; *The Best of SMM*. Ed. Richard Stoner. June 2003. (also reprints from "Ask Uncle Forry" column)

3232 Johnson-Tate, Julie. "An Interview with Forrest Ackerman." *Pulsar*. No. 15. Fall 1989.

3233 Keil, Dave. "A Personal Interview with 4E." *Garden Ghouls Gazette*. No. 9. 1963. pp. 2–3.

3234 Kelley, Mike. "Monster Manse." *Grand Street-Hollywood*. New York: Grand Street Press, Summer 1994. pp. 224–233. (photographs by Daniel Faust captioned by Ackerman)

3235 Kiyonaga, Coco. "Space(Acker)Man Interview: The Greatest Inner View of FJA in 80 years!" *Cult Movies*. No. 21. / *Spaceman*. No. 2. [Hollywood, CA:] 1997. pp. 20–25. (*Spaceman*. No. 2. on reverse side features Ackerman interview)

3236 Lieurance, Charles. "Night of the Ackermonster: Conversations with Science Fiction's #1 Collector." *Amazing Heroes*. No. 153. Ed. Kim Thompson. Westlake Village, CA: Fantagraphics Books, Inc., November 15, 1988. pp. 45–48.

3237 Linaweaver, Brad. "A Conversation with the Master of Metropolis the Very Latest Interview with Forrest J Ackerman." *Cult Movies*. No. 26. 1998. pp. 6–8.

3238 Mayer, Frederick J. "An Interview with Mr. & Mrs. Forrest Ackerman." *The Diversifier*. Vol. 4. No. 5/6. [Whole] No. 26. Ed. C. C. Clingan. Oroville, CA: C. C. Clingan, May/July 1978. pp. 35–37. (mostly with Wendayne concerning her memories of author Clark Ashton Smith)

3239 McCarty, Michael. "Famous Monster Speaks: Forrest J Ackerman." in: McCarty, Michael, Ed. *Modern Mythmakers: Interviews with Horror, Science Fiction and Fantasy Writers and Filmmakers*. Jefferson, NC: McFarland, 2008. pp. 7–14.

3240 McCarty, Michael. "Famous Monster Speaks: Forrest J. Ackerman Talks About His Magazines, Movies, and Monsters." *Dark Regions and Horror Magazine*. No. 12. Concord, CA: Dark Regions Press, Spring 1999. pp. 52-.

3241 McCarty, Michael. "Famous Monsters Speaks! An Interview with Forrest J Ackerman." *Giants of the Genre: Interviews with Science Fiction, Fantasy, and Horror's Greatest Talents*. Holicong, PA: Wildside Press, 2003. pp. 88–90.

3242 Michelucci, Bob. "An Interview with FJA." *The Collectors Guide to Monster Magazines*. Ed. Bob Michelucci. Pittsburgh, PA: Dick Zdinak Associates, 1977. pp. 34–47.

3243 Mothner, Ira. "Those Clean-Living All American Monsters." *Look*. Vol. 28. No. 18. Ed. Daniel D. Mich. Cowles Magazine and Broadcasting, Inc., 8 September 1964. pp. 50, 52.

3244 Robinson, Peter. "Interview with Forrest J Ackerman." 2006. Geekson.com. <http://www.geekson.com/archives/archivedepisodes/2006/episode081808.htm.>

3245 Ross, Jean W. "Interview with Forrest J Ackerman." *Contemporary Authors*. Volume 102. Detroit: Gale Research Co., 1980. pp. 13–16.

3246 Sielski, Mark L. "An Interview with Forrest J Ackerman." *Magick Theatre*. No. 8. Ed. Raymond F. Young. Baldwin, NY: 1987. pp. 13–17.

3247 Simpson, M. J. "It's Superfan!" *SFX Magazine*. No. 21. Bath, UK: Future Publishing Limited, January 1997. p. 28; <http://www.mjsimpson.co.uk/interviews/forrestjackerman.html>

3248 Sims, J. M. "Echoes." *Cinemassacres: A Tribute to Forrest J Ackerman*. Ed. David Byron. Duncan, OK: BearManor Media, 2010. pp. 249–255. (apparently conducted ca. 1995)

3249 Stone, J. Christopher. "Filmfax Hall of Fame: the Most Memorable Hollywood Personalities: It's Finally Official ... Forrest J Ackerman, Filmfan Extraordinaire, Sells His Collection!" *Filmfax: The Magazine of Unusual Film & Television*. No. 17. November 1989. [pp. 32, 34–35, 82, 84.] (on a plan for the disposition of Ackerman's collection)

3250 Tomkins, Dave. "Yo Astro! Embalming Fluid! An Interview with Forrest Ackerman." *Mean*

Magazine. No. 4. Los Angeles, CA: Mean Magazine Inc., 1999. pp. 30–34.

3251 [Unsigned.] "Famous Monsters Revisited Return of the Ackermonster." *Screem*. No. 3. Screemag Publishing, 1994. p. 19.

3252 [Unsigned.] "The Gamma Interview: Forrest J. Ackerman." *Gamma*. No. 4. North Hollywood, CA: Star Press, Inc. February 1965. pp. 77–

3253 [Unsigned.] "The Return of the Monsters." *Look*. Vol. 28. No. 18. Ed. Daniel D. Mich. Cowles Magazine and Broadcasting, Inc., 8 September 1964. pp. 46–49.

3254 Vance, Michael. "The Famous Monster of Filmland Forrest Ackerman." *Baby Boomer Collectibles*. Vol. 1. No. 12. Waupaca, WI: ADD Inc., September 1994. (A Checklist of Published Work Written by Forrest Ackerman) pp. 30–32, 34, 36.

3255 Vance, Michael, and Roy Crane. "Forrest Ackerman Interview." *The Horror Show an Adventure in Terror*. Vol. 6. No. 1. Ed. David B. Silva. Oak Run, CA: Phantasm Press, Spring 1988. pp. 18–

3256 White, Alan. "Meet the Man Who Met the Monsters: FJA'S Monster Memories." *Mr. Monster*. Las Vegas: Alan White, 2009.

3257 White, Alan. "Two Guys Sittting Around Talking About Fandom." *Mr. Monster*. Las Vegas: Alan White, 2009. pp. 13–21. (discusses Guerney's auction)

3258 White, Steve. "Forrest J Ackerman: An Interview with the Publisher of 'Famous Monsters of Filmland.'" *American Pop*. No. 1. Hanover, MA: February 1990.

3259 Woods, Paul A. "The Man Who Created Monster Magic." *Fear!* No. 33. Ed. John Gilbert. West Drayton, Middlesex, England: COMAG, September 1991. p. 10.

3260 Zimmerman, Howard. "Forrest J. Ackerman — The World's Greatest Science Fiction Fan." *Starlog*. No. 13. New York: O'Quinn Studios, Inc., May 1978. pp. 48–53.

WORKS PUBLISHED BY ACKERMAN

3261 *Alden Press*. 1945. (prospectus for a publishing imprint Ackerman intended to launch in tribute to his brother)

3262 *Alden Press*. October 1945.

3263 *Brains for Janes: Stories*. Ed. Ronald Mark and A. Stover. New Orleans: Pirate Press, 1948. (Ackerman was evidently involved in the publication of this book, limited to 200 copies)

3264 *A Checklist of Fantasy Magazines*. 1945 Edition. Los Angeles, The Fantasy Foundation, 1945. 21pp.

3265 *Fancyclopedia*. John Bristol Speer. Los Angeles: Forrest J Ackerman for the Los Angeles Science Fiction Society, 1944. 97 pp. (entries on fan jargon, events)

3266 *Fantasy Annual*. Los Angeles: 1948.

3267 *4sJ Presents, Monsters of the Moon*. Ray Heiz-Mike Frisby. (mock film scenario illustrated with stills from science fiction productions)

3268 *The Hyborian Age*. Robert E. Howard. The Los Angeles — New York Cooperative Publications, Inc., 1938. (Conan the Barbarian creator)

3269 *I Bequeath (...I, Forrest J. Ackerman, Being of Imaginative Mind, Bequeath to the Fantasy Foundation, Upon My Demise, My 1300 Fantasy Books)*. Hollywood, CA: 4 July 1946. (listing of items to start the Fantasy Foundation)

3270 *Index to Science Fiction and Fantasy Magazines and Their Stories [Amazing, Science Wonder,*

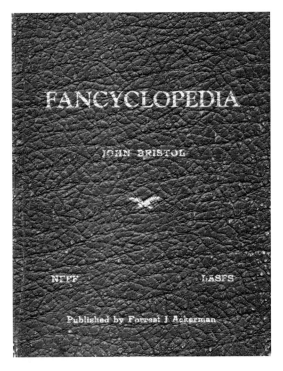

Cover of *Fancyclopedia* [3265]. Ackerman published this detailed lexicography of science fiction fandom in 1944. The author's full name was John Bristol Speer, known in science fiction fandom as "Jack Speer"; it is unknown why he was bylined on the cover as "John Bristol."

Air Wonder, Astounding, Fantasy, Marvel Science, Thrilling Wonder Stories] 1926–1938. Los Angeles, CA: Forrest J Ackerman, 1938. 71 pp.

WORKS ABOUT ACKERMAN

Books

3271 Ackerman, Forrest J. *Forrest J Ackerman, Famous Monster of Filmland.* Pittsburgh, PA: Imagine, Inc. 1986. (covers *Famous Monsters* Nos. 1–50)

3272 Ackerman, Forrest J. *Forrest J Ackerman, Famous Monster of Filmland Volume II.* (Issues #51–100) Universal City, CA: Hollywood Publishing Company, 1991. 162 pp. (covers *Famous Monsters* Nos. 51–100)

3273 Ackerman, Forrest J. *Science-Fiction Fantasy Horror: The World of Forrest J Ackerman at Auction.* New York: Guernsey's, 1987. (illustrated auction catalog) [166 pp.]

3274 Astrella, Al, and James Greene. *House of Ackerman: A Photographic Tour of the Legendary Ackermansion.* Baltimore: Midnight Marquee Press, 2010.

3275 Byron, David, Ed. *Cinemassacres: A Tribute to Forrest J Ackerman.* Duncan, OK: BearManor Media, 2010. (collection of interviews pertaining to Ackerman)

3276 Coker, John L., III, Ed. *Tales of the Time Travelers: Adventures of Forrest J Ackerman and Julius Schwartz.* Orlando, FL: Days of Wonder Publishers, 2009. [Foreword by John Norman and Introduction by Ray Bradbury] (collection of fan writings by Ackerman and Schwartz, material about and remembrances of both)

3277 Daniel, Dennis, et al, Ed. *Famous Monsters Chronicles.* FantaCo Enterprises, 1991. [162 pp.] (tributes from friends and filmmakers, interviews with Warren artists)

3278 Ferry, Ray. *Life Is But a Scream! The True Story of the Rebirth of Famous Monsters of Filmland.* North Hills, CA: Karmanirhara Publications, 2000. (discusses Ackerman extensively throughout, the revival of *Famous Monsters* and subsequent litigation between Ackerman and the author)

3279 Ishida, Hajime. *Forrest J Ackerman's Horror & Sci-Fi Collection Museum.* Japan: Castle Company Ltd., 2009.

3280 Painter, Deborah. *Forry: The Life of Forrest J Ackerman.* Jefferson, NC: McFarland & Company, 2011. 224 pp. (the first full-scale biography of Ackerman)

Profiles/Tributes

3281 Ackerman, Forrest J. "Forrest J Ackerman." *Contemporary Science Fiction Authors II.* Robert Reginald. Detroit: Gale Research Co., 1979; Wildside Press LLC, 2009. pp. 789–790.

3282 Ackerman, Wendayne. "A Word from the World's Greatest Futuria Fantasia Collector." *Futures Past: A Visual Guidebook to Science Fiction History.* Vol. 1. No. 1. Ed. Jim Emerson. Convoy, OH: 1992. p. 39.

3283 Adams, Ron. "4E 4Ever: Forrest J Ackerman Remembered." *Monster Bash.* No. 9. Ligonier, PA: June/July/August 2009. pp. 33–35. (remembrance letters solicited by Ron Adams from HH Wolfman, Joe Moe, Rocky Thein, Michael A., Bruce Tinkel, John P. Miami, Frank Nioletti, Gordon Reid, and Dave Hogan)

3284 Adams, Ron. "Rondo Remembers FJ Always." *Monster Bash.* No. 9. Ligonier, PA: June/July/August 2009. pp. 4–5.

3285 Adler, Dick. "One Man's Monstrous Menagerie." *The Daily Telegraph.* No. 492. London: 10 April 1974. pp. 29–33

3286 Aldiss, Brian. Letter. *Forry! A Special Publication Presented to Forrest J. Ackerman, on the Occasion of the 50th Anniversary of His Birthday, and the 40th Anniversary of His Discovery of Science-Fiction.* Ed. Fred Patten. Los Angeles, CA: Los Angeles Science Fiction Society/A Salamander Press publication, 1966. p. 15.

3287 Arbinger, Blythe. "Monster Trash." *Omni.* Vol. 10. No. 3. Omni Publications International Ltd., December 1987. pp. 28, 30. (on the Guernsey's auction)

3288 Arlt, Martin. "A Tribute to Forrest J Ackerman." *Mad Scientist.* No. 19. Ed. Martin Arlt. Spring 2009.

3289 Ash, Brian. *Who's Who in Science Fiction.* New York: Taplinger, 1976. p. 31.

3290 Asimov, Isaac. Letter. *Forry! A Special Publication Presented to Forrest J. Ackerman, on the Occasion of the 50th Anniversary of His Birthday, and the 40th Anniversary of His Discovery of Science-Fiction.* Ed. Fred Patten. Los Angeles, CA: Los Angeles Science Fiction Society/A Salamander Press publication, 1966. p. 33.

3291 Astrella, Al. "An Ackerfan Speaks." *House of Ackerman: A Photographic Tour of the Legendary Ackermansion.* Al Astrella and James Greene. Baltimore: Midnight Marquee Press, 2010. pp. 15–16.

3292 Babcock, Jay W. "Road Trip: The Ackermansion." *Sci-Fi Universe.* Vol. 3. No. 5. Whole No. 22. February 1997. p. 10.

3293 Basbanes, Nicholas A. *A Gentle Madness: Bibliophiles, Bibliomanes, and the Eternal Passion for Books.* New York: H. Holt and Co., 1995; 1996; *A Gentle Madness: Bibliophiles, Bibliomanes, and the Eternal Passion for Books: With a New Preface.* Macmillan, 1999. pp. 417–418. (Ackerman and his book collection receive mention)

3294 Bear, Greg. "Forrest J Ackerman." *Locus.* No. 576. Vol. 62. No. 1. Ed. Charles N. Brown. January 2009. pp. 59–60.

3295 Bembaron, Jeff. "The House of Ackerman." *House of Frightenstein.* No. 1. Longwood, FL: AC Comics, 1995.

3296 Berry, John. "4e's a Jolly Good Fellow." *Forry! A Special Publication Presented to Forrest J. Ackerman, on the Occasion of the 50th Anniversary of His Birthday, and the 40th Anniversary of His Discovery of Science-Fiction.* Ed. Fred Patten. Los Angeles, CA: Los Angeles Science Fiction Society/A Salamander Press publication, 1966. p. 58.

3297 Beyette, Beverly. "Monster Collection: Los Angeles Man, 75, Amasses Treasures of Horror and Sci-Fi Films." *Houston Chronicle.* Sec. B. 4 January 1993. p. 3.

3298 Biodrowski, Steve. "Obituary: Famous Monsters Founder Forest J. Ackerman." <http://cinefantastiqueonline.com/2008/12/05/obituary-famous-monsters-found-forest-j-ackerman-dead/> 5 December 2008.

3299 Bloch, Robert. "A Brief Ackermention." *Fantasia.* Seattle, WA: Bill Pugmire & Brian Wise. Dec. 1970; *Old Bones.* p. 7.

3300 Bloch, Robert. "From a Friend." *Fantasia.* Seattle, WA: Bill Pugmire & Brian Wise. Dec. 1970.

3301 Bloch, Robert. "Happy Birthday Forry Ackerman." *Outré.* Vol. 1. No. 2. Ed. Al Kracalik. October 1963. pp. 33–34.

3302 Bloch, Robert. "The Many Facets of Forrest J Ackerman." *Lunacon '74 program book. ClaytonCon II Program Book.* 1978.

3303 Bogue, Michael. "Good Things Come in Threes: The Triple Role of FAMOUS MONSTERS in One Fan's Life (A TRIBUTE TO FJA)." *Scary Monsters.* No. 70. Ed. Dennis J. Druktenis. Highwood, IL: Dennis Druktenis Publishing & Mail Order, Inc., April 2009. pp. 84–87.

3304 Bohus, Ted A. untitled tribute. *Scarlet— The Film Magazine.* No. 3. June/July/August 2009. p. 34.

3305 Booe, Martin. "The Monster Maven: Forrest Ackerman, Sci-Fi's Founding Fan." *The Washington Post.* 8 May 1993. pp. G1–G2.

3306 Borst, Ronald V. "Forry Ackerman—'The Man Who Made Us Monsters.'" *Fantasia.* Seattle,

WA: Bill Pugmire & Brian Wise. Dec. 1970. pp. 9–12.

3307 Bradbury, Ray. "All About My Friends, Forry and Julie." *Tales of the Time Travelers: Adventures of Forrest J Ackerman and Julius Schwartz.* Ed. John L. Coker, III. Orlando, FL: Days of Wonder Publishers, 2009. (Introduction)

3308 Bradbury, Ray. "The Beast Upon the Wire." *Forry! A Special Publication Presented to Forrest J. Ackerman, on the Occasion of the 50th Anniversary of His Birthday, and the 40th Anniversary of His Discovery of Science-Fiction.* Ed. Fred Patten. Los Angeles, CA: Los Angeles Science Fiction Society/A Salamander Press publication, 1966. p. 57. (verse)

3309 Bradbury, Ray. "Forrest J Ackerman." Coker, John L. Ed. *A Gathering to Honor Forrest J Ackerman Presented by David A. Kyle and Friends.* Orlando, FL: Days of Wonder Publishers, 2006.

3310 Bradbury, Ray. "Forrie Ackerman." *Lunacon '74 program book*; as "4eword." "*It's Alive!@85.*" Ed. Jeffrey Roberts & George Chastain. A Monster-Boom Special Publication, November 2001. (abridged)

3311 Bradbury, Ray. "From a Friend." *Fantasia.* Seattle, WA: Bill Pugmire & Brian Wise. Dec. 1970. p. 7; as "Dear Bill." *Old Bones.* Ed. Pugmire. p. 7.

3312 Bradbury, Ray. "Happy Birthday Forry Ackerman." *Outré.* Vol. 1. No. 2. Ed. Al Kracalik. October 1963. p. 33.

3313 Bradbury, Ray. "Martian's Chronicle." *Famous Monster, Forry Ackerman.* Byrd, Larry & Ron Haydock (Eds.). (dated November 24, 1960)

3314 Brosnan, Peter L. "King of the Monsters Forrest Ackerman." *Sh-Boom.* February 1990. pp. 56–60.

3315 Brunas, John & Michael. "FM — We're Glad It Was There." *Famous Monsters Chronicles.* Ed. Dennis Daniel with Jim Knusch. [Co-editors: Greg Theakston, Bill Warren] Albany, NY: FantaCo Enterprises, 1991. pp. 167–168.

3316 Buff, Warren. "First Among Equals." *The Drink Tank.* No. 191. Ed. Christopher J. Garcia. 2008. pp. 5–6.

3317 Burns, Kevin. "Famous Last Words." *Famous Monsters of Filmland: The Annotated No. 1.* Movieland Classics, LLC, 2011. p. 159.

3318 Burns, Kevin. "Following Forry." *Famous Monsters of Filmland: The Annotated No. 1.* Movieland Classics, LLC, 2011. pp. 13–18.

3319 Cain, Dana. "Chapter 8: A Tribute to Forrest J. Ackerman and the Ackermansion Collection." *Collecting Monsters of Film and TV: Identification & Value Guide.* Iola, WI: Krause Publications, 1997.

3320 Campbell, Frank. "The Dark Forrest." *The Austin Chronicle.*

3321 Carducci, Mark Patrick. "FM Appreciation." *Famous Monsters Chronicles.* Ed. Dennis Daniel with Jim Knusch. [Co-editors: Greg Theakston, Bill Warren] Albany, NY: FantaCo Enterprises, 1991. pp. 157–158.

3322 Carlson, Michael. "Forrest J Ackerman." *The Guardian.* 8 December 2008.

3323 Carnell, Ted. "The Three Stigmata of Ackerman Forrest." *Forry! A Special Publication Presented to Forrest J. Ackerman, on the Occasion of the 50th Anniversary of His Birthday, and the 40th Anniversary of His Discovery of Science-Fiction.* Ed. Fred Patten. Los Angeles, CA: Los Angeles Science Fiction Society/A Salamander Press publication, 1966. p. 30.

3324 Causey, James. "The Gentle People." *Forry! A Special Publication Presented to Forrest J. Ackerman, on the Occasion of the 50th Anniversary of His Birthday, and the 40th Anniversary of His Discovery of Science-Fiction.* Ed. Fred Patten. Los Angeles, CA: Los Angeles Science Fiction Society/A Salamander Press publication, 1966. pp. 74–80. (short story)

3325 Chaney, Ron. untitled tribute. *Scarlet—The Film Magazine.* No. 3. June/July/August 2009. p. 34.

3326 Charkalis, Diana McKeon. "Movie Fans Flock to a Monster of a Sale." *USA Today.* 11 October 2002.

3327 Cheney, Max. "Forry and Me." *Scary Monsters.* No. 70. Ed. Dennis J. Druktenis. Highwood, IL: Dennis Druktenis Publishing & Mail Order, Inc., April 2009. pp. 101–102.

3328 Clement, Kevin. untitled tribute. *Scarlet—The Film Magazine.* No. 3. June/July/August 2009. p. 35.

3329 Clements, Paul. "Forry's a Jolly Good Fellow." *Famous Monsters Chronicles.* Ed. Dennis Daniel with Jim Knusch. [Co-editors: Greg Theakston, Bill Warren] Albany, NY: FantaCo Enterprises, 1991. pp. 159–161.

3330 Clute, John. "Obituary: Forrest J. Ackerman: Science-fiction Magazine Editor and Collector of Movie Memorabilia." *The Independent.* No. 6931. 31 December 2008. p. 30.

3331 Cohn, Harry. "Personalities of Fandom: No. 7: Forrest J. Ackerman." *British Space Fiction Magazine.* Vol. 2. No. 3. Ed. Vargo Statten. Luton, Beds., U.K: Dragon Press, Ltd., 1955.

3332 Coker, John L. III. "Forrest J Ackerman: A Fan of Many Firsts." *A Gathering to Honor Forrest J Ackerman Presented by David A. Kyle and Friends.* Orlando, FL: Days of Wonder Publishers, 2006.

3333 Corliss, Richard. "Sci-Fi's No. 1 Fanboy, Forrest J Ackerman, Dies at 92." *Time.* Vol. 172. No. 25. 22 December 2008. p. 25.

3334 Corupe, Paul. "Famous Monster." *Rue Morgue Magazine.* No. 83. Toronto, Ontario: Marrs Media Inc., October 2008. pp. p. 17–18.

3335 Cox, Arthur Jean. "A Few Words About an Old Friend." *Locus.* No. 576. Vol. 62. No. 1. Ed. Charles N. Brown. January 2009. pp. 5, 59.

3336 Cox, Jean. "Forrest J Ackerman; May 1945 ... and afterward. *Forry! A Special Publication Presented to Forrest J. Ackerman, on the Occasion of the 50th Anniversary of His Birthday, and the 40th Anniversary of His Discovery of Science-Fiction.* Ed. Fred Patten. Los Angeles, CA: Los Angeles Science Fiction Society/A Salamander Press publication, 1966. p. 54.

3337 Crasdan, Jay. "11 Point Courier New." *The Drink Tank.* No. 191. Ed. Christopher J. Garcia. 2008. p. 6.

3338 Daugherty, Dr. Walter J. "You're a Better Man Than I, Gunga Dhin." *Lunacon '74 program book.*

3339 Davids, Paul. "Preface." *House of Ackerman: A Photographic Tour of the Legendary Ackermansion.* Al Astrella and James Greene. Baltimore: Midnight Marquee Press, 2010. pp. 6–8.

3340 Deluga, Kent R. "'Uncle Forry' or the Man Who Inspired the Scary Monster Kids!" *Scary Monsters.* No. 70. Ed. Dennis J. Druktenis. Highwood, IL: Dennis Druktenis Publishing & Mail Order, Inc., April 2009. pp. 72–73.

3341 Derleth, August. "Message from August Derleth." *Forry! A Special Publication Presented to Forrest J. Ackerman, on the Occasion of the 50th Anniversary of His Birthday, and the 40th Anniversary of His Discovery of Science-Fiction.* Ed. Fred Patten. Los Angeles, CA: Los Angeles Science Fiction Society/A Salamander Press publication, 1966. p. 64.

3342 Dorst, Gary D. "Forry J. Ackermonster the Mini/Maxi/Midi Giant of Monster and Sci-Fi Fandom." *Fantasia.* Seattle, WA: Bill Pugmire & Brian Wise. Dec. 1970. pp. 1, 3–4.

3343 Druktenis, Dennis. "Monster Memories of the Ackermonster." *Scary Monsters.* No. 70. Ed. Dennis J. Druktenis. Highwood, IL: Dennis Druktenis Publishing & Mail Order, Inc., April 2009. pp. 5–11.

3344 Edwards, Bill "Drac." "4E@85." *Scary Monsters Magazine.* No. 43. Highwood, IL: Dennis Druktenis Publishing & Mail Order, Inc., June 2002. pp. 32–35.

3345 Edwards, Bill "Drac." "4E@86 The Day After." *Scary Monsters.* No. 47. Highwood, IL: Dennis Druktenis Publishing & Mail Order, Inc., June/July/August 2003. pp. 83–85.

3346 Edwards, Bill "Drac," and Deborah Painter. "The Stars Came Out For Forrest J Ackerman's Birthday." *Scary Monsters.* No. 47. Highwood, IL: Dennis Druktenis Publishing & Mail Order, Inc., June/July/August 2003. pp. 80–82. (coverage of Ackerman's 86th Birthday Celebration)

3347 Edwards, Malcolm J. "Ackerman, Forrest J." *The Encyclopedia of Science Fiction.* Peter Nicholls. London/New York: Granada, 1979. p. 16.

3348 Edwards, Malcolm J., and John Clute. "Ackerman, Forrest J(ames)." *The Encyclopedia of Science Fiction.* Ed. John Clute and Peter Nicholls. New York: St. Martin's, 1993. pp. 3–4.

3349 Ellers, Marjii. Letter. *Forry! A Special Publication Presented to Forrest J. Ackerman, on the Occasion of the 50th Anniversary of His Birthday, and the 40th Anniversary of His Discovery of Science-Fiction.* Ed. Fred Patten. Los Angeles, CA: Los Angeles Science Fiction Society/A Salamander Press publication, 1966. p. 67.

3350 Enriquez, Sam. "Sci Fi Museum Remains Just a Fantasy." *The Los Angeles Times.* 17 October 1985.

3351 Ernsting, Walter. "Forrest J Ackerman, Biggest Friend of German Fandom!" *Forry! A Special Publication Presented to Forrest J. Ackerman, on the Occasion of the 50th Anniversary of His Birthday, and the 40th Anniversary of His Discovery of Science-Fiction.* Ed. Fred Patten. Los Angeles, CA: Los Angeles Science Fiction Society/A Salamander Press publication, 1966. p. 73.

3352 Essman, Scott. untitled tribute. *Scarlet—The Film Magazine.* No. 3. June/July/August 2009. pp. 32–33.

3353 Evanier, Mark. "Forrest J Ackerman, R.I.P." <http://www.newsfromme.com/archives/2008_12_05.html#016305>

3354 Eyman, Scott. "Forry Ackerman's Fantastic, Horrific Museum" *Cleveland Plain-Dealer.* 16 December 1980.

3355 Farmer, Philip José. "To Forry Ackerman, the Wizard of Sci-Fi." *Lunacon '74 program book*; *Pearls from Peoria.* Burton, MI: Subterranean Press, 2006. (satirical tribute to Ackerman)

3356 Foss, Richard. "The Day After the Night of the Living Dead." *Los Angeles City Beat.* No. 21. Southland Publishing, 2003.

3357 Frank, Mark. "On Forry Ackerman." *Fantasia.* Seattle, WA: Bill Pugmire & Brian Wise. Dec. 1970. p. 6.

3358 Freer, Ian. "Fangs for the Memories." *Empire.* No. 240. UK: June 2009. pp. 164–169.

3359 French, Lawrence. "Supernal Dreams: Prince Sirki calls Forry to the grave." <http://cinefantastiqueonline.com/2008/12/08/supernal-dreams-prince-sirki-calls-forry-to-the-grave/> 8 December 2008.

3360 Garcia, Christopher J. "Forrest J. Ackerman." *The Drink Tank.* No. 191. Ed. Christopher J. Garcia. 2008. pp. 1–8.

3361 Glut, Don. "Thanks, Forry." *Famous Monsters Chronicles.* Ed. Dennis Daniel with Jim Knusch. [Co-editors: Greg Theakston, Bill Warren] Albany, NY: FantaCo Enterprises, 1991. pp. 128–129.

3362 Goingback, Owl. "Dark Light Focus: Forrest J Ackerman." *Writing Horror.* Ed. Mort Castle. Cincinnati: Writer's Digest Books, 1997. p. 155–156.

3363 Goldstone, Cynthia. "4 4ë." *Forry! A Special Publication Presented to Forrest J. Ackerman, on the Occasion of the 50th Anniversary of His Birthday, and the 40th Anniversary of His Discovery of Science-Fiction.* Ed. Fred Patten. Los Angeles, CA: Los Angeles Science Fiction Society/A Salamander Press publication, 1966. p. 50.

3364 Gourlay, Jack. "In Memoriam: FORREST J ACKERMAN." *Scary Monsters.* No. 70. Ed. Dennis J. Druktenis. Highwood, IL: Dennis Druktenis Publishing & Mail Order, Inc., April 2009. pp. 100.

3365 Greene, James. "Dedication." *House of Ackerman: A Photographic Tour of the Legendary Ackermansion.* Al Astrella and James Greene. Baltimore: Midnight Marquee Press, 2010. pp. 11–12.

3366 Griffin, Prof. Anton. "The Professor's Podium: The Man of Magic, Mystery and Wonder Is Gone!" *Scary Monsters.* No. 71. Highwood, IL: Dennis Druktenis Publishing & Mail Order, Inc., June/July/August 2009. pp. 41–42.

3367 Hamilton, Edmond, and Leigh Brackett. Letter. *Forry! A Special Publication Presented to Forrest J. Ackerman, on the Occasion of the 50th Anniversary of His Birthday, and the 40th Anniversary of His Discovery of Science-Fiction.* Ed. Fred Patten. Los Angeles, CA: Los Angeles Science Fiction Society/A Salamander Press publication, 1966. p. 20.

3368 Hammond, Barry. "Children of the Ackermonster: Tribute to Forrest J. Ackerman." *On Spec.* Vol. 20. No. 3. [Whole]No. 75. Ed. Diane L. Walton. Edmonton: The Copper Pig Writers Society, Winter 2008/09. pp. 5–9.

3369 Hanke, Ken. "Forrest J Ackerman." *Scarlet—The Film Magazine.* No. 3. June/July/August 2009. pp. 30, 32–35

3370 Harris, Lee. "Fun Forry Facts to Know and Tell." *Scary Monsters.* No. 70. Ed. Dennis J.

Druktenis. Highwood, IL: Dennis Druktenis Publishing & Mail Order, Inc., April 2009. pp. 70–71.

3371 Haydock, Ron. "From Fandom to Infinity." *Escape! (Into the Whirls of Fandom).* Vol. 1. No. 1. Ed. Ron Haydock & Larry Byrd. Santa Ana, CA: West Coast Zines, January 1961. pp. 13–18.

3372 Hertz, John. [untitled tribute.] *Vanamonde.* No. 853. Ed. John Hertz. 30 September 2009. pp. 1–2; *Uchuujin.* No. 202.

3373 Hillinger, Charles. "FANTASY BUFF: Weird Creatures Crowd Wizard in Monster Mansion." *Los Angeles Times.* Los Angeles, CA: 8 April 1969. B1 p. 2.

3374 Johnstone, Ted. "Forry, Forry, Hallelujah!" *Forry! A Special Publication Presented to Forrest J. Ackerman, on the Occasion of the 50th Anniversary of His Birthday, and the 40th Anniversary of His Discovery of Science-Fiction.* Ed. Fred Patten. Los Angeles, CA: Los Angeles Science Fiction Society/A Salamander Press publication, 1966. pp. 71–72.

3375 Jones, Stephen. "The Ackermonster and Me." *Locus.* No. 576. Vol. 62. No. 1. Ed. Charles N. Brown. January 2009. p. 60.

3376 Jones, Stephen. "The Man Who Bought Bela Lugosi's Trousers or, Ghouls Just Want to Have Fun." *Science Fiction Chronicle.* Vol. 14. No. 12. September 1993. pp. 28, 30. (on the 35th Anniversary *Famous Monsters* convention)

3377 Kemp, Earl & Nancy. "Forrieman Night!" *Forry! A Special Publication Presented to Forrest J. Ackerman, on the Occasion of the 50th Anniversary of His Birthday, and the 40th Anniversary of His Discovery of Science-Fiction.* Ed. Fred Patten. Los Angeles, CA: Los Angeles Science Fiction Society/A Salamander Press publication, 1966. p. 36.

3378 Keppel, Bruce. "Science-Fantasy Artifacts: City Accepts 'Monstrous Collection.'" *Los Angeles Times.* 8 December 1979. (on Mayor Bradley's tentative acceptance of the donation of Ackerman's collection to the City of Los Angeles)

3379 King, Stephen. "The Importance of Being Forry." *Forrest J Ackerman Presents Mr. Monster's Movie Gold: A Treasure Trove of Imagi-Movies.* Ed. Hank Stine. Virginia Beach, VA: Donning Co., 1981. pp. 8–12.

3380 Kirk, Daniel. "How I Met the Man Behind Famous Monsters of Filmland!" *Scary Monsters.* No. 70. Ed. Dennis J. Druktenis. Highwood, IL: Dennis Druktenis Publishing & Mail Order, Inc., April 2009. pp. 52–57. (tribute written by one of the fans whom Ackerman visited on his 1963 cross-country trip and who later illustrated for the revived *Famous Monsters*)

3381 Konigsberg, Eph. "Fahrenheit 98.6 or, The Telemetered Man." *Forry! A Special Publication Presented to Forrest J. Ackerman, on the Occasion of the 50th Anniversary of His Birthday, and the 40th Anniversary of His Discovery of Science-Fiction.* Ed. Fred Patten. Los Angeles, CA: Los Angeles Science Fiction Society/A Salamander Press publication, 1966. pp. 18–20.

3382 Kurta, Jeff. "Sirki Takes a Prince." *Scary Monsters.* No. 70. Ed. Dennis J. Druktenis. Highwood, IL: Dennis Druktenis Publishing & Mail Order, Inc., April 2009. p. 91.

3383 Kyle, David A. "A Fan for All Seasons." *Mimosa.* No. 23. Gaithersburg, MD: January 1999.

3384 Kyle, David A. "Forrest J Ackerman." Coker, John L., Ed. *A Gathering to Honor Forrest J Ackerman Presented by David A. Kyle and Friends.* Orlando, FL: Days of Wonder Publishers, 2006.

3385 Labbe, Rod. "Ack Attack: A Heapin' helpin' of the Fantastic!" *Scary Monsters.* No. 71. Highwood, IL: Dennis Druktenis Publishing & Mail Order, Inc., June/July/August 2009. pp. 90–94.

3386 Labbe, Rod. "Famous Monsters and Me." *Scary Monsters.* No. 39. Highwood, IL: Dennis Druktenis Publishing & Mail Order, Inc., June/July/August 2001. pp. 23–26.

3387 Laemmle, Carla. untitled tribute. *Scarlet—The Film Magazine.* No. 3. June/July/August 2009. p. 34.

3388 Landis, John. "Forry Ackerman: A Loyal and Staunch Friend." *Comic-Con Souvenir Book.* No. 40. 2009. p. 215.

3389 Landis, John. "Introduction." *House of Ackerman: A Photographic Tour of the Legendary Ackermansion.* Al Astrella and James Greene. Baltimore: Midnight Marquee Press, 2010. pp. 13–14.

3390 Langford, David. "The Ackermansion Is Empty." *SFX magazine.* No. 181. April 2009; *Starcombing.* Rockville, MD: Cosmos Books/Wildside Press LLC, 2009. pp. 218–220.

3391 Legge, Michael. "FM: No Static at ALL!" *Scary Monsters.* No. 71. Highwood, IL: Dennis Druktenis Publishing & Mail Order, Inc., June/July/August 2009. pp. 39–40.

3392 Leggett, Paul. untitled tribute. *Scarlet—The Film Magazine.* No. 3. June/July/August 2009. p. 35.

3393 Leiber, Fritz. "Musing from a Parallel Timestream." *Famous Monster, Forry Ackerman.* Byrd, Larry & Ron Haydock (Eds.).

3394 Liebscher, Walt. "4E is a Five-Foot Shelf." *Forry! A Special Publication Presented to Forrest J. Ackerman, on the Occasion of the 50th Anniversary of His*

Birthday, and the 40th Anniversary of His Discovery of Science-Fiction. Ed. Fred Patten. Los Angeles, CA: Los Angeles Science Fiction Society/A Salamander Press publication, 1966. p. 66.

3395 Lilley, Jessie. "Come Out and Play with Me." *Scary Monsters.* No. 70. Ed. Dennis J. Druktenis. Highwood, IL: Dennis Druktenis Publishing & Mail Order, Inc., April 2009. p. 92.

3396 Linaweaver, Brad. "Forry-Word to the Future." *Tropicon III.* 1984.

3397 Linaweaver, Brad. "The Freedom to Remember." *Scary Monsters.* No. 70. Ed. Dennis J. Druktenis. Highwood, IL: Dennis Druktenis Publishing & Mail Order, Inc., April 2009. p. 96.

3398 Lindsay, Ethel. Letter. *Forry! A Special Publication Presented to Forrest J. Ackerman, on the Occasion of the 50th Anniversary of His Birthday, and the 40th Anniversary of His Discovery of Science-Fiction.* Ed. Fred Patten. Los Angeles, CA: Los Angeles Science Fiction Society/A Salamander Press publication, 1966. p. 44

3399 Liu, Caitlin. "Living in a Time Machine." *The Los Angeles Times.* 12 August 2001. (on Ackerman's collection, open houses)

3400 Locke, George. "Collecting..." *Forry! A Special Publication Presented to Forrest J. Ackerman, on the Occasion of the 50th Anniversary of His Birthday, and the 40th Anniversary of His Discovery of Science-Fiction.* Ed. Fred Patten. Los Angeles, CA: Los Angeles Science Fiction Society/A Salamander Press publication, 1966. pp. 59–63.

3401 Lowndes, Robert A. W. Letter. *Forry! A Special Publication Presented to Forrest J. Ackerman, on the Occasion of the 50th Anniversary of His Birthday, and the 40th Anniversary of His Discovery of Science-Fiction.* Ed. Fred Patten. Los Angeles, CA: Los Angeles Science Fiction Society/A Salamander Press publication, 1966. p. 47.

3402 Lucas, Tim. "Childhood's End: Forrest Ackerman 1916–2008." *Video Watchdog.* No. 146. December/January 2009. pp. 4–5.

3403 MacGregor, Hilary E. STYLE & CULTURE: "Welcome to his planet; Forrest J Ackerman, perhaps science fiction's greatest collector, keeps a dwindling trove open to the public." *Los Angeles Times.* 6 January 2003. E.1;

3404 Madle, Robert A. "Inside Science Fiction." *Dynamic Science Fiction.* Vol. 1. No. 3. NY: Columbia Publications, 1953. pp. 105–110. [Ackerman mentioned p. 106.]

3405 Maronie, Samuel J. "In His Mansion, Every Day Is Hallowe'en." *St. Louis Post-Dispatch.* 26 September 1980.

3406 Martin, Robert. "Forry Memories." *Scary Monsters.* No. 70. Ed. Dennis J. Druktenis. Highwood, IL: Dennis Druktenis Publishing & Mail Order, Inc., April 2009. pp. 58–60.

3407 May, B. Hal. "Forrest J Ackerman." *Contemporary Authors.* Volume 102. 1980. Detroit: Gale Research Co., 1980. pp. 12–13.

3408 McCarty, Michael, and Greg F. Gifune[?]. "Interview — Biography of Forry Ackerman." *Mindmares.* No. 8. Ed. Tracy Martin. Brush Prairie, WA: Fall 1999.

3409 McCormack, Ford. "Message from a Mediocre Monster." *Forry! A Special Publication Presented to Forrest J. Ackerman, on the Occasion of the 50th Anniversary of His Birthday, and the 40th Anniversary of His Discovery of Science-Fiction.* Ed. Fred Patten. Los Angeles, CA: Los Angeles Science Fiction Society/A Salamander Press publication, 1966. pp. 51–52.

3410 McLellan, Dennis. "Forrest J Ackerman, Writer-Editor Who Coined 'Sci-Fi,' Dies at 92." *The Los Angeles Times.* 6 December 2008.

3411 McNulty, Thomas. "Legacy of the Ackermonster! an homage to Forrest Ackerman." *Scary Monsters.* No. 38. Highwood, IL: Dennis Druktenis Publishing & Mail Order, Inc., March/April/May 2001. pp. 15–19.

3412 Michaels, Peter. "Famished Monsters of Filmland." *The World of Bela Lugosi.* No. 3. Ed. Gary D. Rhodes. April 1988. p. 4. (on the efforts to find permanent housing for Ackerman's collection)

3413 Michaels, Peter, with Isaac Asimov, Bela Lugosi Jr., and Robert Bloch. "Michaels' Movie Madness." *The World of Bela Lugosi.* No. 4. August 1988. pp. 4–5. (further support for a permanent Ackerman museum)

3414 Moe, Joe. "AckerAfterword: The Monster Demands a Housemate!" *House of Ackerman: A Photographic Tour of the Legendary Ackermansion.* Al Astrella and James Greene. Baltimore: Midnight Marquee Press, 2010. pp. 139–140.

3415 Moe, Joe. "A Famous Monster in Filmland." *Famous Monsters of Filmland.* No. 250. Movieland Classics, LLC., 2010. pp. 4–6.

3416 Moe, Joe. "Foreword: Marching to the Beast of a Different Drummer." *Forry: The Life of Forrest J Ackerman.* Deborah Painter. Jefferson, NC: McFarland & Company, 2011. pp. 1–3.

3417 Moe, Joe. "Friend, Good!" *Rue Morgue Magazine.* No. 83. Toronto, Ontario: Marrs Media Inc., October 2008. pp. p. 17–18.

3418 Moe, Joe. "Imagine a World Without Monsters?" *Famous Monsters of Filmland.* No. 251. Ed. Jessie Lilley and Michael Heisler. Movieland Classics, LLC., July 2010.

3419 Moe, Joe. "In the Beginning, There Was Pulp." *Famous Monsters of Filmland: The Annotated No. 1.* Movieland Classics, LLC, 2011. p. 6.

3420 Moe, Joe. "One Moe Ode to 4E." *Scarlet—The Film Magazine.* No. 3. June/July/August 2009. p. 31.

3421 Moe, Joe. "To Collect and Serve." *Famous Monsters of Filmland: The Annotated No. 1.* Movieland Classics, LLC, 2011. p. 5.

3422 Moffatt, Len. "Forry: Fantastic Traveler." *Forry! A Special Publication Presented to Forrest J. Ackerman, on the Occasion of the 50th Anniversary of His Birthday, and the 40th Anniversary of His Discovery of Science-Fiction.* Ed. Fred Patten. Los Angeles, CA: Los Angeles Science Fiction Society/A Salamander Press publication, 1966. pp. 12–14.

3423 Mollard, Angela. "Roles In Lots of Movies but He's No Star." *NZ Herald.* 29 May 1991. Section 1. p. 20.

3424 Mordair. *Forry! A Special Publication Presented to Forrest J. Ackerman, on the Occasion of the 50th Anniversary of His Birthday, and the 40th Anniversary of His Discovery of Science-Fiction.* Ed. Fred Patten. Los Angeles, CA: Los Angeles Science Fiction Society/A Salamander Press publication, 1966. pp. 38–44.

3425 Murphy, Suzanne. "The Godfather of Sci-Fi." *Westways.* July 1987. pp. 36–38; *Futures Past: A Visual Guidebook to Science Fiction History.* Vol. 1. No. 1. Ed. Jim Emerson. Convoy, OH: 1992. p. 40.

3426 Murray, Doug. "It's All My Parents' Fault!" *Famous Monsters Chronicles.* Ed. Dennis Daniel with Jim Knusch. [Co-editors: Greg Theakston, Bill Warren] Albany, NY: FantaCo Enterprises, 1991. pp. 131–133.

3427 Naha, Ed. "Growing Up a Monster." *Famous Monsters Chronicles.* Ed. Dennis Daniel with Jim Knusch. [Co-editors: Greg Theakston, Bill Warren] Albany, NY: FantaCo Enterprises, 1991. p. 135.

3428 Nahmod, David Alex. "FORRY: My Own Observations of a Gentleman." *Scary Monsters.* No. 70. Ed. Dennis J. Druktenis. Highwood, IL: Dennis Druktenis Publishing & Mail Order, Inc., April 2009. p. 106.

3429 Nesvadba, Josef. Letter. *Forry! A Special Publication Presented to Forrest J. Ackerman, on the Occasion of the 50th Anniversary of His Birthday, and the 40th Anniversary of His Discovery of Science-Fiction. Ed. Fred Patten.* Los Angeles, CA: Los Angeles Science Fiction Society/A Salamander Press publication, 1966. p. 11.

3430 Neville, Kris. "Among the Amazon Headhunters." *Forry! A Special Publication Presented to Forrest J. Ackerman, on the Occasion of the 50th An-* niversary of His Birthday, and the 40th Anniversary of His Discovery of Science-Fiction.* Ed. Fred Patten. Los Angeles, CA: Los Angeles Science Fiction Society/A Salamander Press publication, 1966. pp. 21–29. (short story)

3431 Nolan, Tom. "Through Space and Time with Forrest J Ackerman." *New West.* Vol. 5? No. Beverly Hills, CA: New West Communications Corp.???, 28 January 1980. pp. 128?-13?

3432 Nolan, William F. "Two words — Meaning Friend." in: Waite, Ronald N. "Enchanted Forrest." *Polaris One.* Ed: Colin White and J. Allyson Johnson. Philadelphia, PA: Starfire Press. Vol. 2. No. 1. Spring 1980. pp. 10–11.

3433 Nolan, William F. "A Very Rainy Evening — and other Ackermemories." *Forry! A Special Publication Presented to Forrest J. Ackerman, on the Occasion of the 50th Anniversary of His Birthday, and the 40th Anniversary of His Discovery of Science-Fiction.* Ed. Fred Patten. Los Angeles, CA: Los Angeles Science Fiction Society/A Salamander Press publication, 1966. pp. 48–49.

3434 Norman, John. "A Letter to a Friend, Which He Will Never Read." *Tales of the Time Travelers: Adventures of Forrest J Ackerman and Julius Schwartz.* Ed. John L. Coker, III. Orlando, FL: Days of Wonder Publishers, 2009.

3435 Norman, John. "The Search for Forrest J Ackerman." *Tales of the Time Travelers: Adventures of Forrest J Ackerman and Julius Schwartz.* Ed. John L. Coker, III. Orlando, FL: Days of Wonder Publishers, 2009. (Foreword)

3436 Nuetzel, Charles. "A Twelve-Year Tour with Forry." *Forry! A Special Publication Presented to Forrest J. Ackerman, on the Occasion of the 50th Anniversary of His Birthday, and the 40th Anniversary of His Discovery of Science-Fiction.* Ed. Fred Patten. Los Angeles, CA: Los Angeles Science Fiction Society/A Salamander Press publication, 1966. pp. 68–70.

3437 Painter, Deborah. "Ackermuseum Treasures." *Scary Monsters.* No. 38. Highwood, IL: Dennis Druktenis Publishing & Mail Order, Inc., March/April/May 2001. pp. 26–28.

3438 Painter, Deborah. "The Measure of a Star: A Tribute to Forrest J Ackerman." *Movie Collector's World.* No. 733. July 2009.

3439 Painter, Deborah. "My Book About Dr. Acula." *2010 Scary Monsters Yearbook, Monster Memories.* No. 18. Highwood, IL: Dennis Druktenis Publishing & Mail Order, Inc., March 2010.

3440 Painter, Deborah. "A Tribute to Forry Ackerman at the American Cinematheque. *Scary Monsters.* Highwood, IL: Dennis Druktenis Publishing & Mail Order, Inc., No. 71. June/July/August 2009. pp. 95–99.

3441 Painter, Deborah, Arlene Domkowski, Jeff Barnes, and Cortney Skinner. "Forry Days." *Scary Monsters*. No. 70. Ed. Dennis J. Druktenis. Highwood, IL: Dennis Druktenis Publishing & Mail Order, Inc., April 2009. pp. 65–69.

3442 Palmer, Randy. "The Angel Among Monsters." *Famous Monsters of Filmland*. No. 191. New York: Warren Publishing Company, March 1983. pp. 26–29.

3443 Palmer, Randy. "FM, FJA 'N Me." *Famous Monsters Chronicles*. Ed. Dennis Daniel with Jim Knusch. [Co-editors: Greg Theakston, Bill Warren] Albany, NY: FantaCo Enterprises, 1991. pp. 143–144.

3444 Parla, Paul. "Monster Memories of the Ackermansion." *Scary Monsters*. No. 70. Ed. Dennis J. Druktenis. Highwood, IL: Dennis Druktenis Publishing & Mail Order, Inc., April 2009. pp. 98–99.

3445 Patten, Fred. "Introduction." *Forry! A Special Publication Presented to Forrest J. Ackerman, on the Occasion of the 50th Anniversary of His Birthday, and the 40th Anniversary of His Discovery of Science-Fiction*. Ed. Fred Patten. Los Angeles, CA: Los Angeles Science Fiction Society/A Salamander Press publication, 1966. pp. 7–8.

3446 Pederson, Petrov. (Con Pederson) "The Battle Hymn of the Fanation: The National Fanthem." *The Outlander*. No. 2. May 1949. (lyrical tribute to Ackerman set to the tune of "The Battle Hymn of the Republic")

3447 Pinckard, Terri. "You Can't See the Forrest for the Tease!..." *Forry! A Special Publication Presented to Forrest J. Ackerman, on the Occasion of the 50th Anniversary of His Birthday, and the 40th Anniversary of His Discovery of Science-Fiction*. Ed. Fred Patten. Los Angeles, CA: Los Angeles Science Fiction Society/A Salamander Press publication, 1966. pp. 16–17;

3448 Pinckard, Terri E. "The Message of Scientifictionus Immortalis." *Lunacon '74 program book*.

3449 Platt, Charles. "Inside Science Fiction: Ackermania." *The Magazine of Fantasy and Science Fiction*. Vol. 74. No. 5. May 1988. pp. 93–98. (on Platt's meetings with Ackerman, 1987 auction)

3450 Pugmire, Bill Jr. "Forrest J Ackerman." *Fantasia*. Seattle, WA: Bill Pugmire & Brian Wise. Dec. 1970. p. 5.

3451 Ray, Fred Olen. untitled tribute. *Scarlet— The Film Magazine*. No. 3. June/July/August 2009. p. 33.

3452 Ray, Fred Olen. "Wanted: More Readers Like Fred Olen Ray." *Famous Monsters Chronicles*.

Ed. Dennis Daniel with Jim Knusch. [Co-editors: Greg Theakston, Bill Warren] Albany, NY: FantaCo Enterprises, 1991. pp. 137–138.

3453 Reynolds, Neal Clark. "Monster Movies and Fandom." *Forry! A Special Publication Presented to Forrest J. Ackerman, on the Occasion of the 50th Anniversary of His Birthday, and the 40th Anniversary of His Discovery of Science-Fiction*. Ed. Fred Patten. Los Angeles, CA: Los Angeles Science Fiction Society/A Salamander Press publication, 1966. pp. 34–35.

3454 Rhine, Robert Steven. "A Is for Ackerman." *Girls and Corpses Magazine*. Vol. 2. No. 6. Fall 2008.

3455 Rhodes, Garydon L. "Forrest J Ackerman: Master of Monster Memories." *Magick Theatre*. No. 8. Ed. Raymond F. Young. Baldwin, NY: 1987. pp. 12–13.

3456 Richardson, Mike. "Mike Richardson and John Landis on Forrest Ackerman 3/25/09." <http://www.darkhorse.com/Press-Releases/1698/Mike-Richardson-and-John-Landis-on-Forrest-Ackerman-3-25-09>

3457 Rogers, John. "Sci-Fi Writer Keeps Fantasy Alive." (Associated Press article)

3458 Sackett, Sam. "The Ackerman Story." *Fantastic Worlds*. Vol. 1. No. 2. Fall-Winter 1952. pp. 5–13.

3459 Schlück, Thomas. Letter. *Forry! A Special Publication Presented to Forrest J. Ackerman, on the Occasion of the 50th Anniversary of His Birthday, and the 40th Anniversary of His Discovery of Science-Fiction*. Ed. Fred Patten. Los Angeles, CA: Los Angeles Science Fiction Society/A Salamander Press publication, 1966. p. 65.

3460 Schoepflin, H. V. Letter. *Forry! A Special Publication Presented to Forrest J. Ackerman, on the Occasion of the 50th Anniversary of His Birthday, and the 40th Anniversary of His Discovery of Science-Fiction*. Ed. Fred Patten. Los Angeles, CA: Los Angeles Science Fiction Society/A Salamander Press publication, 1966. p. 53. (author Harl Vincent)

3461 Scrimm, Angus. untitled tribute. *Scarlet— The Film Magazine*. No. 3. June/July/August 2009. p. 34.

3462 Sherman, Jerry. "Mr. Sci-Fi." *Hollywood Post*. Ed. Merlin Snider. Hollywood, CA: August 1983. pp. 4, 6–11.

3463 Shuster, Fred. "Addams family, move over." *L.A. Life*. 31 May 1989. pp. 17–18. (*Los Angeles Daily News* supplement)

3464 Shuster, Fred. "Creature-feature gems, from capes to 'Kong.'" *L.A. Life*. 31 May 1989. p. 18.

3465 Sielski, Mark & Marie. "Our FJA Tributes." *Scary Monsters.* No. 70. Ed. Dennis J. Druktenis. Highwood, IL: Dennis Druktenis Publishing & Mail Order, Inc., April 2009. pp. 76–79.

3466 Silver, Steven H. "Forry and Me: A Memoir of Forrest J Ackerman." *The Drink Tank.* No. 191. Ed. Christopher J. Garcia. 2008. p. 3.

3467 Skerchock, John. "Forry Ackerman: I Wish I'd never met Him." *Scary Monsters.* No. 70. Ed. Dennis J. Druktenis. Highwood, IL: Dennis Druktenis Publishing & Mail Order, Inc., April 2009. pp. 80–83.

3468 Slick, Kevin. "Forry's Fave Five." *Monster Bash.* No. 7. 2007. pp. 20–23.

3469 Slick, Kevin. "untitled tribute." *Scarlet— The Film Magazine.* No. 3. June/July/August 2009. p. 33.

3470 Smith, April. "Citizen Pain." *Rolling Stone.* No. 159. Ed. Jann S. Wenner. Straight Arrow, 25 April 1974. pp. 32–34, 36, 38. (on Warren publishing, contains comments from Ackerman)

3471 Sneary, Rick. Letter. *Forry! A Special Publication Presented to Forrest J. Ackerman, on the Occasion of the 50th Anniversary of His Birthday, and the 40th Anniversary of His Discovery of Science-Fiction.* Ed. Fred Patten. Los Angeles, CA: Los Angeles Science Fiction Society/A Salamander Press publication, 1966. p. 55.

3472 Snider, Merlin, and Jay Hammeran. "Down in Forryland." *Hollywood Post.* Ed. Merlin Snider. Hollywood, CA: August 1983. pp. 5–6.

3473 Spinrad, Norman. "4E's Fantastic Ackermansion." *The Los Angeles Flyer.* 25 May 1972.

3474 Statzer, Bob. "Memories of FAMOUS MONSTERS." *Scary Monsters.* No. 70. Ed. Dennis J. Druktenis. Highwood, IL: Dennis Druktenis Publishing & Mail Order, Inc., April 2009. pp. 103–105.

3475 Sullivan, Tim. "the last famous monster: Forrest J. Ackerman's collected life." *Go Figure!* Vol. 1. No. 1. July-August 1997. Los Angeles, CA: Go Figure! Publications, 1997. pp. 55–60.

3476 Svehla, Gary J. "Forry Ackerman." *Fantasia.* Seattle, WA: Bill Pugmire & Brian Wise. Seattle: Dec. 1970. pp. 4–5.

3477 Tackett, Roy. "Of Time and the Ack." *Forry! A Special Publication Presented to Forrest J. Ackerman, on the Occasion of the 50th Anniversary of His Birthday, and the 40th Anniversary of His Discovery of Science-Fiction.* Ed. Fred Patten. Los Angeles, CA: Los Angeles Science Fiction Society/A Salamander Press publication, 1966. pp. 31–32.

3478 Temple, William F. "Dear Bill." *Old Bones.* Ed. Pugmire. p. 6. (letter in praise of Ackerman)

3479 Theakston, Greg. "The House That Ack Built." *Pure Images.* Vol. 2. No. 1. Ed. Greg Theakston. Pure Imagination, 1986. p. 17.

3480 Thiel, David. "Sci-Fi Forry's a Jolly Good Fellow." *The Drink Tank.* No. 191. Ed. Christopher J. Garcia. 2008. pp. 4–5.

3481 Timpone, Anthony. "One Hundred Most Important People in Science Fiction/Fantasy: Forrest J. Ackerman." *Starlog.* No. 100. O'Quinn Studios, November 1985. p. 39

3482 Tonik, Albert. *A Visit to Two Museums. Science Fiction Collector/Megavore: the Journal of Popular Fiction.* No. 10. Ed. J. Grant Thiessen. Neche, ND: Pandora's Books Ltd, August 1980. p. 34. (Ackermansion and San Francisco Academy of Comic Art).

3483 Triman, Tom. "The Forry Story; A Tribute to Forrest J Ackerman." *Scary Monsters.* No. 70. Ed. Dennis J. Druktenis. Highwood, IL: Dennis Druktenis Publishing & Mail Order, Inc., April 2009. pp. 17–24.

3484 Tuck, Donald H. "Ackerman, Forrest J." *The Encyclopedia of Science Fiction and Fantasy Through 1968: A Bibliographic Survey of the Fields of Science Fiction, Fantasy, and Weird Fiction Through 1968. Vol. I: Who's Who, A–L.* Chicago: Advent Publishers, 1974. pp. 1–2.

3485 [Unsigned.] "Ackerman Auction Successful." *Locus: The Newspaper of the Science Fiction Field.* Vol. 21. No. 1. Whole No. 324. Ed. Charles N. Brown. Oakland, CA: January 1988. p. 5.

3486 [Unsigned.] "Biggest Kid in Los Feliz." *Los Felizian.* Winter 1991.

3487 [Unsigned.] "Collector, Actor, Agent and Sci-Fi'S No. 1 Fan." *San Jose Mercury News.* 9 December 1997.

3488 [Unsigned.] "Forrest Ackerman Rightly Called 'Minister of Sinister.'" *Daily Intelligencer Montgomery Co. Record.* Friday, 14 February 1986. Page 13 B.

3489 [Unsigned.] "Forrest J Ackerman." *The Sunday Telegraph.* 7 December 2008.

3490 [Unsigned.] "Forrest J Ackerman (1916–2008)" *Locus.* No. 576. Vol. 62. No. 1. Ed. Charles N. Brown. January 2009. p. 5.

3491 [Unsigned.] "Forrest J Ackerman, 92, Dies; Coined the Term 'Sci-Fi.'" *The Washington Post.* Vol. 132, No. 2. 7 December 2008. p. C7.

3492 [Unsigned.] "Forrest J. Ackerman: Science-Fiction Writer, Editor and Literary Agent." *The New York Times.* 9 December 2008.

3493 [Unsigned.] "Forry's Fantastic Museum." *Swank*. Vol. 21. No. 4. Ed. Christopher Watson. Magnum-Royal Publications, Inc., April 1974. pp. 90–91.

3494 [Unsigned.] "Goodbye Forry Forrest J Ackerman 1916–2008." *Comic-Con Magazine*. San Diego, CA: San Diego Comic-Con International, Winter 2009.

3495 [Unsigned.] "He's 'Mr. Science Fiction.'" *The Burbank Leader*. 6 December 1997.

3496 [Unsigned.] "Meet the Fan." *Stardust*. Vol. 2. No. 2. Ed. William Lawrence Hamling. Chicago: November 1940. pp. 25–26.

3497 [Unsigned.] "Monster-Movie Guru Wins Appeal." *Los Angeles Daily Journal*. 13 November 2002.

3498 [Unsigned.] "Monsters on the Block." *Locus: The Newspaper of the Science Fiction Field*. Vol. 21. No. 1. Whole No. 324. Ed. Charles N. Brown. Oakland, CA: January 1988. p. 1. (photograph with caption of Ackerman amongst items offered in the Guernsey's auction)

3499 [Unsigned.] "Nobody Rescues Collection Depicting Sci-Fi Era." *San Diego Union Tribune*. 20 September 2002

3500 [Unsigned.] "RIP Forrest J Ackerman." Friday, 5 December 2008 04:52 PM <http://www. fangoria.com/home/news/15-rip/743-rip-forrest-j-ackerman.html>

3501 [Unsigned.] "Scene — When Forrest J. Ackerman Has an Open House, It's Just a Horror Show." *People Weekly*. Chicago: Time, 12 April 1999. p. 110.

3502 [Unsigned.] "Sci-Fi's Grand Old Man, Forrest J Ackerman, Dies." (Associated Press article)

3503 [Unsigned.] STYLE & CULTURE: "The sci-fi museum that never was." *Los Angeles Times*. 6 January 2003. E. 14.

3504 [Unsigned.] "Things That Go Bump in the Night Sci-fi Editor Collects Horror and Fantasy Items." *Glendale News Press*. 23 June 1980.

3505 [Unsigned.] "Whos [*sic*] the Forrest of Them All?" *Screem*. No. 1. Ed. Darryl Mayeski. Wilkes-Barre, PA: Screem Publishing, 1993.

3506 Valley, Richard. "Our Founding Fathers: Forrest J Ackerman, James Warren, Jeremy Brett, and Zacherley." *Scarlet Street*. No. 50. 2004. pp. 16–17. (features a brief congratulatory note from Ackerman on p. 16)

3507 Van Hise, James. "The End of the Ackermansion." *The Road to Veletrium*. No. 47. Yucca Valley, CA: James van Hise, October 2002. (produced for the 177th mailing of the Robert E. Howard United Press Association)

3508 van Vogt, A. E. "Who Is Forrest J Ackerman?" *Lunacon '74 program book*.

3509 Vertlieb, Steve. "The Most 'Famous Monster' of Them All: A Personal Remembrance of Forrest J. Ackerman." <http://thethunderchild.com/Movies/VertliebViews/ForryAckermanTribute.html>; as *Rondo Nominee: The Most "Famous Monster" of Them All*. March 7th, 2010; *From Forry Ackerman to Orson Welles: The Views and Reviews of Steve Vertlieb*. Sacred Poet Press, 2010.

3510 Waite, Ronald N. "Enchanted Forrest." *Polaris One*. Ed: Colin White and J. Allyson Johnson. Philadelphia, PA: Starfire Press. Vol. 2. No. 1. Spring 1980. (profile containing quoted correspondence regarding Ackerman from a variety of figures)

3511 Wallace, Lewis. "Forrest J Ackerman, the Man Who Coined Term 'Sci-Fi,' Dies at 92." <http://www.wired.com/underwire/2008/12/forrest-j-acker/#> 5 December 2008.

3512 Walters, Timothy M. "Monster Memories of Forrest J Ackerman." *Scary Monsters*. No. 71. Highwood, IL: Dennis Druktenis Publishing & Mail Order, Inc., June/July/August 2009. pp. 85–87.

3513 Warren, Bill. "Famous Monsters, Forry Ackerman, & Me." *Forrest J Ackerman Famous Monster of Filmland #2*. Volume II (Issues #51–100) Universal City, CA: Hollywood Publishing Company, 1991. p. 8.

3514 Warren, Bill. "Famous Monsters, Forry Ackerman, and Other Stuff." *Famous Monster Chronicles*. Ed. Dennis Daniel with Jim Knusch. Albany, NY: FantaCo Enterprises, 1991. pp. 165–166.

3515 Warren, Bill. "Forry Before FM." *Scary Monsters*. No. 70. Ed. Dennis J. Druktenis. Highwood, IL: Dennis Druktenis Publishing & Mail Order, Inc., April 2009. pp. 93–95.

3516 Warren, James. "The Best Friend a Monster Fan Ever Had." *Famous Monsters of Filmland Convention Book*. Warren, November 1974.

3517 Warren, James. "Guest of Honor Forrest J Ackerman If He Didn't Exist, Edison & Wankel Couldn't Have Invented Him." *Lunacon '74 program book*.

3518 Wasserman, Harry. [Untitled Tribute.] *Fantasia*. Seattle, WA: Bill Pugmire & Brian Wise. Seattle: Dec. 1970. p. 7.

3519 Weber, Bruce. "Forrest J Ackerman, High Elder of Fantasy Fans, Is Dead at 92." (Obituary). *New York Times*. 6 December 2008. p. A19.

3520 Weiss, Brett. "My Very Scary Week with Uncle Forry." *Scary Monsters Magazine*. No. 61. Highwood, IL: Dennis Druktenis Publishing & Mail Order, Inc., January 2007. pp. 43–44.

3521 White, Alan. "Forrest J Ackerman." *Locus*. No. 576. Vol. 62. No. 1. Ed. Charles N. Brown. January 2009. pp. 60–61.

3522 Wiegand, Steve. "Fear Factors–With a World-Renowned Collection of the Macabre and the Fantastic, Forrest Ackerman is Destined to Fill the Future with Horror." *Sacramento Bee*. 27 October 1992. p. E1.

3523 William, Robert Moore. Letter. *Forry! A Special Publication Presented to Forrest J. Ackerman, on the Occasion of the 50th Anniversary of His Birthday, and the 40th Anniversary of His Discovery of Science-Fiction*. Ed. Fred Patten. Los Angeles, CA: Los Angeles Science Fiction Society/A Salamander Press publication, 1966. p. 11.

3524 Wollheim, Donald A. "Sour Note." *Lunacon '74 program book*.

3525 Wood, Edward. "The Future of Science Fiction." *Forry! A Special Publication Presented to Forrest J. Ackerman, on the Occasion of the 50th Anniversary of His Birthday, and the 40th Anniversary of His Discovery of Science-Fiction*. Ed. Fred Patten. Los Angeles, CA: Los Angeles Science Fiction Society/A Salamander Press publication, 1966. pp. 45–46.

3526 Yerke, T. Bruce. Letter. *Forry! A Special Publication Presented to Forrest J. Ackerman, on the Occasion of the 50th Anniversary of His Birthday, and the 40th Anniversary of His Discovery of Science-Fiction*. Ed. Fred Patten. Los Angeles, CA: Los Angeles Science Fiction Society/A Salamander Press publication, 1966. p. 37.

REVIEWS OF ACKERMAN MATERIAL

3527 Review of *Best Science Fiction for 1973* (New York: Ace, 1973): Delap, Richard. "The 'Best' Anthologies: 1973." *The WSFA Journal* (*The Journal of the Washington S.F. Association*). No. 84. December 1974.

3528 Review of *Best Science Fiction for 1973* (New York: Ace, 1973): Futoran, Gail C. *Luna Monthly*. No. 56. Ed. Ann F. Dierz. Oradell, NJ: November 1974. p. 27.

3529 Review of *Best Science Fiction for 1973* (New York: Ace, 1973): Pierce, J. *Renaissance*. Vol. 5. No. 3. Summer 1973. pp. 11–13.

3530 Review of *Best Science Fiction for 1973* (New York: Ace, 1973): *Publishers Weekly*. 21 May 1973.

3531 Review of *Best Science Fiction for 1973* (New York: Ace, 1973): *Vertex*. Vol. 1. No. 5. Ed. Donald J. Pfeil. Los Angeles: Mankind Publishing Company, December 1973. 1:11 n.g.

3532 Review of *Famous Monsters of Filmland*: Boucher, Anthony. "Recommended Reading." *The Magazine of Fantasy and Science Fiction*. June 1958. p. 104. (discusses *Famous Monsters of Filmland*)

3533 Review of *Forrest J Ackerman Presents Mr. Monster's Movie Gold* edited by Hank Stine (Virginia Beach, VA: Donning Co., 1981): Rovin, Jeff. "The Printed Weird." *Famous Monsters of Filmland*. No. 186. Warren, August 1982. p. 63. (Rovin's column within "The Graveyard Examiner" section mentions *A Reference Guide to American Science Fiction Films*, *Gosh! Wow (Boy-oh-Boy)! Science Fiction*, and *Mr. Monster's Movie Gold*, the latter in the negative)

3534 Review of *The Frankenscience Monster* (New York: Ace, 1969. Paskow, David C. "The Frankenscience Monster." *Luna Monthly*. No. 13. Ed. Ann F. Dietz. Oradell, NJ: June 1970. p. 21.

3535 Review of *Gosh! Wow! (Sense of Wonder)! Science Fiction* (New York: Bantam, 1982). Disch, Thomas M. "*Gosh! Wow! (Sense of Wonder) Science Fiction*." *Rod Serling's The Twilight Zone Magazine*. Ed. T. E. D. Klein. New York: TZ Publications, Inc., May 1982. pp. 6–.

3536 Review of *Science Fiction Worlds of Forrest J Ackerman and Friends* (Powell Publications, 1969). Bear, Greg. "Science Fiction Worlds of Forrest J Ackerman and Friends." *Luna Monthly*. No. 6. November 1969. p. 29.

FANZINE/TRIBUTE PUBLICATIONS

3537 *Acker-monsters' Birthday 'Zine*. Ed. Al Kracalik & R. L. Williams. November 1961.

3538 *The Acker-Zine*. Ed. Bernie Bubnis, Jr. Outside Publishing, ca. 1962. (reprints fanzine articles by Ackerman)

3539 *Famous Monster, Forry Ackerman*. Ed. Larry Byrd & Ron Haydock. November 1960. (celebrating the birthday of "Mr. Monster" tributes by Fritz Leiber and Bradbury)

3540 *Famous Monster of Filmland*. No. 90. 2006. (reproduces original manuscripts for *Famous Monsters* No. 1. in honor of Ackerman's 90th birthday)

3541 *Famous Monster's Birthday*. ca. 1958.

3542 *FOFJA Newsletter*. No. 1. Ed. Douglas Whitenack. January 1993. (Friends of Forrest J Ackerman)

3543 *FOFJA Newsletter.* No. 2. Ed. Douglas Whitenack. March 1993.

3544 *FOFJA Newsletter.* No. 3. Ed. Douglas Whitenack. September 1993.

3545 *Forry! A Special Publication Presented to Forrest J. Ackerman, on the Occasion of the 50th Anniversary of His Birthday, and the 40th Anniversary of His Discovery of Science-Fiction.* Ed. Fred Patten. Los Angeles, CA: Los Angeles Science Fiction Society/A Salamander Press publication, 1966. 82 pp.

3546 *The Forry Ackerman Newsletter.* No. 1. Ed. Verne Bennett. Los Angeles: The Friends of Forrest J Ackerman, July 1969.

3547 *A Gathering to Honor Forrest J Ackerman Presented by David A. Kyle and Friends.* Ed. John L. Coker III. Orlando, FL: Days of Wonder Publishers, 2006.

3548 *"It's Alive!@85."* Ed. Jeffrey Roberts & George Chastain. A MonsterBoom Special Publication, November 2001. (in honor of Ackerman's 85th birthday).

3549 *Movie Collector's World.* No. 729. March 2009. (issue dedicated to "the Most Famous Monster of the All").

3550 *Outlandi.* Los Angeles, CA: Virgin Forrest Publications, 1944. (collection of Ackerman's verse).

3551 *The Sci-Fi Guy: Forrest J. Ackerman.* Lunarians — New York Science Fiction Society, 1974. (*Lunacon '74 Program Book*).

Biography Index to Pages

References are to page numbers. Numbers in ***bold italics*** indicate pages with photographs.

Bibliography Index to Entries

References are to entry numbers in the Bibliography section.